A Guide to College Programs in Culinary Arts, Hospitality, and Tourism

Sixth Edition

A GUIDE TO COLLEGE PROGRAMS IN CULINARY ARTS, HOSPITALITY, AND TOURISM

Sixth Edition

A Directory of CHRIE Member Colleges and Universities

John Wiley & Sons, Inc.

New York · Chichester · Weinheim · Brisbane · Singapore · Toronto

This book is printed on acid-free paper. ♾

Library of Congress Cataloging-in-Publication Data:

ISBN: 0-471-32942-8

Printed in the United States of America.

10 9 8 7 6 5 4 3 2 1

A Guide to College Programs in Culinary Arts, Hospitality, and Tourism

Sixth Edition

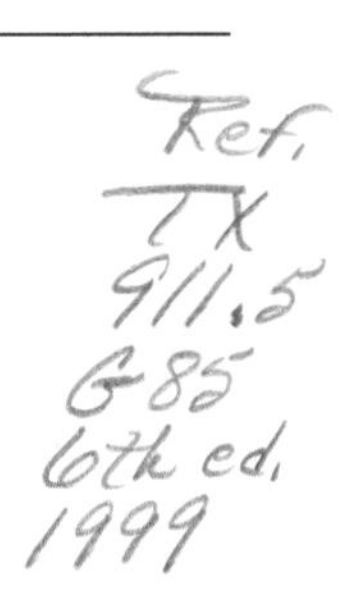

Table of Contents

FOREWORD

The value of any publication rests with the user. Feedback from students, educators, guidance counselors, human relations specialists, and others who have used previous editions of this directory supports the claim that *A Guide to College Programs in Culinary Arts, Hospitality, and Tourism* is the single best source of information regarding education and employment opportunities in these fields. This sixth edition builds on the successes of the past 10 years of work by the staff of the International Council on Hotel, Restaurant, and Institutional Education (CHRIE) in collaboration with John Wiley & Sons, Inc. We are proud of this ongoing effort to guide students to the educational program that best meets their individual needs and, further, to guide recruiters to prospective employees.

The listings of colleges and universities comprise the heart of this publication. Programs are grouped by types of degrees awarded (two-year, four-year, and graduate programs), by geographic location (United States and international), and by specialization (culinary arts, hotel and lodging management, restaurant and foodservice management, travel and tourism management). With information such as this, students and their relatives, counselors, and other advisors can more ably select a program of study that meets their own unique needs. And corporate recruiters can likewise use the *Guide* to select institutions whose students receive the education and develop the skills of paramount importance to specific corporations.

Additionally, the *Guide* contains a wealth of information about career opportunities in culinary arts, hospitality, and tourism; about CHRIE's accrediting commissions; and about CHRIE itself.

Special thanks go to the individuals who spent many hours devoted to the production of this book. Lori Pierelli, CHRIE Publications and Communications Manager, Dina Murray, CHRIE Manager of Member Services, Erin Lynn, CHRIE Publications Assistant, and JoAnna Turtletaub, Senior Editor in the Professional and Trade Division at John Wiley & Sons, Inc.

Readers of this publication are requested to forward comments about the content, format, or other aspects of this publication to CHRIE at 1200 17th Street, NW, Washington, DC 20036-3097; phone 202/331-5990; fax 202/285-2511; e-mail: chrie@erols.com>.

CHRIE is hopeful that this publication leads more and more students to educational institutions that offer lodging, food service, and tourism programs; enables graduates to find gainful employment in their chosen field; and attracts additional members to CHRIE who will recognize this organization as a valuable and valued resource of ongoing benefit throughout their careers.

Dale Gaddy, Ed.D., CAE
Chief Executive Officer

A Guide to College Programs in Culinary Arts, Hospitality, and Tourism

Sixth Edition

Hospitality and Tourism: Careers in the World's Largest Industry

Carl D. Riegel, EdD and Melissa Dallas, JD

The diverse and dynamic hospitality and tourism industry provides challenging and exciting career opportunities for people with a variety of talents and interests. The possibilities for satisfying careers are almost limitless, and the rewards and satisfactions provided by the industry far exceed those found in many other fields of work. For example, the International Council on Hotel, Restaurant, and Institutional Education (CHRIE) divides the industry into five different parts or segments: food services, lodging services, recreation services, travel-related services, and convention and meeting services. Each of these segments includes dozens of subcategories and each subcategory presents numerous career opportunities.

While the different segments of the hospitality and tourism industry have their own unique characteristics, they all share the same mission and heritage - serving the guest. They also possess a common future as one of the most dynamic employment and career fields available to people in the 21st century.

***Food services** include quick service, carry-out, family-style, specialty and fine dining restaurants; private clubs; banquet operations, coffee shops and dining rooms in hotels and lodging facilities; pubs; delis; gourmet shops; nightclubs; catering companies; commercial airlines; and foodservice operations in businesses, schools, colleges and universities, stadiums, convention centers, state and national parks, hospitals and other health-care facilities, and just about any place food is served.*

***Lodging services** include luxury, full-service convention, all-suite, mid-scale and budget hotels; motels; resorts; conference centers; inns; senior-living service; time-shares, condominiums; and bed and breakfast operations.*

***Recreation services** include theme parks and attractions; marinas; sports and leisure management; campgrounds; parks; and casinos.*

***Travel-related services** include domestic and international air-travel, cruise lines, railroads, tour operators and wholesalers, travel agencies and tourism marketing. Convention and meeting services include meeting planning, convention center management, event planning and management, exhibition and trade show planning; and management and convention services in hotels.*

An Evolving Industry

Not so long ago these segments were viewed as distinct and independent, and, in many cases, separate industries. CHRIE's members, who consist of hospitality and tourism educators, industry recruiters, and others who influence educational policy in the hospitality and tourism field, believe differently. As they see it, these segments are components of a single and unified industry. For a long time the industry has suffered from a lack of a common identity, and this has led to confusion among people in government, educators outside of hospitality education, and the general public. This confusion created a lack of awareness regarding the size and scope of the industry, and caused many to underestimate the industry's career producing potential and its impact on both domestic and global economies. It has been a slow process, but the hospitality and tourism industry is finally emerging as a single, important, and global enterprise.

Employment and Economic Importance in the United States

The number of people directly employed in the US hospitality and tourism industry is staggering. Presently, some sources estimate that about 11.4 million people, or over one in eleven workers, is employed in the industry. Of these, approximately 18 - 20% or about 2.2 million people are employees in managerial, professional, or sales and marketing positions. Even more staggering is the fact that by 2005, the US Bureau of Labor and Statistics predicts that the industry will employ around 12.4 million people. This means a 9% increase in jobs over a six-year period.

Many people are indirectly employed in the industry, meaning that their jobs depend on travel and tourism. The Travel Industry Association of America (TIAA) estimates that one in eight US employees are directly or indirectly employed in the industry. This means that the actual number of people working in the hospitality and tourism industry approaches 15.8 million in the United States alone.

Additionally, the industry is one of the largest employers of minorities and women and it affords them the advancement opportunities at levels higher than many other fields of work. For example, the

National Restaurant Association found that 45% of 1.4 million restaurant managers were female, 9% were African-American, and 9% were Hispanic.

Furthermore, the hospitality and tourism industry is the first, second, or third largest employer in 32 states and its employment base is the largest of any in the private sector. By itself, the industry employs more people than the agricultural sector and the steel, textile, auto, and electronics industries combined.

Besides being one of the largest and most important employers, the hospitality and tourism industry generated over $452.5 billion in direct expenditures in 1996, and an additional $186.5 billion in indirect expenditures during the same year. Both of these combined contributed $67.1 billion in tax revenue for local, city, and state governments as well as for the federal government.

Global Economic Importance

The economic impact of the hospitality and tourism industry depends on how it is defined, but according to the World Tourism Organization, global tourism receipts have increased from $205 billion in 1988 to almost $450 billion in 1997. However, when indirect spending is included, this figure increases to approximately $3.5 - $4 trillion, representing over 5.5% of the world's combined gross national product. With respect to employment, estimates suggest that somewhere between 112 and 200 million people are employed either directly or indirectly in the industry. This represents more than 10% of the worldwide workforce. In a nutshell, regardless of the source consulted, travel and tourism is the world's largest industry and rivals any other in terms of size and economic impact.

Other Economic and Social Contributions

In 1998, some 49 million international visitors to the United States spent $81 billion and generated $8 billion in tax receipts. The TIAA expects international expenditures to grow to over $101.5 billion by 2001. In 1997, the WTO estimated that 67 million visitors arrived in France, 33.4 million in Italy, and 24 million in China.

Beyond these economic and employment benefits, the industry provides a good number of social benefits both internationally and domestically. On the domestic front, hospitality and tourism businesses provide entree to the work force for many first-time workers and welfare recipients. They also provide purpose and supplemental income to a growing number of retirees. Furthermore, the hospitality and tourism industry offers many entrepreneurial opportunities which are unmatched by most other types of businesses. For example, four out of ten foodservice establishments are sole proprietorships or partnerships. This means that there is plenty of room for aspiring business owners.

On the global front, the industry contributes to international development and fosters understanding between the nations of the world. As an industry,

hospitality and tourism is dependent upon a variety of external factors and is influenced by economic, social and political trends. However, in recent years, advances in communications technology, transportation, and the industrialization of many previously underdeveloped countries have made tourism truly a global phenomenon. This, coupled with the reduction of many trade and political barriers, has contributed to increased levels of economic prosperity in many countries, while at the same time ensuring the growth of the entire industry.

Finally, tourism is often the first step in the economic development of many poorer or underdeveloped countries. Tourism provides not only a direct economic contribution to developing nations, but also establishes the infrastructure which facilitates the

development of other types of industries. Infrastructure includes things such as airports, more developed roads, utilities, hotels, and restaurants. These serve a dual purpose. First, they allow for tourism to happen and, second, they support other business ventures.

However, mass-market tourism is not always wise. The challenge for many underdeveloped nations is balancing the economic growth spurred by tourism with the protection of their country's ecological and social systems. This has spawned a new industry called "ecotourism." Ecotourism involves low impact development and activities which are friendly to the natural and social environment. Rather than destroy either the habitat or the culture in the interest of gaining increased revenue from tourism, ecotourism permits residents to have it both ways. This creates a "win-win" situation for both traveler and inhabitants alike.

EMPLOYMENT IN THE HOSPITALITY AND TOURISM INDUSTRY

The hospitality and tourism industry has experienced unprecedented growth during the past two decades, and this surge has translated into exceptional opportunities for graduates of hospitality and tourism programs. In the foodservice industry, the employment growth rate is expected to be faster than the average for all occupations through 2006. New managerial jobs in the hotel industry are expected to grow at the average rate.

For the long term, the employment outlook for the industry is good: the managerial job pool is expected to grow at a rate better than the rest of the economy. For the short term, however, employment opportunities are excellent. The hotel industry is recovering at an escalated pace from a downturn in business which began in 1992 and many cities in the U.S. are experiencing higher year round occupancies and rates than ever before. The occupancy rates in 1996 remained stable at 65.2%; however, the occupancy rate in luxury hotels was 74% and is predicted to increase over the short term. Furthermore, the TIAA reports that a 3.6% increase in the supply of hotel rooms is expected in 1999.

As a result, many lodging firms have resumed aggressive recruiting efforts, and prospects for the right people are excellent. Many firms, however, have learned a lesson from the downturn and prefer to hire candidates who have a substantial amount of lodging-related work experience in addition to their education. They prefer to hire people who are ready to assume entry level supervisory or management positions with minimal training. On the other hand, a few firms support management training programs that nurture managerial expertise. Furthermore, the way some lodging organizations are designed is changing (see figures 9 - 12) and advancement opportunities have changed as well.

In foodservices, a substantial number of management positions are available. Many companies have recognized the need for more professional managers who can assume operational, marketing and financial leadership. Furthermore, some segments such as casual dining and contract food service are still growing and many new concepts, including coffeehouses and bagel shops, have emerged.

Large national and multinational corporations have increasingly dominated ownership of hospitality and tourism businesses. This trend has substantially increased the demand for managers with a formal

education in hospitality and tourism management, as well as other skilled employees who are committed to providing high-quality guest service in a professional manner. In short, there is a critical need for people with the general management skills to manage all aspects of the business.

As well, for people who want to run and operate their own business, the hospitality and tourism industry continues to provide a vast array of opportunities for those who possess a strong entrepreneurial spirit. Just about everyone knows at least one "rags to riches" story about a person who has become very successful by operating a business associated with the hospitality and tourism industry. For hard-working, creative, and service-oriented people who want to own and operate their own businesses, the hospitality and tourism industry offers almost unlimited potential.

In many respects, the hospitality and tourism industry is a mature one. However, social and demographic changes suggest that the industry's growth is not over. Growth in the late 1990s and the 21st century will focus on new markets and products such as international expansion, gaming, adventure travel, and senior-living services.

Young people between the ages of 18 and 24 have traditionally been a major source of entry-level labor for the hospitality and tourism industry. But changing demographics suggest a downward trend in the number of young people in this age category through the 1990s. While the 1991-92 recession softened the impact of this labor shortage on the industry, consensus is that under normal employment conditions, an ideal atmosphere for interesting, fast-paced jobs will exist and promotions and increased responsibility will occur quicker in the hospitality and tourism industry than in other fields of employment.

Overall, the forecasts for growth in the hospitality and tourism industry are strong. The TIAA notes that travel expenditures have increased by 44% between 1990 and 1997. As well, airline traffic is expected to increase by 2.8% in 1999 while capacity is expected to increase by 3.2%. Thus for graduates of hospitality and tourism education programs, these are very good times and are likely to remain so for some time to come.

Career Opportunities in Hospitality and Tourism

Graduates of hospitality and tourism programs frequently start their careers in junior management positions such as management trainees, assistant managers or supervisors. Starting salaries compare favorably with those in other business-related occupations, and the potential for advancement is excellent for the capable individual who is willing to work hard. In some restaurant operations, for example, a junior manager may assume full operating responsibility for a million-dollar-plus profit center in as little as two years following graduation, while commanding a salary significantly exceeding those in other industries.

Advancement opportunities in hospitality and tourism extend far beyond the management of individual restaurants and hotels. Opportunities exist in recreation services, gaming operations, cruise lines, tour operations, and destination management to name a few. There are many opportunities for advancement to multiunit management or corporate staffs in major companies. The industry also hires graduates in accounting, marketing and sales, finance, and human resource management. In addition to these positions, many of the vendors who supply products and services for the industry hire graduates of hospitality and tourism programs. Seasoned industry professionals also have the option of pursuing careers in fields like foodservice consulting. Figures 1-8 depict some sample career paths, Exhibits A & B list some key positions, and Figures 9-12 portray possible organizational structures of a large hotel. Finally, Exhibit C details some representative industry salaries.

Will A Career in Hospitality and Tourism Be Right for You?

For all the benefits, careers in hospitality and tourism management are not for everyone. The industry is people and service oriented. Students considering these careers must genuinely like and be able to relate to people. They must be able to quickly solve a variety of problems. Further, aspiring employees should be willing to work flexible hours - the hours, that is, during which people want to be served. Students may have to consider the possibility of relocating, often several times, since many organizations have operations in a variety of geographic locations. Finally, managers are responsible for ensuring that operations run smoothly and effectively at all times, and that means frequently working more than a 40-hour week.

Despite the hard work, a career in hospitality or tourism management is rewarding for those seeking responsibility, opportunity for professional advancement, salary growth and high levels of personal satisfaction.

HOSPITALITY AND TOURISM EDUCATION

In the United States, the number of postsecondary institutions offering hospitality and tourism programs has more than quadrupled during the past 25 years. The combination of this rapid growth and the continually evolving nature of the industry has resulted in hospitality and tourism programs that differ widely in their philosophies and approaches. In view of this diversity, the following information is provided as an overview of hospitality and tourism education. A major portion of the thought and data relating to the concept of career education comes from *Educating for Careers* by Thomas F. Powers.

THE IMPACT OF EDUCATION IN A CHANGING WORLD

The world economy has changed drastically in the years since World War II. The emergence of what Peter Drucker calls the "knowledge worker" has created far-reaching implications for postsecondary education. This growth can be explained in part by efforts to expand access to postsecondary education to a broader population base. But an even larger part of this expansion may be attributed to the growth of career-oriented programs, such as hospitality and tourism education, which in turn are based on the needs of specific industries.

In the United States, for example, two major developments in education have had a significant impact on both the economy and the growth and direction of postsecondary education. First, completion of high school has become the rule rather than the exception. Nearly 75% of today's young people complete high school compared to 50% in 1940.

Although the implications of this are numerous, one major effect is clear: the qualifications of entry-level employees in the United States are now higher than ever before. Second, participation in postsecondary education has more than tripled during this time. About 15% of the young people in the United States participated in higher education in 1945 compared to something on the order of 50% today.
As the workforce becomes better educated, knowledge and skill become more valued by society generally, and this, in turn, increases demand for workers with more education. Similarly, as the opportunity for participation in higher education is extended to an even broader proportion of the population, the decision to pursue further education becomes based more on career and economic goals than on objectives related to cultural or personal development. Finally, as more people travel and experience other cultures, their expectations and demands increase along with their cultural sophistication.

Thus, academic fields like hospitality and tourism education have evolved and matured because they provide career opportunities to students as well as address the labor needs of the industry. It is important to note, however, that career education generally, and hospitality and tourism education specifically, is not vocational in the sense of providing graduates only with the narrow skills necessary to function on a particular job or aggregate of jobs. Rather, the purpose of career education is to produce educated and knowledgeable workers who are capable of growing and maturing, both in their chosen fields and as individuals. This means that career education should provide graduates with a flexible educational background to assure that they can function in the economic mainstream and achieve goals which relate more to themselves and to society at large than to the requirements of any specific labor market.

John Dewey perhaps best summarized this notion when he differentiated between a job and work in *Democracy and Education*. According to Dewey, the term "job" relates to earning a living - the trade-off of time, effort, and, perhaps, skill for wages. It is viewed as something separate from the worker and involves low engagement of self. Work, by contrast, is characterized by an involvement of the self. It includes the worker's purpose in life, the exercise of judgment, and the sense of value accruing to the worker, the economy, and, ultimately, society.

WHAT IS HOSPITALITY AND TOURISM EDUCATION?

Hospitality and tourism education programs, like many other career-oriented programs, are difficult to define. Career education programs have expanded rapidly, but not uniformly, among postsecondary educational institutions. Colleges and universities often respond to demand for new programs by building onto existing programs. As a result, career programs like hospitality and tourism management differ widely and lack the standardization that characterize many traditional fields of study.

However, an emerging view of hospitality and tourism education is that of a field of multidisciplinary study which brings the perspectives of many disciplines, especially those found in the social sciences, to bear on particular areas of application and practice in the hospitality and tourism industry. Furthermore, while hospitality and tourism education may lack some of the formalities of the traditional professions such as law or medicine, it nevertheless lends itself best to educational models followed by these professions.

Professional education consists of three key elements: substantive knowledge, skills, and values. Substantive knowledge is the essential knowledge necessary for practice of the profession; it is the core area upon which instruction is based. The skills component consists of abilities necessary to apply professional knowledge to the field of work. The values component involves the fostering of key career values necessary for success in that field.

The Growing Trend toward Hospitality and Tourism Education

During the past two decades, hospitality and tourism education has grown in tandem with the rapidly expanding industry. In the early 1970s, there were approximately 40 four-year programs in the United States that offered degrees in hospitality management or hotel and restaurant management. As of this writing, CHRIE estimates that there are now almost 170 hospitality programs granting baccalaureate degrees and more than 800 programs offering associate degrees, certificates or diplomas.

Additionally, in recognition of the increasing economic impact of tourism on state, national, and global economies, many institutions have established programs of study in tourism, either as an adjunct to existing hospitality programs; as separate and free-standing programs; or as "umbrella" departments under which hospitality and other programs are housed.

Due to its growing popularity and pervasive presence, hospitality and tourism education is continuing to move more and more toward the mainstream of postsecondary education. With the exception of those courses dedicated directly to or in support of the major, it generally shares degree requirements which are consistent with other university programs. And, like other university programs, graduate and post-graduate degree programs in hospitality and tourism often coexist with undergraduate curricula. The number of universities offering master's degrees and doctoral (Ph.D.) degrees in this field is increasing as witnessed by the section in this directory devoted to those programs.

Furthermore, given the nature of the hospitality and tourism industry and the appeal of the exciting career opportunities offered by the industry, hospitality and tourism programs have achieved substantial popularity among college students. On many campuses, students in other programs take courses in hospitality and tourism management to enhance their future employment prospects.

The Future of Hospitality and Tourism Education

In spite of its rapid growth, hospitality and tourism education is in the process of maturing as an academic field. The future appears to hold bright promise for the discipline. Most programs experience good placement rates for graduates, and more and more hospitality and tourism organizations are seeking candidates with degrees for management positions. The future seems to be one of increasing professionalism for this field.

One sign of the maturation of hospitality and tourism education is the current debate over issues of curricula and faculty credentials. While the field will probably always be marked by diversity with respect to actual program approaches, there is substantial evidence to indicate that the field is of one mind in regard to purpose and standards of education.

In fact, standards for accrediting hospitality programs have been developed and implemented. The Accreditation Commission for Programs in Hospitality

Administration (ACPHA) was formed in 1989 after the members of CHRIE approved proposed changes in CHRIE's Constitution to allow for the creation of a commission to accredit hospitality administration programs at baccalaureate degree-granting institutions. The Commission began accrediting programs in 1991. The accreditation process has succeeded in raising the quality of the hospitality administration programs that have undergone review. Colleges and universities accredited by ACPHA as of December 1998 are identified in their respective listings within this guide.

The Commission for Accreditation of Hospitality Management Programs (CAHM) was formed in 1994 to accredit hospitality management programs at associate degree-granting institutions. The Commission began accrediting programs in early 1996.

Standards for both ACPHA and CAHM focus on core curriculum requirements, faculty credentials, and other measures of program quality, yet still allow for diversity in terms of program goals and philosophy. The enhancement of quality is as important to both accreditation and the commissions as is the more frequently cited role of assessment.

Correspondence regarding the accreditation process should be sent to ACPHA/CAHM, c/o CHRIE, 1200 17th St., NW, Washington, DC 20036-3097.

PROGRAM COMPONENTS

Most hospitality and tourism programs consist of four main areas.
(1) The major.
(2) General education and advanced learning skills.
(3) Electives.
(4) Work experience.

THE MAJOR

The major is the vehicle that brings practical application to the college curriculum. Making up between 25 and 40 percent of the undergraduate curriculum, the major is the true core of undergraduate studies. Students commit to a major by choice, and the major department or program becomes their "home" on campus, because it is a source of social contacts and personal advice, and also because it provides both focus and a sense of purpose for undergraduate life.

Given the diversity among hospitality and tourism programs, it is difficult to present a single description of the major, but, in general, most will resemble, to one degree or another, one of five broad categories or approaches.

(1) *Craft/Skill Approaches.* Programs falling into this category take a no-nonsense, "nuts and bolts" approach to the field. The major is based on the functions and crafts employed in hospitality and tourism operations, and its major focus is on helping students acquire technical operations skills and, in some cases, management and supervisory skills. Craft- and skill-based programs are often found in community and technical colleges, but they exist in some four-year programs as well.

(2) *Tourism Approaches.* These programs primarily emphasize the content of tourism - concepts, trends, economic impact, etc., and the many social sciences which contribute to the tourism field such as sociology, anthropology, and economics. These programs most often include coursework in areas of business administration as well.

(3) *Food Systems/Home Economics Approaches.* Hospitality programs housed or started in colleges of home economics typically employ this approach. These departments typically place heavy emphasis on nutrition and food science, and food production and delivery systems, as well as both the natural and social sciences. Principles of management and administration are also stressed, but to a lesser degree than in business administration programs.

(4) *Business Administration Approaches.* These programs, usually housed in colleges or schools of business administration, tend to pay more attention to the disciplines of administration - management, finance, marketing, operations, accounting, etc. - and less attention to products such as food or rooms.

(5) *Combined Approaches.* Programs fitting into this category will combine two or more of the approaches previously mentioned. This is often the case in independent hospitality schools and colleges with four-year degree programs. For example, some programs may combine a business administration approach with a food systems/home economics approach.

GENERAL EDUCATION AND ADVANCED LEARNING SKILLS

In many respects, the general education component of the college curriculum is what is left of a core liberal arts education, at one time the dominant type of American undergraduate education. However, increasing specialization, an increase in general knowledge, and the emergence of career education have made this type of common learning impractical at most institutions. In place of a uniform liberal arts education, general education acts to ensure that all students obtain some understanding of the skills which will aid them in advanced studies and lifelong learning. This includes knowledge of cultural heritage as it is expressed in the humanities, the social sciences, the arts, and the natural and physical sciences. General education requirements relate more to the individual than to the major, but that does not lessen their importance in educating the total person.

Advanced learning skills have traditionally included English composition, mathematics, physical education, speech, and, in some cases, foreign languages. However, with advances in technology, knowledge, and social responsibility, advanced learning skills have been expanded to include mathematical precision, statistics, practical ethics, and computer literacy. These skills relate directly to both the individual and the hospitality and tourism major.

ELECTIVES

Electives, like the major, are chosen by the student and provide opportunities for broadening the individual's educational experience in a way that he or she might find personally important. For example, electives can be used to acquire additional advanced learning skills which are not part of the required curriculum and to develop interests or talents in the arts. They may also be used to bolster personal competencies in areas which are part of, or related to, the major area of study.

WORK EXPERIENCE

No matter what approach it takes, a hospitality and tourism education program is still no substitute for experience. The industry seldom hires management-level people who lack substantial, varied, and responsible work experience, regardless of a college degree. It is important that prospective managers have a solid commitment to a career in hospitality and tourism and that they have experiential knowledge of the industry. Therefore, most programs require that students undertake and complete significant work experience in the industry before they graduate. This experience is usually paid by an outside employer and typically ranges between 400 and 1,200 clock hours (between one and three summers).

An increasingly popular way of obtaining work experience in the industry involves students taking a semester off and completing an extended internship, often at a facility away from their home state. Both employers and students like this arrangement. For students, it is an opportunity to get a feel for a company and perhaps try their hand at a variety of jobs. For employers, this arrangement permits longer-term staff planning and allows them time to evaluate prospective management employees. This work experience goes by a variety of names - co-op, internship, and practicum.

By definition, co-ops are paid, and the work experience increases in difficulty and responsibility as the student progresses through the different facets of the program. Internships are intended to provide practical experience in a profession. The intern, under the supervision of a professional, acquires operational skills and applies learned theories to actual practice. Under an internship, academic credit and pay or a stipend may or may not be included, and a full-time work experience for a 10- to 12-week period is the norm. Practica refer to career-oriented work experiences that students undertake on a volunteer basis while they are enrolled in classes.

COMPARING AND SELECTING PROGRAMS

There are many dimensions to compare between various hospitality and tourism education programs. We have previously discussed differences among programs with respect to orientation and administrative tradition. However, there are several additional factors one should consider when comparing programs.

LEVELS, TYPES OF PROGRAMS, AND PROGRAM OBJECTIVES

The listings in this guide are cataloged according to program level or those granting associate degrees, diplomas, and certificates; baccalaureate degrees; and graduate degrees.

Although a major difference between levels has to do with when the program is undertaken and the amount of time required for completion, levels are also indicative of a wide variety of other factors, including institutional setting, program objectives, and faculty credentials. In addition to broad-based curriculum objectives, hospitality and tourism programs will also differ in terms of curricular specialization. Some programs, arguing that specialization beyond a degree in hospitality and tourism management is unnecessary at the undergraduate level, will offer a prescribed course of study which all students, regardless of career aspirations, must complete. Others will offer elective courses related to the major, which permit students to either specialize or pursue their specific interests.

At some institutions, the field of hospitality and tourism management is subdivided into specialized areas. After taking a series of core courses, students will choose to specialize or major in one of these tracks. Some examples of hospitality and tourism specializations include hotel management, restaurant management, sales and marketing, attractions management, destination management, or convention and meeting management. Exhibit D outlines key attributes of hospitality and tourism programs.

LABORATORY FACILITIES

Many hotel and restaurant programs have food production laboratories designed to assist the teaching of restaurant and foodservice management by providing an opportunity for students to gain first-hand experience. These laboratories vary from institution to institution and range from supervised work experience in the college dining halls to fully equipped gourmet dining rooms and kitchens. At some colleges, laboratories are used to provide hands-on work experience; at others, they are employed to provide training in the culinary arts; and at still others, laboratories are viewed as vehicles for providing management simulation experience in which students assume full managerial responsibility for production, promotion, and service of a foodservice function.

In addition to foodservice laboratories, some programs are equipped with front office laboratories and beverage-tasting laboratories. In a some cases, hotel or restaurant programs may even be involved in the operation of an actual lodging or dining facility. Finally, given the realities of modern technology, many programs provide computer laboratories with special software dedicated to management and hospitality and tourism functions.

FACULTY CREDENTIALS

Faculty in hospitality and tourism programs are well qualified and dedicated teachers. Qualifications will, as previously mentioned, differ in accordance with program levels and objectives. In general, faculty members hold both academic and experiential credentials; that is, in addition to academic degrees, most faculty members have had some managerial work experience in the hospitality and tourism industry; some have had extensive and upper-level management work experience.

Generally, faculty teaching in these programs hold at least a master's degree. Among faculty at four-year colleges and universities, doctoral (Ph.D.) degrees are becoming common. It should be noted that until recently there were no doctoral degree-granting programs in hospitality and tourism management, which means that most Ph.D.s teaching in hospitality and tourism programs have earned doctorates in other fields. These fields include such areas as business, law, education and nutrition.

PLACEMENT

Job placement for hospitality and tourism graduates has been universally high, but differences do exist from school to school with respect to both the type and scope of companies which employ the graduates of a program. Many programs place graduates with a mixture of national, regional, and local firms; others place graduates primarily with local and regional companies. Usually, the scope of placement is more a reflection of the location of the institution and the characteristics of the student body than of program quality. For example, a program at an institution in a large city might have a mix of older and nontraditional students and, as a result, will focus its attention on the local labor market.

The hospitality and tourism industry is a highly segmented, specialized industry, and the mix of firms recruiting for particular segments also differs across institutions. Programs with an institutional management or foodservice focus are more likely to attract recruiters from foodservice firms than lodging firms. On the other hand, programs with an administration emphasis or which focus on both hotel and restaurant management are more likely to attract corporate recruiters from a variety of firms, including both foodservice and lodging companies. Again, this does not necessarily reflect program quality, but rather the type of the program.

FINANCIAL AID AND SCHOLARSHIP SOURCES

Most programs will have an office of financial aid to assist students in making arrangements to pay tuition and fees. Many programs have scholarships available directly through the school. After reviewing a student's situation, the financial aid officer at a college or university can help decide on the best financial options open to the student. Below is a listing of scholarships available from associations in the United States.

American Culinary Federation (ACF)
The Ray and Gertrude Marshall Scholarship Fund Limited to ACF Junior members enrolled in post-secondary culinary arts programs and ACF apprenticeship programs. Scholarship deadlines are as follows: February 15, June 15, and October 15 of each year. Scholarship awards are announced approximately 45 days after the deadline date. Scholarship

grants are awarded in the amount of $500 with one merit award of $1000 awarded each period. Loans also available for up to $1,500 for ACF members after completing one semester of studies in good academic standing. Loan applications accepted year-round, with awards made in April, August, and December.

American Culinary Federation
10 San Bartola Rd.
St. Augustine, FL 32086-3466
Phone: (904) 824-4468
http://www.acfchefs.org/

American Society for Healthcare Food Service Administrators (ASHFSA)
Grants of up to $1000 for full- or part-time students of institutional foodservice management. Three scholarship funds: one geared to undergraduates at both two- and four-year colleges, and the other two geared toward current hospital foodservice managers furthering their education. Deadline: late April, with awards made in early summer.

Scholarship Committee
American Society for Healthcare
Food Service Administrators
American Hospital Association
840 North Lake Shore Drive
Chicago, Illinois 60611
Phone: (312) 280-0000
http://www.ashfsa.org/

American Society of Travel Agents (ASTA)
Grants of up to $1200 for students with a 3.0 or better grade point average enrolled in a travel and tourism program at a two-year, four-year or graduate institution. Several different scholarship funds are available including an international exchange award. Deadline: early June.

Scholarship Department
American Society of Travel Agents
1101 King Street
Alexandria, Virginia 22314
Phone: (703) 739-2782
http://www.inndirect.com/inndirect/yp/asta.html

Club Managers Association of America (CMAA)
Grants range from $1000 to $2000 and are awarded to sophomores, juniors, and seniors specializing in club management at an accredited college or university. Deadline: May 1.

Club Managers Association of America
1733 King Street
Alexandria, Virginia 22314
Phone: (703) 739-9500
http://www.cmaa.org/

The Cooking Advancement Research and Education Foundation (CAREF)

304 West Liberty Street, Suite 201
Louisville, Virginia 22314
Phone: (502) 587-7953
http://www.gstis.net/~epicure/history.htm

Educational Institute of the American Hotel & Motel Association

Educational Institute of the American Hotel
& Motel Association
800 North Magnolia Avenue, Suite 1800
Orlando, FL. 32708
Phone: (800) 752-4567
http://www.ei-ahma.org/

Hospitality Financial and Technical Professionals (HFTP)
Three scholarships awarded each year to students majoring in either accounting or hospitality management at an accredited college or university. Grants range from $1000 to $1500. Applications must come through an IAHA local chapter president. Deadline: July 15.

Hospitality Financial and Technical Professionals
11709 Boulder Lane, Suite 110
Austin, TX 78726
Phone: (800) 646-4387
http://www.iaha.org/

International Food Service Executives Association (IFSEA)
Two scholarships are awarded in each of eight regions each year to foodservice-related majors. Awards range from $250 to $500. Deadline: February 1.

International Food Service Executives Association
1100 South State Road 7, Suite 103
Margate, Florida 33068
Phone: (305) 977-0767
http://ifsea.org/index.html

National Restaurant Association Educational Foundation (NRA-EF)
Fifteen categories of scholarships for students specializing in foodservice, hospitality management, culinary arts, food technology, dietetics or related degrees. A variable number of scholarships of varying dollar amounts are awarded each year. Deadline: March 1.

Scholarship Department
The Educational Foundation of the National
Restaurant Association
250 South Wacker Drive, Suite 1400
Chicago, Illinois 60606
Phone: (312) 715-1010
http://www.restaurant.org/

National Tourism Foundation (NTF)
Grants of $500 are awarded to juniors and seniors majoring in travel and tourism at an accredited four-year college or university. Deadline: March, with awards made in late spring.

National Tour Foundation
PO Box 3071
Lexington, Kentucky 40596
Phone: (606) 253-1036
http://www.ntaonline.com/www/public/shortcuts/national_tourism_foundation/index.html

Travel and Tourism Research Association (TTRA)
Three awards: Student Travel Research Award ($500), open to graduate or undergraduate students (abstracts due by March 1); Slattery Marketing Award - $1000 - one paper or project submission per institution (projects due by March 1); Dissertation Competition - $1000 - limited to candidates for Ph.D. or Doctor of Business Administration (400-word abstract due by December 1). Winners also receive expense-paid trip to TTRA's annual conference.

Travel and Tourism Research Association
546 East Main Street
Lexington, KY 40508
Phone: (606) 226-4344
http://www.ttra.com/award.html

LOCAL CHAPTER AWARDS

The local chapters of associations related to the hospitality and tourism industry sometimes offer scholarships as well. Quite often these local scholarship funds are subject to fluctuations in the chapter's finances. For a list of local chapters, contact the following:

American Institute of Wine and Food (AIWF)
1550 Bryant Street, Suite 700
San Francisco, California 94103
Phone: (415) 255-3000
http://www.aiwf.org/contact.html

Hospitality Sales and Marketing Association International (HSMAI)
1300 L Street NW, Suite 800
Washington, DC 20005
Phone: (202) 789-0089
http://www.hsmai.org/

CORPORATE SCHOLARSHIPS

Many corporations and foundations give funds for scholarships directly to colleges and universities. What follows is a partial listing of corporations and foundations who have donated funds for scholarships to colleges and universities in the past.

- American Hotel Foundation
- Banfi Vintners
- Four Seasons Hotels
- The Hilton Foundation
- Hyatt Hotels Corporation
- The J. Willard Marriott Foundation
- The Statler Foundation
- Stouffer Hotels and Resorts
- Welch Foods, Inc.
- Westin Hotels

WEB-BASED SOURCES OF CAREER INFORMATION

The following list, albeit short, contains valuable links to trends, happenings, and careers in the hospitality and tourism industry.

http://www.ei-ahma.org/hotels/association.htm
http://www.hospitalityjobs.com/
http://www.nrn.com/
http://www.hotel-online.com/Neo/
http://www.wto.org/
http://www.careersonline.com.au/show/tour/tour.html
http://www.cert.ie/S3P11.HTM
http://www.destination-ns.com/tians/tians.htm
http://www.jobsourcenetwork.com/hospit.html
http://www.hospitalitylink.com/
http://www.gti.co.uk/employers/empfood.htm
http://www.chrie.org/

OTHER SOURCES OF CAREER INFORMATION

Following is a list of associations that may be able to provide additional information about the segment of the hospitality and tourism industry that they represent.

American Culinary Federation (ACF)
10 San Bartolla Rd.
St. Augustine, FL 32084-3466
Phone: (904) 824-4468
http://www.acfchefs.org/

American Dietetic Association (ADA)
216 W. Jackson Blvd.
Chicago, IL 60606-6995
Phone: (312) 899-4895
http://www.eatright.org/

American Hotel & Motel Association (AH&MA)
1201 New York Ave., NW, Suite 600
Washington, DC 20005-3931
Phone: (202) 289-3100
http://www.ahma.com/

American Society of Travel Agents (ASTA)
1101 King St.
Alexandria, VA 22314
Phone: (703) 739-2782
http://www.inndirect.com/inndirect/yp/asta.html

Association for International Practical Training (AIPT)
10 Corporate Center, Ste. 250
10400 Little Patuxent Pkwy.
Columbia, MD 21044
Phone: (410) 997-2200
http://www.aipt.org/

Club Managers Association of America (CMAA)
1733 King St.
Alexandria, VA 22314
Phone: (703) 739-9500
http://www.cmaa.org/

Dietary Managers Association (DMA)
406 Surrey Woods Dr.
St. Charles, IL 60174
Phone: (630) 587-6336
http://www.dmaonline.org/

Educational Institute of the American Hotel & Motel Association
800 North Magnolia Avenue, Suite 1800
Orlando, FL. 32708
Phone: (800) 752-4567
http://www.ei-ahma.org/

Foodservice Consultants Society International (FCSI)
304 W. Liberty St., Ste. 201
Louisville, KY 40202
Phone: (502) 583-3783
http://www.fcsi.org/

Healthcare Foodservice Management (HFM)
204 E St., NE
Washington, DC 20002
Phone: (202) 546-7236
http://www.hfm.org/

Hospitality Financial and Technical Professionals
11709 Boulder Lane, Suite 110
Austin, TX 78726
Phone: (800) 646-4387
http://www.iaha.org/

Hospitality Sales and Marketing Association International (HSMAI)
1300 L St., NW, Ste. 800
Washington, DC 20005
Phone: (202) 789-0089
http://www.hsmai.org/

Hospitality Business Alliance (HBA)
Phone: 1-800-765-2122, ext. 768
Fax: 312-466-1596
http://www.h-b-a.org

Hotel Catering and Institutional Management Association (HCIMA)
191 Trinity Rd.
London SW17 7HN England
Phone: +44 (0) 171-672 4251
http://hcima.org.uk/general/

International Association of Conference Centers (IACC)
243 N. Lindbergh Blvd., Ste. 315
St. Louis, MO 63141
Phone: (314) 993-8575
http://www.iacconline.com

International Executive Housekeeping Association (IEHA)
1001 Eastwind Dr., Ste. 301
Westerville, OH 43081
Phone: (614) 895-7166
http://www.ieha.org

International Food Service Executives Association (IFSEA)
1100 S. State Rd. #7, Ste. 103
Margate, FL 33068
Phone: (305) 977-0767
http://ifsea.org/index.html

International Hotel and Restaurant Association (IH&RA)
251, rue du Faubourg
St-Martin 75010 Paris France
Tel 33 (0) 1 44 89 94 00
http://www.ih-ra.com/

Meeting Professionals International (MPI)
International Headquarters
4455 LBJ Freeway, Suite 1200
Dallas, Texas 75244-5903
Phone: 972-702-3000
http://www.mpiweb.org

National Association of Colleges and University Food Services (NACUFS)
1405 S. Harrison, Ste. 103
Manly Miles Bldg.
Michigan State University
East Lansing, MI 48824
Phone: (517) 332-2494
http://www.nacufs.org/

National Association of Food Equipment Manufacturers (NAFEM)
401 N. Michigan Ave.
Chicago, IL 60611-4267
Phone: (312) 644-6610
http://www.nafem.org/

National Restaurant Association
1200 17th St., NW
Washington, DC 20036-3097
Phone: 1-800-424-5156
http://www.restaurant.org/

National Restaurant Association Educational Foundation
250 S. Wacker Dr., Ste. 1400
Chicago, IL 60606
Phone: 1-800-765-2122
http://www.edfound.org

National Tour Association (NTA)
P.O. Box 3071
Lexington, KY 40596
Phone: (606) 226-4444
http://www.ntaonline.com/

Professional Convention Management Association (PCMA)
100 Vestavia Office Park, Ste. 220
Birmingham, AL 35216
Phone: (205) 823-7262
http://www.pcma.org/

Society for Foodservice Management (SFM)
304 W. Liberty St., Ste. 301
Louisville, KY 40202
Phone: (502) 583-3783
http://www.sfm-online.org/

Travel Industry Association of America (TIA)
1100 New York Avenue, NW, Suite 450
Washington, DC 20005-3934
Phone: (202) 408-8422
http://www.tia.org/

REFERENCES

Dewey, J. 1916. *Democracy and Education*. New York: MacMillan.

Dittmar, H. 1996. "Sustainable Travel and Tourism." *Surface Transportation Policy Protect Progress.* 4(6): 1-2.

Murphy, B. 1996. "Meeting New Berth Demands: Cruise Leaders Require Search for First-Time Businesses". *Maritime Reporter/Engineering News*. July.

Naisbitt, J. 1994. *Global Paradox*. New York: W. Morrow.

National Restaurant Association. 1998. *1998 Pocket Fact Book*. Washington, DC.

Powers, T.F. 1977. *Educating for Careers: Policy Issues in a Time of Change*. University Park, PA: The Pennsylvania State University Press.

Riegel, C.D. 1987. "Doctoral Education for HRI: Defining a Field of Study". *The Cornell Hotel and Restaurant Administration Quarterly. 28* (2): 28–33.

Riegel, C.D., and Dallas, M.B. 1998. *Hospitality and Tourism Careers A Blueprint for Success.* Inglewood Cliffs, New Jersey: Prentice-Hall.

Rodriguez, C. "Travel and Tourism Forecasts: 2000 and Beyond." *Viewpoint* 1(2): 34-40.

Tourism Works for America Council. 1997. *Tourism Works for America 1997 Report*. Washington, D.C.

Travel Industry Association of America. 1998. *Economic Impact*. http://www.tia.org/press/fastfacts1.stm.

Travel Industry Association of America. 1998. *Latest Reports: 1999 Outlook for Travel and Tourism.* http://www.tia.org/research/forecasts.stm.

United State Bureau of Labor Statistics. 1998-99 *Occupational Outlook Handbook*. http://www.stats.bls.gov.

Williams, A. 1992. "Preparing for Your Field Experience AKA Co-op, Practicum or Internship". *Hosteur (2,)* 1.

World Tourism Organization. 1997. *Tourism Highlights 1997*. http://www.world-tourism.org/esta/monograf/hl97/higlig97.pdf.

FIGURES 1–8: SAMPLE CAREER LADDERS

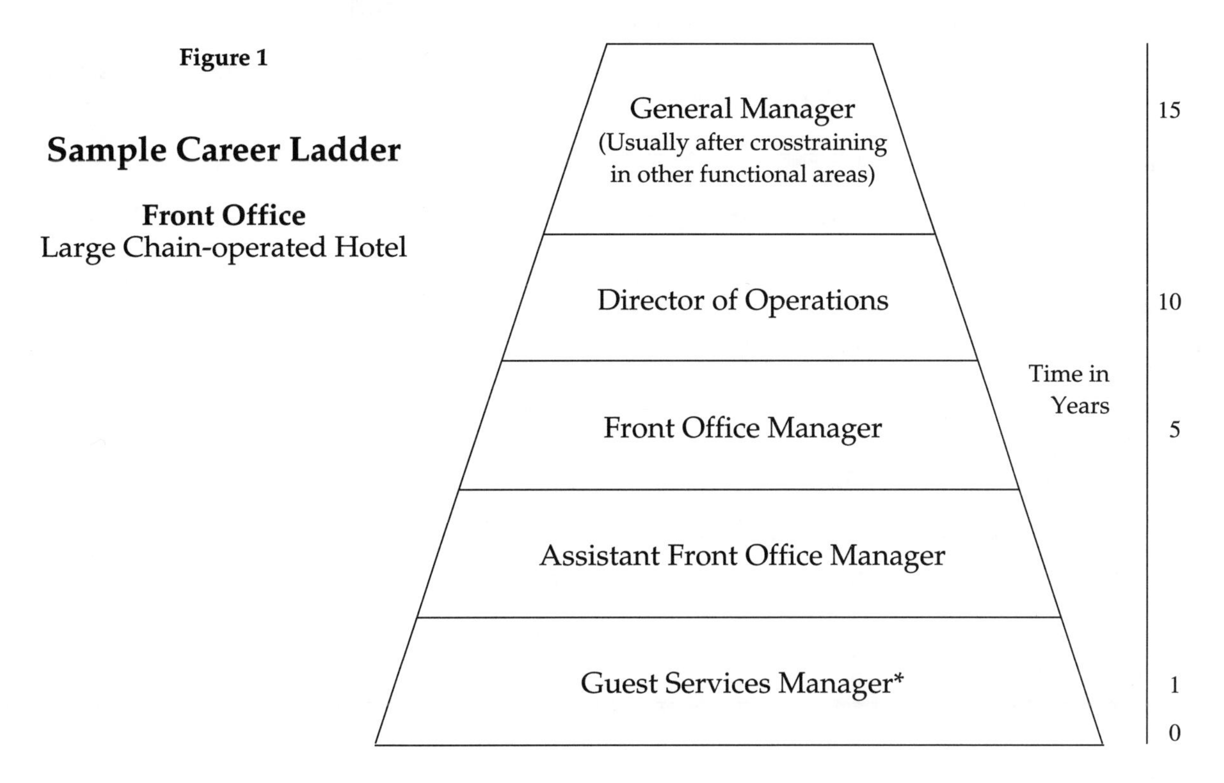

*Assumes previous front office operations experience.

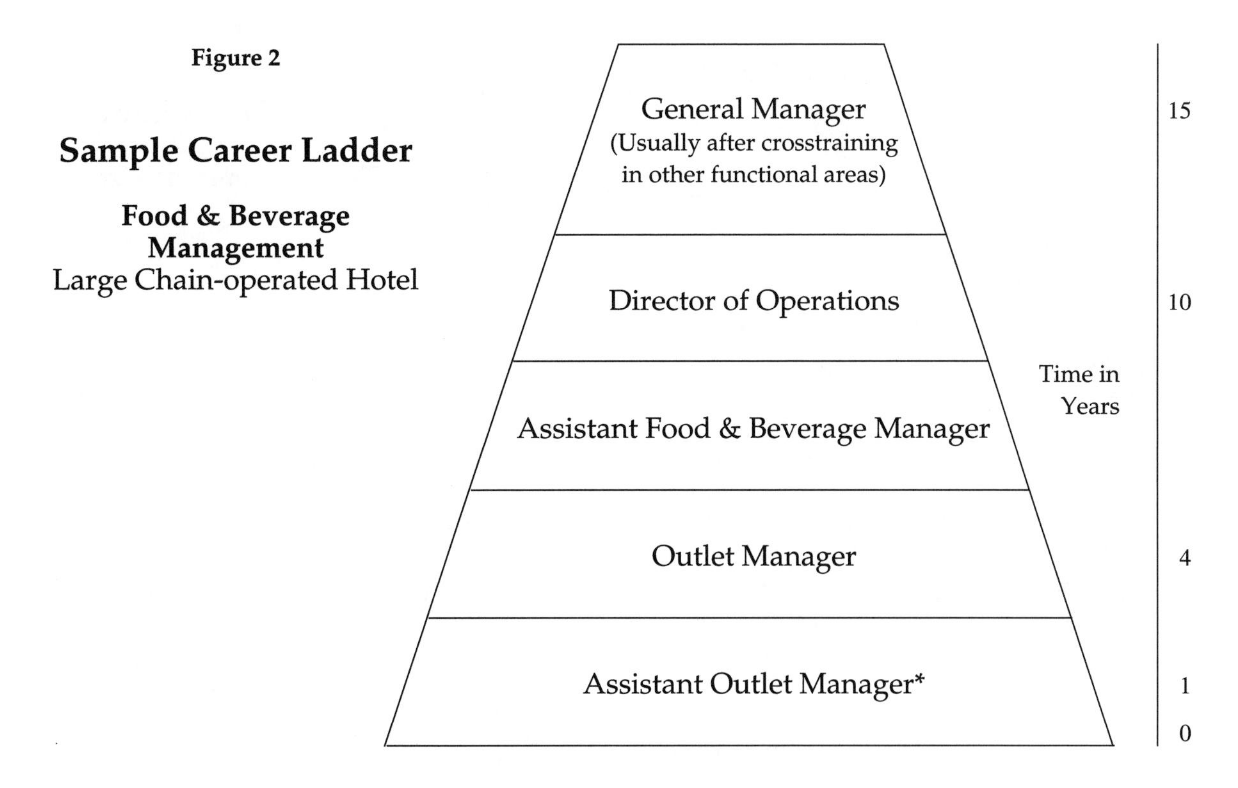

*Assumes previous food & beverage operations experience.

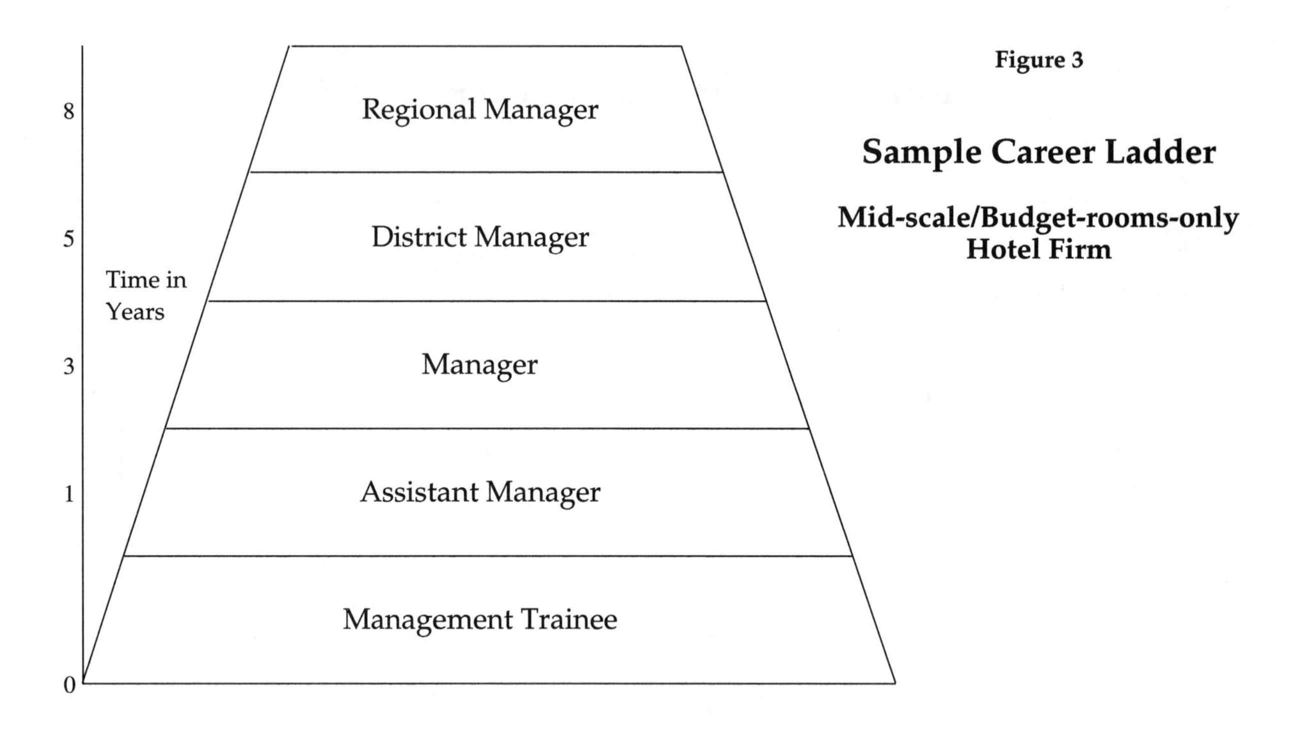

Figure 3

Sample Career Ladder

Mid-scale/Budget-rooms-only Hotel Firm

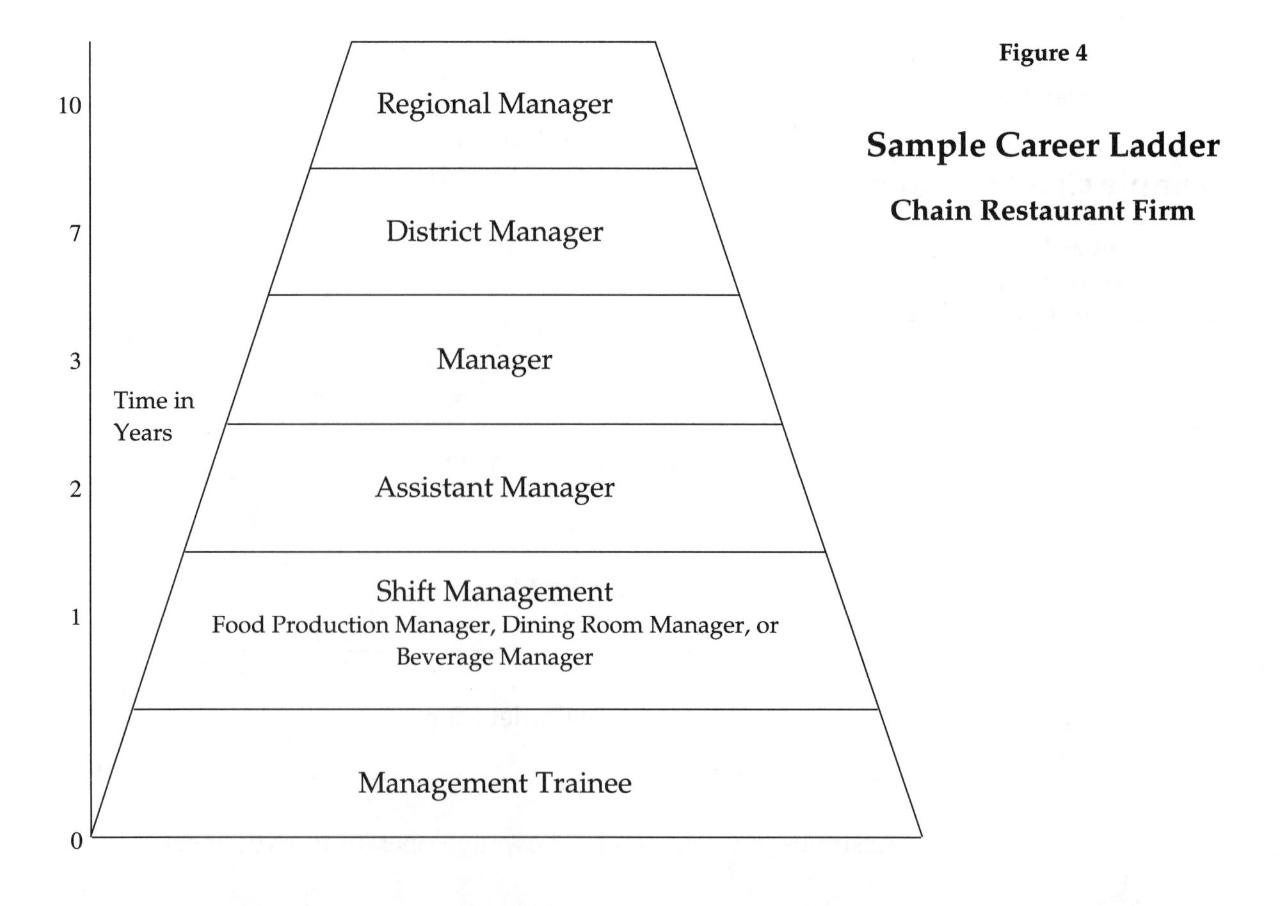

Figure 4

Sample Career Ladder

Chain Restaurant Firm

Figure 5

Sample Career Ladder

Chain Travel Agency

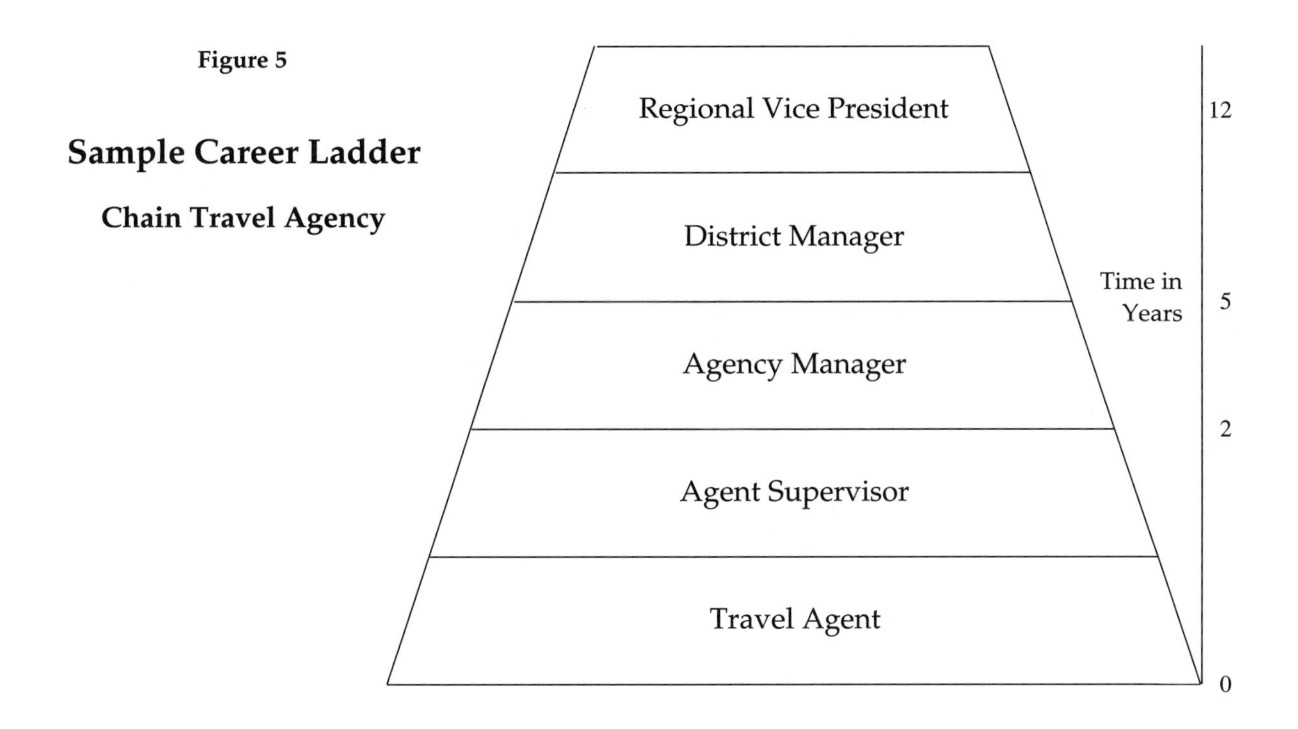

Figure 6

Sample Career Ladder

Airline Sales and Marketing

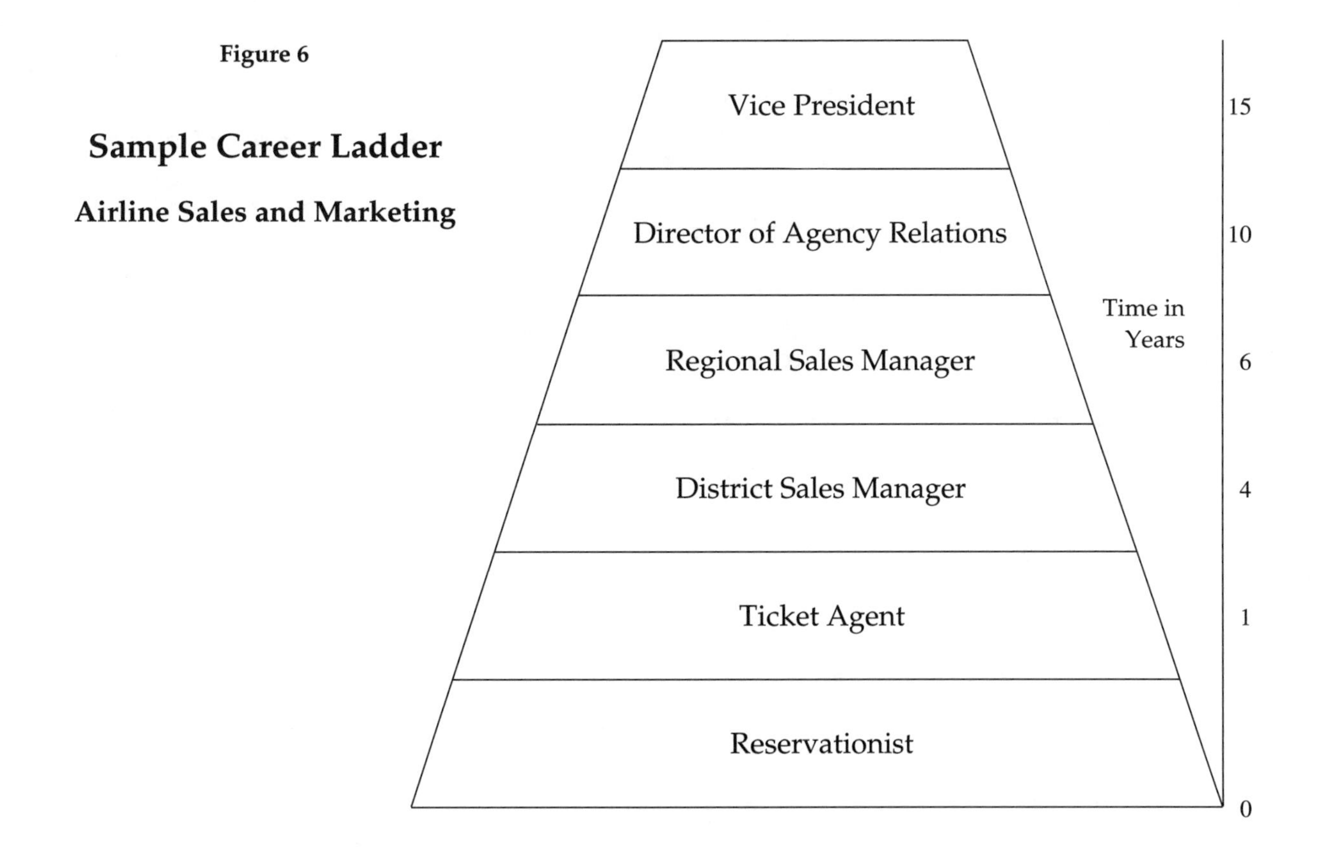

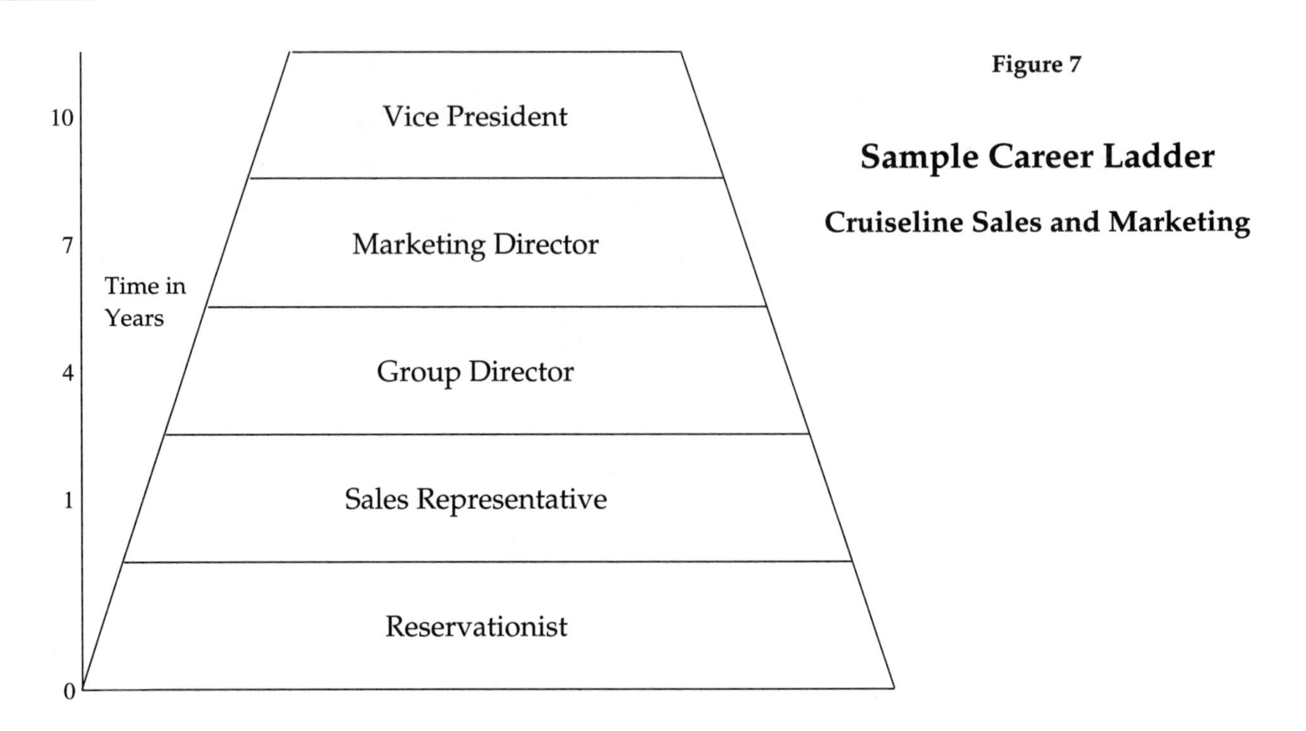

Figure 7

Sample Career Ladder

Cruiseline Sales and Marketing

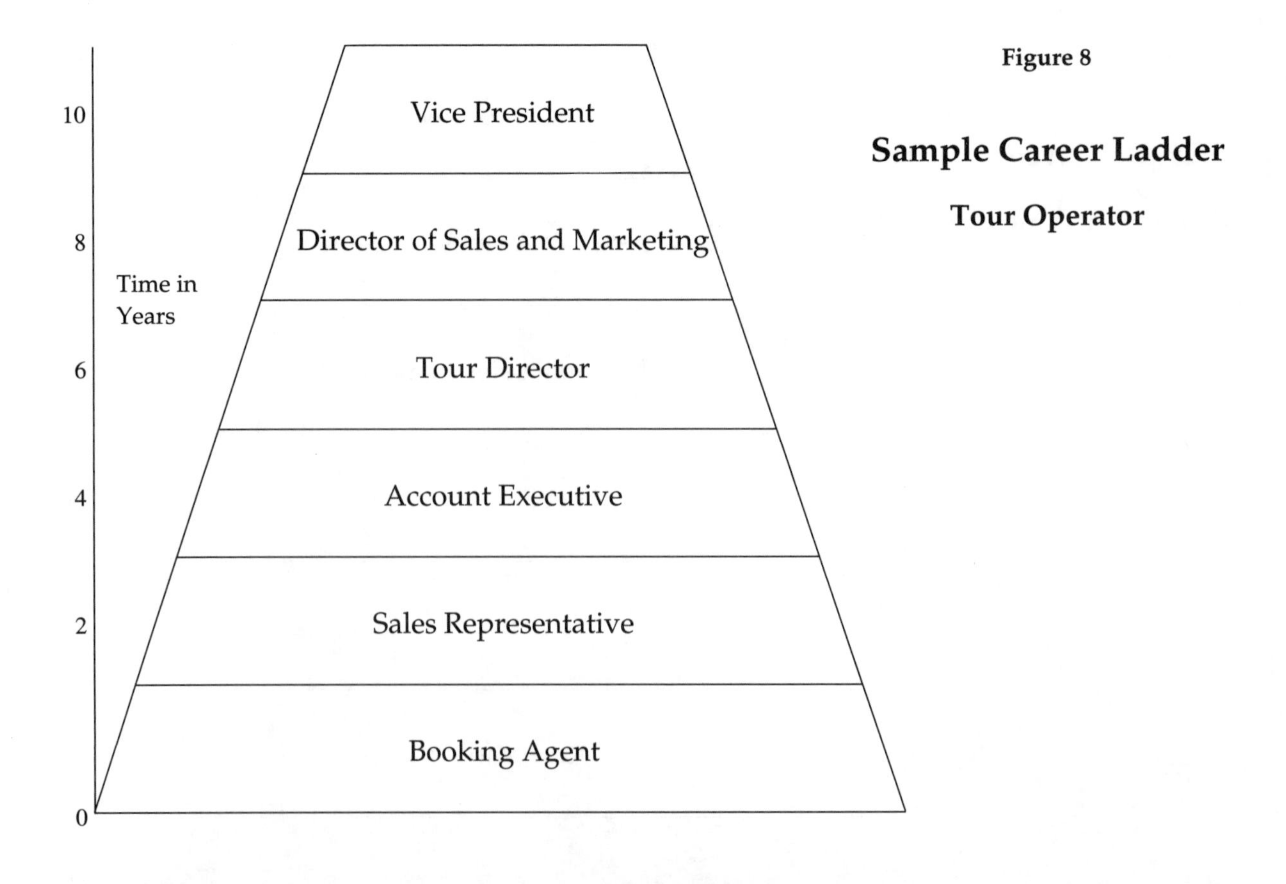

Figure 8

Sample Career Ladder

Tour Operator

Figure 9: Sample Organizational Chart for a Large Hotel Property Traditional Organization

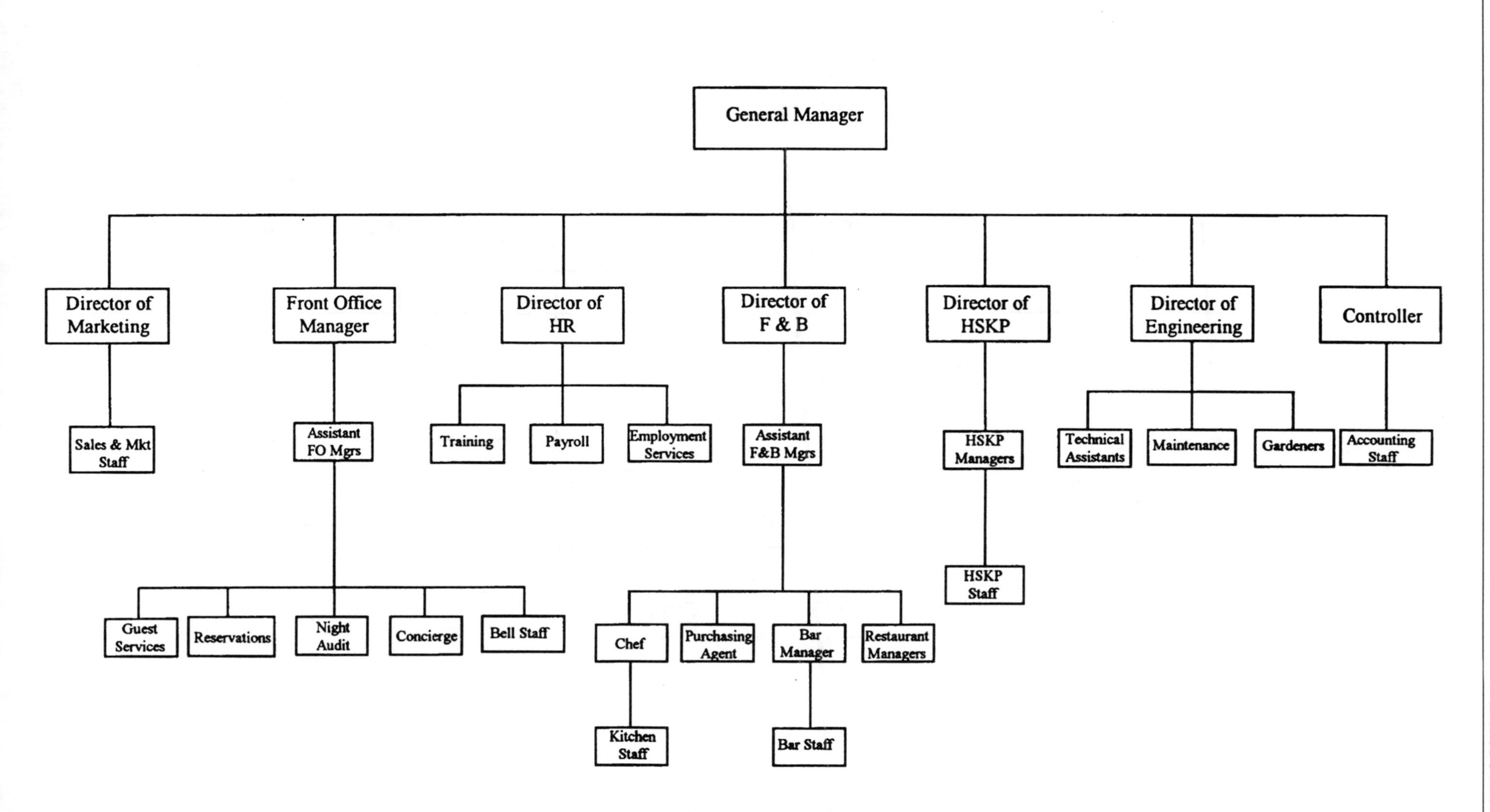

FIGURE 10: SAMPLE ORGANIZATIONAL CHART FOR A LARGE HOTEL PROPERTY
ALTERNATIVE ORGANIZATION

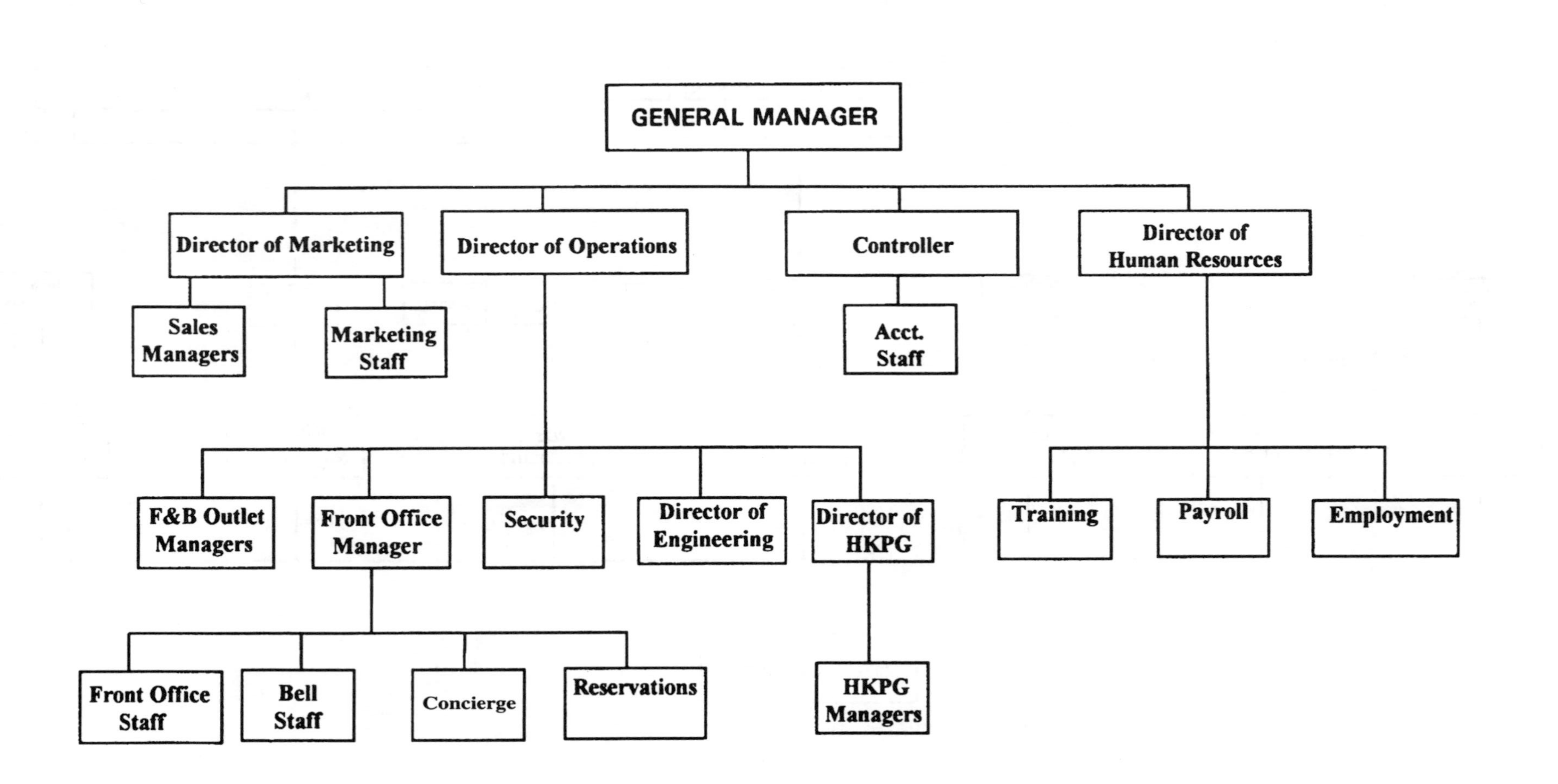

FIGURE II: SAMPLE LARGE HOTEL INDIVIDUAL BUSINESS UNIT STRUCTURE

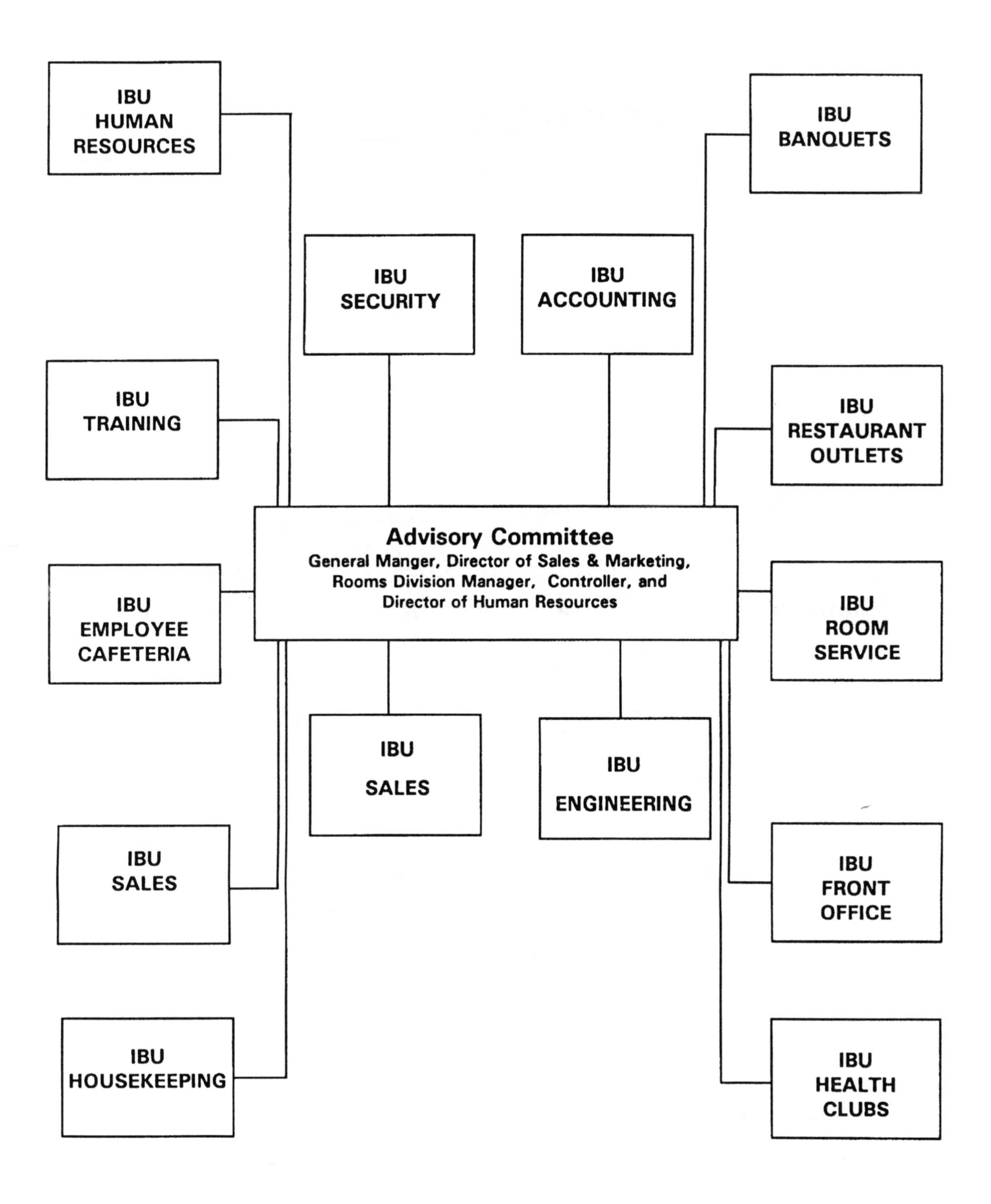

Figure 12: Sample Hotel Limited Service Structure (rooms only)

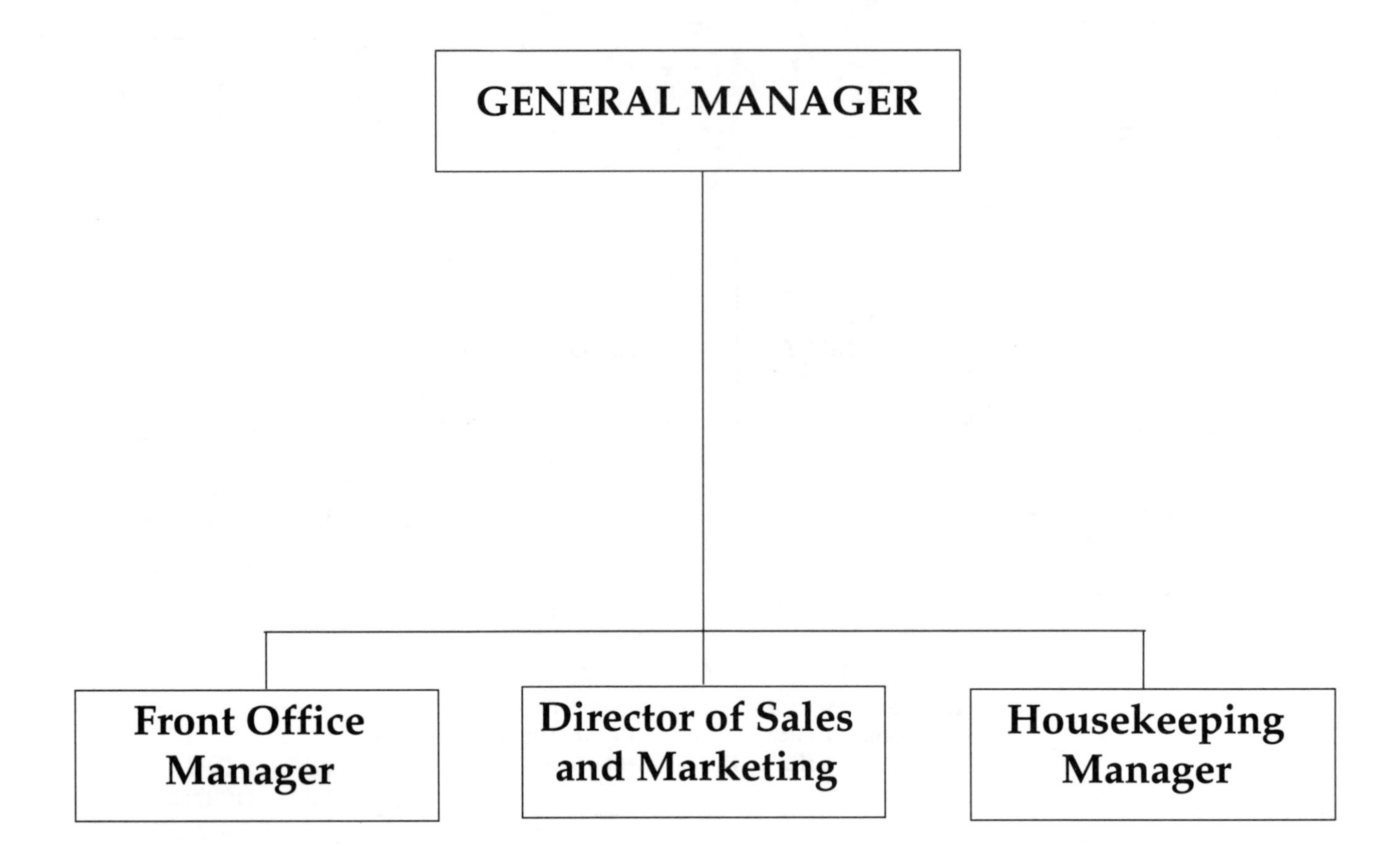

Exhibit A: Key Hotel Management Positions

Title	Department	Description	Advancement Opportunity
Food and Beverage Controller	Accounting	Controls Food and Beverage costs through menu planning and pricing/purchasing decisions, storage, issuing. Works closely with management and provides advice through consultation and reporting.	Assistant Controller
Assistant Controller	Accounting	Functions as office manager with responsibility for preparation of financial statements.	Controller
Controller	Accounting	Acts as financial advisor to management in achieving profit objectives through detailed planning, controlling costs and effectively managing assets and liabilities of the hotel.	Area/Regional Controller
Director of Operations	Administration	Usually the number two manager in a hotel, responsible for the management of all operating departments, such as Food and Beverage, Housekeeping, etc.	General Manager
General Manager	Administration	Supervises all activities within the hotel. Responsible for the coordination of all departments.	Regional and Corporate Positions
Director of Engineering	Engineering	Responsible for the maintenance of the physical and mechanical plant.	Regional Team
Steward	Food and Beverage	Purchases and supervises the receipt and storage of food beverage for the hotel.	Restaurant Manager
Director of Food and Beverage	Food and Beverage	Oversees entire food and beverage department.	General Manager
Catering Manager	Food and Beverage	Sells banquest and supervises banquet services.	Director of Food and Beverage
Convention Services	Food and Beverage	Acts as liaison between meeting planners and the hotel. Responsible for execution of major functions.	Catering, Manager/Director of Food and Beverage

Title	Department	Description	Advancement Opportunity
Front Office Manager	Front Office	Acts as a liaison between the guest and the hotel for reservation, registration and information.	Cross-training in other divisions—Director of Operations
Reservations Manager	Front Office or Marketing	Oversees reservations functions, plans for reservations and yield management.	Front Office, Manager/Director of Marketing
Housekeeping Manager	Housekeeping	Supervises the work of room attendants and housepersons in assigned areas.	Director of Housekeeping
Director of Housekeeping	Housekeeping	Supervises all housekeeping personnel. In charge of all renovation and purchases of housekeeping supplies.	Cross-training in other divisions—Director of Operations
Director of Marketing	Marketing	Oversees all marketing and sales functions, develops marketing and sales plans.	Director of Operations with cross-training in other divisions
Director of Sales	Sales	Sells convention facilities for meetings, banquets and receptions. Sells rooms to volume purchasers such as corporate travel directors of large companies.	Director of Marketing

EXHIBIT B: POSITIONS AVAILABLE IN TRAVEL-RELATED BUSINESSES

Tourist Bureau Manager
Travel Journalist/Writer
Promotion/Public Relations Specialist
Marketing Representative
Group Sales Representative
Tour Operator
Travel Agency Manager
Recreation Specialist
Tour Escort
Retail Store Manager
Incentive Travel Specialist
Consultant
Translator
Planner
Sales Manager
Policy Analyst
Campground Manager
Research/Statistical Specialist
Marina Manager
Economist
In-Transit Attendant
Resident Camp Director
Motor Coach Operator
Concession Operator
Auto-Recreation Vehicle Rental Agency Manager
Destination Development Specialist
Information Officer
Travel Agent
Travel Counselor/Sales Manager
Tour Wholesaler
Reservation Agent
Interpretive Specialist (Museums, Destination Information, Crafts, Art, etc.)
Curriculum Specialist
Business Travel Specialist
Financial Analyst
Teacher/Instructor
Transfer Officer
Market Researcher
Group Sales Manager
Association Manager
Tour Broker
Public Relations Officer
Tour Operator
Receptionist
Tour Leader
Meeting/Conference Planner
Guide
Ski Instructor
Advertising Agency Account Executive
Convention Center/Fair Manager
Sales Representative
Guest House/Hostel Manager
Entertainer
Program Specialist
Recreation Facility/Park Manager
Promoter

EXHIBIT C: REPRESENTATIVE INDUSTRY SALARIES (IN US$ THOUSANDS)

Hotel Salary Guideline
Low represents 100–400 rooms
Medium represents 400–700 rooms
High represents 700–1,000 rooms

Hotel Positions–Corporate	Low	Medium	High
CFO	87	112	157
Corporate Controller	52	64	87
Vice President–Operations	64	85	124
Vice President–Sales/Marketing	61	88	122
Corporate Food & Beverage Director	53	73	105
Corporate Chef	56	69	97
Director of Development	58	71	90
Director of Construction	52	72	98
Director of Human Resources	43	58	79
Director of Purchasing	34	46	73
Regional Manager	50	75	102

Hotel Positions–Operations	Low	Medium	High
General Manager	45	63	97
Assistant Manager	31	45	67
Controller	37	50	69
Human Resources Manager	31	39	58
Rooms Division Manager	31	46	59
Front Office Manager	29	35	46
Food & Beverage Director	35	50	74
Restaurant Manager	25	32	45
Maitre d'	25	34	47
Beverage Manager	28	35	49
Banquet Manager	34	41	52
Director of Catering	27	38	59
Catering Sales	32	38	47
Executive Chef	37	52	72
Sous Chef	29	37	49
Pastry Chef	24	31	50
Banquet Chef	27	31	37
Director - Sales/Marketing	35	44	73
Sales Manager	28	38	51
Conference Manager	32	35	53
Executive Housekeeper	29	38	53
Assistant Housekeper	21	27	41
Chief Engineer	23	29	43

Motels/Resorts	Low	Medium	High
Guest Services Manager	28	42	46
Motel Manager	29	35	49
Motel Manager (Couples)	32	42	52

Country Clubs (Golf)	Low	Medium	High
Manager (500+ Members)	49	65	87
Manager (250–500 Members)	39	53	58
Clubhouse Manager	36	43	54
Athletic/City Club Mgr.	37	61	81

Foodservice	Low	Medium	High
Regional Manager	47	58	69
District Manager	44	57	73
Foodservice Director	35	45	68
Cafeteria Manager	30	44	58
Production Analyst	37	49	56
Unit Manager	28	42	61
Assistant Manager	25	30	37

Restaurant/Fast Food Corporate	Low	Medium	High
Chief Operating Officer	90	119	161
Division Manager	73	93	118
Regional Manager/Vice President	66	89	109
Marketing Director	51	69	101
Controller	46	58	69
Human Resources Director	39	53	68
Training Director	35	45	57
Purchasing Director	37	50	68
Real Estate Manager	58	81	104

Operations	Low	Medium	High
Operations Director (Chain)	54	71	89
District Manager (Multi-unit)	44	64	75
General Manager (Fast Food)	31	38	47
Assistant General Manager (Fast Food)	24	27	35
General Manager (R - Non-Liq)	35	46	65
Assistant Manager (R - Non-Liq)	25	31	41
General Manager (R - w/Liq)	37	42	69
Assistant Manager (R - w/Liq)	28	35	46
Chef	34	49	64
Sous Chef	28	35	44
Kitchen Manager	27	32	39
Pastry Chef	25	34	43
Banquet Manager	27	31	39

Multiunit Foodservice Guideline
FF = Fast Food Restaurant
R - Non-Liq= Restaurant not serving liquor
R - w/Liq = Restaurant serving liquor

Source: Roth Young Wage and Salary Review (1997)
Adjusted for inflation and market demand to reflect 1999 average estimated salaries

EXHIBIT D: KEY ATTRIBUTES OF HOSPITALITY AND TOURISM PROGRAMS BY TYPE OR LEVEL

Program Type	Institutional Settings	Curriculum Objectives	Completion Time	Faculty
Certificate and Diploma* Programs	Business, Technical and Career Institutes	To provide students with specialized skills for specific hospitality and tourism jobs.	1–3 years	Primary industry experience and training. Many also have baccalaureate degrees, and some have graduate degrees.
Associate and Diploma* Programs	Community Colleges and Technical Institutes	To provide training and education necessary for hospitality and tourism management careers. Emphasis is on career education and technical skills, but curricula includes general education components. Some degrees can be transferred to baccalaureate programs.	2 years	Combination of industry skills and experience with combined undergraduate and, in many cases, graduate training.
Baccalaureate Degree Granting Programs	Four-year Colleges and Universities	To provide career education in combination with a broad general studies component and advanced learning skills. Emphasis on developing conceptual abilities and integrating knowledge of hospitality and tourism with other disciplines.	4 years	Combination of industry experience and graduate education. Heavy emphasis on graduate education.
Graduate Degree Granting Programs	Universities	To provide advanced education for specialized industry positions or for future educators. Emphasis on creating an interdisciplinary base for applied and research, policy analysis, planning and theoretical education.	1–2 years (master's) 3–5 years (doctorate)	Doctoral education with some industry experience. Industry experience not always required.

*Diplomas at some Canadian community colleges and European technical colleges are awarded for completion of a course of study which meets or exceeds requirements for an associate degree in the United States.

ACCREDITATION

Accreditation is a status granted to an educational institution or program that has met or exceeded stated standards of educational quality. Accreditation has long been accepted in the United States but is generally unknown in other countries. The United States has always preferred to keep governmental restrictions on institutions of post-secondary education to a minimum and has encouraged the voluntary system of accreditation in promoting quality education without inhibiting innovation. This system of accreditation has helped to ensure that post-secondary education in the United States maintains the highest quality both in the field of education and in the field of research.

Accreditation has two fundamental purposes: to assure the quality of the program and to assist in the improvement of the institution or program. Accreditation accomplishes these two purposes by requiring each program seeking accreditation to:

— Define its educational mission, goals, and purposes in writing after consultation with students, faculty, alumni, and the hospitality industry.

— Translate its mission into educational outcomes that can be objectively and clearly assessed.

— Assure the Commissions that the hospitality program has the administrative, financial, and academic support to achieve its educational mission.

— Ascertain, by sending a team of qualified educators to the program campus, the degree to which the program has translated its mission into educationally appropriate outcomes. This team also provides the experience and knowledge of peers to help guide the program toward continuous improvement of program quality.

— Affirm, through Commission action and annual reviews, that the program meets a standard of educational quality and will maintain a programmatic commitment to continually improving that quality.

CHRIE has set up two autonomous accrediting bodies: The Accreditation Commission for Programs in Hospitality Administration (ACPHA) which accredits hospitality administration programs at the baccalaureate level and the Commission for Accreditation of Hospitality Management Programs (CAHM) which accredits hospitality management programs at the associate degree or equivalent level.

Ongoing funding assistance for the development of the accreditation process was being provided through a series of grants from the Educational Foundation of the National Restaurant Association. A portion of the Commission's operating expenses are also being offset by fees collected from institutions seeking accredited status.

The members of CHRIE approved proposed changes in CHRIE's Constitution during the Spring of 1989 to allow for the creation of a commission to begin accrediting hospitality education programs at baccalaureate degree-granting institutions. After the proposed Constitutional changes were accepted by the members of CHRIE, the Accreditation Commission for Programs in Hospitality Administration (ACPHA) was formed during the Fall of 1990, and the commission began accrediting hospitality management programs at institutions granting baccalaureate degrees in 1991.

The Commission for Accreditation of Hospitality Management Programs (CAHM) was formed in January, 1994. The Commission began accepting applications for accreditation from hospitality management programs granting associate degrees (or the equivalent) in late 1994.

Questions concerning the accreditation process should be directed to Dorothy C. Fenwick, Ph.D., ACPHA/CAHM at 1-800-257-7657 or fax at (410) 226-0177. A complete application packet including the "Handbook on Accreditation," "Self-Study Guide" and Appendices, the Team Manual and Policies and Procedures is available for a fee of US$125. Requests for only the Self-Study Guide and Appendices are mailed free of charge. The "Handbook of Accreditation" contains the criteria for eligibility, objectives of the accreditation process, and the standards for accreditation of hospitality management programs. As they were developed, the standards outlined in the "Handbook of Accreditation" were published in various stages in the CHRIE Communique. CHRIE members were asked to review the proposed standards and respond in writing with comments to the CHRIE office. Feedback received from CHRIE members was used to make revisions in the proposed standards.

The "Self-Study Guide" describes the purposes of self-study in accreditation, the Commission's expectations of self-study, guidelines for organizing, planning, and conducting the self-study, an application for accreditation, and other forms to be used in completing the self-study. All written communication to ACPHA or CAHM should be sent to the Commission office at P.O. Box 278, Oxford, Maryland 21654. Please note: fees listed below are subject to change. Contact the Commission office for current fees.

ACPHA

The current fees for the accreditation process for hospitality management programs at baccalaureate degree-granting institutions are as follows:

Application Fee: US$300, payable upon application submission.
Self-Study Fee: US$2,500 payable when the completed Self-Study for accreditation or re-accreditation is submitted. Accredited status is normally granted for a seven-year period. The fee makes a contribution to ACPHA's cost in processing the Self-Study and preparing for the site visit.
Site-Visit Expenses: The program being evaluated bears the travel, food, and lodging expenses for the members of the site-visit team. This will normally be a three-person team, but may include as many as five members depending on the size and scope of the program.
Annual Maintenance Fee: The annual accreditation maintenance fee is US$300. This fee provides a portion of the funds required for the Commission's ongoing operations.

CAHM

The current fees for the accreditation process for hospitality management programs at associate degree-granting institutions:

Application Fee: US$125, payable upon submission.
Self-Study Fee: US$500, payable when the completed Self-Study for accreditation or re-accreditation is submitted. Accredited status is normally granted for a seven-year period. The fee makes a contribution to CAHM's cost in processing the Self-Study and preparing for the site-visit.
Site-Visit Expenses: The program being evaluated bears the travel, food, and lodging expenses for the members of the site-visit team. This will normally be a three-person team, but may included as many as five members depending on the size and scope of the program.
Annual Maintenance Fee: US$400. This fee provides a portion of the funds required for the Commission's ongoing operations.

About CHRIE

Founded in 1946 as a not-for-profit 501(c)3 organization, the International Council on Hotel, Restaurant, and Institutional Education (CHRIE) has long been respected as the leading organization for educators and industry professionals involved in the broad spectrum encompassing hospitality and tourism education. CHRIE's mission is to "advance quality education through proactive professional development, research, coalitions, and networks for association members and constituencies." CHRIE currently has more than 2,400 members in 52 countries, and that number continues to grow as the field expands. CHRIE's interdisciplinary focus provides a distinct advantage that no other organization has—that of a powerful catalyst that blends the various disciplines within the hospitality and tourism industry through communications, volunteer programs, and our annual conference.

CHRIE is governed by a volunteer Board of Directors charged with the responsibility for policy decisions and oversight of all CHRIE activities. Elected officers are supported by a professional staff headquartered in Washington, DC.

Membership Categories

There are two primary categories of membership in CHRIE: individual and institutional/corporate/organizational. CHRIE's membership is international in scope and includes: individual educators; hospitality and tourism industry professionals; colleges and universities granting baccalaureate and graduate degrees; institutions granting associate degrees, certificates and diplomas; hospitality and tourism industry corporations; and related companies, associations and organizations. CHRIE also offers a student membership.

Membership in CHRIE affords many opportunities:

• continuing education is available through CHRIE's publications and conferences;

• professional interaction provides an opportunity to exchange innovative ideas with colleagues in addition to creating valuable business and social contacts; and

• members participate in the development and expansion of hospitality and tourism education as a discipline and in maintaining high standards within the profession.

The number of CHRIE members around the world continues to increase at a rapid pace. To meet the varying needs of its members, CHRIE provides a wide range of member services designed to accomplish the organization's goals and objectives.

Publications

CHRIE Communique

A monthly newsletter which includes timely news and information about the world of hospitality and tourism education, special features, and a "Professional Opportunities" section listing employment opportunities for hospitality and tourism educators.

Journal of Hospitality & Tourism Education

CHRIE's refereed, interdisciplinary quarterly which features informative articles by leading sources covering a wide range of topics related to hospitality and tourism, including teaching techniques, curriculum development, trends in education and industry, industry practices and human resource development.

Journal of Hospitality & Tourism Research

Published four times annually and widely recognized as a specialized journal of record, the *Journal of Hospitality & Tourism Research* provides CHRIE members with a medium for sharing "cutting edge" research, theoretical developments and innovative methodologies. Publication is carefully guided by editors and a board of reviewers consisting of leading hospitality and tourism educators.

HOSTEUR™ Magazine
Published twice per year, *HOSTEUR* is the only internationally distributed career and self-development magazine for the more than 112,000 students at CHRIE member schools preparing for careers in the hospitality and tourism industry.

A Guide to College Programs in Culinary Arts, Hospitality, and Tourism
This directory of CHRIE member schools features a detailed program description including information on curriculum, size of program, admission requirements, availability of scholarships or internships, etc. The guide is marketed internationally to prospective students, guidance counselors, and hospitality and tourism industry employers.

Member Directory and Resource Guide
An annual listing of individual, institutional, and corporate members of CHRIE. Includes biographical data on individual members. Distributed free of charge to CHRIE members, with individual copies available for sale to the general public.

ANNUAL CONVENTION

Without a doubt, CHRIE's annual convention is the most important event of the year for hospitality and tourism educators. Several hundred educators and industry professionals meet in a highly charged atmosphere of seminars, panel discussions, paper presentations, general sessions, and social functions. The annual conference has become a "must-attend" event for the hospitality and tourism educators and the industry professionals that CHRIE serves.

MEMBERSHIP INFORMATION

Anyone concerned with hospitality and tourism education will want to take advantage of the many benefits offered to members of CHRIE. Questions concerning member benefits and annual membership fees can be directed to the CHRIE headquarters office at 1200 17th St., NW, Washington, DC 20036-3097; phone (202) 331-5990; fax (202) 785-2511; e-mail: chrie@erols.com. Please visit our website at http://www.chrie.org.

Associate Degree, Certificate, and Diploma-Granting Programs

Please note: All listings are correct at time of publication based on information submitted by each school.

The Academy of Hotel Management and Catering Industry in Poznań

Hospitality Management and Marketing, Tourism Industry Service, Hotel Management and Catering Industry

Program Enrollment:110 Hospitality Management and Marketing; 210 Tourism Industry Service; 240 Hotel Management and Catering Industry
Institutional Enrollment: 540
Degrees Awarded: Certificate, Diploma, Higher Diploma and Postgraduate Diploma
Degree Categories: Certificate in F&B Management, Certificate in Rooms Division Management, Diploma in Hotel Operations, Higher Diploma in Hotel and Tourism Management - License & two years MA Degree, Postgraduate Diploma in Hotel and Tourism Management
Emphases/Specializations: Certificate and Diploma in Hospitality Management and Marketing, Diploma in Tourism Industry Service, Diploma in Hotel Management and Catering Industry
Institutional Accreditation: State Department of Education, The Association of European Hotel and Tourism Schools in Strasbourg
Contact: Anna Przybylak ,BA, The Academy of Hotel Management and Catering Industry in Poznań, ul. Nieszawska 19, 61-022 Poznań, Poland; phone (061) 8771082, 8791481, fax. 8771711

Institution Description
The Academy of Hotel Management and Catering Industry in Poznań is the first such institution of higher education in Central-Eastern Europe. Our school has excellent facilities and very high training quality while the costs are among the lowest and students' tuition is used for further development of the school.

Program Description
The syllabus has been worked out on the basis of the latest models of the world and European education. The students are obliged to study English, French and German as well as computer science and they go through two obligatory practices at home and abroad.

Special Features
Our mission is to provide the best career education possible, that is why our principle is that the whole theoretical knowledge should be verified through practical experience.

Financial Aid and Scholarships
The Academy is pleased to provide Qualified students with complete financial aid program including, loans, scholarships or training abroad during which students can earn enough to pay their tuition fee.

Approximate Tuition and Fees
In-state: $4,960 plus $450 entrance fee.

Admissions
We have an open admissions policy. Applicants must have completed high-school or have successfully passed a college placement test or an equivalent examination and be full of enthusiasm.

Graduation Requirements
To graduate a student must: complete all required courses with a passing grade, go through two obligatory practices home and abroad and meet all financial obligations to the school.

Algonquin College

Hotel and Restaurant Management, Travel and Tourism, Culinary Management

Program Enrollment: 750
Institutional Enrollment: 10,000 undergraduate; 60,000 continuing education
Degrees Awarded: Diploma; Certificate
Degree Categories: Diploma in Hotel and Restaurant Management, Tourism and Travel, Culinary Management; Certificate in Chef Training, Baking Techniques, Festivals and Community Events Management, Patisserie, Retail Meat Cutting, Bartending, Sommelier, Conventions and Meetings Management, Rooms Division Management, Catering and Banquet Management, and Restaurant Management

Program Accreditation: Ministry of Education, and Training
Contact: Rick Reid, Director, Hospitality and Tourism Sector, Algonquin College, 1385 Woodroffe Ave., Nepean, Ontario, Canada K2G 1V8; phone (613) 727-4723, ext. 7761

Institution Description

Algonquin College serves eastern Ontario with campuses in Ottawa, Pembroke and Perth. It offers over 180 post-secondary, apprentice and tuition short programs in the English language. Funded by grants from the provincial government, Algonquin offers nationally recognized programs in the fields of hospitality and tourism, applied arts, business administration, health sciences, and technology and trades. A co-op educational program and an apprenticeship program, coordinated with provincial aid, are also offered for the mature student who wishes to combine academic studies with full-work terms.

Program Description

The Hospitality and Tourism Sector offers full-time diploma programs in Hotel and Restaurant Management, Tourism and Travel and Culinary Management. Hotel and Restaurant Management students concentrate on practical areas such as dining room service, food and beverage control, mixology/oenology, and food preparation. Their education is rounded out with classes in marketing, hospitality law, hotel accounting procedures, front office skills, and human resource management. Tourism and Travel students achieve competence in marketing and sales techniques, airline systems, tourism geography, travel industry automation, and tour selection planning. Students in the Culinary Management Program concentrate on food preparation, theory and kitchen management. Students in all programs will also take one course each semester in general education. Festivals and Community Events Management, a one year post diploma certificate program develops the skills necessary to organize, plan and produce festivals and community events.

Special Features

Algonquin College and the Hospitality and Tourism Sector announced the opening of their Hospitality Centre in September, 1990. This new facility houses a demonstration theatre, kitchen labs, baking and pastry labs, computer centre, travel agency and sommelier lab. Students will be involved in the managing and staffing of a full-service dining room also located in this new facility. Algonquin students who successfully pass the required courses for their diplomas have enjoyed a 90 percent placement rate in the industry upon graduating.

Approximate Tuition and Fees

For Canadian students, tuition, fees and books will cost approximately US$3,5000 per year. For international students, tuition, fees and books are approximately US$13,500 per year.

Admissions

Admission to the Hospitality and Tourism programs is based on the successful completion of the Ontario Secondary School diploma or equivalent, or mature student status.

Graduation Requirements

Graduation for a diploma requires the successful completion of 1,300 semester hours, which includes 100 hours of general study, 600 hours of professional skill development, and 600 hours of management students.

Alpine Center for Hotel & Tourism Management Studies

Associate Institute of IHTTI Switzerland

Program Enrollment: 230
Institutional Enrollment: 230
Degrees Awarded: Diploma; Certificate
Degree Categories: Diploma in Hotel Management leading to the Bachelor of Arts degree in Hospitality Management after an additional 6 months of study in Switzerland; HND in Travel & Tourism Management; IATA/UFTAA Standard and Advanced Diplomas; Certificate in Hotel Operations; Certificate in Catering Management; Certificate in Chef Training (Culinary Arts)
Emphasis/Specialization: Hotel and Tourism Management
Program Accreditation: Diploma is recognized by 20 Cantons and the Republic of Neuchâtel, Switzerland. Hotel Management program is fully accredited by the Hotel, Catering and Institutional Management Association of Great Britain. Alpine is an authorized IATA/UFTAA Training Center. Alpine is an approved Edexcel Center, UK
Insitutional Accreditation: EFAH—European Foundation for the Accreditation of Hotel School Programs; HCIMA of Great Britain; Canton of Neuchâtel, Switzerland; IATA/UFTAA; Edexcel, UK
Contact: Sybil Hofmann, Managing Director, The Alpine Center, 70 Possidonos Avenue, 166 75 Glyfada, Greece; Tel: +30 1 8983 210/022; Fax: +30 1 8981 189; e-mail: shofmann@alpine.edu.gr

Institution Description

Privately owned, Alpine Center was founded in Greece in 1987 and is an associate institute of International Hotel and Tourism Training Institutes of Switzerland (IHTTI), offering programs of study in English which are identical to those of IHTTI. Alpine prepares its students for an international career and assists in job placement throughout the world.

Program Description

During the first two years, the Hotel Management course emphasizes the operational aspect of the business, and leads to a Certificate in Hotel Operations. The third year is devoted entirely to business administration, management and a detailed project.

Graduates may continue their studies and earn a BA degree in Hospitality Management in Switzerland with the University of Bournemouth and at the same time receive the Advanced Hotel Management Diploma. The HND in Travel and Tourism Management course requires two years. Graduates may continue and gain entry onto the last year of the program leading to the award of the BA in Tourism Business Management in UK. It incorporates the IATA/UFTAA Standard Diploma course in the second year, which is optional. A third year Management Diploma course includes the Advanced IATA/UFTAA Diploma course. The Chef Training course is two years and leads to the Certificate in Culinary Arts.

Special Features

Featuring a truly international environment, Alpine runs its courses in a hotel where students live and receive their practical and theoretical training and education. A Career and Placement Office assists students in job placements worldwide.

Financial Aid and Scholarships

No financial aid is available; however, work-study programs are offered to a few needy and capable students.

Approximate Tuition and Fees

Hotel Management Tuition and Fees: US$ 8,500 per year; Room and board: US$2,500. Travel and Tourism: US$4,300 per year, room and board: US$3,100. Chef Training: US$6,400 per year, room and board: US$2,500. Other fees: US$600 for books and uniforms.

Admissions

A student must have a high school diploma, be at least 17 years old, speak fluent English, and pass a placement test and personal interview.

Graduation Requirements

Students must complete the set program, inducing one foreign language (French or German), and 11 months of internship for the diploma in Hotel Management, five months for the Catering Management Certificate, 10 months for the Chef Training Certificate, and eight months for the Travel and Tourism Management. Students must attain an average of five (of 10) in all academic, practical and attitude marks.

American Hospitality Management College

Hotel and Restaurant Management

Program Enrollment: 226
Institutional Enrollment: 226
Degree Awarded: Associate of Sciences; Diploma; Certificate; Bachelor of Hospitality Management
Degree Categories: Hotel and Restaurant Management
Emphasis/Specialization: Foodservice Management; Food and Beverage Management; Bar and beverage Management; Hotel and Lodging Management; Human Resources Management ; Mixology and Bartending Practice; Prevention Service and Risk Management: Marketing and Feasility Study
Institutional Accreditation: Full College's Professional Management Development Program Partners agreement with the Educational Foundation of the National Restaurant Associate of U.S.A.

Contact: David Wen-Wei Chou, MHM, Professor and Director, Department of Hotel and Restaurant Management, American Hospitality Management College, 300 Hanko Rd. Sec4, Taichung, Tawan 404, phone (886)4-2328119; fax (886)4-2328093, Email: AHMCUSER@msll.hinet.net

Institution Description

Since 1995, AHMC has been devolping programs of professional study and creative concepts of training, especially designed for Chinese students who are interested in Hotel and Restaurant management. AHMC is located n the heart of Taiwan, only 15 minutes from Taichung airport. AHMC is famous for its progressive quality programs and super facilities. Our bartender training facility is the best in China and a dedicated faculty and staff offer a wealth of credentials. Costs are among the lowest and training quality is among the highest in China.

Program Description

The curriculum is two years or sixteen months of intense study and practice. AHMC offers two paid internship of two months. Our hospitality management program prepares students for management careers. Students may specialize in hotel, restaurant, bar, or club management business. Our program is well structured so that students may enter the profession or transfer to a four-year instuition such as Johnson & Wales and Lynn Universities in the United States. Certainly, our credits can be transferred to numerous professional universities in the U.S.A. and the U.K.

Special Features

The program began as a partnership with the United States National Restaurant Association (NRA), and that vital link thrives today. The best from two continents—AMHC's combination of China and American education. Our student orginization "hospitality entrepreneurs" is active in many ongoing community projects. Cooperative education and internships are available to all students.

Financial Aid and Scholarships

Financial aid is available to all eligible full-time students. Contact our financial aid office for details.

Approximate Tuition and Fees

Tuition per semester (18 weeks) was US$1,695 in 1999/2000. Courses commence every spring and fall in February and September.

Admissions

AHMC has an open admissions policy. Applicants for the A.S. degree course must have completed high-school or have succesfully passed a college placement test or equivalent examination. In addition, they must be at least 16 years of age, and full of enthusiasm.

Graduation Requirements

The AS degree in Hotel and Restaurant Management requires completion of 99 credit hours. Required courses in general studies, hospitality management and specific area of study must be completed prior to receiving the Associate of Science degree. A minimum cumulative grade point average of 2.0 is also required, AHMC will accept transfer credits in equivalent work from other educational instuitions provided the grade achieved was a C or better.

Andalus Institute for Technology and Training (AITT)

Program Enrollment: 40
Institutional Enrollment: 6400
Degree Awarded: Diploma
Degree Specialization: Hospitality
Program Accreditation: General Organization for Technical Education and Vocational Training (GOTEVT)
Contact: Mr. Ahmad M. Banaweer - Hospitality Division Director Tel. (9662) 6519393-6514931-6514696 Fax. (9662) 6514990 P.O. Box 32379 Jeddah 21428 Saudi Arabia

Institution Description

Founded in 1994, AITT offers a variety of training programs in the Hospitality Industry. AITT believes in developing new technology in training materials through its consultants of higher degrees in their specializations, or through it membership in CHRIE, AH&MA, and ASTD. AITT has also a good cooperation with different academic associations all over the world.

Program Description

Hospitality Diploma Program gives students the skills required for supervising major hospitality service operations. The two-year diploma program offers courses in front office operations, housekeeping, food & beverage service operations, sales and marketing, human resource and financial management, and facilities management. There are many opportunities for cooperative educational work experiences as well.

Special Features

The program is the first of its kind in Saudi Arabia started on September 1997.

Admissions

Secondary school graduates or equivalent.

Graduation Requirements

Diploma degree requires the successful completion of 69 credits, the graduation project, and on the job training program (OJT).

Aruba Hotel School

School of Hotel Management

Institutional Enrollment: 200
Degree Awarded: Associate of Sciences in Hotel/Restaurant Management; Associate in Applied Science, Certificate in Continuing Education Courses
Institutional Accreditation: Government Board of Education
Contact: Tony A.D. Green, B. A., M.A., Ph. D. Cand., Director, Aruba Hotel School, P. O. Box 5019, L. G. Smith Blvd. 35, Oranjestad, ARUBA, Dutch Caribbean Area; phone (297) 838600; fax (297) 835157

Hospitality Sector
Aruba Hotel School

Institution Description

The Aruba Hotel School, School of Hotel Management is located near the hotel strip on Aruba's white sand beaches and is an integral part of Aruba's Post Secondary Educational System (EPI) which is comprised of 3 other distinct programs. The Aruba Hotel School is the Hospitality School within the EPI Educational System. Founded in 1982, the Aruba Hotel School continues to attract students from the Caribbean region as well as from as far away as India, Italy, Norway, The Netherlands, the U.S.A., Africa, Suriname, Peru, and other lands. A new program added in 1990, a Continuing Education program, designed to sharpen the skills of hospitality employees unable to enroll in a traditional program, have greatly enhanced the school's outreach and effectiveness.

In the 1997 Fall semester, another new concentration was added to the Aruba Hotel School, namely an Immediate Employment (IE) program with a Food Service and Food Production major. The new program, complementing the already existing Further Study (FS) program, will prepare graduates for immediate employment for entry level positions. Graduates of the FS program are prepared for further study to upper level degree programs.

Active member of CHRIE since 1983. Member of World Tourism Organization. Active member of the Caribbean Association of Hotel Schools (CHOCHS). The school maintains a close working relationship with the Florida International University, University of Las Vegas, Hotel Management School Leeuwarden in the Netherlands, University of Northern Arizona and others.

Program Description

A comprehensive curriculum compatible with any U.S. college curriculum of laboratory classes, industry work practicums, theoretical hospitality classes, and general education courses, from the basis for the two or three years' programs (two years for students applying with 12th grade U. S. high school diplomas or 2 "A" levels or their equivalent) leading to the internationally recognized Associate of Science degree in the FS program, or the Associate of Applied Science in the IE program.

Special Features

The unique cooperation between the Aruba Hotel School and the Aruba Hotel and Tourism Association with their over 7000 luxury hotel rooms and their exquisite restaurants provides students with the most ideal learning environment in all phases of resort operation. Through the Aruba Hotel School's Internet connection, students have access to a world-wide wealth of research information.

Approximate Tuition and Fees

Tuition and fees per school year is US$6800. This fee includes school uniforms, textbooks, accident insurance, module practicums. Room and board (off campus) is estimated at $3,000 per year. Both programs require extensive hands on practicums for a designated amount of weeks in real-to-life hotel/restaurant environments with the FS program affording graduates almost automatic transfer into most U.S. hospitality bachelors programs.

The Aruba Hotel School is committed to creating professionalism and personality.

Asheville-Buncombe Technical Community College

Hotel and Restaurant Management, Culinary Technology

Program Enrollment: 90
Institutional Enrollment: 6,300
Degrees Awarded: Associate of Applied Science; Certificate
Degree Categories: Associate in Hotel and Restaurant Management, Culinary Technology; Certificate in Baking and Pastry Arts
Institutional Accreditation: Commission on Colleges of the Southern Association of Colleges and Schools

Contact: Sheila A. Tillman, Chairperson, Department of Hospitality Education, Asheville-Buncombe Technical Community College, 340 Victoria Road, Asheville, NC 28801; phone (828) 254-1921

Institution Description

Asheville-Buncombe Technical Community College (A-B Tech) is a state and county funded, two-year community college offering programs in hospitality education, culinary technology, business education, health care, law enforcement, engineering and applied technology. A-B Tech offers 35 associate degree programs and diploma programs in four specialty program divisions.

Program Description

The Hotel and Restaurant Management (HRM) curriculum prepares students to enter the hospitality industry as management trainees in hotels, restaurants and clubs. Areas of study include hotel accounting/front office procedures, advertising, personnel management, housekeeping, food and beverage purchasing and cost control, and food preparation. An internship program in the field is required. The Culinary Technology curriculum provides students with the knowledge and skills to become a chef. This is accomplished through a combination of course work, in-house observation, laboratory practice, and supervised work experience in the field.

Special Features

An on-campus motor lodge, operated and maintained by HRM students, provides "live project" experience under the direction of college faculty. The culinary facility includes a fully equipped kitchen and two large dining room laboratories.

Financial Aid and Scholarships

The college maintains a financial aid office and offers grants-in-aid, loans and scholarships. The HRM and Culinary Technology programs offer several loans and scholarships.

Admissions

Asheville-Buncombe Technical Community College has an open-door admissions policy. High school graduation or its equivalent is required for admission to any curriculum. The college begins accepting applications on September 15, and early application is advised for the Culinary Technology program.

Specialization Areas

Hotel and Lodging Management
Restaurant and Foodservice Management
Culinary Arts

Graduation Requirements

Of the 75 semester hours required for graduation, 60 hours are devoted to major area courses. The balance of 15 hours are in the area of general education. Additionally, there must be 300 plus hours of successfully completed hospitality work experience.

Atlantic Tourism & Hospitality Institute (An Affiliate of Holland College)

Culinary, Tourism & Hospitality Management Programs

Program Enrollment: 500
Institutional Enrollment: 500
Degrees Awarded: Diploma, Certificate
Degree Categories: College Diplomas in each of the above mentioned programs
Emphases/Specializations: Culinary Arts, Pastry Arts, Hotel and Restaurant Management, Golf Club Management, Tourism and Travel Management, Events and Conventions Management, Recreation and Leisure Management, Tourism Marketing and Advertising Management
Institutional Accreditation: Member of the Association of Canadian Community Colleges (ACCC)

Contacts: Holland College Admissions Centre
305 Kent Street, Charlottetown, PEI C1A 1P5
Phone: (902) 629-4217 Fax: (902) 629-4239, Toll Free: 1-800-446-5265 (press 2), Web Site: http://www.hollandc.pe.ca, E-mail: info@hollandc.pe.ca
For further detailed program information ask to speak with Jim Fraser, ATHI Programs Manager - E-mail: Jfraser @ATHI.pe.ca

Institution Description

The Atlantic Tourism and Hospitality Institute (ATHI) was created in 1995 as an affiliate of the Holland College School of Applied Arts and Technology, located in beautiful Charlottetown, Prince Edward Island, Canada. The renowned **Culinary Institute of Canada** Programs are the cornerstone of ATHI and it has been training aspiring chefs since 1984. State of the art Tourism and Hospitality Programs are designed to enable students to develop the necessary skills that will lead the industry into the 21st Century.

Program Description

Culinary Arts along with the many specific Tourism and Hospitality related management diploma programs are two years of intense study and practice. All programs require a minimum 16 weeks of Internship with Industry. Credits are transferrable to a number of Canadian universities.

Special Features

ATHI Programs are competency based and designed to enable graduates to compete in the global marketplace. The Institute offers hands-on food and beverage training in its kitchens and dining room facilities.

Admissions

High school diploma or recognized adult education equivalent.

Tuition and Fees - International

- Culinary Arts and Pastry Arts - Tuition $11,500 (Cdn) approx. $7,600 (U.S.)
- Hotel & Restaurant Management, Golf Club Management, Tourism & Travel Management, Events and Conventions Management, Recreation and Leisure Management, Tourism Marketing and Advertising Management - Tuition $8,500 (Cdn) approx. $5,600 (U.S.).

Additional fees to cover texts, and lab fees are specific to each program.
(US currency exchange rates subject to fluctuation.)

Graduation Requirements

Must successfully complete all theory and practical courses plus complete a 16 week work Internship.

Bahamas Hotel Training College

Applied Associates of Arts Degree in Hospitality Operations
Applied Associates of Arts Degree in Culinary Arts

College: College of Hospitality and Culinary Arts
Program Enrollment: 67
Institutional Enrollment: 301
Degrees Awarded: Applied Associates of Arts Degree in Hospitality Operations, Applied Associates of Arts Degree in Culinary Arts
Program Accreditation: Hotel Catering and Institution Management Association (HCIMA)
Institutional Accreditation: Commission on Occupational Education (COE)
Contact: Mrs. Iva Dahl-Brown, Executive Director , or Mrs. Anna-Marie Albury, Registrar, The Bahamas Hotel Training College, PO Box N-4896, Nassau, Bahamas. Phone (242) 323-5804; fax (242) 325-2459; e-mail: bhtc@bahamas.net.bs

Institution Description
Established in 1973, the Bahamas Hotel Training College (BHTC) is a hospitality and culinary arts training institution which is governed by an independent council. Applied Associates of Arts Degree and short courses in Hospitality Operations and Culinary Arts are offered. Graduates easily transfer to prestigious colleges and universities in America and the United Kingdom.

Program Description
The BHTC's Applied Associates of Arts Programs have been created on the premise that practical and technical skills are viable paths toward successful careers.

Approximate Tuition and Fees
Bahamian Nationals US $2,500 per year; Non-Bahamian Nationals US $6,000 per year

Admissions
Admissions to the BHTC is based on quality of high school performance, recommendations from the applicant's teachers and counselors, and the applicant's ability to successfully complete the admissions interview process.

Graduation Requirements
In order to graduate , full-time students must successfully complete 432 clock hours of liberal art courses, 336 clock hours of in the hotel and catering industry. Students must complete: liberal arts courses, business courses, hospitality of hospitality operations courses: 8 weeks of internship and 96 clock hours elective courses. Part-time students must complete requirements within five years industry internship, and elective courses consultation with their program coordinator.

Special Features
All courses at the BHTC are interfaced with interaction, laboratory work and theoretical instruction. Placement in internship and student government involvement provide further development.

Bakersfield College

Foods and Nutrition Program

Program Enrollment: 55
Institutional Enrollment: 12,829
Degrees Awarded: Associate of Science, Certificate of Achievement
Degree Categories: Associate degree in Foodservice Management; Certificates in Culinary Arts, Dietetic Services, and Child Nutrition Management
Emphases/Specializations: Foodservice Management Degree with options in Culinary Arts, Foodservice Management and Child Nutrition Management
Program Accreditation: Western Association of Schools and Colleges; National Restaurant Association (Professional Management Development Program)
Institutional Accreditation: Western Association of Schools and Colleges
Contact: Gayla Anderson, Chair, Family & Consumer Education Division, Bakersfield College, 1801 Panorama Drive, Bakersfield, CA 93305; Phone (805) 395-4561; fax (805) 395-4241; e-mail gaanders@bc.cc.ca.us

Institution Description
Bakersfield College, established in 1918, is one of the oldest two-year community colleges in the nation. Bakersfield College, a commuter oriented community college, has continued to grow and to meet the educational needs of Kern county, an area noted for its rich agricultural and petroleum industries.

Program Description
Program provides educational opportunities and professional development for new students and working professionals in the foodservice field to increase knowledge, skills, and attitudes to ensure optimal job performance. Program combines hands-on training with classroom lecture. Work experience is required.

Special Features
Program is able to integrate the classroom theory courses with practical experience in the program's student operated restaurant and campus cafeteria.

Financial Aid and Scholarships
The Office of Financial Aid offers financial assistance to students, a variety of grants scholarships, loans and part-time employment opportunities are available for qualifying students.

Admissions
Students can enroll if they are 18 years of age. New students are required to take the assessment test and provide a TB clearance.

Approximate Tuition and Fees
In-state: $12 per unit.

BCA Business Studies Department of Hotel and Tourism Management

Hotel and Tourism Management

Program Enrollment: 105

Institutional Enrollment: 1700 undergraduates and 40 postgraduates

Degrees Awarded: Certificate, Diploma of Higher Education

Degree Categories: Diploma of Higher Education in Hotel and Catering Management with Tourism and Leisure by the University of Huddersfield, UK, after two years of study in Athens, leading to the final year of study at the University of Huddersfield for a Bachelor (Hons) Degree in: i) Hotel and Catering Management with Tourism and Leisure ii) International Hotel and Catering Management iii) Hotel and Catering Operations Management

Emphases/Specializations: Hotel, Tourism, Catering and Leisure Management

Program Accreditation: The academic program is the result of a franchise arrangement with the University of Huddersfield, therefore it is recognised by all the EU countries

Contact: Elena Venturatos, Director of Hotel and Tourism Management Department, BCA Business Studies, P. Psychico campus 2, Elikonos str. 15452 Athens, Greece. Phone: 00301 6726815 Fax: 00301 6748177

Institution Description

With 30 years of tradition in education, BCA offers the following programmes: Hotel and Tourism Management with the University of Huddersfield, Shipping and Transport (BSc and MSc) with London Guildhall University and Business Administration and Marketing with Plymouth University. BCA's educational activities include an English speaking primary and secondary school as well as a Health Care Educational Institution in collaboration with the best private hospital in Greece.

Program Description

BCA's Hotel and Tourism Management program is delivered in English and focuses on the skills and techniques necessary for the management of Hotel and Tourism business. These are supplemented by a coherent program of modules that allow students to develop knowledge of specialist environments. A Foundation year is also available.

Special Features

In order for students to acquire additional practical skills and industry experience, they have to complete a period of industrial placement within leading hotel and tourism companies in Greece and overseas. Additionally the program is supported by extensive industry visits, field trips and partner hospitality companies.

Admissions

A high school diploma or its equivalent and proof of fluency in English

Tuition & Fees

US$ 5,300 per academic year. No Room and Board offered.

Specialization Area

Hotel and Catering Management, Tourism and Leisure Management

Graduation Requirements

Diploma students must successfully compete the required number of modules and the industrial placement period as prescribed in the BCA and University of Huddersfield curricula.

The Beachcomber Training Academy

Basic and Advanced Level in Food and Beverage and Room Division; Supervisoy and Managerial Level

Program Enrollment : 1300 in 1998
Institutional Accreditation : Industrial and Vocational Training Board (I.V.T.B) - National board which controls all training institutions in Mauritius
Degrees Awarded : Certificates
Emphases / Specializations : Restaurant service / Kitchen production / Pastry and Bakery / Bar / Room Service / Front Office / Stewarding / Housekeeping / Guest Relations / Safety and Security Hygiene / Customer Care

Contact : Director : Tiburce Plissoneau Duquène (Mhcima), Beachcomber Training Academy, Robert Edward Hart Street, Curepipe - Mauritius, phone: (230) 601-3232, Fax : (230) 675-3240

Institution Description

BTA is the training school of the Beachcomber Group, one of the biggest hotel groups of the Republic of Mauritius. The seven hotels of the group have an overall capacity of 1300 rooms and have a workforce of 2800 persons. This private training school registered in 1996 with the Industrial and Vocational Training Board (I.V.T.B) of Mauritius, and is owned and operated through Beachcomber Training Academy Ltd.

The BTA section at the Beachcomber head office houses a training room and a library. Audio-visual equipment includes TV sets, video and a camera video. Two sets of mobile language laboratory accommodating 24 persons at one sitting are used. Practical training is carried out on the different hotels and at our head office. Trainers and equipment can be transferred easily to any location.

Program Description

Custom Tailored Programs: Proficiency courses are conducted for different categories of personnel at all levels of the hotel and catering industry. Duration of courses vary from a minimum of 30 hours to a maximum of 300 hours. BTA offers the same services to small, medium, and large firms in the hotel and catering industry in Mauritius and in the neighboring countries of the Southwest Indian Ocean, including Madagascar, Comores and Seychelles.

1300 persons were trained in 1998, including those following a full 52-week part-time training course for supervisors. BTA has also trained shop assistants for the Beachcomber Boutiques, Tropical Elegance, Galaxy, Hostess and Drivers for Mauritours (Local tour operator) and Boat skippers for fishing.

Approximate Tuition and Fees

According to course duration and content.

Graduation Requirements

School leavers or people with industrial experience.

Briarwood College

Hospitality Management: Hotel and Restaurant Management, Travel and Tourism Management

Program Enrollment: 24
Institutional Enrollment: 530
Degrees Awarded: Associate of Applied Science
Emphases/Specialization: Hotel and Restaurant Management, Travel and Tourism Management
Program Accreditation: New England Association of Schools and Colleges, Connecticut Board of Higher Education

Contact: Richard Dyer, Program Director, Hotel and Restaurant Management, Briarwood College, 2279 Mount Vernon Road, Southington, CT 06489; phone(860)628-4751 or(800)952-2444; fax (860)276-8838; e-mail rwdyer@snet.net

Institution Description
Briarwood College is a small private, coeducational campus in Southington, Connecticut. The institution is approximately 80% commuter-oriented. There are 26 other programs offered including child care, business management, dental assisting, mortuary science, office administration, legal assistant/paralegal, and occupational therapy assistant. The College has an excellent reputation.

Program Description
Emphasis is placed on development on independent thinking skills and decision-making managers. Very specific industry courses are designed to acquaint students with the necessary hospitality skills, knowledge and attitudes. Articulation agreements have been signed with many colleges and universities for students who wish to transfer to a 4-year program.

Special Features
Internship experiences are part of both program requirements. Placement is available. "Education for Life" enables qualified graduates to return for any courses tuition free.

Financial Aid and Scholarships
Federal Pell grants are available for eligible students upon completion of the FASA application. Stafford student loans are available as well as many scholarships.

Admissions
Open admissions policy. A high school diploma is required. SATS are not required.

Tuition and Fees

In-State	$10,605
Out-of-State	$10,605
Room and Board	$ 2,396
Other Fees	$ 270

Specialization Area
Hotel and Lodging Management
Restaurant & Foodservice Management
Travel & Tourism Management

Graduation Requirements
General education requirements require 28 hours, program area requirements are 34 hours for a combined total of 62 credit hours required for graduation in a two-year program.

Broome Community College

School of Hotel-Restaurant Management

College: Business Department
Program Enrollment: 105
Institutional Enrollment: 3,900 full time; 2,900 part time
Degree Awarded: Associate of Applied Science
Degree Category: Hotel-Restaurant Management
Emphases/Specializations: Hotel and Lodging Management; Restaurant and Food service Management; Travel and Tourism Management; Dietary Management
Program Accreditation: Full partners with the Educational Foundation of the National Restaurant Association; Certification for Dietary Management with the Dietary Managers Association
Institutional Accreditation: Middle States Association of Colleges and Schools
Contact: Rey C. Wojdat, Coordinator, Hotel-Restaurant Management, Business Department, Broome Community College, Front St., Box 1017, Binghamton, NY 13905; phone (607) 778-5171; fax: (607) 778-5170; email: wojdat_r@sunybroome.edu

Institution Description

Established in 1946, Broome Community College is a comprehensive community college. It has programs designed to prepare graduates for immediate employment or for transfer to four year institutions. BCC has historically attracted about two-thirds of its student body from Broome County and one-third from outside the country.

Program Description

BCC's Hotel-Restaurant Management (HRM) Program builds on a solid academic foundation of business course offerings including: accounting, marketing, human resources management, law and selling fundamentals. Course offerings in the HRM Program include: managerial accounting, cost control, hospitality law, food production, sanitation, menu management and purchasing. A certificate in Dietary Management can be obtained by completing required coursework and sitting for the accreditation exam prepared by the Dietary Managers Association.

Special Features

The Hotel-Restaurant Management Program is part of a highly reputable and strong Business Department, offering courses in accounting, business administration and marketing/management. In addition, the College-onthe-Weekend program offers students the opportunity to take classes which meet only every third weekend for a total of only six weekends per semester.

Financial Aid and Scholarships

BCC's financial aid office makes available numerous opportunities to receive both financial aid and scholarships, as does the Division of Business and the HRM Program.

Approximate Tuition and Fees

In-state:$1,100 per semester; out-of-state: $2,200 per semester. Room and board: $2,300 per semester (estimate). Other fees: $140

Admissions

Students are selected as they apply, complete the admissions process, and are found qualified for a particular program. More information may be obtained from the Admissions Office, phone (607) 778-5000, ext.5001.

Graduation Requirements

Graduation requires the successful completion of 66-67 semester hours, which includes approximately twenty hours of business courses, six hours of Humanities courses, six hours of social science courses, eight hours of math or science courses, three hours of computer science, and twenty six hours of HRM courses.

Canberra Institute of Technology

Faculty of Tourism, Retail and Hospitality

Program Enrollment: 2,000 +
Institutional Enrollment: 20,000
Degrees Awarded: Graduate Certificate, Advanced Diploma, Diploma, Certificate
Emphases/Specializations: Business in Hospitality; Food and Beverage Studies; Retailing; Travel; Tourism; Bakery; Butchery; Commercial Cookery Studies; Catering and Nutrition.
Program Accreditation: Australian Council Accrediting Tertiary Awards; Tourism Training Australia Accreditation Committee; Australia Hospitality Review Panel (AHRP) Tourism Training Australia; Travel Training Review Panel; The Canberra Institute of Technology Advisory Committee under delegation from the ACT Accreditation and Registration Council

Contact: Mrs Lyn Smith, Dean, Faculty of Tourism, Retail and Hospitality, Canberra Institute of Technology, GPO Box 826, Canberra ACT 2601; Australia; Phone: +61 2 6207 3125. Fax: +61 2 6207 3209 or email: lyn.smith@cit.act.edu.auHome Page: http://www.cit.act.edu.au/tnh/welcome.htm

Institution Description

Canberra Institute of Technology is located in Canberra, the National Capital of Australia. Canberra is a modern, well-planned city of over 350,000 people located in the Australian Capital Territory (ACT). It is approximately 300 kilometres southwest of Sydney. The Faculty of Tourism, Retail and Hospitality is one of five faculties and one school at the Canberra Institute of Technology. The Faculty facilities are the most up-to-date of its kind in Australia. The Faculty is the largest provider of vocationally oriented skills specific to education and training in hotel management, food and beverage services, tourism, retail and catering in the ACT and surrounding Region.

Program Description

The Faculty offers a wide variety of courses which may be taught in a series of commercial outlets, from Certificate, Advanced Diploma and Graduate Certificate level, and conducted by full-time and part-time academic staff. Lecturers have relevant academic and discipline qualifications in their area of expertise and extensive experience in the tourism, retail and hospitality industry.

Special Features

Facilities include computer laboratories, four commercial restaurants, front office and club & gaming rooms, six state-of-the-art food production laboratories, four beverage merchandising laboratories, gourmet food outlet, butchery laboratory, as well as other dedicated classrooms. Many graduates transfer to major universities to complete a bachelor's degree in their field.

Financial Aid and Scholarships

Financial aid and industry scholarships are available to eligible students.

Admissions

Places in the Faculty are highly competitive; entry requirements vary for different courses. As a guide, satisfactory completion of a senior high school program is required. Mature age entry will be considered for all courses.

Graduation Requirements

As an example, the Advanced Diploma of Hotel Management requires the successful completion of two years of study in all subjects, plus 600 hours of supervised industry placement.

Cape Fear Community College

Hotel-Restaurant Management Program

Program Enrollment: 100
Institutional Enrollment: 6,500
Degrees Awarded: Associate of Science
Degree Categories: Business Administration; Hotel Restaurant Management; Culinary Technology
Emphases/Specializations: Hotel-Restaurant Management
Institutional Accreditations: Southern Association of Schools and Colleges

Contact: Diane Sinkinson, Lead Instructor, Hotel-Restaurant Management Program, Cape Fear Community College, Wilmington, NC 28401; phone (910) 251-5172; fax (910) 763-2279 or Valerie Mason, (910) 251-5960

Institution Description

Cape Fear Community College, located in downtown Wilmington, North Carolina, was established as the Wilmington Industrial Education Center in 1959 and raised to technical institute status in 1964. In 1988, the school officially became Cape Fear Community (CFCC). CFCC is one of 59 such institutions operated by the state under the direction of the State Board of Community Colleges and administered by a local Board of Trustees. The College offers 52 different programs conferring two degrees, one-year diplomas or certificates. AA/EOC

Program Description

A Department within the Business Division, the Hotel-Restaurant Management (HRM) curriculum prepares students to work as supervisory and management personnel in hotels, restaurants, resorts and clubs. Visit our Web Page for more information on our program: http://cfcc.wilmington.net

Special Features

CFCC's HRM program offers certificate courses from the Educational Institute of the American Hotel and Motel Association and is a Diploma partner with the Educational Foundation of the National Restaurant Association. The Wilmington area has an abundance of restaurants, hotels and other varieties of tourism businesses that provide the student with co-operative education and employment opportunities. The program has a dining room/food lab facility located on the Riverwalk of the Cape Fear River at the Wilmington downtown campus.

Financial Aid and Scholarships

The Financial Aid Office at CFCC administers grants and scholarships, part-time work and low- interest educational loans. During 1997-98, CFCC processed financial assistance for scholarships, grants, loans, work study, and $2.9 million in financial aid to 2,023 students. Some scholarships are specifically for the HRM program.

Approximate Tuition and Fees

Tuition is established by the North Carolina State Legislature and is subject to change. Full-time in-state student tuition is approximately $280 per semester.

Admissions

Prospective students must submit the following materials: application for admission; official high school transcript and official college transcripts. Assessment testing for admission will be completed by the College.

Graduation Requirements

Graduation requires the successful completion of at least 69 semester credit hours with courses in Hotel-Restaurant Management, Business and General Education. The Culinary Technology degree also requires 69 semester credit hours.

CENCAP International School of Hotel and Tourism Management

Hotel and Food and Beverage Administration

Program Enrollment: 500
Institutional Enrollment: 500
Degrees Awarded: Diplomas, Certificates
Degree Categories: Final Degree: Superior Technician in Hotel and Food and Beverage Administration (3 years). Intermediate Degree: Technician in Hotel and Food and Beverage Administration (2 years)
Emphases/Specializations: Once students have obtained their intermediate degree of Technician in Hotel and Food and Beverage Administration, they may undergo a 2 year program of curricular articulation with the Universidad Nacional de General San Martín (National University of General San Martín) in order to receive their Bachelor's degree in Hotel and Food and Beverage Administration
Institutional Accreditation: DEGEP (Dirección General de Educación de Gestión Privada). Ministry of Education and Culture of Argentina
Contact: Debora Freidkes, Director of International Relations, CENCAP School of Hotel and Tourism Management. Av. Córdoba 1555, Buenos Aires Argentina (1055); phone (54 1) 816-6263/6264; fax (541) 814-0434

Institution Description
CENCAP is one of the most prestigious institutions of Hotel and Food and Beverage Administration in the country. Our students learn the technical aspects of the profession as well as the concepts of attitude, aptitude and courtesy.

Program Description
The curriculum is three years of intense studies and internships. Students are required to complete 500 hours of internships in order to graduate. Students can also continue their studies to acquire their Bachelor and Masters Degrees abroad.

Special Features
The combination of theory and internships within the industry provide the student with an excellent foundation for a successful career either in Argentina or abroad.

Admissions
High school diploma, personal interview, introductory course.

Tuition
US$4,000 annually.

Specialization Areas
Hotel Management
Food and Beverage Management

Graduation Requirements
Students must successfully complete 96 weeks of classroom theory as well as 500 hours of internships.

Centennial College

Hospitality and Tourism Administration

Program Enrollment: 450
Institutional Enrollment: 10,000 full-time; 50,000 part-time
Degree Awarded: Diploma
Degree Category: Hotel and Tourism Administration
Emphases/Specializations: Hotel, Restaurant, Tour Operations; Convention Management
Institutional Accreditation: Association of Canadian Community colleges; Association of Colleges of Applied Arts and Technology in Ontario

Contact: Doug Rapley, BA, BEd, Chairperson Hospitality and Tourism Administration, School of Applied Arts and Health Sciences, Centennial College, P.O. Box 631, Station A, Scarborough, Ontario, Canada M1K 5E9;phone (416)289-5311, fax (416)289-5354

Institution Description
Centennial College is a provincially funded, comprehensive college with courses in applied arts, business and health sciences. It provides high quality, career-oriented education.

Program Description
Centennial College's three-year Hospitality and Tourism Administration Program is built on a solid foundation of liberal education, business education and practical work experience. Students pursue specialized hospitality and tourism industry study in restaurant, hotel and tour operations, as well as convention management. In addition, students complete four-month internship.

Special Features
Four specialized teaching labs: kitchen, recipe development, dining room/foodservice, front office simulation. A compulsory 16 week internship.

Financial Aid and Scholarships
Financial aid is available to Ontario residents through the Ontario Student Assistance Program. Some provincial assistance is available from other provinces. Limited scholarships are available.

Approximate Tuition and Fees
Tuition is approximately US$1500 per year. Costs for uniforms, supplies and books are approximately US$200.

Admissions
Ontario Grade 12 or equivalent, or mature student status (Over 19 years of age) and satisfactory completion of an English test and orientation/interview.

Graduation Requirements
Must complete 10 quarters of study and two quarters of internship within five calendar years.

Center for Culinary Arts, Manila

Culinary School

Program Enrollment: 80 - 100 students admitted to the diploma and certificate program, annually

Courses Offered: Diploma in Culinary Arts and Technology Management; Certificate in Baking and Pastry Arts

Institutional Accreditation: Educational Foundation of the National Restaurant Association; Northern Alberta Institute of Technology (NAIT)

Contact: Corazon F. Gatchalian, Ph.D.,Director, 287 KatipunanAvenue, Loyola Heights, Quezon City, Philippines, phone: (632) 426 4841/426 6681 - 89 local

Institution Description

CCA, Manila is the first and only culinary school in the Philippines dedicated to professional chefs' education. The school occupies more than 1,500 square meters within the Cravings Center. It has ideal facilities for instruction, which includes professionally equipped kitchen laboratories and bakeshops.

Diploma/Certificate Programs

Diploma in Culinary Arts and Technology
This is a two-year comprehensive program, the first year aims to build strong foundation on the culinary principles and provide intensive hands-on training in procedures and techniques. The second year offers more advanced culinary courses combined with professional manaement courses.

Certificate in Baking and Pastry Arts

This is a twelve month program designed to provide students with strong foundation on the principles and techniques in baking. Emphasis is on providing hands-on laboratory experience as well as externship training for a thorough mastery of procedures and techniques.

Tuirition/Fees

PhP 175,000.00 per year

Admissions

Classes begin on the second Monday of june of each year. Application perion starts on the first week of November of each year (eight months before the start of classes) and ends on the last working day of February. Applications after this period will be subject to availability of slots.

Requirements

Official transcript of records from last school attended.
An essay of approximately 500 words on the topic specified in the application form. Three (3) letters of recommendation from former instructors and employers (for those previously employed). Medical certificate from accredited establishments of CCA, manila. Accomplished application form. Application fee of Php 200.00

Other Continuing Education Programs Offered

Professional Management Development Courses
CCA offers a series of courses covering the following functional management are: Foodservice Cost Control; Restaurant: Concept to Operations; Catering Management; Quantity Food Production.
The above courses are geared towards raising the level of competence of professionals in the foodservice / lodging industry in Restaurant association.

Fundamentals of Cooking and Baking The following are a few of the courses offered under this program: Fundamentals of Cooking; Fundamentals of Baking; Commercial Baking; International Entrees for the professional chefs.
The courses are capsualized four-day programs aimed to provide foundation skills in culinary / baking that combines lectures and actual hands-on training. The courses are conducted by highly competent chefs of the Center for Culinary Arts.

Specialized Culinary and Baking Courses
A few of the courses offered under this program are the following: Pasta Masterclass; Pizza Masterclass; Cooking with Herbs and Spices; Cooking with Flavored Oils; Sweet Sensation; Heavenly Breads.
These are two-day courses focusing on varied themes for culinary enthusiast. A 100% hands-on experience is used to maximize the learning experience of the participants. The courses are conducted by the chef instructors of CCA, manila and various chefs of different key hotel and restaurants in the Philippines.

Central Arizona College

Hospitality: Hotel & Restaurant Management and Culinary Arts

Program Enrollment: 28
Institutional Enrollment: 2,327
Degrees Awarded: Associate in Arts, Associate in Applied Science, and Certificates
Degree Categories: Hotel and Restaurant Management, Cook's Apprenticeship/Culinary Arts
Emphases/Specialization: Associate in Arts - Hotel and Restaurant Management; Associate in Applied Science - Hotel and Restaurant Management; Associate in Applied Science - Culinary Arts Certificate; Hotel and Motel Management Certificate; Restaurant Management Certificate; Cook's Certificate
Program Accreditation: The Educational Foundation of the National Restaurant Association ProManagement Option is available on certain certificates and degrees
Program Accreditation: North Central Association of Colleges and Secondary Schools
Contact: Janice Pratt, CHA, CHE, Professor of Hotel and Restaurant Management, Business Division, Central Arizona College, 8470 N. Overfield Road, Coolidge, AZ 85228; phone (520) 426-4403; fax (520) 426-4259; e-mail janice_pratt@python.cac.cc.az.us

Institutional Description
The HRM/Culinary programs are offered at the Signal Peak campus located on a desert mountain at the heart of Arizona, 60 miles from Tucson, and 45 miles from Phoenix. The natural beauty of the college, combined with the small student to teacher ratio, create an oasis for learning and growing.

Program Description
Certificate programs prepare the student for direct employment. The Applied Science Degree prepares the student for supervisory to managerial industry positions. The Culinary Degree follows the guidelines established by the Educational Foundation of the American Culinary Federation and includes the apprenticeship. The Associate in Arts Degrees transfers to university programs.

Special Features
Partnerships with Sodexho Marriott, the National Restaurant Association, and the Resort and Country Club Chef's Association of the New Southwest to enhance the learning environment.

Financial Aid
Subject to eligibility, awards are available through Federal Programs such as Pell, work-study, Veterans Administration, etc. Private, industry, and association foundation scholarships are also available.

Admissions
Central Arizona College adheres to an open door concept that provides educational access opportunities for people with diverse interests, talents, abilities, ages, cultural backgrounds, and ethnic views. A high school diploma or GED is required. Students are also evaluated for level placement in the areas of Reading, English, and Mathematics.

Tuition and Fees

In State	14-20 credit hours is $426
Out of State	For 14-20 credit hours is $2,722
Room Fees	$610 per semester plus deposits
Board Fees	$1,030 per semester
Other Fees	Lab fees (when applicable) $38/credit hour

NTR prefix courses add $8 for instate, $33 out of state, per credit hour.

Specialization Area
Hotel & Lodging Management; Restaurant & Foodservice Management; Culinary Arts.

Graduation Requirement
The Hotel and Restaurant Management Associate in Arts Degree is 64 credit hours. The Associate in Applied Science Degree in Hotel and Restaurant Management is 66 credit hours. The Associate in Applied Science Degree in Culinary Arts is 66 credit hours. The certificates range from 16 to 31 credit hours.

Central Institute of Technology, New Zealand

Hospitality Management, Hotel Reception, Travel Consultancy, Tourism

Program enrollment: 60 Hospitality Management, 20 Hotel Reception, 50 Travel Consultancy, 30 Tourism
Institutional enrolment: 1500
Degrees Awarded: Bachelors, National Diploma, Certificate
Degree Categories: Bachelor of Hospitality Management, National Diploma in Hospitality Management, Certificate in Travel Consultancy,
Emphases/Specializations: Hotel and Lodging, Management, Restaurant and Food Service Management, Travel and Tourism Management, Culinary Arts
Program Accreditation: New Zealand Qualifications Authority (NZQA)
Institutional Accreditation: NZQA
Contact: Centre for Hospitality and Tourism Management, Central Institute of Technology, PO Box 40-740, Upper Hutt, Wellington, New Zealand, phone: 64 (04) 527-6357, fax 64 (04) 527-6364

Institutional Description

The Central Institute of Technology was established in 1960 and has a special two-fold mission (1) to provide advanced level programs for which the demand is spread thinly across the country, and (2) to recognise that for many students, gaining a polytechnic education requires leaving home. For this reason, the Central Institute of Technology provides a 500-bed residential facility where students can live in quality, friendly, and favorably priced accommodations. The institution specializes in the following programs: management and computing, hospitality and tourism management, health sciences, health professions, pure science, engineering, electronic and electrical engineering.

Program Description

The Centre for Hospitality and Tourism Management offers a variety of programs: a 3 year Bachelors Degree in Hospitality Management, a Diploma in Hospitality Management and various Certificate courses in Front Office Operations, Hospitality Operations, Travel, Tourism, Cookery and Foodservice.

Special Features

All programs have a co-operative education component. This provides students the opportunity to obtain first-hand industry experience, a saleable commodity. Secondly, it allows the Centre to become closely related the industry and to receive feedback on its education program from industry practitioners.

Financial Aid and Scholarships

At this time, this is little financial aid or scholarship work available in New Zealand at this level. Although student aid is on the increase, individual students need to approach organizations that are offering scholarships.

Approximate Tuition and Fees

Tuition fees for the National Diploma in Hospitality Management are approximately NZ$3,000 per year. Other costs involved with the program include the purchasing of uniforms and textbooks. Tuition and fees for a Certificate in Front Office or Travel Consultancy range from NZ$3,000-NZ$4,000. Other costs associated with these programs include textbooks and workbooks.'

Admissions

The Admissions Committee is interested in: the academic quality of all applicants; the suitability of applicants for the hospitality/tourism service industry; recommendations provided by the applicant's counsellors or teachers; and the depth of involvement in extracurricular activities indicating leadership, and organizational and problem-solving skills.

Graduation Requirements

Graduation requires successful completion of all the units of learning for each program. Students are required to attain the recommended pass mark for each unit.
Graduation requires successful completion of all the units of learning for each program. Students are required to attain the recommended pass mark for each unit.

Cloud County Community College

Hotel/Hospitality Management, Recreation/Leisure Management

Program Enrollment: 40
Institutional Enrollment: 4000
Degrees Awarded: Associate of Applied Science; Associate of Science (Transfer Degree)
Degree Categories: Associate of Applied Science in Hotel/Hospitality Management; Associate of Applied Science in Recreation/Leisure Management; Associate of Science in Hotel/Hospitality Management (Transfer Degree); Associate of Science in Recreation/Leisure Management (Transfer Degree)

Institutional Accreditation: North Central Association of Colleges and Schools, Kansas State Department of Education
Contact: Glenn Baron, Instructor, Department of Tourism, Cloud County Community College, 2221 Campus Dr. Concordia, KS 66901-1002; phone (800) 729-5101or (785) 243-1435; fax (785) 243-1043; Internet http://www.cloudccc.cc.ks.us

Institutional Description
Founded in 1965, Cloud County Community College is a public two-year student centered learning college centrally located in the USA.

Program Description
The Hotel/Hospitality Management and Recreation/Leisure Management programs enable graduates to enter the specialized area of their choice. The curriculum is industry driven and competency based with a theme of quality and leadership. The in-class learning is reinforced with a cooperative education internship in industry. Articulation with Kansas State University's Hotel, Restaurant, Institutional Management and Dietetics program has been established, as well as, out-of-state articulations with various colleges and universities. Students have the opportunity to obtain membership in various professional organizations and participate with on-campus clubs.

Special Features
Students may enroll in a unique Hotel Site Visits course. Class sizes are small and personal attention is guaranteed. The Cloud County Community College Career Assistance Center provides information about careers and organizations; opportunities to meet with prospective employers; and assistance to students and alumni in assessing their career decisions. Historically, the program has had a solid placement record.

Financial Aid and Scholarships
Cloud County Community College maintains a financial aid office on campus. There are a variety of financial aid programs available.

Admissions
Cloud County Community College has open and rolling admissions. A high school diploma or GED is required. Persons not meeting the above requirements should contact the Admissions Office.

Tuition and Fees
In-State $1513
Out-of-State $2980
Room and Board $1980 includes 5 meals per week
Other Fees $50

Specialization Area
Hotel & Lodging Mgmt.
Restaurant & Foodservice Mgmt.

Graduation Requirements
The completion of 68 semester credit hours. This includes 47 credits in management and hospitality or recreation, 18 credits in general education, and 3 credits for the cooperative education internship.

Colorado Mountain College

Resort Management, Culinary Arts

Program Enrollment: 50
Institutional Enrollment: 1,500 full time
Degrees Awarded: Associate of Applied Science; Certificate
Degree Categories: Associate in Culinary Arts, Resort Management; Certificate in Resort Management, ACF Certification of Culinary Apprenticeship
Emphases/Specializations: Resort Management; Rooms Division Management
Program Accreditation: American Hotel and Motel Association; American Culinary Federation Pending
Institutional Accreditation: North Central Association of Colleges and Schools
Contact: Teri Masten, Director of Pre-Enrollment Services, Colorado Mountain College, P.O. Box 10001, Department HO, Glenwood Springs, CO 81602; phone (800) 621-8559

Institution Description

Colorado Mountain College is a publicly supported, two-year college enrolling students from the Central Colorado Rockies, all of Colorado, 38 states and several foreign countries. Residential campuses are located in Glenwood Springs, Steamboat Springs, and Leadville. Other programs include Associate of Arts in ski business, ski area operations, photography, graphic design, environmental technology, and business.

Program Description

The Resort Management program gives basic instruction in resort and lodging operations, resort specialty subjects, management concepts, accounting and related resort coursework. The world-class resort of Steamboat Springs gives students a wide range of hands-on experiences. Culinary Arts offers three years' apprenticeship program at Keystone Resorts and in Vail.

Special Features

Students are able to apply what they learn in the classroom through internship programs in the resort industries and through the ACF Apprenticeship Program.

Financial Aid and Scholarships

Each year more than 50 percent of our students receive some form of financial assistance. Grants, loans, work programs and scholarships, as well as opportunities for part-time employment, are available to help students meet educational expenses.

Approximate Tuition and Fees

For 1998-99, $38 per credit for Colorado Mountain District residents; $65 per credit for in-state residents; $210 per credit for out-of-state residents.

Admissions

Colorado Mountain College is an open enrollment community college. We admit all who demonstrate a desire to learn and the ability to profit from our educational programs. Academic testing is administered at the time of enrollment. Some of CMC's programs, like culinary arts, have selective admission.

Columbus State Community College

Hospitality Management

Program Enrollment: 375
Institutional Enrollment: 17,000
Degrees Awarded: Associate of Applied Science; Certificate
Degree Category: Hospitality Management
Emphases/Specializations: Associate in Foodservice/ Restaurant Management, Travel/Tourism/Hotel Management, Chef Apprenticeship, Dietetic Technician, Certificate in Dietary Manager
Program Accreditation: Chef Apprenticeship and Fooservice/Restaurant Management majors by American Culinary Federation Accrediting Commission
Institutional Accreditation: North Central Association of College and Schools

Contact: Carol Kizer, Chairperson, Hospitality Management Department, Columbus State Community College, 550 East Spring St., Columbus, OH 43215; phone (800)621-6407 or (614)287-2579

Institution Description

Columbus State is a public, two-year state community college offering affordable pre-baccalaureate and technical two-year associate degree programs, general education studies, supportive programs and services, and community services. The college currently offers more than 50 associate degrees, certificates and continuing education programs.

Program Description

Columbus State's Hospitality Management programs prepares students for supervisory positions in a wide range of establishments serving guests away from home. The curriculum includes classes in communications, social and behavioral sciences, physical science, humanities, business management, as well as technical courses. Over 100 industry sites cooperate with CSCC to provide the supervised and coordinated work experiences, which are required by the program.

Special Features

Students receive instruction in well-equipped, small- and large-quantity food preparation laboratories. A computer laboratory provides hands-on experiences with lodging, foodservice, and travel reservation systems.

Financial Aid and Scholarships

The college maintains a fully staffed financial aid office. Professional and community groups fund many scholarships, particularly for students who have completed at least one quarter of coursework.

Approximate Tuition and Fees

Ohio residents: $61 per credit hour to a maximum of $732 per quarter for students scheduling 12-18 credit hours. Non-Ohio U.S. residents: $134 per credit hour to a maximum of $1608 per quarter. International students: $162 per credit hour to a maximum of $1944 per quarter.

Admission

Columbus State Community College is committed to the selection of students without regard to color, age, race, sex, creed, sexual orientation, national origin, marital or veteran's status as defined by law. Columbus State maintains an open door policy, which means that most programs are open to anyone with a high-school diploma or the equivalent. Placement tests assess abilities in math and English, ans some prerequisite coursework may be required prior to enrollment in the technical program.

Graduation Requirements

Graduation requires the completion of 104-110 quarter credit hours depending upon the major. Fifty-five to 65 credit hours are technical courses, with a minimum of 22 credits in general studies and 21 credits in basic studies necessary for career competency. The Chef Apprenticeship Program requires three years or 6,000 hours of on-the-job training, in addition to the associate degree requirements.

The Cooking and Hospitality Institute of Chicago

Associate of Applied Science in Culinary Arts

Program Enrollment: 750
Institutional Enrollment: 1000
Degrees Awarded: Associate of Applied Science; Certificate
Degree Categories: Associate in Culinary Arts; Certificate in Professional Cooking, Baking and Pastry, Restaurant Management
Program Accreditation: Accreditation Commission for Schools and Colleges of Technology, American Culinary Federation
Institutional Accreditation: Accrediting Commission for Schools and Colleges of Technology
Contact: James Simpson, Executive Vice President, The Cooking and Hospitality Institute of Chicago, 361 W. Chestnut, Chicago, IL 60610; (312) 944-0882; fax (312) 944-8557

Institutional Description
Established in 1983, The Cooking and Hospitality Institute of Chicago has developed into a strong training center focusing on culinary and hospitality education. Located in the heart of Chicago's River North community, the modern facility includes three commercial kitchens and an on-premise restaurant.

Program Description
Students can choose among a variety of certificate programs, including professional cooking, baking and pastry, and restaurant management. An associate degree program in culinary arts is also offered.

Special Features
The Institute has an on-premise restaurant that serves as the advanced laboratory for culinary students. An active placement service is maintained with the Chicago area hospitality industry.

Financial Aid and Scholarships
The institute's financial aid office makes available federal Title IV opportunities. Scholarships are available from the Illinois Restaurant Association, Les Dames D'escoffier, CAREF.

Approximate Tuition and Fees
$300 per credit hour, plus books and materials.

Admissions
Students must complete a formal application and submit high school transcripts or GED scores.

Graduation Requirements
Satisfactory completion of 69 credits, which includes 15 credits in general education.

County College of Morris

Hospitality Management Program

Program Enrollment: 150
Institutional Enrollment: 10,000
Degree Awarded: Associate of Applied Science
Degree Category: Hospitality Management
Institutional Accreditation: New Jersey State Department of Higher Education; Middle States Association of Colleges and Secondary Schools

Contact: Professor Edward B. Pomianoski, Director Hospitality Management Program, County College of Morris, 214 Center Grove Road, Randolph, NJ 07869-2086. Phone: (973) 328-5669

Institution Description

County College of Morris is a two-year community college essentially dedicated to meeting the needs of students and employers for educational advancement and career training, and to foster social and cultural enlightenment within the community it serves.

Program Description

The County College of Morris Hospitality Management Program functions as an integral part of the department of Business Administration and provides academic and practical training which prepares graduates for hospitality management career opportunities. These opportunities encompass career paths in the Hospitality Industry within the lodging segment including luxury, convention, all-suite, gaming, and resort hotels, and in the food service segment including restaurants, catering, and institutional and business food service management. Students also study travel and tourism, recreation and leisure management (theme parks, clubs, and public parks), meeting and event sales, planning , and management, senior living services, healthcare, and retirement community management, and the support infrastructure as the balance of the seven areas which comprise the main business segments of the hospitality industry.

Special Features

The Hospitality Management Program provides the following distinctive features: paid one semester cooperative work experience, state-of-theart culinary facilities, catering club, and practical applications of classroom and laboratory instruction.

Financial Aid and Scholarship

Financial assistance consists of scholarships, loans, grants and part-time employment, and includes: Pell Grants, OEF, the New Jersey Garden State Scholarship Program, TAG, the guaranteed student loan program, NDLS, and supplemental educational opportunity grants.

Approximate Tuition and Fees

Tuition is $924 per semester for county residents, $1,728 per semester for in-state, out-of-county residents, and $2,328 per semester for outof-state residents.

Admissions

A basic requirement is graduation from an approved secondary school or a high school equivalency certificate. Admission to a full-time program of study is based on a review of the high school academic record, counselor recommendations, and where appropriate, the applicant's maturity and interest as may be determined during his or her admissions counseling interview. High school seniors are recommended to submit official test scores of the scholastic aptitude test of the college Entrance Examination Board. Admission to part-time study is open to both high school and nonhigh school graduates.

Graduation Requirements

To be eligible for a degree, the student must be in good standing and have completed the general and prescribed curriculum coursework for his or her major with a 2.0 or better cumulative grade point average. All degree students must complete at least 30 of the last 38 credits at the County College of Morris.

The Culinary Institute of America (CIA)

Associate Degree Program

Program Enrollment: 2,000
Institutional Enrollment: 2,150
Degrees Awarded: Associate in Occupational Studies (Bachelor of Professional Studies also offered, see next section)
Degree Categories: Culinary Arts, Baking and Pastry Arts
Emphases/Specializations: Cooking, Baking, Foodservice
Program Accreditation: New York State Department of Education
Institutional Accreditation: Accrediting Commission of Career Schools and Technology (ACCSCT); Candidate for Accreditation Status, Commission on Higher Education (Middle States Association of Colleges and Schools)

AMERICA'S CENTER FOR CULINARY EDUCATION SINCE 1946

Contact: Doug Thompson, Vice President of Enrollment Planning, The Culinary Institute of America, 433 Albany Post Road, Hyde Park, NY 12538-1499; phone 914-452-9430 or 1-800CULINARY; e-mail: Admissions@culinary.edu; Web site: www.ciachef.edu

Institution Description

An independent, not-for-profit institution of higher education committed to providing the world's best professional culinary arts and science education; degree and continuing education programs provide students with the opportunity to acquire the general knowledge and practical skills they need to build successful careers in an ever-changing foodservice and hospitality industry.

Program Description

Hands-on teaching of cooking and baking; students build essential culinary skills in a logical sequence in the college's 38 professional kitchens and bakeshops, and gain invaluable experience cooking and serving in the college's four fine-dining public restaurants on campus.

Special Features

An 18-week paid externship at an off-campus foodservice establishment; sixteen entry dates a year for culinary arts and eight entry dates a year for baking and pastry arts.

Financial Aid and Scholarships

A variety of federal, state, and CIA aid for those who qualify, including Federal Pell Grants, Federal SEOGs, college work-study, Federal Perkins Loans, parent loans, Veterans Administration educational benefits, vocational rehabilitation grants, and emergency student loans.

Admission

The Admissions Committee seeks candidates who have demonstrated a commitment to a culinary career and have the personal initiative, confidence, and motivation to succeed. The basic requirements are successful completion of a secondary school education or its equivalent and some experience in the foodservice and hospitality industry. The applicant's educational record is evaluated on the basis of overall performance and the type of program taken.

Tuition and Fees

Tuition is $15,400 a year; residence hall rates average about $3,000 a year; fees for supplies, student activities, and practical exams average $725 per year; one-time fees include application ($30), enrollment ($100), externship ($350), and graduation ($220).

Specialization Area

Culinary Arts

Graduation Requirements

Successful completion of the entire course of study: four on-campus semesters of 15 weeks each (approximately 1,820 hours) plus one 18- to 21-week semester of an approved externship (600 hours); completion of 69 credits, maintaining a grade point average of at least 2.00.

Domino Carlton Tivoli International Hotel And Business Management School (DCT)

Hotel Management Diploma Program, Culinary Arts Certificate; A.A. in General Business Administration

Program Enrollment: 275
Degrees Awarded: Diploma in International Hotel Management; Diploma in Hotel Management; Diploma in Food and Beverage Management; Graduate Entry Diploma in Hotel Management
Degree Category: Hotel Management; Culinary Arts; General Business

Contact: Walter Spaltenstein, Director, Carlton Tivoli International Hotel Management Career Centre, Haldenstrasse 57, CH-6002 Lucerne, Switzerland; phone 41-41-4180707; fax 41-41-4109754

Institution Description

Established in 1992, the DCT Hotel Management Career centre is part of a large, privately owned Swiss company that specialises in the hospitality sector. The centre is a residential college specialising in hotel management. Because of its commitment to excellence, DCT is rapidly gaining a reputation as one of the finest Swiss hospitality management institutions. It has an outstanding location and resources, as well as top-quality faculty, all of which ensures a first-class hospitality education. The quality of DCT's programs have been recognised by government offices in several European countries, and by professional associations in the United States. DCT is accredited through the Association of Collegiate Business Schools and Programmes and by CHRIE.

Program Description

DCT's programs are structured so that theoretical and practical learning are both balanced and interrelated. These two main components are complemented by periods of experimental learning in hotels where the nexus and interdependence of skills and hands-on competencies; as well as creative and analytical thinking and problem-solving, can be made operational. DCT's modular program places emphasis on both the practical skills necessary for graduates to succeed in the hospitality industry and on management skills which will ensure that successful students are not only competent practitioners, capable of dealing with real-life problems and acting creatively in many situations, but are also thinking and caring people, able to plan effectively, analyse clearly and make judgements related to finances and people's welfare and comfort.

Special Features

Industrial internships are co-ordinated through DCT's Career Planning and Placement Office, and students are guaranteed placement in leading Swiss hotels. Career guidance and job placement throughout the graduates' career is also organised through this organisation. Classes are small, using the most up-to-date equipment, and student learning is enhanced by using the parent organisation's facilities for pre-Industry training.

Approximate Tuition and Fees

Tuition per term (11weeks) is SFr 8,400 board and lodging per term is SFr 1,500. Courses commence every quarter in January, April, July and October.

Admissions

Applicants for the Associate Degree/Diploma courses must have completed high school or have successfully passed on equivalent examination. In addition, they must be at least 18 years of age and have a minimum TOEFL score of 500. Applicants for the Graduate Entry Diploma course must have a recognised bachelor's degree and a TOEFL score of at least 550. For GE-S program, a Diploma from an accredited college or university.

Graduation Requirements

Graduation requires an aggregate grade of C or above in academic and operational units, and successful completion of the industrial internship periods in Swiss hotels. DCT is an educational partner with Florida International University for a joint Diploma-Bachelor of Science Degree in International Hospitality Management on our Luzern campus.

Delaware County Community College

Hotel-Restaurant Management

Program Enrollment: 105
Institutional Enrollment: 9,650
Degrees Awarded: Associate of Science; Certificate
Degree Category: Hotel-Restaurant Management
Institutional Accreditation: Middle States Association of Colleges and Schools
Contact: Robert Bennett, Professor, Hotel-Restaurant Management, Deleware County Community College, 901 S. Media Line Road, Media, PA 19063; phone (610) 359-5267; fax (610) 325-2813

Institution Description

Deleware County Community College's (DCCC) main campus is located on a 123-acre site at Route 252 and Media Line Road in Marple Township. The college offers over 45 degree programs leading to associate degrees or transfer to other four-year schools.

Program Description

The Hotel-Restaurant Management Program at DCCC requires 60 credits and the option of an internship.

Special Features

A culinary internship program, in conjunction with local restaurant owners, and a kitchen laboratory provide the training students want.

Financial Aid and Scholarships

DCCC is committed to the ideal that no student will be denied an education because of limited financial resources.

Approximate Tuition and Fees

Tuition for residents of sponsoring school districts is $700.00 per semester; for Pennsylvania residing in an area that does not sponsor a community college, $2,000 per semester; and for non-Pennsylvania residents, $1,400 semester.

Admissions

DCCC provides equal opportunity to all. The open-door policy allows the college to admit any high school graduate or person who has passed the GED exam.

Graduation Requirements

The 60 credits required for the degree in hotel-Restaurant Management include courses in beverage, computers and catering, sanitation, food production, and hotel supervision.

Educational Institute of the American Hotel & Motel Association

Hospitality Management

Degrees Awarded: Hospitality Management Diploma; Hospitality Operations Certificate; Certificates of Specialization

Professional Certifications Awarded: Certified Hospitality Educator (CHE); Certified Hotel Administrator (CHA); Certified Lodging Manager (CLM); Certified Rooms Division Executive (CRDE); Certified Human Resources Executive (CHRE); Certified Food and Beverage Executive (CFBE); Certified Engineering Operations Executive (CEOE); Certified Hospitality Housekeeping Executive (CHHE); Certified Hospitality Sales Professional (CHSP); Certified Hospitality Technology Professional (CHTP); Certified Hospitality Supervisor (CHS); Registered Guestroom Attendant; Registered Front Desk Representative; Registered Restaurant Server

Emphases/Specializations: Rooms Division Management; Food and Beverage Management; Marketing and Sales Management; Human Resources Management; Accounting and Financial Management; Club Management

Program Accreditation: Every course counts toward initial certification or certification renewal at any level through the American Culinary Federation Educational Institute (ACFEI)

Contact: Mari Behrendt, Manager, Academic Programs, Educational Institute of AH&MA, PO Box 1240, East Lansing, MI 48826; phone (800) 344-4381 or (517) 372-8800; fax (517) 372-5141

Institution Description

The Educational Institute (EI) is a nonprofit educational foundation of the American Hotel & Motel Association. Since 1953, EI has been a bridge between academia and industry. The Institute's role is to help satisfy the need for trained hospitality professionals by preparing individuals for hospitality careers and career advancement.

Program Description

EI courses cover every area of hospitality management. Programs and courses can be integrated into existing hospitality or tourism curricula, or serve as the basis for a new program.

Special Features

Leading educators and industry professionals work with EI to develop instructional resources. Companion materials, including CD-ROMs, videos, and case studies, add a real-life perspective to course material. Course materials can also be delivered via the Internet.

Financial Aid and Scholarships

The American Hotel Foundation (AHF) offers the American Express Scholarship and the Ecolab Scholarship, which may be used toward EI Distance Learning programs and professional certification.

Admissions

EI has an open admissions policy. Students participate in courses at over 1,200 academic institutions and through training programs and thousands of hotels, restaurants, and governmental agencies worldwide. Courses may also be taken through EI. No previous training or experience is required.

Tuition & Fees

Tuition and fees vary based on programs. Contact the Institute for specific information.

Specialization Area

Hotel and Lodging Management

Graduation Requirements

The Hospitality Management Diploma program requires completion of 12 courses. The Hospitality Operations Certificate program consists of eight courses. Each Certificate of Specialization program includes five courses.

Erie Community College, City Campus

Hotel Technology; Culinary Arts

Program Enrollment: 125
Institutional Enrollment: 14,000
Degrees Awarded: Associate (A.A.S.), Hotel Technology; Associate (AOS,) Culinary Arts
Degree Categories: Associate, Hotel Technology Associate, Culinary Arts
Emphases/Specialization: Hotel Technology; Culinary Arts; Baking
Institutional Accreditation: Middle State Association of Colleges and Schools; The State University of New York (SUNY)

Contact: Paul J. Cannamela, C.C.E., A.A.C., Department Chair, Hotel Technology & Culinary Arts, Erie Community College, City Campus, 121 Ellicott St., Buffalo, New York 14203, Phone (716)851-1035, Fax (716)851-1129, E-mail: Cannamela@cstaff.sunyerie.edu

Institution Description
Erie Community College (ECC.), established in 1946 is New York's first multi-campus public community college outside of New York City. ECC offers degrees in Associate in Arts (AA), Associate in Applied Science (AAS), Associate in Occupational Studies (AOS), Associate in Science (AS) in over 80 programs within the Allied Health, Business and Public Service, Engineering Technologies and University Parallel Divisions. The Hotel Technology & Culinary Arts programs are located in the heart of downtown Buffalo New York.

Program Description
ECC's Hotel Technology and Culinary Arts Programs objective is to provide students with the necessary managerial and practical skills to enter a variety of jobs in accordance with their career aspirations and the job opportunities available in the Hotel and Culinary industry. Both programs combine the theory of classroom work with practical experience in management and food and beverage.

Special Features
The Hotel Technology and Culinary Arts program strength lies in the fact that E.C.C. is able to integrate the classroom theory courses with practical experience through the use of local hotels and an on-campus student operated restaurant.

Financial Aid and Scholarships
ECC has a comprehensive program of students aid including federal and state subsidized programs, loans, work study and scholarships. In addition the Hotel Technology & Culinary Arts program administers a number of scholarship programs including a Statler Foundation Scholarship.

Admissions
ECC provides educational opportunities for all qualified students who seek post secondary education on either a part-time or full-time basis. To qualify for admission; individuals must hold a High School Diploma or General Education Diploma (GED). Take the Math and English pretests and achieve certain levels of competency. Complete all admissions forms.

Tuition and Fees
Erie County Resident: $2500 per year;
Out-of-County: $5000 per year;
Out-of-State: $5000 per year;
International: $5000 per year;
Other Fees: approximately $250 per year

Specialization Areas
Hotel & Lodging Management; Culinary Arts; Baking.

Graduation Requirements
Graduation requires the successful completion of all courses listed under the specific Degree Program; attain a cumulative GPA of 2.0 or above and demonstrate proficiency in algebra at the level of MT106.

Faulkner State Community College

Hotel/Restaurant Management, Culinary Arts, Condominium/Resort Management

Program Enrollment: 100
Institutional Enrollment: 4,000
Degrees Awarded: AAS Degree; Certificate
Emphases/Specializations: Hotel/Restaurant Management, Culinary Arts, Condominium/ Resort Management
Institutional Accreditation: Faulkner State College is accredited by the Commission on Colleges of the Southern Association of Colleges and Schools.
Program Accreditation: Faulkner State has a "Full Academic Partnership" agreement with the Educational Institute of the American Hotel & Motel Association and the Educational Foundation of the National Restaurant Association.

Contact: Edward W. Bushaw, Program Coordinator, 3301 Gulf Shores Parkway, Gulf Shores Campus, Gulf Shores, Alabama 36542; phone (334) 968-3104; fax (334) 968-3120; e-mail: ebushaw@faulkner.cc.al.us

Institution Description
Faulkner State is a public two-year institution located in Baldwin County in Southwest Alabama. Faulkner's Hospitality Management Center is located on the Gulf Shores Campus. Two miles from the Gulf of Mexico, this facility houses offices, classrooms and laboratory facilities for Culinary Arts and Hotel/Restaurant and Condo Management.

Program Description
The Hotel/Restaurant Management and Culinary Arts programs at Faulkner were initiated to provide educated and trained individuals for management positions in resorts, hotels, restaurants and recreation facilities along the Gulf Coast Region. The programs hold strong support from local and regional industry who provide excellent management training opportunities.

Special Features
Faulkner's hospitality program offers students real-life industry experience through state-of-the-art computer and laboratory facilities as well as required internships of 2,100 hours in the field. The program boasts a 96% placement rate for graduates.

Specialization Area
Hotel/Restaurant Management; Culinary Arts; Condominium/Resort Management

Graduation Requirements
Students must complete courses within a general education core, courses within major, and field experience to123 quarter hours.

Financial Aid and Scholarships
Financial aid is provided in the form of Federal Pell Grants, Federal Work Study Jobs, Institutional Work-Ship and Scholarships. Through the hospitality industry, unlimited resources are available for qualified applicants.

Admissions
In keeping with the philosophy that the capabilities of each individual should be developed, Faulkner State operates under an "open-door" admissions policy. This policy grants admission to entering freshmen, transfer students, transient students, audit students, accelerated high school students and international students as well as any student seeking re-admission.

Tuition and Fees
In-State, $32.50 per credit hour; Out-of-State, $57.50 per credit hour; Room & Board, $725.00/quarter. (These rates include all applicable fees).

Galway-Mayo Institute of Technology

School of Hotel and Catering Studies

Program: BA in Hotel and Catering Management; National Diploma in Hotel and Catering Management (Full-time); National Diploma in Hotel and Catering Management (Block-release); National Certificate in Hotel Accommodation and Languages; National Certificate of the NTCB: Professional Cookery; Advanced Kitchen Programmes; Retail Butchery; Supervision of Restaurant Service Operations; Supervision of Bar Service Operations; Hospitality Skills; Advanced Restaurant Service Skills and Bar Service.

College: School of Hotel and Catering Studies

Program Enrollment: Master's - n/a; Doctorate- n/a

Institutional Enrollment: Undergraduate - 1200; Graduate - n/a

Degree Awarded: BA in Hotel and Catering Management;

Degree Categories: Business Administration

Emphasis/Specializations: Master's - n/a; Doctorate - n/a

Program Accreditation: n/a

Institutional Education: n/a

Contact: Secretary, School of Hotel and Catering Studies, Galway-Mayo Institute of Technology, Dublin Road, Galway, Ireland. **Telephone:** +353-91-770555 x2236; **Fax No:** +353-91-758411; **e-mail:** liam.hanratty@gmit.ie

Institution Description

The School is one of Ireland's leading hotel schools, offering a wide range of courses in the Hotel, Catering and wider Hospitality industries and comprises two departments. The Department of Hotel and Catering Management concentrates on courses for future managers at all levels – from department head of a small unit to general management of a large hotel or group, while the Department of Hotel and Catering Operations offers courses in Professional Cookery, Retail Butchery, Food and Beverage Supervision, Restaurant Operations, Bar Operations, Accommodation Services and Hospitality Skills.

Special Features

All programs involve periods of industrial attachment.

Financial Aid and Scholarships

n/a

Admissions

Admissions to Courses in BA in Hotel and Catering Management, National Diploma in Hotel and Catering Management (Full-time) and National Certificate in Hotel Accommodation and Languages in the Department of Hotel and Catering Management is through the CAO/CAS National System. Interviews are carried out for the National Diploma in Hotel and Catering Management (Block-Release).

Admission to courses in the Department of Hotel and Catering Operations is through CERT, CERT House, Amiens Street, Dublin 1, Ireland. **Telephone:** +353-1-855 6555.

Tuition & Fees

In-State: Details available from college

Out-of-State: Contact Registrar, Mr Tony Quinlan

Telephone: +353-91-770555 x2327

Specialization Area

Hotel and Lodging Management; Restaurant & Foodservice Management; Culinary Arts

Graduate Requirements

n/a

Garland County Community College

Certificate of Proficiency in Hospitality Administration

Program Enrollment: 42
Institutional Enrollment: 2,000
Degrees Awarded: Certificate
Degree Categories: Certificate of Proficiency in Hospitality Administration
Emphases/Specializations: Hospitality Administration
Program Accreditation: Business Division – ACBSP – The Association of Collegiate Business Schools and Programs

Institutional Accreditation: The North Central Association of Colleges and Schools
Contact: Allen Powell, Hospitality Administration Coordinator-Instructor, Garland County Community College, 101 College Drive, Hot Springs, Arkansas 71913, Telephone (501) 760-4277, FAX (501) 760-4261

Institution Description

Garland County Community College was established in 1973 as a public two-year college to provide post-secondary educational opportunities to the citizens of Garland County and surrounding areas. The College is located in mid-America Park just outside the city limits of Hot Springs, America's oldest national park.

Program Description

The Hospitality Administration Program was developed by industry professionals to meet the needs of the Hot Springs community. The Certificate of Proficiency in Hospitality Administration is awarded after successful completion of 18 semester hours of hospitality courses. Most classes will transfer to four-year hospitality programs nationwide.

Special Features

Hot Springs is Arkansas' premier tourist destination, with over 3 million visitors a year. Internships are offered in a wide variety of hospitality businesses.

Financial Aid and Scholarships

The college's financial aid office makes available federal Title IV opportunities, work-study, grants, scholarships for admission, and loans. Scholarships are also available from local hospitality employers.

Admissions

Students must submit a formal application, official high school transcript or proof of GED, ASSET Test scores, and proof of immunization. College transfer students must send transcripts from each institution attended.

Tuition & Fees

Tuition is $37 per semester credit-hour, based on twelve (12) semester hours per semester for Garland County residents. Students are also assessed a $10 registration fee each semester.

Maximum tuition per year is:

In State -	$ 888
Out-of-County -	$ 1,104
Out-of-State -	$ 2,760
Other Fees -	$ 20

Specialization Area

Hotel & Lodging Management; Restaurant & Foodservice Management; Travel & Tourism Management

Graduation Requirements

To be eligible for the Certificate of Proficiency in Hospitality Administration, students must successfully complete 18 semester hours of hospitality courses. Students must have a cumulative grade point average of 2.00 or higher for graduation.

Gateway Technical College

Hotel/Hospitality Management

Program Enrollment: 40
Institutional Enrollment: 26,000
Degrees Awarded: Associate of Applied Science
Degree Categories: Hotel/Hospitality Management
Emphases/Specialization: In addition to the Associate degree, certificates in Hospitality Services, Hotel Food Services, and Hotel Rooms Division Management are available.

Institutional Accreditation: North Central
Contact: Randy Mueller, Instructor-Hotel/Hospitality Management, Gateway Technical College, Racine, WI, 53403. Telephone: (414)631-7396; Fax: (414)631-1075

Institution Description

Gateway Technical College is located in-between Chicago, Ill. and Milwaukee, WI. The full program is offered in Racine, on the shores of Lake Michigan. A majority of courses are also made available at the urban campus of Kenosha, as well as the Elkhorn campus in the Geneva Lakes resort area.

Program Description

Since 1973 the program has focused on lodging management. In recent years we have expanded that focus to include food service management positions that require a minimal amount of culinary skills. The core skills of the program are also applicable to a number of other tourism-related management positions.

Special Features

Potential local internship sites include Dairyland Greyhound Park; Six Flags Great America; Marriott, Radisson, Marcus, and other hotels; numerous restaurants; three convention & visitors bureaus.

Financial Aid and Scholarships

Wisconsin Innkeepers Association; Wisconsin Association of Convention & Visitors Bureaus; Racine County Convention & Visitors Bureau; Gateway Foundation; federal grants.

Admissions

Potential students need to fill out an application, submit transcripts of prior high school and any college work, submit scores or take either the ACT, SAT, or CLEP test. Life (career) experience may be submitted for Advanced Standing credits. Wisconsin Hotel/Motel Youth Apprenticeship credits accepted.

Tuition & Fees

In-state tuition: $60.00 per credit, ca. $1,800 per full-time year (30 credits)
Out of state: ca. $500.00 per credit
Books/Supplies: ca. $600.00 per year

Specialization Area

Hotel & Lodging Management

Graduation Requirements

64 credits; 2.0 or higher GPA in core courses.
2 years minimum (Associate degree); must complete one field experience and one full internship as part of the 64 credits.

George Brown College
Hospitality Centre

Program Enrollment: 2,200 full time, 4,000 part time
Institutional Enrollment: 10,000 full time, 30,000 part time
Degrees Awarded: Management Diploma; Skill Program Certificate
Degree Category: Diplomas: Hotel Management. Culinary Management, Food and Beverage Management, Certificates: Food and Nutrition Management, Sommelier, Baking and Pastry Arts, Culinary Arts-Italian. Cook Apprenticeship, Chef Pre-Employment, Chef Pre Employment-Aboriginal, Foodservice and Bartending, Chinese Cuisine, Baker Apprenticeship
Program Accreditation: Canadian Food and Nutrition Management Society, Canadian Guild Sommelier, Canadian Pastry Chefs Guild, Canadian Federation of Chefs de Cuisine
Institutional Accreditation: Ontario Ministry of Skills Development; Ontario Ministry of Colleges and Universities; Ontario Training and Adjustment Board
Contact: Ron Thompson, Dean, Hospitality & Tourism Centre, George Brown College, 300 Adelaide St. E., Toronto, Ontario, Canada, M5A 1N1; phone (416) 415-2230; fax (416) 415-2501

Institution Description
George Brown College, the downtown City Community College of Toronto, is one of 23 community college is Ontario, Canada. It offers diversified educational programs in business, fashion, technology, health science, graphic arts, hospitality, and performing arts on four major campuses.

Program Description
The Hospitality & Tourism Centre at George Brown College is Canada's largest culinary and hospitality training facility offering thirteen specialized management, apprenticeship and tuition short programs. Students gain opportunities to complete a series of undergraduate and post diploma programs delivered through a skill-based curriculum offered in a block delivery system.

Special Features
Contemporary CDN$14 million campus with state-of-the-art cooking and computer facilities, 66 full-time faculty and staff.

Financial Aid and Scholarships
Industry scholarships, awards and bursaries for hospitality students. Government loans, income support and apprenticeship sponsorships for Canadian students.

Approximate Tuition
Hotel Management, Food & Beverage Management, and Culinary Management tuition is CDN$2100 per year.

Admissions
Canadian students requirements for program: Grade 12 for the management programs. mature students enter through functional testing and interviews. Modularized bock courses encourage graduates to graduate from multiple program specialization. Apprentice cooks often graduate in Culinary Management, etc. Post-diploma specializations in industry certified programs.

Golden Gate University

Hotel Restaurant and Tourism Management

College: School of Technology and Industry
Program Enrollment: 30
Institutional Enrollment: 4,000 Undergraduates; 5,500 Graduates.
Degrees awarded Certificate in Hotel Management, Certificate in Restaurant Management, Certificate in Tourism Management.
Emphases/Specializations: Hotel Management; Restaurant Management; Tourism Management.
Institutional Accreditation: Western Association of Schools and Colleges.
Contact: John T. Self, Ph.D. Department Chair, Hotel, Restaurant and Tourism Management, Golden Gate University, 536 Mission Street, San Francisco, CA 94105; Phone (415) 442-7802; Fax (415) 442-7049

Institutional Description

Founded in 1853, Golden Gate University is the fourth oldest and fifth largest private university in California. Its mission is to prepare students for successful careers in professional fields through programs of exceptional quality that integrate theory with practical experience.

Program Description

San Francisco provides a unique opportunity to study in the one of the most exciting hospitality oriented cities in the world. With small classes, taught by leading hospitality professionals drawn from executives practicing in the field, make the program unique. The HRTM department offers the finest internships available and an advisory board of Industry leaders available for mentoring.

Special Features

The HRTM program emphasizes working closely with each student on their career advising and placement needs, which is exemplified by a placement rate exceeding 96 percent.

Financial Aid and Scholarships

The financial aid office makes available numerous opportunities and the HRTM Program offers several scholarships based on academic achievement, financial need and hospitality industry experience.

Approximate Tuition Fees

Tuition for both in-state and out-of-state undergraduate classes is $1,059 per course.

Admissions

Admission to Golden Gate University is based on evidence of a student's ability to benefit from its educational programs. Such evidence typically includes the official academic record at other institutions, scores on any required tests and stated educational objectives.

Graduation Requirements

There are two certificates available. The Entry-level Certificate requires 24 credit hours and the Advanced Certificate requires 39 hours.

Grand Rapids Community College

Hospitality Education Department

Program Enrollment: 360
Institutional Enrollment: 13,900
Degrees Awarded: Associate of Applied Arts and Sciences, Certificate of Completion
Degree Categories: Associate in Culinary Arts, Culinary Management, Certificate in Baking and Pastry Arts
Program Accreditation: American Culinary Federation Educational Institute Accrediting Commission
Institutional Accreditation: Commission on Colleges and Universities of the North Central Association of Colleges and Secondary Schools

Contact: Robert B. Garlough, Director, Hospitality Education Department, Grand Rapids Community College, 151 Fountain, NE, Grand Rapids, MI 49503-3263; phone (616) 234-3690; fax (616) 234-3698

Institution Description

Grand Rapids Community College (GRCC), founded in 1914, is one of the oldest junior colleges in the nation. It is known for its strong transfer programs and extensive offering of up-to-date occupational programs. The liberal arts and occupational courses number more than 1,000. Associate degrees or certificates are offered in 52 occupational programs.

Program Description

The Hospitality Education Department (HED) offers Associate degrees in Culinary Arts, Culinary Management and a Certificate in Baking & Pastry Arts. A strong emphasis on Technical skills is supported by courses in finance, marketing, personnel management, nutrition, food science and purchasing. The college has transfer agreements with four state colleges and universities, and numerous out-of-state universities. A Certificate of Completion is offered in Baking and Pastry Arts.

Special Features

Students operate a retail deli/bakery, a fine dining public restaurant, a catering/banquet facility, a Victorian conference center an American bistro as part of their supervised hands-on training. The department occupies 58,000 square feet of instructional and laboratory space in four campus buildings. Courses are taught by an instructional staff consisting of nearly 20 degreed and highly experienced professionals. Students may participate in many extracurricular club activities, international culinary-study tours, and international student exchanges. The Hospitality Education Department is very involved in local, national and international culinary salon activities. The college serves as the Center for the International Consortium of Hospitality and Tourism Educators.

Financial Aid and Scholarships

A broad range of financial aid resources and scholarships is available. The HED also administers numerous scholarships given by local food and wine organizations.

Approximate Tuition and Fees

Tuition is $54, $80, or $91 per credit depending on students' residency status. Chef and tableservice uniforms; $275; chef cutlery kit: $190.

Admissions

GRCC has an open admissions policy, but the HED requires a minimum 2.0 GPA from high school or the successful completion of the Academic Foundation Courses before entering into either hospitality curriculum.

Graduation Requirements

An Associate in Applied Arts and Sciences degree requires the successful completion of 73 credits for Culinary Management and 73 credits for Culinary Arts and for Culinary Management. A certificate in Baking and Pastry Arts requires successful completion of 40 credits. A three-credit cooperative education experience of 240 hours is required during the summer session, where students participate in paid food service related work experience.

Guam Community College

Tourism and Hospitality

Program Enrollment: 70
Institutional Enrollment: 4,000
Degrees Awarded: Associate of Science & Certificate
Degree Categories: Hotel Operations, Food & Beverage Operations, Travel Agency Management
Emphasis/Specialization: Hotel/restaurant management and travel management
Program Accreditation: N/A

Institutional Accreditation: Western Association of Schools and Colleges
Contact: Eric Chong, CHE, CRDE, Tourism Department Chair/Assistant Professor, P.O. Box 23069, Barrigada, GU 96921, telephone/fax: (671) 735-5629

Institutional Description

Guam Community College is a multifaceted public vocational education institution created in 1977. It operates secondary and post-secondary vocational programs, adult and continuing education, and also short-term, specialized training. The College offers over 50 courses of study which are job related.

Program Description

Tourism and Hospitality Program was established in the mid 1980's to provide training and education for the hospitality industry. For graduation, students are required to acquire work experience in the field to supplement their classroom learning. The program uses resources from the Educational Institute of the American Hotel & Motel Association.

Special Features

The program also oversees the Hospitality Institute which offers short, intensive training and the Tour Guide Certification Training. 80% of faculty have earned CHE designations.

Financial Aid and Scho larships

Students may apply for a variety of financial assistance offered through the Federal Student Aid Programs. Various scholarship programs are also available.

Admissions

GCC has an open admissions policy. Placement testing is not mandatory for admission but useful to measure student's level in reading, mathematics, and grammar skills. Advisors use test results in helping students with course selections.

Tuition & Fees

Resident student - $40 per semester hour; non-resident student - $55 per semester hour; and foreign students - $70 per semester hour.

Specialization Area

Hotel & Lodging Mgmt., Restaurant & Foodservice Mgmt., Travel & Tourism Mgmt.

Graduation Requirements

To receive a Certificate, students need to earn 33 semester credits in technical requirement courses. Students may continue to pursue an Associate of Science degree by completing the general educational requirements in addition to the technical requirements, a total of 60 semester credits is required.

Harcum College

Hospitality/Tourism Program

Program Enrollment: 25
Institutional Enrollment: 650
Degree Awarded: Associate of Science
Degree Categories: Hospitality; Travel/Tourism
Emphases/Specializations: Hospitality; Tourism; Meeting/Convention Management

Institutional Accreditation: Middle States Association of Colleges and Secondary Schools; State Council of Education in Pennsylvania; U.S. Office of Education
Contact: Frank L. Smith, Jr. CTC, Program Director, Harcum College, 750 Montgomery Ave., Bryn Mawr, PA 19010; phone (610) 526-6073 fax (610) 526-6031

Institution Description

Harcum College is a two-year, private women's college offering 22 different degree programs. The programs are based in the Business, Fine and Applied Arts, Health Sciences, Animal Sciences and Liberal Arts divisions. The institution offers students both residential and commuter opportunities. The college is committed to preparing women to live and work effectively in the contemporary world.

Program Description

Tourism and Hospitality are among today's fastest growing and changing fields. Well-trained professionals are needed in travel agencies, hotels, airlines, convention centers and corporate travel offices. The program trains students for position in the hotel and travel fields, providing the hands-on sabre computer reservation systems and the opportunity of an internship.

Special Features

This program provides the student with the opportunity of an internship in the hotel and travel field. The program offers a travel club that students may be involved with and elected to hold office in. The faculty has experience in the travel and hotel field and provides students with all the help they can.

Financial Aid and Scholarships

There are two basic types of financial aid: gift aid and self-help aid. Gift aid consists of scholarships and grants which do not have to be repaid. Self-help aid includes student employment and loans which must be repaid.

Approximate Tuition and Fees

Tuition for full-time resident students is $8,310; room and board, $5,080; general fees, $630. Tuition for full-time commuter students is $8,310; general fees, $498. Tuition for part-time students is $296 per credit.

Admissions

Harcum operates under a rolling admissions policy. There is no deadline for the receipt of applications, but students are advised to apply early. Students are encouraged to visit the campus and talk with an admissions counselor. A $25 application fee (nonrefundable) is due with application, along with a copy of the high school transcript and letters of recommendation. A deposit will be required once accepted. SAT scores are required for certain programs.

Graduation Requirements

Sixty credits are required for graduation with about a 30/30 split in the average in most programs. Thirty credits general education and 30 credits major area of work. Two Physical Education credits are required for graduation. It generally takes students two years to complete the program.

Highline Community College

Hotel & Tourism Management Program

Program Enrollment: 30
Institutional Enrollment: 10,000
Degrees Awarded: Certificate in Hotel & Tourism Management; AAS – Associate of Applied Science Degree in Applied Science
Emphases: none at the moment outside of Internship Experiences
Accreditation: no current special accreditation

Institutional Accreditation: Northwest Association of Schools and Colleges, and the Higher Education Coordinating Board's State Approving Agency for the State of Washington.

Contact: Mr. Chris Brandmeir, Program Manager for the Hotel & Tourism Management Program; 2400 S. 240th St, P.O. Box 98000, MS 18-1, Des Moines, WA 98198-9800. (206) 878-3710, ext. 3855, Fax (206) 870-4850, E-mail cbrandme@hcc.ctc.edu

Institution Description

Since 1961, Highline has served the greater Seattle, Washington area. A non-residential campus on 80-acres overlooking Puget Sound just south of Seattle-Tacoma International Airport, there are 450 faculty in over 45 transfer and occupational programs with a diverse student body of all ages, from many states and different countries.

Program Description

The Program is designed to provide students with both practical and theoretical training to start their career. Courses are completed in managing front desk operations, food and beverage operations, housekeeping management, customer service, computers, communications, business and management. Instruction is augmented by required internships in the industry.

Special Features

With 103 credits in communications, business, accounting, microcomputers, and international business; students also complete a 22 credits in industry internships to obtain practical experience.

Financial Aid

Highline Community College participates in a number of financial aid programs and information is available directly from the financial aid office.

Highline Community College operates on an open admissions policy using an on-campus placement test to determine appropriate class placement. Transcripts of work to date as well as a completed admissions form are required for entrance at any quarter. International applicants must meet English proficiency requirements or study ESL on campus.

Tuition & Fees

In State Resident:	10-18 credits	$505.00
Non Resident:	10-18 credits	$1987.00

Specialization Area

Hotel & Lodging Management, Restaurant & Foodservice Management, Travel & Tourism Management.

Graduation Requirements

Graduates complete 103 quarter credits with at least 22 credits in industry Internships, and 48 quarter credits in: written and oral communications, labor relations, management, accounting, business law & ethics, computers, and international business. Students usually complete the program in seven(7) quarters.

HOSTA Hotel and Tourism School

Hotel Operations and Mangement, Tourism

Program Enrollment: 200
Institutional Enrollment: 200
Degree Awarded: Diploma
Degree Categories: Hotel Operations; Hotel Management; Travel and Tourism Operations; Travel and Tourism Management
Program Accreditation: Hotel, Catering, and Institutional Management Association (HCIMA); European Foundation for the Accrediation of Hotel School Programmes (EPAH)
Institutional Accreditation: IATA/UFTAA
Contact: David C. Nott, FHCIMA, Academic Dean, HOSTA, 1854 Leysin, Switzerland; phone (24) 693-1717; fax (24) 493-1727

Institution Description

HOSTA is situated in the French-speaking ski resort of Leysin. The school began in 1959 with programs offered in German, but now the Hotel and Tourism Programs are both taught in English. The student body is international, with most students coming from Europe.

Program Description

Hotel Program: Two semesters are devoted to Swiss hands-on skills courses (kitchen, resteraunt, governance, front office, etc.) followed by a six-month internship. The next two semesters are U.S. style management courses. Transfers to and from U.S. programs are possible. Travel and Tourism programs: Two semesters prepare students for full travel agency operations and travel consultancy (and official IATA/UFTAA Travel Consultant's course). Two semesters Travel and Tourism Management.

Special Features

Both the Hotel operations and Travel and Tourism programs include 180-300 hours of foreign languages chosen from French, German, Spanish and Italian.

Financial Aid and Scholarships

As HOSTA is a private institution without state or other outside funding, financial aid is very limited.

Approximate Tuition and Fees

US $10,000-10,500 per semester depending on program and exchange rate. This amount includes tuition, room and board.

Admissions

Admission is open to those 18 years old and above with a high school diploma or equivalent such as HAVO, mittlere Reife. A high level of English is required.

Graduation Requirements

To graduate from the hotel Operations, Hotel Management or Tourism Programs, a student must gain an overall average grade of 3.5 with a maximum one course failure. Hotel diplomas are only awarded after completion of the required in-training.

Hotel Institute Montreux (HIM)

Hotel Management

Program Enrollment: 200
Institutional Enrollment: 200
Degrees Awarded: Diploma; Bachelor of Science Degree in Association with the University of South Carolina.
Degree Categories: Hotel Management (three years)
Emphases/Specializations: Hotel Management
Program Accreditation: Educational Institute of American Hotel and Motel Association
Institutional Accreditation: New England Association of Schools and Colleges Inc. (NEASC), Swiss Hotel Schools Association (ASEH), European Foundation for Accreditation of Hotel School Programmes (EFAH).
Contact: E.P.O. Dandrieux, Director, Hotel Institute Montreux, 15 Avenue des Alpes, 1820 Montreux, Switzerland; phone ++41 21 963-7404; fax ++41 21 963-8016; e-mail Web page http://www.him.ch

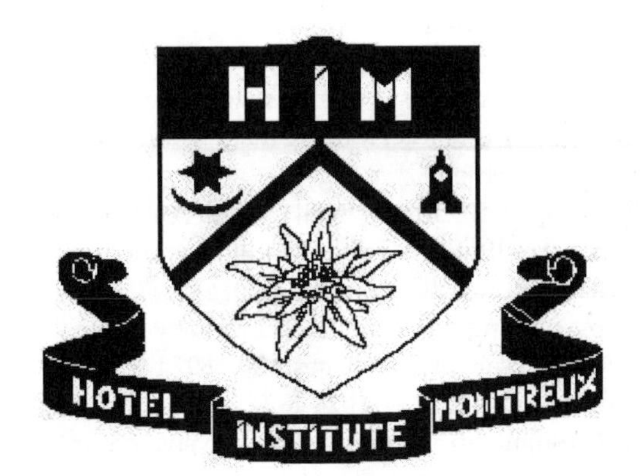

Institution Description
Hotel Institute Montreux (HIM) is an English-speaking hotel management institution situated in Montreux, Switzerland, one hour by train from Geneva airport. In principle, all programmes are residential, but non-residential students are accepted. HIM's three year Hotel Management Program is the major program.

Program Description
JOINT DEGREE PROGRAM: HIM offers a 3-year Bachelor's Degree in association with the University of South Carolina, consisting of 2.5 years in Switzerland (including two internships), and two semesters at University of South Carolina on Hilton Head Island. The graduate receives the HIM and AH&MA Diplomas, and a Bachelor of Science from USC.

Special Features
The practical workload is predominant in the first year. Swiss or American trained faculty, specialized kitchens, dining rooms, library, computer lab and classrooms offer an ideal working environment.

Financial Aid and Scholarships
As with all Swiss hotel institutes, HIM does not offer scholarships. Students are permitted to settle fees on an installment basis.

Admissions
All of HIM's programs require a high school education as well as an excellent command of the English language. Students come from over 30 countries. HIM has representatives in most of these countries who interview students and screen admissions for HIM.

Tuition and Fees
In-state $10,000
Out-of-State $10,000
Room and Board $3,000
Other Fees $2,000 deposit for books, uniform, insurance, etc.

Specialization Area
Hotel & Lodging Management

Graduation Requirements
All subjects are obligatory. Continuous assessment takes the form of progress tests or quizzes, and final exams are required in all subjects. Maximum grades are 100 percent, minimum passing grades are 70 percent overall. A maximum of two failures in minor subjects is allowed.

Hotel Consult SHCC "Cesar Ritz" Colleges

Program Enrollment: 200
Institutional Enrollment: 200
Degrees Awarded: Swiss Hotel Management Diploma
Degree Categories: Hotel Management; Food and Beverage Management
Emphases/Specializations: Swill Culinary Art and Service
Program Accreditation: City and Guilds of London; ASEH, Switzerland; ACICS, Washington, DC
Contact: Wolfgang D. Petri, Ph.D., President, HotelConsult SHCC "Cesar Ritz" Colleges, CH-1897 Le Bouveret, Swizerland; phone: + 41 24 482 8282; fax: + 41 24 482 8899; e-mail: hoco.admissions@ritz.vsnet.ch

Institution Description

Institute Hotelier "Cesar Ritz" is operated by HotelConsult SHCC Colleges and is a pioneer in combining the European art of hospitality with the American science of management. The college offers a residential program in quality hotel style condition located on the shores of Lake Geneva in Switzerland. The school offers a complete range of facilities and conditions for a most desirable and positive learning environment.

Program Description

Two years in length, the program is places special emphasis on European food and beverage operations combined with the American style of management. The program includes two periods of paid internship in hospitality operations.

Special Features

Emphasis in the program is placed on European culture and environment and on the development of professional attitude and discipline through supervised internships within the Swiss industry. Exchange option with Swiss Hospitality Institute "Cesar Ritz in Washington, Connecticult and the "Cesar Ritz" Program at the International College of Tourism and Hotel Management, Sydney, Australia. Qualified students can further their studies at the International College of Hospitality Administration, Brig, Switzerland, toward a Bachelor of Arts degree offered by Washington State University.

Financial Aid and Scholarships

The school awards scholarships to students achieving high academic and professional standards for continuing their education on completion of their diploma.

Admissions

Successful completion of high school (or equivalent) and fluency in English. (Exemption of the first year of studies may be granted in cases of applicants who have equivalent academic or professional experience).

Graduation Requirements

Successful completion of study program with a GPA of 2.0 or better and internship requirements relevant to the program followed, and a pass in professional attitude test.

Humber College - HRT Alliance

Hospitality, Recreation and Tourism Industries Training

Institutional Enrollment: 11,500 full-time: 75,000 part-time
Degrees Granted: Diploma, Post-Graduate Diploma and Certificate
Degree Categories: Hospitality, Recreation and Tourism Management (On-line), Ecotourism and Adventure Recreation(Post Diploma), Fast Track Recreation and Leisure(Post Diploma), Chef/Culinary Management, Chef Training, Cook Apprentice, Hospitality Management, Tourism and Travel, HRT Sectoral, Recreation and Leisure Services, Sports Equipment Specialist and Tourism and Travel, Life Long Learning Certificates including Small Business Development, Bar Operations, Tourism Industries Certificate and Managing You Own Tour Group.
Institutional Accreditation: Ontario Ministry of Education and Training

Contact: John Walker, Director, HRT Alliance, Humber College of Applied Arts and Technology, 205 Humber College Blvd., Toronto, Ontario, Canada M9W5L7
phone (416) 675-6622 ext. 4550; fax: (416) 675-3062;
E-mail: JOWALKER@ADMIN.HumberC.ON.CA

Institution Description

Since first opening our doors in 1976, Humber College has grown into one of Canada's largest and most respected community colleges. The main campus is located in the west end of Toronto and includes a 300 acre Arboretum. Humber's 135 full time programs, 4,000 different specialty courses, learning partnerships with recognized Universities and Colleges and active student life all contribute to the essence of life at this dynamic campus.

Program Description

With the active participation of over 500 industry partners, HRT Alliance provides a dynamic learning environment supported by state-of-the-art facilities and a dedicated faculty team. Students who study with us benefit from market-related curriculum, laboratory work which provides practical skills and real life industry Traineeship experiences. Our graduates are the preferred choice of industry's leading employers.

Special Features

HRT Alliance's innovative resources include: The Catering and Learning Center, Tall Hats (upscale retail food service operation) bar and wine operations, computer labs, Training Kitchens including baking and pastry arts, a la carte restaurant operations and small quantity cuisine production and Tourism and Travel laboratory featuring live reservations links. Learning is achieved through a variety of medians including distance learning, custom designed, learning in industry and traditional, in-class.

Financial Aid and Scholarships

Financial assistance is available under the Ontario Student Assistance Program or the Canada Student Loans Plan. In addition, a large number of scholarship, bursaries and special industry awards are offered annually.

Admission

An Ontario Secondary School Diploma at or above general level (grades are reviewed for suitability), or equivalent, or mature student status is required for admission to any of the diploma programs. University or college graduation or equivalent experience is required for post-diploma programs. The Cook Apprentice program requires current employment in a kitchen for a minimum length of 8 weeks, and grade 10 education.

Graduation Requirements

Graduation requirements vary slightly between programs. On average, a diploma programs requires 9 credits in general education and 76 credits in core subject areas.

ICS Learning Systems

Hospitality Management

Institutional Enrollment: Over 200,000
Degrees Awarded: Associate in Specialized Business Degree
Degree Categories: Hospitality Management
Institutional Accreditation: Distance Education and Training Council, Licensed by the Pennsylvania State Board of Private Licensed Schools

Contact: Tanya Horsfield, Chief Instructor, Hospitality Management, ICS Learning Systems, 925 Oak Street, Scranton, PA 18515; phone (570) 342-7701; fax (570) 961-4038

Institution Description

ICS has developed into a wordwide educational system headquartered in Scranton, Pennsylvania. It is a non-traditional proprietary institution offering postsecondary career education in business and technology. Established to provide a learning system based on guided independent study, it offers for those unable or unwilling to pursue their educational goals through traditional means an opportunity to earn an ASB or AST degree.

Program Description

The Hospitality Management curriculum prepares graduates for entry-level management positions in the hotel and restaurant fields. ICS aims to provide specialized education designed to fulfill practical needs, career, job advancement, and self-improvement—without sacrificing the ultimate goals of education, personal growth, and enrichment.

Special Features

Distance education.

Financial Aid and Scholarships

ICS does not participate in any financial aid or scholarship programs. A no interest payment plan is offered to students.

Admissions

To qualify for open admission, the applicant must submit proof of high school graduation or a GED Equivalency Certificate. Advanced standing may, on approval, be granted to those applicants who have completed comparable work with a C grade or higher from accredited institutions.

Tuition & Fees

Current tuition information is available by calling (800) 233-4191.

Specialization Area

Hotel & Lodging Management, Restaurant & Foodservice Management.

Graduation Requirements

Students must complete a minimum of 60 credit hours in a CDS degree program with a Cumulative Quality Point Average of 2.0 or higher in all studies. A minimum of 50% of the total credit hours must be completed through ICS.

Indiana University of Pennsylvania Academy of Culinary Arts

Culinary Arts Program

Program Enrollment: 100
Institutional Enrollment: 14,000
Degree Awarded: Certificate
Degree Category: Culinary Arts
Program Accreditation: American Culinary Federation Educational Institute Accrediting Commission
Institutional Accreditation: Middle States Association of Colleges and Schools
Contact: Debbie Osikowicz, Admissions Coordinator, IUP Academy of Culinary Arts, 125 South Gilpin Street, Punxsutawney, PA 15767; phone (800-438-6424); fax (814-938-1159); e-mail culinary-arts@grove.iup.edu

Institution Description

Indiana University of Pennsylvania is Pennsylvania's fifth largest university and one of the nation's academic best. *Barron's Guide to the Most Prestigious Colleges* recently lists IUP among the most academically competitive colleges and universities in the country.

Program Description

The academy's philosophy is learning through a three-step process. The first step is comprehensive instruction to understand the "why," called theory. The second is demonstration and application. The third is proficiency, often referred to as mastery. All comprehensive skills are enhanced by a four-month paid externship incorporated into the program. Academy graduates can receive 42 credits advanced standing in IUP's Bachelor of Science degree program in Hotel, Restaurant, and Institutional Management.

Special Features

The program features a modern, state-of-the-art facility, including five gourmet instructional kitchens, two lecture/demonstration classrooms, a computer laboratory, a culinary library and a fine dining restaurant operated by students. Unique individual attention through very low student-to-instructor ratios is emphasized. Lifetime job referral assistance is available for graduates.

Financial Aid and Scholarships

Financial aid in the form of grants, loans and scholarships is available to those students who qualify.

Admissions

Admission requirements include an application, high school diploma or GED, entrance exam, interview and letters of recommendation.

Approximate Tuition & Fees

Both in-state and out-of-state instructional costs are $4700 per academic semester. There is a one-time supply package charge of $1400. Additional fees are calculated on a semester basis: optional health fee $50-$80 depending on plan selected. Room: $968 per double occupancy room. Board: meal plans range from $630-$741. Off-campus housing is also available in the Punxsutawney area.

Graduation Requirements

Graduation requires the successful completion of 2,250 hours of laboratory, classroom, and related outside projects, including a 450-hour externship.

International Center for Hotel and Tourism Training MODUL Vienna

Training Programs on Secondary and Post-Secondary Level for the Hospitality and Tourism Industries

Institutional Enrollment: 2,100 in the last 3 years
Degrees Awarded: Matura; Diploma of Hospitality Management; Certificate of International Hotel Management; Mag. (FH)
Emphases/Specializations: Austrian and international hospitality management; restaurant and kitchen management; travel and transport; tour operation; tourism and resort management, conference management
Institutional Accreditation: Federal Ministry of Education; Vienna Chamber of Commerce; Federal Ministry of Science for Fachhochschulstudiengang
Contact: Dr. Erich Auerbäck, Principal, International Center for Hotel- and Tourism Training MODUL, Peter-Jordanstraße 78-80, A-1190 Vienna, Austria; Phone: ++43-1-47670; Fax: ++43-1-47670/217; e-mail: whabitzl@modul.at

Institutional Description

The International Center for Hotel- and Tourism Training MODUL is run by the Vienna Chamber of Commerce. It is situated in a residential area in the green belt of Vienna. The institute was founded in 1908 as one of the first hotel schools in Europe. The institute is a private operation under public law.

Program Description

Besides a 5-year Higher Secondary School for Hospitality and Tourism, which ends with a 'Matura' (GCE-A level), the center also runs a 4-semester Post-Secondary Course in Hospitality Management, a 4-semester International Course in Hotel Management, taught entirely in English, and a 'Fachhochschulstudiengang für Tourismus-Management', which lasts 7 semesters and which offers academic and professional training at university level. Graduates of this course are awarded the academic title 'Mag. (FH)'.

Special Features

The institute is connected to a four-star hotel, which is also operated by the Vienna Chamber of Commerce, and which enables our students to apply theoretic knowledge in real-life situations. Compulsory placements during the academic year and in the summer holidays guarantee up-to-date professional training. The teaching staff comprises academically trained personnel as well as professionals from the hospitality and tourism industries.

Financial Aid and Scholarships

For Austrian and EU-students the governmental system of grants is applicable.

Admissions

Admission to the 5-year course is free. For the Post-Secondary Course in Hospitality Management Matura (GCE-A level) is required; for the Fachhochschulstudiengang the above or 3 years' professional experience are required. All applicants have to pass an entrance examination. For the International Course in Hotel Management an international baccalaureate/GCE-A level or 3 years' work experience plus a good command of English are required. Due to a limited number of places admission interviews are held for the three programmes mentioned last.

Tuition & Fees

Tuition fees range from ATS 19,500 to 81,000 according to the course chosen. Attendance of the Fachhochschulstudiengang is free. Meals can be taken at the school cafeteria at reduced rates.

International College of Hospitality Management, *"Cesar Ritz"*

Institutional Enrollment: 120
Degree Program: Associate of Science
Degree Category: Hospitality Management
Emphases/Specializations: Hotel and Lodging Management; Restaurant and Foodservice Management
Institutional Accreditation: New England Association of Schools and Colleges; Connecticut State Department of Education
Contact: Marilyn H. Ciccone, Vice President for Enrollment Management, International College of Hospitality Management, *"Cesar Ritz"*, 101 Wykeham Rd., Washington, CT 06793; phone: (860) 868-9555; toll free: (800) 955-0809; fax: (860) 868-2114; e-mail: admissions@ichm.cc.ct.us; internet: www.hotelconsult.com or www.ichm.cc.ct.us

Institution Description

The International College of Hospitality Management, *"Cesar Ritz,"* located in Washington, Connecticut, midway between New York City and Boston, is the only Swiss college of hospitality management in the United States. It is one of the four internationally acclaimed HOTELCONSULT colleges, with affiliate campuses located in Le Bouveret and Brig, Switzerland and Sydney, Australia. The mission of the College is to prepare students for successful careers in the hospitality industry around the world by combining the renowned Swiss art of hotellerie with American management techniques. With just 120 residential students on a 27-acre campus in Connecticut's beautiful Litchfield Hills, the College provides intensive course work and practical experience, along with highly personalized career training on two paid internships at prestigious hotels, restaurants, resorts, and hospitality-related businesses in the United States and abroad.

Program Description

The two-year Associate of Science in Hospitality Management degree program is designed to provide students with a sound basis in hotel, restaurant, and tourism management. The first year of the program includes courses in the liberal arts, food and beverage operations, and practical courses in the kitchen and service departments. After the first two terms in residence, students have the skills and professional knowledge to begin their first paid internship in a hotel, resort, restaurant, or business-related hospitality operation. The internship is a carefully structured and supervised part of the program, bringing to life what has been learned in the classroom. In the second year of the program, students develop greater skills in hospitality management, service, planning, computer applications, and financial control. Students also study a foreign language. The year concludes with a second paid internship. A one-year Certificate in Hospitality Management program is available to students who hold a bachelor's or master's degree in a field other than hospitality management or have extensive professional experience in the hospitality industry.

Special Features

Study abroad is available to students who choose to spend their second year at one of the College's affiliate campuses in Le Bouveret, Switzerland or Sydney, Australia. Some graduates may elect to pursue a Bachelor of Arts degree in hotel and restaurant management awarded by Washington State University at HOTELCONSULT's International College of Hospitality Administration in Brig, Switzerland, or transfer to a college or university in the United States.

Financial Aid and Scholarships

The College has several types of financial assistance programs, including scholarships and grants, low-interest loans, and employment opportunities, to assist all eligible part-time or full-time students in meeting their educational expenses. In many cases, the College's financial aid officer will award a qualified student a financial aid package that may include all three types of financial aid. Of special note are Presidential Scholarships in the amount of $5,000. per year and Cesar Ritz Scholarships in the amount of $2,250. per year which are available to qualified students who are residents of the USA.

Tuition and Fees

Expenses for the academic year include tuition, $13,000., and room and board, $4,250. Each student is required to have an operating account of $1,500. to cover books, uniforms, and supplies.

Admission

The College welcomes applications from students all over the world who are serious about succeeding in the hospitality industry. Applications are accepted for enrollment in four academic terms: fall, winter, spring, summer. A completed application form, $25. application fee, official high school transcript or GED scores, and a letter of recommendation are required. SAT I scores are not required but are highly recommended. Students for whom English is not the native language are required to submit TOEFL scores to show proof of English competency. Applicants are strongly encouraged to schedule an on-campus interview, and interviews can be arranged off-campus, if necessary. All prospective students are welcome as guests for campus meals and/or overnight accommodation.

Graduation Requirements

A cumulative grade point average (GPA) of 2.0 or higher is required for graduation, along with fulfillment of internship requirements, professional attitude assessment, and all required courses.

J. Sargeant Reynolds Community College

Hospitality Management and Culinary Arts Program

Program Enrollment: 110
Institutional Enrollment: 11,000
Degrees Awarded: Associate Degree; Certificate; Career Studies Certificate
Degree Categories & Specializations: Associate in Applied Science Degree – Culinary Arts; Lodging Operations Specialization; Hospitality Entrepreneurship Specialization; Food Service Management Specialization; Dietetic Technician Specialization; Career Studies Certificate – Nutrition Assistant; Career Studies Certificate – Dietary Manager

Program Accreditations: American Culinary Federation; Educational Institute of AH&MA; American Dietetic Association; Dietary Managers Association
Institutional Accreditation: Southern Association of Colleges and Schools
Contact: David J. Barrish, CHA, Program Head, Hospitality Management and Culinary Arts, J. Sargeant Reynolds Community College, P.O. Box 85622, Richmond, Virginia 23285-5622; phone (804) 786-2069; fax (804) 786-5465; http://www.jsr.cc.va.us/dtcbusdiv/hospitality

Institution Description
Established in 1972, J. Sargeant Reynolds Community College (JSRCC) is a three-campus institution and the third largest college in the Virginia Community College System. The College provides for occupational-technical education, workforce development, college transfer, and various community services. JSRCC actively supports educational reforms in such diverse areas as tech prep, distanced learning and quality management. JSRCC is an affirmative action/equal opportunity educational institution.

Program Description
The purpose of the Hospitality Management and Culinary Arts is to provide students the opportunity to master industry-validated competencies that prepare them for lifelong career progression within the allied hospitality industries. Goals of the Program are designed to yield a measurably superior hospitality management education, enhance accessibility to students of varying preparedness levels, ensure accountability for education and employment outcomes, and promote education as a lifelong endeavor.

Special Features
Classes are taught at the JSRCC **Center for Hospitality Development**, which consists of lecture, laboratory and food services spaces. A complete food preparation facsimile exists at the Center and is utilized to permit students in the curriculum to develop their technical skills in a sophisticated and realistic setting. Innovative class scheduling enables students to earn degrees by attending classes one day a week.

Financial Aid and Scholarships
Program students are eligible for semiannual awards of the American Hotel Foundation Scholarship, the Virginia Hospitality and Travel Association Scholarship, the Virginia Restaurant Association Scholarship, the Educational Foundation of the National Restaurant Association Scholarship, as well as numerous other general scholarships offered through the College. The JSRCC Student Financial Aid Office assists students with the acquisition of local, state and Federal loans and grants.

Tuition and Fees
In-state tuition is US$49.55 per semester credit. Out-of-state tuition is US$163.25 per semester credit.

Admissions
Any person who has a high school diploma, its equivalent, or is 18 years of age and is able to benefit from instruction at JSRCC may be admitted when required items as listed in the College Catalog are received by the JSRCC Office of Admissions and Records.

Graduation Requirements
To be awarded an associate degree, students must have fulfilled all of the course requirements of the curriculum as outlined in the College Catalog with a minimum of 15 semester hours acquired at the college. This is customarily achievable over a 2 to 3 year period.

Johnson & Wales University

College of Culinary Arts/The Hospitality College

Program Enrollment: 4,601 in College of Culinary Arts; 2,733 in The Hospitality College; at campuses in Rhode Island, South Carolina, Florida, Virginia*, and Colorado*
Institutional Enrollment: 11,599
Degrees Awarded: Certificate; Associate in Applied Science; Associate in Science; Bachelor of Science; Master of Business Administration; Master of Arts; Doctor of Education (Ed.D.)
Degree Categories: (see Baccalaureate Degrees section for bachelor's degrees offered) Baking & Pastry Arts; Culinary Arts; Food & Beverage Management; Hotel-Restaurant Management; Recreation/Leisure Management; Restaurant/Institutional Management; Travel-Tourism Management
Institutional Accreditation: Johnson & Wales University is accredited by the New England Association of Schools and Colleges, Inc., and is accredited as a senior college by the Accrediting Council for Independent Colleges and Schools. In addition, the hospitality programs at the Providence, R.I. campus are accredited by the Accreditation Commission for Programs in Hospitality Administration.

Contact: Ms. Caroline A. Cooper, Dean, The Hospitality College; Chef Jean-Michel Vienne, Dean, College of Culinary Arts; Johnson & Wales University, 8 Abbott Park Place, Providence, RI 02903; phone Dean Cooper (401) 598-1475; Dean Vienne (401) 598-1130; South Carolina campus (800) 868-1522; Florida campus (800) 232-2433; Virginia campus (800) 277-2433; Colorado campus (970) 476-2993

Institutional Description

Johnson & Wales is a private, coeducational institution offering practical career education in food service, hospitality, business and technology. J&W's associate, bachelor's and graduate degree programs prepare students to enter the work world. Technology and graduate programs are offered at the Providence campus only.

Program Description

J&W hospitality and culinary programs offer an opportunity for students to combine academics with hands-on training in one of the University's three hotel/food service properties. Students take courses in their major during their first year. A four-day school week allows students to put academics into practice on the long weekends.

Special Features

Johnson & Wales University's upside down curriculum and hands-on training facilities allow students to gain experience in their fields before graduation. Corporate partners, including American Express Travel, Radisson and Marriott, also give students experience. J&W boasts a 98% graduate employment rate within 60 days of graduation.

Financial Aid and Scholarships

J&W has a fully staffed financial aid and planning office to assist qualified students in meeting educational expenses by putting a financial aid package together for them. J&W awarded over $25 million in institutional aid to students at all campuses last year.

Approximate Tuition and Fees

Undergraduate tuition for the culinary program at J&W's Providence, R.I. campus for 1999-2000 is $15,840; hospitality program $13,824. Room & Board ranges from $5,829 to $7,050; general and orientation fees are $525 and $140, respectively. Tuition varies at other campuses and in the Alan Shawn Feinstein Graduate School. J&W's Guaranteed Tuition Plan freezes tuition at the first year enrollment rates.

Admissions

Admission to J&W requires a high school diploma or its equivalent. Although not required, the University encourages applicants to submit SAT or ACT test scores. An applicant's motivation and interest in succeeding in a chosen field are also given strong consideration.

Graduation Requirements

Degree candidates must successfully complete the required number of courses and/or term hours as prescribed in the various curricula with a minimum average of 2.0. All students graduating with an associate degree are eligible to continue on to a four-year degree program.
**Culinary Arts program only.*

Johnson County Community College

Hospitality Management

Program Enrollment: 500
Institutional Enrollment: 15, 500
Degree Awarded: Associate of Applied Science
Degree Categories: Hospitality Management, Culinary Arts
Emphases/Specializations: Food & Beverage Management; Chef Apprenticeship; Hotel Management
Program Accreditation: American Culinary Federation Educational Institute Accrediting Commission
Institutional Accreditation: North Central Association of Colleges and Schools
Contact: Jerry Vincent, Program Director, Hospitality Management, Johnson Community College, 12345 College Blvd., Overland Park, KA 66210; phone (913) 469-8500, ext. 3250

Institution Description

The Hospitality Program at Johnson County Community College is structured with more than 42 hours of hospitality courses. The program has three teaching kitchens as well as four dining rooms. The program has articulation agreements with several major universities.

Special Features

Program faculty average 20 years of industry experience before entering the educational field. Placement of graduates is 100 percent to date with annual salaries ranging from $24,000 to $26,000.

Financial Aid and Scholarships

The college has a well-staffed aid office with various forms of student assistance. Scholarships are also available from local professional organizations.

Approximate Tuition and Fees

Tuition is $46 per credit hours for Kansas residents and $120 per credit hours for out-of-state residents.

Admissions

Any person seeking admission to Johnson County Community College must meet one of the following requirements: be a high school graduate, have passed the GED exam, or reached the age of 18 and demonstrated the ability to benefit through the Johnson County Community College student assessment process.

Graduation Requirements

The 64 hours of credit necessary to complete the Associate of Applied Science degree shall include the following general education distribution requirements: communications-three hours, social science and/ or economics-three hours, humanities and/ or art— three hours, mathematics—three hours, health and physical education—one hour.

Keystone College

Hotel, Restaurant and Food Service Management/Culinary Arts/ Travel and Tourism

Program Enrollment: 45
Institutional Enrollment: 700 full time; 425 part time
Degree Awarded: Associate in Applied Science (AAS)
Degree Category: Hotel/Restaurant Management; Food Service Management; Culinary Arts; Travel/Tourism Management
Institutional Accreditation: Middle States Association of Colleges and Schools

Contact: Janet De Andrea, Director of Admissions, or Patricia Davis, Division Chair of Business, Office Technology, and Hospitality, Keystone College, La Plume, PA 18440

Institution Description

Keystone College is a residential, coeducational, private two-year college, located 15 miles north of Scranton, Pennsylvania in the beautiful Pocono Northeast. Sixty-five percent of the graduating class transfer to fouryear colleges and universities with full junior status. Others go on to full-time careers. The academic strength of the institution lies in its strong emphasis on quality teaching and genuine concern for the individual student. Keystone's intimate small college atmosphere provides for an interaction between professor and student which extends fay beyond the classroom.

Program Description

The Hotel/Restaurant/Food Service Management, Culinary Arts and Travel and Tourism Programs are geared towards management positions and preparing students for two options: entering a career immediately after graduation or transfer to a four-year college or university. Students are required to complete a 500-hour supervised, salaried internship.

Special Features

Students in the Hospitality/Culinary Arts/Travel/ Tourism Program at Keystone have added opportunities for awards based on academic ability, interest in the field, and motivation to succeed in an academic and work environment. Student membership in the Society of Hosteurs and the honor society AXT is a great advantage to our students. Students at Keystone can take advantage of career planning and placement services to secure employment upon graduation or transfer to a four-year college or university.

Financial Aid and Scholarships

It is the goal of Keystone College to make sure that qualified applicants are never denied admittance because of inability to pay. The financial aid program at Keystone ensures need-based financial assistance made up of grants, loans, scholarships and work study to qualified applicants. In addition to need-based assistance, Keystone offers three merit-based scholarship programs: the Commuter Scholarship, the Nokomis Scholarship and the Departmental Scholarship. These scholarships, which range from $2,000 per year to $5,000 per year, are made available to students who are in the upper two fifths of their high school graduating class.

Approximate Tuition and Fees

The 1000-2000 tuition and fees (resident or commuting) are $9,800. Room and board $6,200.

Admissions

Keystone will consider applicants who meet the following criteria: graduation from an approved secondary school or the equivalent; satisfactory scores on the SAT or ACT; evidence of potential for successful college achievement.

Graduation Requirements

Students successfully completing the 69-73 credit hours with at least a 2.0 cumulative GPA are awarded an associate degree. Hospitality students also must complete a 500-hour internship/ practicum.

Swiss Hotel Association Hotel Management School *Les Roches*

Swiss Hotel Association Hotel Management Diploma, Associate Diploma Program

Program Enrollment – 900
Institutional Enrollment – 1000
Degrees Awarded: Bachelor of Science(Honours), Swiss Hotel Association Diploma, Associate of Science, Post Graduate Diploma.
Emphases/Specializations: International Hospitality Management, Hotel Management, Culinary Arts, F & B Operations.
Program Accreditation: Swiss Hotel Association.
Institutional Accreditation: New England Association of Schools and Colleges (NEASC), Swiss Hotel Association, State (Canton) of Valais.

Contact: Admissions Office, Les Roches, CH-3975 Bluche-Crans-Montana, Valais Switzerland Tel:(+41) 27 485 96 00, Fax: (+41) 27 485 96 15; e-mail: admin.roches@roches.vsnet.ch

Institution Description
Les Roches Hotel Management School is located in the small village of Bluche. In the center of the Valaisan Alps at an altitude of 4,200 feet, Bluche is less than two miles from the international ski resort of Crans-Montana. Students live in chalet-style accommodation, with modern, comfortable living quarters. A quality working environment together with extensive study and information technology network offer each student the best conditions for the successful completion of their studies.

Program Description
The "International Hospitality Industry Management Programme" offered in Bluche has been designed in collaboration Swiss, English and American industry and educational partners. It reflects our willingness to draw on the expertise of each partner in specific areas of education. Students completing this program will receive state of the art courses in culinary arts corresponding to the Swiss Hotel Association standards combined with the best college level management courses from the United Kingdom and the United States. The program is international through its design, course content and faculty experience and nationality, and student body which is drawn from some seventy countries.

Special Features
The program is run over a period of four years for Bachelor of Science (Honours) degree, three for the Swiss Hotel Association Hotel Management Diploma and two for the Associate Degree in Food and Beverage Operations. Each year of the first three years are divided into two 21-week semesters spent alternatively on campus and practising within the industry on paid (if accomplished in Switzerland) internships. The fourth year is based on two 16 week sessions spent on campus.

Financial Aid and Scholarships
All inquiries should be sent in writing to the School Board at the above address.

Admissions
The admission decisions are given taking into account the international origins of our applicants. Determining factors which are taken into consideration are the candidate's successful completion of high school, SAT scores, high school recommendation and personal interview results with one of our accredited agents.

Tuition & Fees
Tuition, room, board and books, per annum is approximately US$15,000.

Specialization Area
Hotel & Lodging Mgmt.

Lexington College

Hotel, Restaurant and Institutional Management Program

Program Enrollment: 50 full time
Institutional Enrollment: 50 full time
Degrees Awarded: Associate of Applied Science
Degree Categories: Food service and Lodging
Emphases/Specializations: Hotel, Restaurant and Institutional Management
Program Accreditation: Illinois Board of Higher Education, Commission on Institutions of Higher Education of the North Central Association of Colleges and Schools
Institutional Accreditation: Illinois Board of Higher Education, Commission on Institutions of Higher Education of the North Central Association of Colleges and Schools
Contact: Susan E. Mangels, President, Lexington College, 10840 S. Western Avenue, Chicago, IL 60643-3294

Institution Description

Lexington College is a private, two-year accredited college for women interested in hospitality management. Lexington is located in a residential area of Chicago, with many hospitality establishments nearby in which students can work as part of their studies. Facilities include a beautiful 40-acre, off-campus site, the Shellbourne Conference Center.

Program Description

Lexington's curriculum prepares students to be hospitality industry professionals with an openness to the cultural diversity within our own country and an international understanding of others. Lexington addresses the needs of women today, preparing each student to successfully meet life's challenges - both personal and professional.

Special Features

Lexington is the only women's hospitality college in the United States. Lexington is a single-purpose college, so the program is concise and compact. Graduates are prepared for both immediate opportunities and lifelong applications. With a 5:1 student to faculty/staff ratio, the college offers students the guidance and attention to cultivate their talents. The college boasts a 95% job placement rate.

Financial Aid and Scholarships

Federal, state and institutional financial assistance is available, as well as scholarships sponsored by the hospitality industry.

Admissions

Women who are high school graduates or hold a high school equivalency certificate are eligible. The ACT, SAT or other college placement test is recommended for admission.

Tuition & Fees

In-State: 1998-1999 tuition $6,900 per year.
Out-of-State: 1998-1999 tuition $6,900 per year.
Room and Board: 1998-1999 $3,300 per year.
Other Fees: Average $400 per year.

Specialization Areas

Hotel & Lodging Mgmt., Restaurant & Foodservice Mgmt.

Graduation Requirements

Graduation requires the completion of 64 semester hours which includes 17 hours of general education, 32 hours of management and business courses, and 15 hours of hospitality electives. A 240-hour externship is required.

Lincoln Land Community College

Hospitality Management and Services

Program Enrollment: 50 (new program 1994)
Institutional Enrollment: 30,000
Degrees Awarded: Hospitality Management and Services Associate in Applied Science Degree; Food and Beverage Certificate of Completion; Hotel-Motel Management Certificate of Completion
Degree Category: Hospitality Management
Degree Specializations: Hotel-Motel Management, Culinary Arts, Travel/Tourism, Dietary Manager
Institutional Accreditation: North Central Association of Colleges and Universities
Contact: Jay Kitterman, Hospitality Management Director, Lincoln Land Community College, 5250 Shepherd Road, P.O. Box 19256, Springfield, IL 62794-9256; phone (217) 786-2772, 1-800-727-4161, ext. 772; fax (217) 786-2495

Program Description

The associate degree program combines a strong business base with professional courses in lodging, food service, culinary skills, and tourism. Emphasis is placed on acquiring operational skills for persons entering this field. Persons already in the industry will find these courses instrumental in advancing their careers. Pro Management Program of the National Restaurant Association.

Special Features

Students receive instruction in a state-of-the-art display kitchen and computer labs. Students are required to complete paid internships at area hotels and restaurants. Emphasis is placed on career planning and placement. Because Springfield was the hometown of Abraham Lincoln, many local sites draw tourists from around the world.

Financial Aid and Scholarships

A growing number of financial aid programs are available for students who are eligible on the basis of demonstrated financial need. Scholarships are also available, awarded for general academic superiority, academic excellence in particular subject areas, and for outstanding performance in a variety of areas.

Tuition and Fees

In-district tuition is US$39 per credit hour. Out-of-district residents tuition with chargeback authorization is US$39 per credit hour. Out-of-district residents without chargeback authorization and all out-of-state students will pay additional tuition charges which will be revised based on per capita costs as defined in Illinois statute. Other fees are US$1.00 per credit hour activity fee and US$3.00 per credit hour laboratory/technology fee.

Admissions

Students must be age 18 or older to apply for admission to the college; however, special admission procedures are available for high school juniors and seniors.

Graduation Requirements

To earn an associate in applied science degree, each student must successfully complete 62.5 hours or more in the planned program including 15 hours in general education courses and 45+ hours in hospitality management and services and commercial cooking courses. A food and beverage certificate of completion requires 25 hours of hospitality management and services and commercial cooking courses. A hotel-motel management certificate requires 30.5 hours of hospitality management and services, business, and accounting courses.

Louisiana State University at Eunice

Hospitality Management

Program Enrollment: 47
Institutional Enrollment: 2,700
Degrees Awarded: Associate in Management
Degree Categories: Associate in Management and the Rooms Division Certificate from the Educational Institute of the American Hotel and Motel Association
Emphases/Specializations: Hotel and Restaurant Management
Program Accreditation: Not eligible for specialized accreditation until 2005
Partnership Agreements: Educational Institute of the American Hotel and Motel Association in Rooms Division Management
Institutional Accreditation: Commission on Colleges of the Southern Association of Colleges and Schools.
Contact: Dr. Fred Neal Landry, Head, Division of Business and Technology, Louisiana State University at Eunice, PO Box 1129, Eunice, LA 70535, phone: 318-550-1313; fax 318-546-6620

Institution Description

LSUE offers a wide range of courses and programs for the student wishing to pursue a four-year degree as well as for the student wishing to prepare for a career in two years or less of study. The campus is located in Acadia Parish; Eunice, Louisiana.

Program Description

The Hospitality and Tourism Industry plays an important role in academia. Students who choose hospitality management will learn the knowledge and skills needed by hotels, restaurants, clubs, resorts, and other service providers in the hospitality industry. Courses cover such areas as hotel, restaurant, club, convention and resort management.

Special Features

The program provides the Educational Institutes Specialization's Certificate in Rooms Division Management and Course Certificates in Travel and Tourism, Food and Beverage Management, Club Management, Convention Management, Resort Management and Human Resources Management. Additionally, each student is given the opportunity to focus on marketing, accounting, and/or management information systems.

Financial Aid and Scholarships

LSUE administers a broad program of financial aid and employment opportunities to help deserving students who need assistance to continue their education.

Admissions

LSUE provides educational opportunities for all qualified students who seek postsecondary education. LSUE assures equal opportunity for all qualified persons without regard to race, color, religion, sex, national origin, age, handicap, marital status, or veteran's status in the admission to, participation in, or employment in its programs and activities.

Tuition and Fees

In State: $48.50 for each semester hour.
Maximum tuition is $582.00 per semester.
Out-of-State: $158.80 for each semester hour.
Maximum tuition is $1,320 for each semester.
Room and Board: N/A
Other Fees: $97.00 to $100.00 for each semester.

Specialization Areas

Hotel and Lodging Management
Restaurant Management
Club Management
Resort Management
Accounting/Management Information Systems
Convention Management and Marketing

Graduation Requirements

Graduation requires the completion of 69 credit hours, which include 48 hours in the business and hospitality areas and 21 hours of general education courses. Students must achieve an overall average of 2.0 (C average) or better on all college work attempted, plus a minimum grade-point average of 2.0 on all work taken at LSUE.

Luzerne County Community College

Hotel, Restaurant and Institutional Management

Program Enrollment: 200
Institutional Enrollment: 6100
Degrees Awarded: Associate of Applied Science; Certificate of Specialization
Degree Categories: Associate in Hotel and Restaurant Management, Food Production Management, Tourism and Travel Management
Emphases/Specializations: Hotel and Restaurant Management; Food Production Management; Tourism and Travel Management
Institutional Accreditation: Middle States Association of College and Schools; State Board of Education—Commonwealth of Pennsylvania
Contact: William Bruce Neil, Ph.D. CHA Hotel, Restaurant and Institutional Management, Luzerne County Community College, 1333 South Prospect Street, Nanticoke, PA 18634; phone 570-740-0514; fax 570-740-0553

Institution Description

Luzerne County Community College is a public two-year, comprehensive community college. A variety of educational programs and support services are offered in an attempt to provide an opportunity for persons to pursue an education consistent with their interests and capabilities. Local industry executive serve on advisory committees ensuring that programs meet industry needs.

Program Description

The Hotel, Restaurant and Institutional Management Department prepares students for entry-level positions in the hospitality industry. Many students enter the work force directly from the program; other students transfer to hospitality programs in four-year colleges throughout the country. Certificate programs are designed to enhance the skills of currently employed hospitality workers.

Special Features

Faculty have industry experience and under their supervision students receive hands-on experience, using existing industry computer software and instruction within our major food production laboratories.

Financial Aid and Scholarships

LCCC maintains a fully staffed financial aid office which provides information on scholarships, loans, grants, work-study jobs and veteran's benefits.

Admissions

The college has a policy of open admissions for residents of Luzerne County and surrounding areas. Students from outside the county are encouraged to apply. Admissions standards for both county and out-of-county applicants are the same. Limitations of space or special requirements of individual curricula impose some restrictions. Certain programs may require specific prerequisites and alternative programs are available for the student that does not meet requirements.

Tuition and Fees

Tuition for residents of Luzerne County is $53 per semester hour each semester. For residents of Pennsylvania who don't have a community college in their area, tuition is $106 per semester hour. Out-of-state residents pay $159 per semester hour.

Specialization Area

Hotel & Restaurant Management; Food Production Management; Travel & Tourism Management.

Graduation Requirements

Students are required to successfully complete the recommended program of studies leading to the Certificate of Specialization or Associate of Applied Science, including any work experience practicum and/or clinical requirements. Students are required to make application for the receipt of certificates and/or degrees by the dates specified in the college academic calendar.

Macomb Community College

Culinary Arts/Hospitality

Program Enrollment: 200
Institutional Enrollment: 32,00 Degree credit students
Degrees Awarded: Associate of Applied Science, NRA Diploma, NIFI Sanitation Certificate, State of Michigan Sanitation Certificate, Practicum Completion Certificate
Degree Category: Associate of Applied Science in Culinary Arts/ Hospitality
Degree Specializations: Culinary Arts/Hospitality, ACF Apprenticeship Program
Institutional Accreditation: North Central Association of Colleges and Schools, American Culinary Federation Educational Institute
Contact: David F. Schneider, C.E.C., C.C.E., Faculty/ Department Coordinator. Macomb Community College, 44575 Garfield Road, Clinton Township, MI 48038; phone (810) 286-2088

Institution Description

Macomb Community College is the largest of Michigan's community colleges and ranks as the third largest multi-campus community college in the nation. The college's 126 degree credit programs offer a balance between liberal arts courses geared for students' first two years of a four year degree, and training for occupational careers.

Program Description

The program is designed to meet the needs of the current job market. Twenty three credit hours of management instruction builds the 44 credit hour core of the Associate Degree. Daily and evening Department-run restaurant gives the student much needed "hands-on" front and back of the house experience.

Special Features

The program requires students to work two hours practical experience for every credit hour taken (58 hours total) in Department restaurant or catering functions. The Curriculum includes the NRA diploma program and is an ACFEI accredited program.

Financial Aid and Scholarships

Macomb College's financial aid office has a policy of open admissions to applicants with a high school diploma or the equivalent, or who are at least 18 years of age. Assessment test required prior to admission to assist with placement.

Graduation Requirements

Forty-four credit hours in program core and 18 credit hours in general education for 62 hours total. Fifty-eight hour Practicum Certificate, NIFI Certificate, State Sanitation Certificate, 2.0 Grade Point Average.

Manchester Community Technical College

Hospitality Management Programs

Program Enrollment: 175
Institution Enrollment: 9,000
Degree Awarded: Associate of Science; Certificate
Degree Categories: Associate in Foodservice Management, Hotel-Tourism Management; Certificate in Culinary Arts
Program Accreditation: Board of Governors for Higher Education; American Culinary Federation Educational Institute Accrediting Commission

Institutional Accreditation: New England Association of Schools and Colleges
Contact: Jayne Pearson, Department Chair, Hospitality Management Programs, Manchester Community-Technical College, 60 Bidwell St., Manchester, CT 06045; phone (860)647-6311; fax (860) 647-6238

Institution Description

Manchester Community-Technical College offers career and transfer curricula leading to Associate of Arts and Associate of Science degrees, or certificates in the following program categories: hospitality management, business, computer and information sciences, education, allied health, liberal/general studies, human services and social science.

Program Description

MCTC's Hospitality Management Programs and Culinary Arts Program prepares students for entry-level management and supervisory positions, in addition to providing a strong academic base for a smooth transfer into a four year institution. A cooperative work experience emphasis, coupled with strong academic courses, provides students with many career avenues to pursue.

Special Features

Students are able to take a wide selection of food-preparation production courses in a modern, 8,000 square-foot facility, which includes two fully equipped kitchens, three dining rooms, dishroom, and a storeroom. These courses, plus the cooperative work experience program, provide strong management skills.

Financial Aid and Scholarships

Manchester Community-Technical College offers financial assistance in the form of grants, part-time employment, loans and tuition waivers/remission to insure that students who exhibit financial need will have the means to provide for their education expenses.

Approximate Tuition and Fees

Full-time (minimum 12 credits): in-state, $760 per semester; out-of-state, $2,296 per semester.

Admissions

MCTC has an open admissions policy. Anyone with a high school diploma or GED, or veterans and adults (age 21 or over) without a diploma, may be admitted to the college.

Graduation Requirements

Associate degree students must complete 62 academic credits, which includes 41 credits in their core curricula, with the balance in humanities, social science, natural science and liberal arts credits. The certificate course requires 30 credits in several specialized areas.

Massachusetts Bay Community College

Hospitality Management

Program Enrollment: 100
Institutional Enrollment: 3,800
Degree Awarded: Associate of Science
Degree Category: General Business Administration
Emphases/Specialties: Hotel Rooms Division Management; also Meetings Management and Regional Tourism Management

Institutional Accreditation: New England Association of Schools and Colleges
Contact: Prof. Edward G. McCourt, CHE
Massachusetts Bay Community College, 50 Oakland Street, Wellesley, MA 02481-5357; voice: 781-239-2207, fax: 781-416-1607; email: mccourte@mbcc.mass.edu

Institutional Description
Massachusetts Bay Community College is a publicly supported, associate degree and certificate granting institution. The college was founded in 1961 and has had a prominent presence in the west-of-Boston suburbs since the early 1970's. Career and transfer, associate degree and certificate programs are offered as well as opportunities for part-time study and personal and professional enrichment through noncredit courses.

Program Description
The Hospitality Management Program presents the broad spectrum of hospitality and tourism. While the key program focus is rooms division management, opportunities for meetings and regional tourism studies and experiences are provided. Content courses are balanced with courses in business administration and the liberal arts.

Special Features
Students complete an intensive field experience that includes, at minimum, 120 hours in a hotel, meetings or regional tourism setting.

Admissions
The college maintains an open-door admissions policy. Each student is admitted on a first-come, first-serve basis, provided the application and all supporting materials are complete and there is a vacancy in the program for which the student has applied. The office of admissions begins processing applications early in the fall for entry to all programs in the succeeding fall semester. A high school diploma or GED is required.

Graduation Requirements
Demonstrated academic competency in English, reading, mathematics and computer literacy, a cumulative grade point index of 2.0 or better and completion of the specified number of credit hours are all required.

Middlesex County College

Hotel, Restaurant, and Institution Management

Program Enrollment: 250
Institutional Enrollment: 5,500 full time; 4,500 part time
Degrees Awarded: Associate in Applied Science; Certificate of Achievement and Technical Certificate
Degree Categories: Associate in Hotel, Restaurant and Institution Management; Dietetic Technology Certificate of Achievement in Culinary Arts; Technical Certificates in Hotel Management Operations and Restaurant Operations
Emphases/Specializations: Options in Hotel Management, Restaurant/Foodservice Management, and Culinary Arts Management for Associate Degree
Institutional Accreditation: Middles States Association of Colleges and Secondary Schools
Contact: Marilyn Laskowski-Sachnoff, Associate Professor and Chairperson, Hotel, Restaurant and Institution Management Department, Middlesex County College, 2600 Woodbridge Avenue, PO Box 3050, Edison, New Jersey 08818-3050; phone: 732-906-2538; fax 732-906-7745 and e-mail: Sachnoff @email.njin.net

Institution Description

Middlesex County College offers more that 550 courses, including co-op work experiences, clinical involvement and laboratory assignments that parallel classroom studies. Students may choose career or job-oriented programs in business, health, engineering and science technologies.

Program Description

The Hotel, Restaurant and Institution Management Program provides students with the necessary skills for employment. The Culinary Arts Program was designed to provide the student with the knowledge and skills to become a professional in the field of food preparation and production. The Dietetic Technology Program prepares the student for a career in foodservice management and nutrition care.

Special Features

Clinical experience for students in dietetic technology; professional faculty who blend theory and practice through lecture-demonstration; employment along with college credit though cooperative education; a newly renovated State of the Art commercial food laboratory.

Financial Aid and Scholarships

Middlesex County College makes every effort though its financial aid program to overcome financial barriers that may prevent students from completing their education. Funds from federal, state and college sources are available to those who have need and meet eligibility requirements.

Admissions

Enrollment at Middlesex County College is open to high school graduates; persons who have met criteria for an equivalency diploma; or non-high school graduates who are 18 years of age or older. Prospective students may obtain the appropriate application materials by contacting the Office of Admissions by telephone, mail or in person, or by calling the HRI Department.

Graduation Requirements

Satisfactory completion of all courses in an approved program which requires not less than 60 nor more than 70 semester credit hours, except when required for licensing, accreditation or transfer to full junior status; minimum grades of C in English courses; minimum cumulative grade point average of 2.0; residency requirements.

Milwaukee Area Technical College

Culinary Arts

Institutional Enrollment: 10,000
Program Enrollment: 120
Degrees Awarded: Associate Degree; Certificate
Degree Categories: Culinary Arts
Program Accreditation: North Central Association of College and Schools; American Association of Community Colleges; American Culinary Federation, National Restaurant Association

Contact: Dean, Consumer and Hospitality Division, Milwaukee Area Technical College, Culinary Arts, 700 W. State Street, Milwaukee, WI 53233; phone (414) 297-6255; fax (414) 2297-7733

Institution Description

Milwaukee Area Technical College (MATC) is recognized for it's national leadership in offering a wide range of quality post secondary academic and technical courses and programs.

Program Description

As a technical college, MATC has courses designed to prepare you for immediate entry into specific occupations and careers. One hundred and four advisory committees, consisting of employee and employer representatives, guide the content of MATC programs to assure their quality and relevance to the workplace.

Special Features

MATC's Culinary Arts program provides chefs for the area's finest restaurants, and has consistently ranked among the top programs in the country.

Financial Aid and Scholarships

"Support Services for Students" are designed to assist students with financial, academic or personal assistance.

Admissions

Requirements for admission to the program are as follows: a high school diploma or GED; demonstration of proficiency in basic skills through admission assessment; good health as evidenced by a medical examination; proper immunizations. In addition, you will need an ability to relate to others, reading aptitude and basic math problem-solving skills. A high level of physical stamina and the ability to work rapidly for extended periods of time are important.

Graduation Requirements

Students graduating in the program must successfully complete 32 credits in technical courses, 12 credits in technical support courses, six credits in electives and 15 credits in liberal arts.

Mission College

Hospitality Management

Program Enrollment: 80 full time; 120 part time
Institutional Enrollment: 11,000
Degrees Awarded: Associate of Science; Certificate
Degree Categories: Associate in Food Service and Restaurant Management; Certificate in Food Service and Restaurant Management, Dietetic Supervisor
Emphases/Specializations: Culinary Apprenticeship Program in conjunction with the state of California
Program Accreditation: Western Association of Schools and Colleges

Institutional Accreditation: Western Association of Schools and Colleges
Contact: Haze Dennis, Department Chair, Hospitality Management, Mission College, 3000 Mission College Blvd., Santa Clara, CA 95054-1897, phone (408) 988-2200 X3280, 3283; fax (408) 567-2877; e-mail: haze_dennis@wvmccd.cc.ca.us

Institution Description
Mission College is a commuter-oriented community college in the heart of Silicon Valley. Besides providing a comprehensive academic curriculum, it offers a variety of vocational/technical programs.

Program Description
The Hospitality Management Program is housed in a modern, state-of-the-art building. Besides regular classrooms, it has large kitchens, dining rooms and support facilities. Students operate a cafeteria in the Fall and a first-class restaurant in the Spring semester. Transfer credits are accepted by most four-year schools with comparable programs.

Special Features
Besides a core curriculum, a number of optical courses are offered, such as cuisine, baking and pastry work, chocolate creations, wines and spirits of the world.

Financial Aid and Scholarships
The college maintains a Financial Aid Office that assists students in applying for loans, grants and scholarships.

Approximate Tuition and Fees
In-state: $13 per unit; out-of-state: $123 per unit. Student health fee: $7.50 per semester. Campus center fee: $5 per semester. Parking fee: $1 per day or $20 per semester. Fees and charges are subject to change.

Admissions
Mission College is an open enrollment institution. New students are required to take assessment tests in English and math for level placement.

Graduation Requirements
Associate of Science degree: 48 units of major coursework, plus general education work, plus 400 hours of work experience, all with a 2.0 GPA. Food service supervisor certificate: 48 units of major coursework, plus 400 hours of work experience. Each course must be completed with a grade of C or better.

Mohawk Valley Community College

Hospitality Programs

Program Enrollment: 150
Institutional Enrollment: 8,500
Degrees Awarded: Associate in Applied Science; Associate of Science; Associate in Occupational Studies; Certificate
Degree Categories: Associate in Occupational Studies in Food Service; Associate in Applied Science in Food Administration; Restaurant Management; Associate in Applied Science in Hotel Technology: Meeting Services Management; Certificate in Food Service Chef Training; Certificate in Hotel Technology: Front Office Technology
Emphases/Specializations: Associate: Foodservice Administration, Restaurant Management, Hotel Management/Meeting Services Management Certificate: Chef Training, Hotel Technology/Front Office Management
Institutional Accreditation: Middle States Association of Colleges and Schools
Contact Mark E. Waldrop, Interim Director, Hospitality Programs, Mohawk Valley Community College, 1101 Floyd Ave., Rome, NY 13440; phone (315) 334-7710; fax (315) 334-7762

Institution Description

MVCC was founded in 1946 as the New York State Institute of Applied Arts & Sciences at Utica. At present, MVCC, a unit of the 64-campus State University of New York, is a publicly supported community college. The college offers two-year degree programs that prepare students for technical and semi-professional careers in business, industry, social service and health care, or for further college study. Several shorter length certificate programs are also offered.

Program Description

The program offers three associate degrees in varying fields of hospitality. The Restaurant Management degree option prepares the student for middle management and supervisory positions in the field of restaurant and hospitality operations. The Food Service degree option prepares students for entry positions in the foodservice industry including food preparation, baking and catering. The Hotel Technology: Meeting Services Management option prepares students for employment in front office management, hotel food and beverage managment, housekeeping management or convention services.

Special Features

A practicum course of 225 hours of supervised work experience is part of the Food Service and Hotel Technology degree programs and is an option for the restaurant management degree. Many students use this experience as a stepping stone for permanent positions upon graduation.

Financial Aid and Scholarships

A variety of financial aid programs including EOP, TAP and PELL are available, as are a variety of grants and scholarships. A detailed list can be obtained from the financial aid department, and are also listed in the college catalog. MVCC offers a comprehensive financial assistance program of scholarships, grants, loans and other opportunities including work-study for qualified students.

Admissions

Admission to MVCC is on the basis of individual student records. Because MVCC is a county-sponsored institution, residents of Oneida County are given first preference. We accept many students from other parts of New York State as well as from other states and other countries.

Tuition and Fees

In-State: $1,250 per semester
Out-of State: $2,500 per semester
Student Activity Fee: $16 per year

Specialization Area

Hotel & Lodging Management; Restaurant & Foodservice Management

Graduation Requirements

The Food Service degree option requires the successful completion of 67-69 credit hours of study and includes elective and physical education requirements. The Restaurant Management degree option requires 70-71 credit hours of study and includes courses from liberal arts and sciences. The Hotel Technology degree option requires 65-68 credit hours of study and includes courses in business management. All three degrees require a minimum of two year of full-time study to complete.

Monterey Peninsula College

Hospitality/Restaurant Management

Program Enrollment: 60
Institutional Enrollment: 6000
Degrees Awarded: Associate in Science, Certificate of Achievement
Degree Categories: Associate in Hospitality Operations, Associate in Hospitality Management, Associate in Restaurant Management, Certificate in Hospitality Operations
Institutional Accreditation: Western Association of Schools and Colleges

Contact: Mary Nelson, Life Science Division, Monterey Peninsula College, 980 Fremont St., Monterey, CA 93940-4799. Phone (831)646-4134, Fax (831)645-1353, E-mail: mary@ultimanet.com, Web site: www.mpc.edu

Institution Description

Monterey Peninsula College is part of California's public community college system responding to the educational, cultural, and recreational needs of students and community members. MPC has provided over 50 years of service and quality educational programs. Located immediately off of Highway 1 in Monterey, the college has a beautiful view of Monterey Bay. The Monterey area is a premier resort, ecotourist, and golf destination. MPC has a diverse student population including over 300 international students from 45 countries. Extensive English and other support services are available.

Program Description

The mission of the program is to prepare students for transfer to four-year universities and to provide hospitality employees with continuing education and professional development. Courses offered include front office, housekeeping, food and beverage service management, sanitation, and a full range of culinary arts short courses. Students also take courses in business.

Special Features

Working with the Monterey County Hospitality Association and the American Culinary Federation, the program offers opportunities for students to participate in industry events and activities. Students in the golf management program can elect an emphasis in hospitality. MPC has an outstanding beverage service management instructor and recently added courses in special event management and professional meeting management. The culinary arts classroom has been completely remodeled this year.

Financial Aid and Scholarships

Financial assistance in the form of grants, loans, scholarships, and part-time jobs is provided to those who qualify. Many local groups provide scholarships. Jobs are numerous since Monterey is a destination resort area.

Admissions

Anyone who is 18 years of age or older and who is capable of profiting from instruction, or anyone who has a high school diploma or Certificate of Proficiency is eligible to attend MPC. An application for admission is required as part of the admissions process.

Tuition & Fees

Resident: $12 per unit
Non-resident: $121 per unit
Health fee: $11 per semester
Building fee: $10 per semester

Specialization Area

Hotel & Lodging Management, Restaurant & Foodservice Management

Graduation Requirements

Satisfactory completion of 60 units of college work. Twenty-one units are general education requirements; the remainder are hospitality, business and computer courses. Four units of cooperative work experience is also required.

Mt. Hood Community College

Hospitality and Tourism Program

Program Enrollment: 115
Institutional Enrollment: 25,000
Degree Awarded: Associate of Applied Science
Degree Category: Hospitality and Tourism Operations
Emphases/Specializations: Hotel and Motel Operations; Travel and **Tourism Operations;** Food Service Management; Convention and Meetings Management; Recreation and Leisure Management

Program Accreditation: Oregon State Department of Education
Institutional Accreditation: Northwest Association of Schools and Colleges
Contacts: Courtland Carrier, Program Director, Hospitality and Tourism Program, Mt. Hood Community College, 26000 S.E. Stark St., Gresham, OR 97030; phone (503) 667-7486

Institution Description

Mt. Hood Community College (MHCC) is a regionally based community college located in Gresham, Oregon, and part of the Portland metropolitan area. It is an equal distance to the resort areas of the Oregon Coast, Cascade Mountains and the Columbia Gorge National Scenic Area. MHCC offers over 78 different transfer programs, and 50 vocational-technical programs leading to associate degrees.

Program Description

MHCC's Hospitality and Tourism Program highlights the high technology application in many industry-specific courses, combined with the "high touch" of a people-oriented industry. Students pursue industry-specific courses in management, marketing, law, convention and meeting planning, computers, human resources, hotel/motel operations, travel geography, food service operations, and practical work experience, in addition to liberal arts.

Special Features

The MHCC program offers students technical training combined with remarkable work experience opportunities in the center of Oregon's hospitality industry. MHCC is now a licensed school for the institute of certified travel counselor (CTC) and destination specialist (DS) programs.

Financial Aid and Scholarships

MHCC maintains a fully staffed financial aid office and the Hospitality and Tourism Program pursues industry related scholarships and grants dependent on both academic achievements and work experience.

Approximate Tuition and Fees

$1,620 academic year resident tuition (Oregon, Washington, Idaho). $115 per credit out-of-state; $135 per credit international residents. Additional $1 per credit student fee.

Admissions

MHCC offers an open admissions policy, and all courses are designed to progress from the introductory level to progressively more difficult courses.

Graduation Requirements

Graduation requirements include the completion of 93-96 credit hours. This includes 40 hours of hospitality management and business administration, 24 hours of general education, 10 work hours of related electives, and two cooperative education work internships.

Nassau Community College

Hotel Technology Administration

Program Enrollment: 450
Institutional Enrollment: 23,000
Degree Awarded: Associate of Applied Science
Degree Category: Hotel Technology Administration, Food Service Management Administration
Emphases/Specializations: Restaurant Management; Hotel Management

Institutional Accreditation: Middle States Association of Colleges and Secondary Schools
Contact: Donald Bennett, Chair, Hotel and Restaurant Management, Nassau Community College, One Education Drive, Bldg. K, Garden City, NJ 11530; phone (516) 572-7344; fax (516) 572-9739

Institution Description

Nassau Community College is part of the State University of New York. It is a comprehensive, full-opportunity institution of higher education. The college is dedicated to providing high quality, low-cost education and career preparation that responds to the needs and interests of the community which it serves.

Program Description

Nassau Community College's Hotel and Restaurant Management Program is focused on instructing students in management and technical knowledge. The faculty prepares students for leadership roles and decision-making positions in the hospitality industry.

Special Features

The program received the 1987-88 National Restaurant Association's Award for Academic Excellence. The department offers an extensive cooperative work-study program, transfer counseling, placement services and a Hotel and Restaurant Club. Student may elect to enroll in two-week study programs and summer work-study program in Europe.

Financial Aid and Scholarships

The college maintains a fully staffed financial aid office, and the Hotel and Restaurant Management Program offers scholarships based on academic achievement and industry involvement.

Admissions

Open enrollment.

Graduation Requirements

Graduation requires the completion of 68 semester hours, which includes 35 semester hours of general education and business courses and 33 hours of hotel and restaurant management courses. A 350-hour of cooperative work experience is also required.

National Restaurant Association Educational Foundation

Foodservice and Hospitality Management

Degrees Awarded: Course and Program Certificates of Completion; Foodservice Management Professional® Certification

Degree Categories: Foodservice Management; Administrative Management; Financial Management; Human Resources Management; Marketing Management; Operations Management

Program Accreditation: Management and Applied Foodservice Sanitation courses are accepted by the American Culinary Federation, American School Food Service Association, Dietary Managers Association, International Food Service Executives Association, International Military Club Executives Association and National Food Brokers Association

Contact: John Gescheidle, Academic Sales Leader, National Restaurant Association Educational Foundation, 250 South Wacker Drive, Suite 1400, Chicago, IL 60606-5834; (312) 715-1010; fax (312) 715-0220

Institution Description

The National Restaurant Association Educational Foundation is a not-for-profit subsidiary of the National Restaurant Association. The Foundation develops, promotes and provides educational and training solutions for the restaurant and hospitality industry. As a leading education and training organization, the Foundation offers nearly 70 years of knowledge and expertise in the industry.

Program Description

The Educational Foundation's Professional Management Development (ProMgmt.SM) program addresses areas critical for foodservice students in their pursuit of educational and career success. Courses can be easily integrated into existing degree or certificate programs. Students receive certificates for the successful completion of each course. One of the featured courses is the ServSafe® food safety training program, the nation's most widely accepted course in foodservice sanitation for than more 20 years. In addition, students who successfully complete eight courses receive the industry-recognized National Restaurant Association Certificate.

Special Features

The Foundation assembles advisory committees comprised of educational leaders and solicits input from top industry professionals to ensure thorough course development. The Foundation's courses use the most current textbooks available and are developed to decrease the instructor's development time while enabling an individualized instructional style. The ServSafe coursebook and exam are also available in Chinese, Korean, French-Canadian and Spanish.

Scholarships

With $600,000 to award for the 1999/00 school year and more than $1 million to award for 2000/01, the Foundation encourages higher education among the restaurant and hospitality industry's professionals, educators, administrators and graduate and undergraduate students.

Approximate Tuition and Fees

Course fees: one course, $41-$150; eight-course ProMgmt. program, $375-$1,000. Course fees are subject to change.

Admissions

The Foundation has an open admissions policy. Students may participate in courses at more than 350 degree-granting institutions. Courses may also be taken through independent study or corporate/association-sponsored programs. Previous training or experience is not required.

Graduation Requirements

The Foundation's ProMgmt. program requires a student to successfully complete eight courses within the five Degree Categories stated above.

Naugatuck Valley Community Technical College

Hospitality Management

Program Enrollment: 120
Institutional Enrollment: 6,000
Degrees Awarded: Associate in Science
Degree Categories: Food Services Management; Hotel Management
Emphases/Specializations-Certificates: Culinary Arts; Dietary Supervision
Program Accreditation: Connecticut Board of Higher Education
Institutional Accreditation: New England Association of Schools and Colleges

Contact: Todd B. Jones, Coordinator, Hospitality Management Programs; Naugatuck Valley Community-Technical College; 750 Chase Pkwy; Waterbury, CT 06708; Telephone (203) 575-8175; Admissions: (203) 575-8078; e-mail: mt_markos_17@apollo.commnet.edu; Internet: http://www.nvctc.commnet.edu/ and http://nvmcc.commnet.edu/hpc/

Institution Description

Naugatuck Valley Community-Technical College is a state community college housed in the modern Central Naugatuck Valley Higher Education Center in suburban Waterbury, Connecticut. The college has an excellent academic reputation with its associate degree, certificate and nontraditional learning programs in business, mathematics, technology, science, arts and humanities, nursing and allied health, early childhood education, criminal justice, horticulture and automotive technology.

Program Description

The nationally recognized, award-winning Hospitality Management Programs combine foodservice, hotel, business, general education and work experience courses in food preparation and service, cost controls and accounting, sanitation, nutrition, hospitality law, catering and event management, wine & beverage, management, economics, computer science, tourism, and hotel operations and marketing/sales. Certificates are offered in Culinary Arts and Dietary Supervision.

Special Features

All students are evaluated on their performance in a student managed catering business and sommelier society which operate in a state-of-the-art commercial kitchen on campus, and in Terrace Six, a 100-seat fine dining facility.

Financial Aid and Scholarships

It is the policy of the college that no student be denied a chance to enroll because of lack of funds. Tuition and fees are kept to a minimum and there are diversified financial aid and scholarship programs.

Approximate Tuition and Fees

Full-time (12 credits or more): $907 per semester. Part-time, per three-credit course: $243 (price per credit declines as number of credits taken increases).

Admissions

Naugatuck Valley Community Technical College has an "open-door" admissions policy. Anyone who has a high school diploma, GED, or is a veteran or an adult, age 21 or over, without a diploma may be admitted to the college. Individualized programs are designed in consultation with Program Coordinator for those interested in Hospitality Management.

Graduation Requirements

An Associate of Science Degree in either Food Services Management or Hotel Management is awarded upon completion of the required 60 semester hours, which includes 30 hours in hospitality courses, 18 hours in business courses, and 15 hours in general education.

New Brunswick Community College - St. Andrews

Hospitality & Tourism

Program Enrollment: 180
Institutional Enrollment: 500
Degrees Awarded: Diploma
Degree Categories: Hospitality and Tourism
Emphasis/Specializations: Restaurant and Culinary; Hotel and Restaurant; Facilities and Accommodation; Travel and Tourism; Adventure and Recreation

Program Accreditation: ACCESS (CITC/ACTA)
Institutional Accreditation: NB Department of Education
Contact: John W. Ferguson, Department Head, Hospitality and Tourism, New Brunswick Community College - St. Andrews, P.O.Box 427, St. Andrews, New Brunswick, Canada E0G 2X0

Institution Description

Located in a popular resort community, the college is one of 10 New Brunswick Community Colleges. The college is working to maintain a base of 500 full time students in a combination of Hospitality & Tourism, Trades & Technology, and Marine related programs. The college uses facilities at both its main campus and the Algonquin Hotel, a national tourism icon.

Program Description

The Hospitality and Tourism faculty offers 5 options in its Diploma program. Graduates have direct access to year 3 of the Bachelor of Applied Management in Hospitality and Tourism program at the University of New Brunswick. Options include Travel and Tourism, Restaurant and Culinary, Hotel and Restaurant, Facilities and Accommodation, and Adventure and Recreation.

Special Features

Lead by faculty drawn from industry, the diploma includes practical skill development using a real hotel, live Apollo reservations access, and applied field trips.

Financial Aid and Scholarships

The program meets eligibility requirements for student aid programs offered by provincial governments.

Admissions

Applicants must have a high school graduation certificate or equivalent. Admission is competitive based upon academic achievement and/or demonstrated interest in the field.

Tuition & Fees

Canadian $2,400 CDN ($1,500 US$ approx)
International $5,000 CDN ($3,200 US$ approx.)
Other Fees Student fee, Books & supplies $600-800 CDN ($400-500 US$)

Specialization Area

Hotel & Lodging Mgmt.; Restaurant & Foodservice Mgmt.; Travel & Tourism Mgmt.; Culinary Arts

Graduation Requirements

In order to receive a diploma the student must complete the full core curriculum and all course units assigned to their specific option.

New England Culinary Institute

Culinary Arts

Program Enrollment: 560
Institutional Enrollment: 280 in residency; 280 on internship
Degree Awarded: Basic Cooking Skills Certificate, Associate of Occupational Studies; Bachelor of Arts
Degree Category: Culinary Arts; Service Management
Program Accreditation: ACCSCT; State of Vermont
Contact: Admissions Director, New England Culinary Institute, 250 Main St., Montpelier, VT 05602-9720; phone (802) 223-6324

Institution Description

Founded in 1980, New England Culinary Institute is a small proprietary school staffed by extremely talented and committed chefs offering comprehensive, hands-on training in the culinary arts. The institute has two campuses situated 45 minutes apart. One is located in Montpelier, Vermont and the other campus is in Essex, Vermont. The institute is accredited by ACCSCT, certified by the State of Vermont, and approved by the Veterans Administration. Both professional and nonprofessional continuing education courses are also offered. The new certificate program allows students to learn basic cooking skills without having to commit to two years.

Program Description

All programs emphasize hands-on training, very low seven-to-one student/teacher ratio provides personal instruction from excellent chefs in very small classes. Each program offers at least one term on a paid, closely supervised internship anywhere in the United States. The associate's degree program is 2 years in length. The bachelor's degree program is 1 1/2 years in length. The certificate program is 11 months in length.

Special Features

Internships enable students to broaden their view of the food service industry and be exposed to the skills and knowledge of other chefs. One hundred percent placement rate for qualified graduates. Advanced placement program for qualified applicants.

Financial Aid and Scholarships

Financial Aid is administered by the Vermont Student Assistance Corporation. Students can apply for loans and scholarships from the federal government, private sources, and New England Culinary Institute.

Approximate Tuition and Fees

A comprehensive fee of $20,945 per year covers tuition, room and board, and fees for the culinary arts program. The annual comprehensive fee of $21,155 covers tuition, room and board, and fees for the bachelor's degree program.

Admissions

Admission to the institute requires: application, short essay, recommendations and a high school transcript or equivalent. Rolling admissions process until class is filled.

Graduation Requirements

Graduation requires the completion of all blocks of study throughout the resident terms as well as successful completion of internships.

Northern Virginia Community College

Hospitality Management/Dietetic Technology/ Culinary Arts/Travel and Tourism

Program Enrollment: 425
Institutional Enrollment: 32,000
Degrees Awarded: Associate in Applied Science, Certificate
Degree Category: Business Management
Emphasis/Specialization: Associate in Hotel Management, Food Service Management, Dietetic Technology, Travel and Tourism; Certificate in Hotel Management, Food Service Management, Culinary Arts, Travel and Tourism, Convention and Exposition Management
Institutional Accreditation: Southern Association of Colleges and Schools; State Council of Higher Education for Virginia
Contact: Janet M. Sass, Program Head, Hospitality Management, Dietetic Technology and Culinary Arts, phone (703)323-3457, e-mail: nvsassj@nv.cc.va.us; Michael Freiband, Program Head, Travel and Tourism, phone (703)323-3457, e-mail: nvfreim@nv.cc.va.us; fax 703-323-3509; 8333 Little River Turnpike, Annandale, VA 22003

Institution Description

Northern Virginia Community College (NVCC) is one of 23 two-year colleges in the Virginia Community College system. Founded in 1966, NVCC is a comprehensive institution of higher education, offering programs of instruction in over 100 specializations. A commuter institution, the college is dedicated to making a high quality education accessible to all.

Program Description

The Hospitality Management/ /Travel and Tourism/ Dietetic Technology/Culinary Arts (HRI/TRV/ DIT)Program prepares its students to enter executive training and management position in the hospitality, healthcare and travel industries. The curriculum is a blend of professional, technical and liberal arts courses which enables graduates to successfully deal with the complexities of the field.

Special Features

NVCC's HRI/TRV/DIT Program offers a variety of laboratory and computer classes, along with cooperative education work experiences throughout the metropolitan Washington, D.C. area.

Financial Aid and Scholarships

NVCC has financial aid counselors to provide information about financial aid programs, application procedures and eligibility. The HRI/TRV/DIT Program offers several scholarships for academic excellence.

Admissions

NVCC has a policy of open admissions to applicants with a high school diploma or the equivalent, who are at least 18 years of age. International students should contact the college for additional admission requirements.

Tuition and Fees

Virginia residents - $48.50 per semester credit hour. Out of state residents - $162.20 per semester credit hour.

Specialization Area

Hotel Management; Foodservice Management; Travel and Tourism; Culinary Arts; Dietetic Technology; Convention and Exposition Management

Graduation Requirements

Graduation requires the completion of 65 semester hours with a minimlum cumulative grade point average of 2.0. The associate degree is comprised of 18 credits of general education (English, speech, math, social science, etc.) and 47 credits of professional and technical courses in the field of HRI, TRV, and DIT. The certificate requires the completion of 30 semester hours.

Northern Alberta Institute of Technology

Culinary Arts

Program Enrollment: 168 Certificate/Diploma: 240 Apprentices

Institutional Enrollment: 6,900 Full Time. 6,700 Apprentices, 32,000 Continuing Education Registrants

Degrees Awarded: 1 Year Cooking Certificate; 2 Year Culinary Arts Diploma; Apprentice Cooks I, II, III

Degree Specializations: Graduates of the Culinary Arts Program find employment in a number of areas in the hospitality industry. These may include: cooks in hotels, restaurants, clubs, convention centers, institutions (hospitals, schools), cafeterias, resorts, travel service (cruise ships, flight kitchens), catering firms, and various food chains, representatives/ consultants in sales, research and development, marketing and merchandising firms in the foodservice industry; entrepreneurship; public health inspector (additional training required)

Contact: Ralph Walker, Program Head, Culinary Arts, 11762— 106 Street, Edmonton, Alberta, Canada, T5G 2R1; phone (780) 471-8679; fax (780) 471-8914

Institution Description

Established in 1982, the Northern Alberta Institute of Technology is a modern multi-campus institution offering a wide range of job-oriented educational programs. NAIT offers a wide range of two-year diploma and one-year certificate programs in Business, Architectural Technologies, Engineering Technologies, Envrionmental and Laboratory Technologies, Health and Sciences Technologies, Hospitality and Applied Arts, and Pre-Technologies. NAIT is dedicated to offering quality career education that fulfills the goals and expectations of students while serving the needs of the economy.

Program Description

The Cooking Certificate offers a one-year course of study which leads to a two year diploma in Culinary Arts. The curricula are designed to meet the needs of students who wish to pursue a career in the food service industry. The basic philosophy of both programs is to expose the student to many aspects of the industry; and by this process, successfully prepare him/ her to enter the world of food service.

Special Features

NAIT is the second largest technical institute in Canada. The strength of the programs offered at NAIT lies in the ability to provide hands on learning experience in fully modernized food facilities and working one-on-one.

Financial Aid and Scholarships

Financial assistance to needy students is available in a number of forms: loans, grants, bursaries, awards and scholarships.

Tuition and Fees

Tuition Fees are CDN$2,013 annually (may be subject to change); books and supplies approximately CDN$600.

Admissions

Prerequisites for the Culinary Arts Program is Grade 10 or equivalent including English 10 or 13 and mathematics 10 or 13. Competitive selection criteria has been completion of grade 12 with English and math.

Graduation Requirements

Graduation requires the successful completion of all components of the 924 Hours/ First Year for Certificate and 924 Hours/ Second Year for Diploma with not less than a 50% mark in each course.

Norwalk Community-Technical College (NCTC)

Hospitality Management and Culinary Arts Programs

Program Enrollment: 120
Institutional Enrollment: Approximately 5,300 full- and part-time students in credit programs and approximately 4,000 in noncredit programs
Degrees Awarded: Associate in Arts, Associate in Science, Associate in Applied Science, Certificates
Degree Categories: AS in Hotel/Motel Management, AS in Restaurant/Foodservice Management, Culinary Arts Certificate
Emphases/Specialization: none
Program Accreditation: none
Institutional Accreditation: New England Association of Schools and Colleges; Connecticut Board of Governors for Higher Education; Technology Accreditation Commission of the Accreditation Board for Engineering and Technology, Inc.
Contact: Tom Connolly, Coordinator, Hospitality Management and Culinary Arts Programs, Norwalk Community-Technical College, 188 Richards Avenue, Norwalk, CT 06854-1655; phone (203)857-7355 or 7158; fax (203)857-3327

Institutional Description
Public, two-year college, nonresidential. Norwalk Community College and Norwalk State Technical College were founded in 1961; in 1992 the colleges merged to become Norwalk Community-Technical College. There are 43 career and transfer programs, including an Honors Program, 16 certificate programs, professional and continuing education programs, Business and Industry Services Network courses, Workforce Institute and Global Business Institute.

Program Description
The Hospitality Management and Culinary Arts Programs are designed for the individual seeking professional knowledge, skills and techniques required for entry-level management or hourly positions in either the Foodservice, Lodging or Travel & Tourism industries. Successful completion of the program leads to either an Associate of Science degree or a Culinary Arts Certificate.

Special Features
The Hospitality Management and Culinary Arts Programs are housed in a state of the art facility which includes a demonstration and instructional kitchen adjacent to a 72 seat instructional dining room.

Financial Aid and Scholarships
Financial assistance is available in four forms: grants, scholarships, college work-study and loans. Several scholarships are available for students from Connecticut industries.

Admissions
NCTC has an open admissions policy. Applicants are urged to apply early to receive the appropriate advisement. Most students are required to take a placement test. Full-time Culinary Arts students must complete a college application by July 1st for the fall semester and January 1st for the spring semester. Only sixteen full-time Culinary Arts Students are excepted per semester.

Tuition & Fees
In-state; part-time, $243 per three-credit course, including fees; full-time, and $907 per semester, including fees. Out-of-state: part-time, $696 per three credit course, including fees; full-time, $2719 per semester, including fees.

Specialization Area
Hotel & Lodging Mgmt.; Restaurant & Foodservice Mgmt.; Travel & Tourism; Culinary Arts

Graduation Requirements
Student are required to complete 22 courses and 68 semester hours of credit for the Restaurant/Foodservice Management Program; 22 course and 65.5-66.5 semester hours of credit for the Hotel/Motel Management Program; 9 courses and 30 semester hours of credit for the Culinary Arts Certificate Program; and minimum Grade Point Average of 2.0

Nova Scotia Community College Akerley Campus

Baking and Pastry Arts, Cooking, Food and Beverage Service, Hotel-Restaurant Management

Program Enrollment: 125
Institution Enrollment: Full Time: 1200, Part Time: 500
Degree Awarded: Diploma/Certificate
Degree Category: Food Service and Business
Emphasis/Specialization : Red Seal, Chef Certification
Institutional Accreditation: Canadian Federation of Certified Chefs (CFCC)

Contact: Student Services Department Akerley Campus, Nova Scotia Community College, 21 Woodlawn Rd, Dartmouth, Nova Scotia, B2W 2R7, Canada, Phone: (902) 491-4961, Fax (902) 491-4903

Institution Description

The Akerley Campus of the Nova Scotia Community College offers educational opportunities in over 30 occupational fields. Officially opened in 1969, the campus has graduated thousands of men and women who have achieved success in their chosen fields. This success has led many employers to return, year after year for new graduates. Many of today's employers are former graduates themselves.

Program Description

The College offers four hospitality-related semester programs. **Baking and Pastry Arts** students acquire the theory and practical skills to prepare various types of bake goods, pastries and desserts. The **Cooking** Program prepares students for careers as professional cooks and future chefs; the course emphasizes both institutional and gourmet cooking. **Food and Beverage Service** offers four interrelated disciplines, professional table service, hosting and staff supervision, bartending and mixology, and cash register procedures and graduates top quality, knowledgeable foodservice personnel for the hospitality industry. In **Hotel- Restaurant Management**, students acquire a thorough understanding of the operational and management principles of hotels, tourist resorts and restaurants.

Special Features

Students prepare food and bake goods for the cafeteria in a modern cooking lab and a production kitchen. The fully licensed dining room offers gourmet meals five days a week.

Financial Aid and Scholarships

Students attending the Nova Scotia Community College are eligible to apply for student loans under the Canada Student Loan program.

Approximate Tuition and Fees

Tuition: one-year programs, CDN $ 1200 per year; two year programs, CDN $ 1200 for each year.
Books: reference books required for each course may be purchased from the campus bookstore at the time of enrollment.

Admission

Acceptance into any course is based on the applicant's probability of successful completion of the specific program and entry into the field of choice.

Graduation Requirements

Progress of students is assessed on the basis of a continual testing and evaluation process. Each subject area of a course is divided into sections, students are required to make a passing grade in each section. The passing mark is 60%.

Ott College

Hotel Management, Culinary Arts

Program: Hospitality
Program Enrollment: 150
Institutional Enrollment: 300
Degrees Awarded: Hotel Management, Culinary Arts
Degree Categories: Hotel Management, Culinary Arts
Emphases/Specialization: Hotel Management, Associate and Diploma, Culinary Arts Diploma

Institutional Acreditation: Buenos Aires Provincial Education Board DIEGEP-4708, City Of Buenos Aires Education Board DGEP-B1049
Contact: Verónica Ferreyra, Dean, Eduardo Costa 848, tel/fax number : 792-1958 / 792-2337, e-mail address: ott@ciudad.com.ar

Institution Description

Ott College was founded in 1966 and was the first College to offer courses in Hospitality and has now a successful culinary program as well.

It is well known in the Argentine Community and has strong links with foreign Universities. Students live off-campus in nearby private family housing.

Program Description

A two-year / three-year up-to-date and dynamic training in international hotel management. The areas of study are Accommodation and Food and Beverage Management and hospitality business administration, including Accounting and Finance. Practical work experience is required and offered for graduation. Classes are taught in Spanish.

Special Features

International students are offered 1-3 months language courses in Spanish and Portuguese as well as living with a student family.

Financial Aid and Scholarships

On request, according to academic achievement; limited number available.

Admissions

High School diploma

Tuition & Fees

In-state : $ 4.200
Out-of-state : $4.200
Room and Board (if applicable)
Other Fees : Special International courses.

Specialization Area

Hotel & Lodging Mgmt.; Restaurant & Foodservice Mgmt; Travel & Tourism Mgmt.; Culinary Arts

Graduation Requirements

For the degree, both years must be completed and all examinations passed. For International short courses, full attendance is required.

Oxnard College

Hotel and Restaurant Management

Program Enrollment: 80
Institutional Enrollment: 7,000
Degrees Awarded: Associate of Science; Associate of Arts; Certificate
Degree Category: Culinary Arts; Hotel Management; Restaurant Management
Institutional Accreditation: Western Association of Schools and Colleges

Contact: Frank Haywood, Facilitator, Hotel and Restaurant Management, Oxnard College, 4000 S. Rose Ave., Oxnard, CA 93033; phone (805) 9865869; fax (805) 986-5865

Institution Description

Oxnard College is a commuter-oriented small college with strong programs in both academics and vocational programs. The college has outstanding programs in a number of vocational areas in addition to the HRM program (i.e., Fire Technology, Legal Assisting, Auto Mechanics/Auto Body, Electronics).

Program Description

Oxnard's College's HRM program puts heavy emphasis on hands-on training. Our state-of-the-art training kitchen provides students the opportunity to study all phases of food preparation from fast foods to classical cuisine. We are fully articulated with California Polytechnic University's program in Hospitality Management.

Special Features

Second year hotel students complete internships at local hotels getting experience in various departments. We run the "Strawberry Shortcake" booth for the city at the California Strawberry Festival. O.C. HRM Program is now in partnership with the National Restaurant Association and the American Hotel and Motel Association offering certificate courses and management diplomas.

Financial Aid and Scholarships

Depending on eligibility , HRM students can get assistance from a variety of student financial assistance programs. Students also generate scholarship money through HRM Club activities and many others.

Approximate Tuition and Fees

$12 per unit for resident students. $115 per unit for out-of-state and international students. $10 mandatory health fee per student. Culinary students will need to spend an additional $400 for uniforms, tools and books.

Admissions

Students can enroll at the college if they are 18 years of age. HRM students are required to have a clear TB test prior to entering the food labs. No special examinations are administered prior to registration.

Graduation Requirements

While Culinary Arts students could complete the 23 units (8 courses) in less time, most students finish in two to three years. Both the Hotel and Restaurant Management programs require 10 courses (27 and 26 units respectively).

Parkland College

Program Enrollment: 110
Institutional Development: 8,500
Degrees Awarded: Associate in Applied Science (A.A.S.); Certificate
Degree Categories: Restaurant Management (A.A.S.); Food Service (Certificate); Hotel/Motel Management (A.A.S. and Certificate); Travel and Tourism (Certificate)
Program Accreditation: Commission on Accreditation of Hospitality Management Programs (CAHM)
Institutional Accreditation: North Central Association of Colleges and Schools, Illinois Community College Board
Contact: Peter T. Tomaras, CHA, FMP, Program Director, Hospitality Industry, Department of Business and Agri-Industries, Parkland College, 2400 W. Bradley Avenue, Champaign, IL 61821; phone (217) 351-2378; fax (217) 373-3896; e-mail: ptomaras@parkland.cc.il.us

Institution Description

A commuter-oriented community college opened in 1967, Parkland serves more than 225,000 inhabitants in 12 counties in East Central Illinois. The award-winning, 223-acre campus is at the northwest corner of Champaign, readily accessible from interstate highways 72,74, and 57.

Program Description

Parkland instructors bring decades of practitioner experience to their classrooms. The teaching emphasis is on quality and professionalism through enlightened management of human resources. Through academic partnerships students earn course certifications from the Educational Institute of AH&MA and the Education Foundation of the NRA.

Special Features

Both certificate and degree students serve a mandatory sixteen-week work-experience internship. Students may participate in the Hospitality Industry Club.

Financial Aid and Scholarships

Parkland administers comprehensive financial aid programs including grants, loans, part-time employment and scholarships. Students may apply for $10,000 in program-specific scholarships.

Tuition and Fees

For the 1999-2000 school year, in-district tuition is $51 per credit hour for district residents, plus variable course fees in the $4-8 range. Out-of-district tuition is approximately $185 for Illinois residents, $240 for out-of-state students. There are no dormitories.

Graduation Requirements

Associate in Applied Science degrees require 60-62 semester hours, including a substantial general education base. Certificate requirements are 30 semester hours, including 7-9 hours of general education.

Paul Smith's College of Arts & Science The College of the Adirondacks

Hospitality Management and Culinary Arts

Program Enrollment: 400
Institutional Enrollment: 800
Degrees Awarded: Bachelor of Science, Bachelor of Professional Studies, Associate in Applied Sciences
Degree Categories: Culinary Arts and Service Management; Culinary Arts; Culinary Arts/Baking; Hotel, Resort & Tourism Management; Hotel and Restaurant Management; Tourism Management
Emphasis/Specialization: Management, Leadership, Culinary, Baking
Program Accreditation: American Culinary Federation Accrediting Commission
Institutional Accreditation: New York State Department of Education; Middle States Association of Colleges and Schools

Contact: Professor Paul Sorgule, CCE, AAC, Assistant Dean, Hospitality/Culinary, P.O. Box 265, Paul Smith's College Paul Smiths, New York 12970; (518) 327-6215; (518) 327-6369 FAX; e-mail: sorgulp@paulsmiths.edu; College Web Page: www.paulsmiths.edu

Institution Description
Paul Smith's Colege is a residential campus located in the heart of the Adirondack Mountain Olympic Region. It is situated on the northern shore of the Lower St. Regis Lake on the site of the original Paul Smith's Hotel. Surrounding this waterfront site are 14,000 acres of college-owned forests and lakes.

Program Description
Paul Smith's is one of the oldest two-year colleges of hospitality management in the U.S. And one of the newest and most innovative four-year institutions offering degrees in hospitality and culinary arts. The college enjoys an outstanding reputation in the industry as proven by over 14,000 graduates. Paul Smith's prides itself in the experiential emphasis of all of its programs that include internship and externship semesters.

Special Features
There are six state-of-the-art kitchens on the campus, a high-tech computer classroom, full scale retail bakery, a 92 room hotel used for training, and plans for a training restaurant and food technology laboratory in it's Statler Hospitality Center. Students in the college hotel are trained on the Springer-Miller Property Management System.

The college offers internship options in its hotel, in the Burgundy Region of France, and on-campus in its full-scale bakery. Students enjoy more than 300 choice properties for externship throughout the United States.

Financial Aid and Scholarships
Paul Smith's College maintains a full-time financial aid office prepared to assist parents, as well as prospective and enrolled students with information concerning the various avenues through which they may receive assistance in meeting the cost of an education. In addition, scholarships are available from the industry and private individuals.

Approximate Tuition and Fees
Tuition is $12,500 per year, room and board is approximately $6,000 per year, and lab fees between $450 and $800 per semester. Books, tools, and uniforms are extra.

Admissions
Admission to Paul Smith's College os based on academic ability and aptitude as well as character, related work experience and extracurricular activities. SAT or ACT test scores are required.

Transfer students are very welcome from institutions offering similar degrees. AAS and AOS two-year degree graduates can bridge into baccalaureate programs with relative ease.

Graduation Requirements
Cumulative Grade Point Average of 2.0; complete minimum credit hours for degree; college core liberal arts to include English, Math, and Social Sciences.

Other
14:1 students to faculty ratio. Laboratory classes carry a cap of 15 and most lecture classes accommodate less than 25. Paul Smith's has a 99% placement rate.

Pennsylvania College of Technology

Hospitality

Program Enrollment: 150
Institutional Enrollment: 4,850
Degrees Awarded: Associate of Applied Science, Bachelors of Arts
Degree Categories: Food and Hospitality Management, AAS; Culinary Arts, AAS, BS; Baking and Pastry Arts, AAS; Dietary Manager Technology, AAS
Program Accreditation: American Culinary Federation Educational Institute Accrediting Commission (CA,BK) CAHM (FH)
Institutional Accreditation: Middle States Association of Colleges and Secondary Schools
Contact: Mr. William C. Butler, Dean School of Hospitality, One College Avenue, Williamsport, PA 17701; phone (570) 327-4505; fax – 1-570-327-4503; E-mail: bbutler@pct.edu

Institution Description

As a Penn State affiliate, Penn College is realizing its full potential as Pennsylvania's premier technical college. Continuing in a tradition of excellence, Penn College is a strong force in higher education in Pennsylvania, offering certificate, associate and baccalaureate degree programs. Students from around the state, the nation, and the world are enjoying the benefits of state-of-the-art programs in traditional and emerging technologies.

Program Description

Culinary Arts – This program prepares the students in fine product preparation and presentation. Extensive practical experience with the variety of cuisine and techniques is available through hands-on instruction. The program is fully accredited by the American Culinary Federation Educational Institute Accrediting Commission. Food and Hospitality Management – This program includes academic classroom study and practical laboratory work in business and personnel management, food preparation and supervision, and related subjects. Guest speakers, field trips and directed community field work experiences expand students' learning opportunities. Baking and Pastry Arts – This program prepares the student to produce a full range of baked goods and pastries, classical and contemporary. Extensive practical hands-on experience is enhanced by classroom instruction. The program is fully accredited by the American Culinary Federation Educational Institute Accrediting Commission. Dietary Manager Technology – This program prepares students to perform as a key link between Dieticians and cooks in health care and institutional facilities. It combines culinary skills with strong theoretical and clinical education in nutrition.

Special Features

Students have an opportunity to become Junior Members of the American Culinary Federation, West Branch Chapter, which enables them to become certified in various levels within the organization. Students participate in food show competitions, end-of-the-semester projects and culinary salons throughout the area. Other opportunities are available including: The Visiting Chef Series, California Winery Association Events, the NRA Salute to Excellence, The Kentucky Derby, The Breeder's Cup and Hunt Country Vineyard's Weekend Open House, and assisting on "You're the Chef", our syndicated PBS series.

Financial Aid and Scholarships

Recognizing that the cost of education is often greater than the student and his/her family can afford without help, the Financial Aid Office helps students obtain financial assistance through Grants and Scholarships (College and School possibilities), Loans, College Work Study Programs, Veteran's Benefits, Vocational Rehabilitation Sponsorship and part-time employment.

Admissions

Committed to serving the educational needs of students from all walks of life, Pennsylvania College of Technology operates under an "open door" admissions policy and is open to anyone with a high school diploma or its equivalent. An adult who does not have a high school diploma or its equivalent may be admitted as a "special student." Acceptance to some programs of study, including baccalaureate degree programs, is based upon the applicant's meeting the requirement including necessary academic skills and prerequisites of the specific program of study. The College reserves the right to deny admission or readmission to any student if, in the opinion of College authorities, his/her admission is not in the best interest of the student or the College. Equal opportunity for admission is offered without regard to age, sex, handicap, race, religion, creed, national origin, veteran status, or political affiliation. The College will provide opportunities to develop the basic skills necessary to enroll in degree and certificate courses to those who demonstrate such needs of the College's placement tests.

Tuition and Fees

Application Fee – applicants for status as full-time students in degree or certificate programs must include a non-refundable application fee with their Admissions Application. You are required to pay this non-refundable fee only once (unless you are enrolling after more that two years). IN-STATE STUDENTS: tuition and fees will total approximately $7,000 per year in 1998-99.* OUT-OF-STATE STUDENTS; tuition and fees will total approximately $8,300 per year in 1998-99. * The College reserves the right to change tuition and other fees as required. For the latest information, please contact the Office of Admissions.

Pensacola Junior College

Culinary Management

Program Enrollment: 40
Institutional Enrollment: 34,000
Degrees Awarded: Associate of Science
Degree Categories: Associate of Science in Culinary Management
Emphasis/Specializations: Culinary arts, baking and dining room service

Program Accreditation: Southern Association of Colleges and Schools, Florida State Department of Education
Contact: Howard Aller, CEC, CCE, Director, Culinary Management Department, Pensacola Junior College, 1000 College Blvd., Pensacola, FL 32504; phone (850) 484-1422, fax (850) 484-1543, email: haller@pjc.cc.fl.us

Program Description

The Culinary Management program prepares individuals for careers in several areas of the culinary industry. Students gain a unique combination of comprehensive theoretical knowledge and hands-on training. Students master the fundamentals of culinary production in an environment that builds teamwork while gaining practical and individualized experience.

Institution Description

Founded in 1948, and Florida's first junior college, Pensacola Junior College is a public, 2-year institution located in Florida's sparkling white sand coast with a year-round temperateclimate and a relaxed pace of living. PJC is a commuter campus with no on-campus housing

Special Features

Students have the opportunity to display their culinary skills at both lunch and dinner in the department's public dining room; one term of each is required for graduation. The lunches, planned, prepared, and served by one class, change themes and menus weekly. The multi-course dinners include tableside service and a pastry cart, all presented by students in the advanced classes

Financial Air and Scholarships

Pensacola Junior College maintains a financial aid office on campus and all Culinary Management students are eligible for a full range of financial assistance. There are some limited scholarships for culinary management majors only.

Admissions

Pensacola Junior College maintains an open admissions policy- a high school diploma or GED is required. Placement tests are mandated for all first-time students and college prep classes are offered for those needing them.

Tuition and Fees

The Pensacola Junior Colle Culinary Management Program costs are approximately $2000 per year for in-state students and $5000 per year for out of state students. This covers all tuition, fees, and books.

Graduation Requirements

The two-year program requires the completion of 64 hours in culinary, baking, and other specialized classes and 3 credit hours on-the-job internship experience.

Philadelphia OIC Opportunities Inn: The Hospitality Training Institute

Culinary Arts, Front Office Operations, Housekeeping, Food Service, Travel & Tourism

Program Enrollment: 450
Institutional Enrollment: 4,680
Degrees Awarded: Certificate of Completion
Degree Specializations: Culinary Arts, Front Office Operations, Housekeeping, Food Service, Travel & Tourism
Institutional Accreditation: Pending 1999 approval

Contact: Gregory L. DeShields, General Manager, Philadelphia OIC Opportunities Inn; The Hospitality Training Institute, 1231 North Board Street, Philadelphia, PA 19122, phone (215) 236-7700; fax (215) 236-0841; web site: www.philaoic.org; E-mail: jobs@philaoic.org

Institution Description
The mission of the Philadelphia OIC is to assist the unemployed and under-employed, the homeless, and disadvantaged youth and adults achieve self-sufficiency and empowerment, primarily through education, training, and job placement, and through supportive human services, housing and economic development.

Program Description
Opportunities INN: The Hospitality Training Institute is a division of the Opportunities Industrialization Center, Inc. (OIC), devoted to providing the Philadelphia and Regional hospitality industry with a skilled workforce for the 1990's and the new millenium. Since its inception in 1989, Opportunities Inn has provided training in the 5 components of Culinary Arts, Front Office Operations, Housekeeping, Food Service and Travel Tourism graduating over 150 students annually with a job placement rate of 75%. Emphasis for all courses is on the "service attitude" as well as the development and refinement of interpersonal and communication skills that are critical to advancement and success within the hospitality industry.

Special Features
As a part of their technical education, students receive hands-on-experience in a simulated hotel environment to be able to perform to the standard of the hospitality industry under smiliar workplace conditions. Students also receive life skills and academic instruction, counseling, internship, job placement assistance and the opportunity to join the alumni association. Opportunities Inn is a member of the Philadelphia Convention & Visitors Bureau, Multi-Cultural Affairs Congress, Greater Philadelphia Hotel Association, Deleware County Convention & Visitors Bureau, American Hotel & Motel Association, Philadelphia Resteraunt Association, Greater Philadelphia Restaurant Purveyors Association, CHRIE, Greater Philadelphia Chamber of Commerce and the Association of Culinary Federation.

Tuititon Fees
The Pennsylvania Convention Center Authority endorses and financially supports Opportunities Inn. Because of that support, training is offered at no cost to the students. Culinary Arts students are, however, required to purchase their uniform and utensils (approximately $200).

Admissions
Entrance requirements are dictated in part by the employment placement standards established by the hospitality industry. They include: High School Diploma or GED; interview, positive communication and interpersonal skills and appropriate overall appearance; literacy testing; Math and English tests; no felony convictions or substance abuse; positive references.

Specialization Area
Hotel & Lodging management: Travel & Tourism Management; Culinary Arts

Graduation Requirements
Graduation requires the successful completion of all course subjects; a cummulative GPA of 2.5 or above; regular attendance and punctuality; and internship.

Pima County Community College District

Program Enrollment: 350

Institutional Enrollment: 33,000 (14,800 full time student equivalent)

Degrees Awarded: Associate of Applied Science; Basic Certificate; Advanced Certificate

Degree Categories: Associate and Certificate in Hotel Industry Operations and Management, Restaurant Industry Operations and Management, Tourism and Travel Industry Management; Certificate in Hospitality Industry Operations, Sales and Marketing, Housekeeping Executive Industry Operations and Management, Meetings and Conventions Operations and Management, Culinary Arts

Program Accreditation: National Executive Housekeepers Association

Institutional Accreditation: North Central Association of Colleges and Schools

Contact: Dr. Camille Stallings, CHA, CHSE, CHE, Chairperson, Hospitality Department, Pima County Community College District, 1255 N. Stone Ave., Tucson, AZ 85709-3030; phone (520) 206-6341, fax (520) 206-6201

Institution Description

Pima County Community College, through its diverse educational programs, strives to prepare students to function effectively in a highly complex and technological society; assists all students in reaching their highest potential; and contributes to the educational, social and cultural development of Pima County.

Program Description

Program options are designed to prepare students to enter the hospitality work force and/or to update those already employed in the industry. Program options include six major specialties.

Special Features

Coursework in all options emphasizes communications, decision making, problem solving, ethics, and other successful job skills. Many of the major courses in the program area are taught by professionals in the field. Other types of support provided by local industry include classroom locations, training, jobs, etc. Cooperative education opportunities are available. Faculty advisors in the program area are located at the Downtown Campus.

Financial Aid and Scholarships

Several Sources of financial aid are available from national, state, and local hospitality industry professional associations.

Approximate Tuition and Fees

Tuition for residents is $33 per credit hour through 12 credits; for outof-state students, $56 per credit hour for out-of-state/country

Admissions

The college is open to high school graduates; recipients of a GED certificate; transfer students from an accredited college; non-high school graduates between the ages of 16 and 18 who have officially withdrawn from high school; students currently enrolled in high school who present written approval from the students' principals and parents or legal guardians; and international students. For all programs, preference in admissions shall be given to Pima and Santa Cruz County residents.

Graduation Requirements

Students are required to apply for the receipt of certificates and/or degrees by the dates specified in the college academic calendar. Failure to do so may result in a delay in processing until the following semester.

Purdue University

Restaurant, Hotel, Institutional, and Tourism Management (RHIT)

Institutional Enrollment: 30,159 undergraduate; 6,719 graduate
Degrees Awarded: Associate of Applied Science
Degree Categories: Food Service and Lodging Supervision
Institutional Accreditation: North Central Association of Colleges and Schools
Contact: Raphael R. Kavanaugh, Ed.D., CHA, FMP, Head, Department of Restaurant, Hotel, Institutional, and Tourism Management, Purdue University, 1266 Stone Hall, West Lafayette, IN 47907-1266; phone (765) 494-4643; fax (765) 494-0327; e-mail brubakerm@cfs.purdue.edu; website http://www.cfs.purdue.edu/RHIT/

Institution Description

Located in the heart of the Midwest, Purdue was founded in 1869 as a land-grant university. As one of the 25 largest schools in the nation, its alumni include Nobel Prize winners, astronauts, three U.S. Secretaries of Agriculture, literary figures, and college and corporate presidents. Purdue offers students infinite social and cultural events as well as some of the best athletic facilities in the Big Ten. This beautifully landscaped campus is located in a major metropolitan center 125 miles southeast of Chicago and 65 miles northwest of Indianapolis.

Program Description

The Associate of Applied Science in Food Service and Lodging Supervision is a two-year program that prepares students to assume the responsibilities of middle manager or supervisor in a variety of foodservice and lodging operations. This program requires many of the same courses required for the four-year degree. All credits earned for the AAS degree may be applied to further study toward the four-year BS degree in RHIT.

Special Features

The RHIT Computer Resource Center integrates the latest computer technology into classroom usage. The RHIT Café and restaurant kitchens provide a state-of-the-art training facility for students, as well as public dining, in which students gain hands-on and management experience. RHIT students develop industry networks through unique interaction with the RHIT Advisory Board and the annual RHIT Career Day. The RHIT Recruiting Center provides internship opportunities and coordinates interviewing and job placement for RHIT students.

Financial Aid and Scholarships

Purdue University's Office of Financial Aid provides students with information on many sources of financial assistance. In addition, over $60,000 in merit scholarships and financial assistance are awarded annually to students within the RHIT Department.

Admissions

Admission to Purdue is dependent on class rank in high school, probability of success, grade average, trends in achievement, strength of college preparatory program, and ACT or SAT score are required.

Approximate Tuition and Fees

In-state tuition is $3,564 per year; out-of-state tuition is $11,784 per year.

Specialization Area

Hotel & Lodging Mgmt., Restaurant & Foodservice Mgmt., and Travel & Tourism Mgmt.

Graduation Requirements

Graduation requires 68 hours, which includes 24 hours of general education and 44 hours of restaurant, hotel institutional, and tourism management core courses. A minimum 300-hour work experience or internship is required.

Red Deer College

School of Hospitality and Tourism

Program Enrollment: 150
Institutional Enrollment: 6,500
Degrees Awarded: Diploma; Certificate
Degree Category: Hospitality and Tourism Management
Emphases/Specializations: Diploma in Food and Beverage Management, Accounting and Financial Management, Marketing and Rooms Division Management; Certificate in Food and Beverage Management; Accounting and Financial Management; Marketing and Rooms Division Management
Contact: Bill Alcorn, Chairperson, Hospitality and Tourism, Red Deer College, P.O. Box 5005, Red Deer Alberta, Canada, T4N 5H5; phone: (403) 342-3355; fax: (403) 340-8940

Institution Description

The main campus of Red Deer College is located within the city of Red Deer. Red Deer College is a student-oriented institution that offers many on-campus facilities and services. It focuses primarily on college preparation, university transfer and business programs.

Program Description

The Hospitality and Tourism Program is organized around three comprehensive areas of specialization: marketing and rooms division management; food and beverage management, and accounting and financial management. Students may complete the one year certificate or two year diploma in the area of their choice. The certificate program prepares the student for an entry-level position. The diploma prepares the student for a supervisory or junior-management position in the hospitality industry.

Special Features

Red Deer College and the hospitality industry have formed a partnership that benefits the student and the industry. Both partners contribute to all aspects of the program, from development to accreditation. The student will receive working experience in some of the finest hospitality establishments in the world.

Financial Aid and Scholarships

Financial aid and a variety of scholarships are available. Contact Student Services at (403) 342-3300.

Approximate Tuition and Fees

Canadian citizen: CDN$55.25 per credit hour; international student: CDN$159.25 per credit hour.

Admissions

Students may enter the program under one of two categories: high school graduate or adult status (19 years of age or greater) with a minimum 60 percent GPA, with no mark below 50 percent in math, 30/33 and English 30/33.

Graduation Requirements

To graduate from either the diploma or certificate programs, students must acquire a minimum grade of D in all courses and a minimum 2.0 GPA.

Regal Constellation College of Hospitality

Hotel and Restaurant Operations/Culinary Arts

Program Enrollment: 25-100
Institution Enrollment: 160
Degree Awarded: Diploma
Degree Category: Diploma in Hotel and Restaurant Operations and Culinary Arts
Program Accreditation: Ontario Ministry of Education and Training
Institutional Accreditation: Ontario Ministry of Education and Training; Member of National and Ontario Associations of Canadian Career Colleges; Canadian Restaurant & Foodservices Association; Ontario Tourism and Education Council
Contact: Sharon Turner Director, Constellation College of Hospitality, 900 Dixon Road., Toronto Ontario, Canada M9W 1J7; phone (416) 675-2175; fax (416) 675-6477; E-mail: college@regalconstellation.com

Institutional Description

Private Career College established and registered in 1982 with the Ontario Ministry of Education and Training. Owned and operated through Regal Hotels International. On site at the Regal Constellation Hotel, Canada's largest hotel convention facility.

Program Description

The Diploma Program in Hotel and Restaurant Operations is a 32-week program featuring on-site practicum in hotel departments. Credits may be transferred to Johnson and Wales University, USA; or HOSTA in Switzerland. The Diploma Program in Culinary Arts, (Basic and Advanced) include application study in the main kitchens of the Regal Constellation Hotel for three months.

Special Features

The Regal Constellation College of Hospitality is part of Regal Hotels International and students take their practicum on site at the Regal Constellation Hotel, Canada's largest convention hotel. Practical hands-on experience is offered in a variety of departments so that students can learn the basic fundamentals in operations. Class sizes are small and students get personalized attention. There are frequent start dates every six weeks during the year. Our instructors are Hospitality professionals, with many years of industry experience. Short term courses are offered which focus on specific areas of expertise such as Resort Management; Hospitality Supervision; Financial Accounting and Computer Basics. The Post Graduate Support Program provides guidance and assistance in preparation of resumes and interview skills. Additionally, the college provides students with information on job opportunities available in the industry through the Job Opportunity Listings. Graduates are offered lifetime assistance in Placement Support.

Approximate Tuition and Fees

Hotel and Restaurant Operations: Canadian Residents: CDN$5,295; International students: CDN$7,800.
Culinary Arts: Canadian Residents: CDN$3,495; International students: CDN$5,195
Room and Board: CDN$9,600.

Graduation Requirements

A pass mark of 70 percent. Attendance is mandatory.

The Restaurant School

Hotel Management, Restaurant Management, Culinary Arts, Pastry Arts

Program Enrollment: School of Culinary Arts: 400
School of Management: 100
Institutional Enrollment: 500
Degrees Awarded: Associate in a Specialized Technology (AST); Associate in a Specialized Business (ASB); AST in Culinary Arts, Pastry Arts and Restaurant Management; ASB in Hotel Management
Program Accreditation: Accrediting Commission of Career Schools and Colleges of Technology (ACCSCT)
Institutional Accreditation: Accrediting Commission of Career Schools and Colleges of Technology (ACCSCT)
Contact: Karl D. Becker, Director of Admissions, The Restaurant School, 4207 Walnut Street, Philadelphia, PA 19104; phone toll free (877) 925-6884; fax (215) 222-4219

Institutional Description

Established in 1974, The Restaurant School is dedicated to inspiring the future of the restaurant and hotel industry through training that is dynamic, timely and insightful, with a commitment of service to its students. It has been cited in several national publications as one of the top five schools in the country.

Program Description

There are four majors: Hotel Management, Restaurant Management, Culinary Arts and Pastry Arts. Each major provides the student with a broad-based knowledge of the overall workings of a fine restaurant or hotel. Beyond that, the programs prepare the student with the day-to-day skills and specific knowledge needed for a successful career.

Special Features

The Restaurant School was the first school in the country to offer a travel experience as part of a curriculum. Culinary and pastry students travel to France, while the hotel and restaurant management students participate in an Orlando resort and cruise tour.

Financial Aid and Scholarships

The school is approved to participate in federal loan programs, federal grant programs, and state grant programs. In addition, the financial aid office can provide guidance on organizations that provide scholarships.

Admissions

Application for admission to the School is available to any individual with a high school diploma or its equivalent and an interest in developing a career or ownership options in hotels, fine restaurants, food service or hospitality. Two references, high school transcripts and a personal interview are required.

Tuition & Fees

In-state: $9,750 per academic year; Out-of-state: $9,750 per academic year. Room and board: varies. Other fees: Application fee, $50; registration fee, $150; books, supplies, equipment, uniforms, $1,400.

Specialization Area

Hotel and Lodging Management, Restaurant and Foodservice Management, Culinary Arts

Graduation Requirements

Graduation requires the successful completion of all courses in the selected major and be current with all financial obligations.

Santa Barbara City College

Hotel, Restaurant and Culinary

Program Enrollment: 50 new students per semester; 200 full time
Institutional Enrollment: 13,000
Degrees Awarded: Associate of Science; Certificate of Completion
Degree Categories: Restaurant Culinary and Hotel Management
Emphases/Specializations: N/A
Program Accreditation: American Culinary Federation
Institutional Accreditation: Western Association of Schools and Colleges
Contact: John Dunn, Chairperson, Hotel, Restaurant & Culinary Department, Santa Barbara City College, 721 Cliff Dr., Santa Barbara, CA 93109; phone (805) 965-0581, ext. 2458; fax (805) 963-7222

Institution Description
Santa Barbara City College was established in 1909. The campus is situated on a 74-acre site overlooking the Pacific Ocean. The college offers programs preparing students for transfer to four-year colleges and universities, and for the upgrading of employment skills needed for career advancement and personal development.

Program Description
The Hotel, Restaurant and Culinary (HRC) Department prepares students for employment in the hospitality industry. Many students enter the work force directly from the program, gaining immediate employment in restaurants, clubs, hotels and so forth. Other students continue to complete the Associate of Science degree and transfer to four-year college and university hospitality programs throughout the country.

Special Features
The college's food facilities, snack shop, cafeteria, coffee shop and gourmet dining room function as labs for the program. Second-year industry-based internships are available.

Financial Aid and Scholarships
The HRC Department awards several scholarships each semester, varying from $50 to $1,500. Other major categories include grants, loans and college work-study programs.

Admissions
Enrollment is open to any student with a high school diploma or equivalent who can benefit from a college education.

Tuition & Fees
The tuition cost is $11 per unit for California residents, $140 per unit for out-of-state and international students.

Specialization Area
Restaurant Culinary and Hotel Management

Graduation Requirements
A Certificate of Completion is awarded if a student successfully completes all required HRC courses, with an overall GPA of 2.0. An Associate of Science degree may be earned by passing all required general education courses, plus the required units in the HRC Department, with an overall GPA of 2.0.

Schenectady County Community College

Department of Hotel, Culinary Arts and Tourism

Program Enrollment: 550
Institutional Enrollment: 3,150
Degrees Awarded: Associate of Occupational Studies (AOS); Associate of Applied Science (AAS); Certificate
Degree Categories: Associate of Occupational Studies in Culinary Arts; Associate of Applied Science in Hotel and Restaurant Management, Travel and Tourism; Food Sales and Distribution;Institutional Accreditation: Middle States Association of Colleges and Schools; Commission on Higher Education; American Culinary Federation Educational Institute
Contact: Anthony (Toby) J. Strianese, Chairperson and Professor, Department of Hotel, Culinary Arts and Tourism, Schenectady County Community College, 78 Washington Ave, Schenectady, NY 12305; phone (518) 381-1391; fax (518) 346-0379

Institution Description

Schenectady County Community College (SCCC) is part of the State University of New York system. SCCC provides comprehensive higher education and adult education opportunities of the highest quality through academic, career-technical, professional and personal enrichment programs in response to local educational needs and at low cost to students.

Program Description

All four degree programs provide students with practical and theoretical knowledge in preparation for immediate employment. The Culinary Arts program emphasizes skills needed to begin a career in culinary arts. Students in the AAS programs are also able to transfer to a four year college.

Special Features

SCCC has seven food labs (four gas, three electric) and two dining rooms. The education is rounded out through a series of management and liberal arts courses. Intern opportunities are provided.

Financial Aid and Scholarship

Monetary assistance is provided through a college work-study program, an Educational Opportunity Program, and Perkins Loans and Supplemental Educational Opportunity Grants to qualified matriculated students.

Approximate Tuition and Fees

In-state,$2,200; out-of-state, $4,400. Other fees, $200.

Admissions

SCCC has an open admissions policy. Anyone who can profit from SCCC's programs and services is admitted up to the college's capacity.

Graduation Requirements

All degrees and certificates require a minimum 2.0 GPA. The Hotel and Restaurant Management and Culinary Arts programs require a 600-hour work experience in the industry. Degrees can be completed in two years, while certificates can be completed in one.

Schiller International University

International School of Tourism and Hospitality Management (I.S.T.H.M.)

College: International School of Tourism and Hospitality Management (I.S.T.H.M.)
Program Enrollment: 176 undergraduates; 32 graduates
Institutional Enrollment:934 undergraduate; 254 graduate
Degrees Awarded: Associate of Science; Bachelor of Business Administration: Master of Business Administration; Master of Arts; Diploma
Degree Categories: International Hotel and Tourism Management
Emphases/Specializations: International residence and foreign languages, international internships
Program Accreditation: Accrediting Council for independent Colleges and Schools; Hotel, Catering and Institutional management Association (London) Travel and Tourism (London)
Contact: Wilfried Iskat, PhD, CHA, FMP, FHCIMA, Dean, international School of Tourism and Hospitality Management , 453 Edgewater Drive, Dunedin, FL 34698; phone (727)736-5082; fax (727) 736-6263; tollfree (USA only) 1(800) 336-4133; email: ISTHM@msn.com or wilfred_iskat@schiller.edu

Institution Description

Founded in 1964, and with students from more than 100 nations enrolled, SIU offers the opportunity for an American education in an international setting with English as the language of instruction at all eight campuses in six countries: Tampa Bay Area, Florida, USA; Central London, England; Paris and Strausbourg, France; Heidelberg, Germany; Engelberg and Leysin, Switzerland; and Madrid, Spain. Students are encouraged to transfer freely between SIU's campuses.

Program Description

SIU offers two-year Associate of Science degrees in Hospitality Management and International Tourism Management. These programs combine a full range of professional focused courses, plus courses in international business administration, general education and a language. They also include a series of short term internships in either hotel/restaurant operational areas or tourism management areas. An intensive one-year diploma in hotel Operational Management, a series of special hotel management study-abroad programs (USA, Switzerland and France) are also available.

Special Features

SIU operates two full service hotels in Switzerland and a castle hotel in the Black Forest of Germany, in addition to a restaurant and bistro in Strasbourg. these provide students with international internship opportunities. SIU also maintains close relationships with many international hotels and restaurants which offer internships and guest speakers. Students may move freely between campuses in different countries while studying for their degrees.

Financial Aid and Scholarships

Schiller offers both scholarships and work-study opportunities and participates in government-sponsored loan programs.

Approximate Tuition and Fees

No in-state-out-of-state differentials, but the fee structure applies to the Florida and European campuses. 1999-2000 undergraduate per academic year: Florida, US$12,400; Europe, US$13,400. Room and board: Florida US$5,200; Europe, US$8,700. other fees: US$390.

Admissions

For undergraduate degrees and diplomas: successful completion of 12 years of formal education. Students need an advanced knowledge of English, but those with a good intermediate knowledge can take a course in English as a Foreign Language while beginning work on their degree. Others can enroll initially at one of our English Language Institutes.

Graduation Requirements

Associate degrees: 62 semester credit hours, including eight to nine hotel or tourism management courses, three to five business courses, nine to 10 general education courses, and three to eight semester hours of internships. Diploma: 31 semester credit hours, plus a six-month

School for Tourism—Vienna

Tourism Management

Program Enrollment: 150
Institutional Enrollment: 630
Degrees Awarded: Certificate, Diploma
Degree Categories: University Entrance Level (Matura), Certificates of Specialization
Emphases/Specialization: Marketing and Management of Tourism Institutions, City Tourism and Event Management, Languages and Business
Institutional Accreditation: State department of Education, European Association of Hotel and Tourism Schools, Austrian Association of Hoteliers-AEHT, European Association for Tourism and Leisure Education-ATLAS

Contact: Ms. Victoria Kriehebauer, Headmaster School for Tourism Vienna 21, Wassermanngasse 12, A-1210, Vienna, Austria; phone (0043) 1-2584160; fax (0043) 1-258160-35; e-mail: office@hlt-wien21.ac.at

---

Institution Description

The School for Tourism is located near the headquarters of the United Nations in the cultural city of Vienna.

Program Description

The curriculum is five years of intense study and eight months practice.

Special Features

The School for Tourism offers training-firms, a coffee-house, a training-restaurant, Internet-courses, rhetoric-courses and cooperates with the leading hotels in Vienna.

Specialization Area

Restaurant & Food Management; Travel & Tourism Management.

Admissions

Entrance examination, interviews, knowledge in languages, age 14-19.

Graduation Requirements

The students have 150 hours of classroom theory, 35 hours of practical training in school and eight months of practical work (paid in training).

SENAC – CET - Center of Studies in Tourism and Hotel Management

Superior Course in Hotel Administration / Superior Course in Tourism Technology / Bachelor Course in Hotel Management

Program Enrollment: 270
Institutional Enrollment: 780
Degrees Awarded: Associate and Bachelor
Degree Categories: Hotel Management
Emphases/Specializations: none
Program Accreditation: Brazilian Ministry of Education
Contact: Luiz Gonzaga Godoi Trigo, Director, Av. Francisco Matarazzo, 249, 05001-150, São Paulo – SP Brazil, Tel: (55) (11) 263-2511; Fax: (55) (11) 864-4597; e-mail: cet@sp.senac.br

Institution Description

The Center of studies in Tourism and Hotel Management (CET) is an Institution maintained by Senac. It offers Undergraduate and graduate programs, continuing education and extention courses, international seminars and work training programs for the hotel, tourism and catering industries. CET offers its students the opportunity to practice skills at internships in our Model Hotel Schools.

Program Description

The Superior Course in Hotel Administration available in São Paulo, Águas de São Pedro and Campos do Jordão, provides opportunities to students who want to become professional in this field and able to perform middle management positions. The Superior Course In Tourism technology is starting this year in Águas de São Pedro. The Bachelor Course in Hotel Management is offered only in the capital and prepares students for leading positions.

Special Features

Superior Course in Hotel Administration – Food and Beverage laboratory / Housekeeping lab / internship at the hotel school. Superior Course in Tourism Technology – Computer lab applied to tourism / Professional Practice at the hotel school. Bachelor Course in Hotel Management – Cooking lab / Computer Lab applied to the industry / Housekeeping lab.

Financial Aid and Scholarships

SENAC offers limited financial aid, based on the student's financial situation and scholatic achievement. This student will be developing a research in the field.

Admissions

Students applicants with a high school diploma will be admitted according to their ranking as determined by scholastic aptitude exams

Specialization Area

Hotel and Lodging Management and Travel & Tourism Management

Graduation Requirements

In order to graduate the student must successfully pass all course requirements and complete a 450 hour externship in the field or hospitality institution of his choice.

Sinclair Community College

Hospitality Management, Culinary Arts Option, Bakery Arts, Travel & Tourism

Program Enrollment: 125
Institutional Enrollment: 1800
Degrees Awarded: Associate of Science, Certificate
Degree Categories: Applied Science Hospitality Management, Culinary Arts Option, Certificate in Food Service Management; Associate Hospitality Management, Hospitality Management/Culinary Arts Option; Diploma; The Educational Foundation of the National Restaurant Associate Certificate Program; Certificate: Food Service Management

Institutional Accreditation: North Central Association of Colleges and Schools, Association of Collegiate Business Schools and Programs, American Culinary Federation Education Institute
Contact: Steven Cornelius, Chairperson, Hospitality Management Department, Sinclair Community College, 444 W. Third Street, Dayton, Ohio 45402-1460, phone (937) 512-5197, fax (937) 512-4530, scorneli@sinclair.edu

Institution Description
Sinclair Community College is recognized as one of the leading two-year institutions of higher learning in the entire nation. Sinclair offers affordable quality education, fully qualified faculty, low student/faculty ratio, low cost, convenient class schedules, and innovative teaching techniques, diverse student body, and state-of-the art facilities.

Program Description
Sinclair's Culinary Arts option offers students a valuable hands-on experience and knowledge, using the latest equipment in a new facility. Students will build a solid foundation for a career by mastering the fundamentals. The teaching faculty is experienced and dedicated to the preparation of professions. ACFEI Accredited Program.

Special Features
The Bakery Arts program is approved by the Retail Bakers Association and provides hands-on education in the art of baking.

Financial Aid and Scholarships
Sinclair offers many types of Financial Aid including Federal Pell Grant, OIG, FSEOG, Federal Direct Student Loans, and a wide array of scholarships.

Admissions
Applicants begin their relationship with Sinclair at the Office of Admissions by calling (937) 512-3000. Admission to the college is open to all applicants. All students must participate in placement testing, then attend an orientation session to receive information about Sinclair. Finally, students see an academic counselor for advising and registration.

Tuition and Fees
Montgomery County: $31 per credit hour; Other Ohio: $49 per credit hour; Out of State & Foreign: $80 per credit hour; other fees: $10 application fee.

Specialization Area
Restaurant and Food Service Management, Culinary Arts

Travel & Tourism
Travel and tourism students gain a knowledge of the basic theory of travel and skills of travel professionals. Students complete practical exercises that simulate real work experience. Sinclair's airline computer classroom features live airline reservation terminals. The internship program provides an opportunity to gain on-the-job experience before graduation. Some employment opportunities within the growing travel industry include travel agents, airline agents, flight attendants, car rentals agents, hotel front desk or reservations, tour guides, cruise ships, and convention and visitor bureau managers.

Graduation Requirements
The specific requirements of the program include the successful completion of the Culinary Arts Option curriculum which is 97 credit hours. Also, a minimum of 2.0 grade point average out of a 4.0 possible is required.

Southeast Community College

Food Service

Program Enrollment: 65
Institutional Enrollment: 4,500
Degrees Awarded: Associate of Applied Science; Diploma; Certificate
Degree Category: Food Service
Emphases/Specializations: Food Service Management; Culinary Arts; Dietetic Technology
Program Accreditation: American Culinary Federation; American Dietetic Association; Dietary Managers Association

Institutional Accreditation: North Central Association of Colleges and Schools; Nebraska Department of Education
Contact: Jo Taylor, MA, RD, Food Service Chair, Southeast Community College, 8800 "O" Street, Lincoln, NE 68520; phone (402) 437-2456; fax (402) 437-2497

Institution Description

The Lincoln campus is a modern, single-unit facility on the eastern edge of Nebraska's capital city. The campus offers academic transfer and 26 vocational/technical programs in the areas of business, health, home economics, trade/ industrial and service occupations. It is a commuter campus with no on-campus housing.

Program Description

This program prepares students for employment in the foodservice industry and provides an opportunity to increase job knowledge and skills for those already employed in foodservice. The program provides training in basic foodservice knowledge and skills related to quantity and quality food preparation and service, sanitation and safety, menu planning, culinary arts and business management.

Special Features

Southeast Community College provides up-to-date laboratory facilities. The outstanding, award winning staff works closely—one-on-one—with students in professional and career advising, job placement and hands-on lab experience.

Financial Aid and Scholarships

The financial aid program's goal is to make college affordable to every student. Students must complete the FAF. Assistance is available through gift aid, work programs and loans.

Approximate Tuition and Fees

In-state:$2,805 per year; out-of-state: $3,315 per year. Room and board: estimated single living along $6,000 per year. Other fees: books, tools and supplies, $1,500 per year.

Admissions

All applicants for admission to Lincoln campus programs must have graduated from an accredited high school or have completed an approved high school equivalency examination. Applications are accepted on a first-come, first-served basis according to date of application. All admissions requirements, including any special entrance requirements, must be completed according to established deadlines.

Graduation Requirements

To fulfill graduation requirements, students must successfully complete the following: Associate of Applied Science degree—102 quarter credits; Diploma——70 quarter credits; Certificate—35 quarter credits. A grade of C is required for all required foodservice program courses. Minimal cumulative grade point average for graduation is 2.0.

Southern Alberta Institute of Technology

Hospitality Careers

Program Enrollment: 600 Full time and 400 part-time
Institutional Enrollment: 6,903 in diploma and certificate programs; 4,007 registrations in Apprenticeship and Pre-Employment Programs and 46,659 in Earned Revenue Programs/Courses
Degrees Awarded: Diploma; Certificate
Degree Categories: Diploma in Professional Cooking; Certificate in Commercial Baking, Retail Meat Cutting, Pastry Chef, and Culinary Management
Institutional Accreditation: Alberta Education and Career Development – Apprenticeship and Industry Training Division
Contact: Reg Hendrickson, Dean, Hospitality Careers Department, Southern Alberta Institute of Technology, 1301 – 16th Avenue NW, Calgary, Alberta, Canada T2M 0L4; phone (403) 284-8612; fax (403) 284-7034

Institution Description
Established in Calgary in 1916, Southern Alberta Institute of Technology was Canada's first institute of technology. Over the years, SAIT's programming has evolved from its initial offering of steam engineering and motor mechanics to today's sophisticated selection of programs. SAIT offers up-to-date career training using the finest technical equipment and facilities available.

Program Description
The Hospitality Careers Department features state-of-the-art cooking and production labs, plus a variety of specialized facilities. These include The Highwood Dining Room, a test/demo kitchen, an ice plant, a retail meat outlet, know as the Calorie Counter, blast freezer technology, as well as a computer lab donated by the Calgary Academy of Chefs and Canadian Pacific Hotels.

Special Features
SAIT's Hospitality Careers Department is one of the best "hands–on" culinary training schools in Canada. We aim for excellence, and we have a history of achieving results. SAIT has been involved in hospitality and culinary training for over 40 years. The proof of SAIT's culinary expertise is evident in our feature showcase of trophies, awards and 98% graduate employment rate. Our students, staff and teams have crossed the globe to challenge their skills against the best chefs the world has to offer. Our industry advisory committees shape our programs to maintain relevancy in the field. If you seek hospitality expertise, look no further than SAIT.

Admissions
A minimum of 35 Alberta high school credit (Grade 10) or the equivalent, including English and Mathematics are required for admission into Professional Cooking, Commercial Baking, and Retail Meat Cutting. Admission to the apprenticeship program varies to the trade.

Financial Aid and Scholarships
SAIT administers a variety of scholarships and bursaries to encourage superior academic achievement and to assist students in need of financial aid. The Students Finance Board provides Alberta and Canada Student loans to students. International students that attend SAIT may be eligible to apply for student loans from their country of origin.

Approximate Tuition and Fees
Present fees for international students, including a lab and linen fee, are:
• *Professional Cooking*: CDN$12,750 and CDN$700 for books/supplies;
• *Commercial Baking:* CDN$8,500 and CDN$600 for books/supplies;
• *Retail Meat Cutting:* CDN$4250 and CDN$300 for books/supplies;
• *Pastry Chef*: CDN$8500 and CDN$1000 for books/supplies.
Present fees for Canadian students are:
• *Professional Cooking:* $4650 and $700 for books/supplies;
• *Commercial Baking:* $3100 and $600 for books/supplies;
• *Retail Meat Cutting:* $2050 and $400 for books/supplies;
• *Pastry Chef:* $3500 plus $1000 for books/supplies.

Graduation Requirements
Student must successfully complete all courses (by credit or examination) to qualify for a SAIT diploma or certificate.

Spokane Community College

Hotel/Restaurant Management, Culinary Arts, and Commercial Banking

Program Enrollment: 90
Institutional Enrollment: 5,000
Degrees Awarded: Associate in Applied Science
Degree Categories: Hotel and Restaurant Management, Culinary Arts, and Commercial Baking
Institutional Accreditation: Northwest Association of Schools and Colleges, American Culinary Federation Educational Institute Accrediting Commission

Contact: Duane Sunwold, Department Chair, Hospitality Careers, Spokane Community College, N. 1810 Greene St., Spokane, WA 99217, phone (509) 533-7337

Institution Description
Spokane Community College (SCC) is a comprehensive two-year community college known for its strong vocational programs. SCC offers 62 degree programs and 29 certificate programs.

Program Description
SCC's Hotel and Restaurant Management Program provides students with fundamental knowledge of all front- and back-of-the-house operations as well as tourism, management and communications. Twenty-one specialty courses help prepare students for employment in the hospitality field.

Culinary Arts Program: Basic and Advanced procedures in food preparation are included in the two-year culinary arts program. A detailed study is made of the various cookery methods for meat, fish, poultry, vegetables, soups and sauces. Menu terminology and cooking terms are defined and illustrated. Students are given the opportunity to study management factors affecting food cost control, specifications and standards for foods, sanitation, kitchen planning, kitchen equipment and personnel policies. Students train in a live restaurant setting on campus. Students may enter in any quarter.

Commercial Banking Program: This program prepares students for employment opportunities in the retail, hotel and wholesale bakery fields and cake catering services. The course provides practical and theoretical training in personal hygiene, laws regulating sanitation in the baking industry, use of various types of baking machinery and production training in the baking of breads, rolls, coffee cakes, pies doughnuts and cookies. Decorating, including the proper procedure of piping, use of tubes, making flowers and decorations, mixing of colors and the principles of design, is also included. Baking management is stressed, covering such areas as product control, production per man-hour, cost factors, percentages, purchasing, receiving and storing supplies and the science and care of handling and keeping a perpetual inventory.

Financial Aid and Scholarships
The college financial aid office provides grants, scholarships, supplemental loans and work-study positions.

Admissions
SCC has an "open door" admissions policy for those who are high school graduates or have a GED certificate.

Graduation Requirements
Graduates must complete two years (six quarters) of required classes.

St. Louis Community College at Forest Park

Hospitality Studies/Tourism

Program Enrollment: 350
Institutional Enrollment: 7,500
Degrees Awarded: Associate of Applied Science; Certificate of Proficiency
Degree Category: Applied Science
Emphases/Specializations: Hotel/Restaurant Management; Culinary Arts; Travel Agency Management; Tourism Business Management
Program Accreditation: Missouri Vocational Association
Institutional Accreditation: North Central Association of Colleges and Secondary Schools
Contact: Kathleen Sokol, Department Chair / Professor of Hospitality/ Restaurant Management, St. Louis Community College at Forest Park, 5600 Oakland Ave., St. Louis, MO 63110; phone (314) 644-9751; fax (314) 9519405; email: ksokol@fp-mail.stlcc.cc.mo.us

Institution Description

Adjacent to a major health, cultural and entertainment center in the west central city, Forest Park is an essential part of the St. Louis community. Programs are offered for a diverse student population in such topics as business, social sciences, humanities, science, engineering, technology and more than a dozen allied health areas.

Program Description

Forest Park's Hospitality Studies/Tourism Program provides students with the technical competence and skills necessary for management positions in the hospitality industry. Students learn to perform management functions through related coursework in quantity food production, menu planning, hotel operations, attractions, destination and special events management, food purchasing and sanitation, housekeeping administration, accounting and cost control, supervision, sales and marketing, casino management, and riverboats & land based casino.

Special Features

Forest Park has a new 30,000 sq ft facility. It includes 4 kitchens, computer lab, and electronic classrooms.

Financial Aid and Scholarships

Scholarships are offered by state and local chapters of the Missouri Restaurant Association and by local chapters of national hospitality organizations. Grants, scholarships and loans also are available through the college's financial aid office.

Approximate Tuition and Fees

Tuition for students in the school's service area is $42 per credit hour. Tuition for other Missouri residents is $53 per credit hour, and for out-ofstate residents $67 per credit hour. There is a $1 per credit hour parking fee.

Admissions

Forest Park has an open admissions policy in keeping with its original purpose to provide quality, low-cost education to all area residents.

Graduation Requirements

Graduates must complete 70 semester hours, which include 20 hours in general education and 50 hours in hospitality studies course.

State University of New York College of Agriculture and Technology at Cobleskill

Culinary Arts, Hospitality and Tourism Department

College: College of Agriculture and Technology
Program Enrollment: 250
Institutional Enrollment: 2300
Degrees Awarded: Associate of Applied Science; Associate of Occupational Studies
Degree Categories: Hotel Technology; Culinary Arts, Travel and Resort Marketing; Restaurant Management; Institutional Foods Management
Program Accreditation: American Culinary Federation Educational Institute Accrediting Commission
Institutional Accreditation: Middle States Association of Secondary Schools and Colleges
Contact: Alan Roer, Department Chair, Culinary Arts, Hospitality and Tourism, State University of New York (SUNY) Cobleskill, NY 12043

Institution Description

Two-year residential college offering programs in agriculture and natural resources, business, early childhood, culinary arts, hospitality and tourism, and the liberal arts and sciences. The Bachelor of Technology degree is offered in agriculture.

Program Description

Courses are designed to prepare graduates for middle management and supervisory positions. Three student-operated restaurants. Required work experience. Articulation agreements with four-year institutions. Overseas study exchange in England.

Special Features

Student Fine Foods Association, Junior ACF, C.H.A.T. and Orange Key student organizations. Internships with a variety of hotel, restaurant and recreation companies. Travel lab, hotel computer reservations system, front office and five laboratory kitchens. Culinary Arts Program accredited by the American Culinary Federation Educational Institute (ACFEI) Accrediting Commission.

Financial Aid and Scholarships

Full-time financial aid office. Scholarship awards for incoming first-year students. Scholarships from hotel and restaurant companies.

Approximate Tuition and Fees

Tuition for New York State residents is $3,300 per year; for out-of-state residents $5,000 per year. Room and board is $2,460 per semester. Books and supplies are $300; fees, $275.

Admissions

Admissions are based on qualifications without regard to race, color, creed, sex, age, national origin, handicap or marital status. An application must be a high school graduate or hold a High School Equivalency Diploma. The SAT or ACT is recommended.

Graduation Requirements

Sixty-six credits. In the Association of Applied Science degree, 22 credits must be in general education. A minimum 400-work experience with approved reports is also required.

State University of New York College of Technology, Delhi, NY

BBA in Hospitality Management

Program Enrollment: 65
Institutional Enrollment: 2,100
Degrees Awarded: Bachelor of Business Administration
Degree Categories: Bachelor of Business Administration in Hospitality Management; with concentrations in Hotel & Resort Management, Restaurant; Management, and Travel & Tourism Management
Emphases/Specializations: Associate; Diploma; Certificate
Program Accreditation: Middle States Association of Secondary Schools and Colleges, A.S.T.A. Travel School
Contact: Rosalie Higgins, Department Chair and Professor

Institution Description

Established in 1913, the College of Technology at Delhi offers Baccalaureate and Associate Degrees in a residential setting. A unit of the State University of New York, it is a leader in technical education.

Program Description

Building on a foundation of 50 years of hospitality education, Delhi's new Bachelor of Business Administration Degree prepares graduates for management positions in the industry. Study abroad is available and professional internship is required.

Special Features

Delhi's state-of-the-art Alumni Hall Hospitality Center houses a hospitality lobby, housekeeping laboratories, banquet and catering facilities, beverage laboratory, AAA Travel Branch Office, and a student restaurant. Delhi maintains strong industry relationship through three leading hospitality travel associations. Delhi's over 3,500 successful hospitality management alumni provide curriculum advisement and employment assistance.

Financial Aid and Scholarships

The college financial aid office, hospitality industry, and various associations offer financial aid and scholarships to deserving students.

Admissions

Students applying for enrollment as freshmen must be graduates of an accredited secondary school or have an equivalent education. The following high school course distribution is recommended: 4 units of English, 3 units of social science and at least 4 units of math and science (with a minimum of 2 units in each of those areas). An Admissions Committee will review applications for transfer students. A 2.3 cumulative grade point average is recommended. An interview is also recommended. Previous study in hospitality is not required for transfer students. Students with an associate's degree in liberal arts, business and related areas are encouraged to apply.

Tuition & Fees

In-State	$3,400
Out-of-State	$5,000
Room and Board	$5,300
Other Fees	$1,000±

Specialization Area

Hotel & Lodging Mgmt.; Restaurant & Foodservice Mgmt.; Travel & Tourism Mgmt.

Graduation Requirements

Graduation requires 128 credit hours. General education, 43 hours; hospitality management core, 28 hours; business management core, 21 hours; specialization core, 36 hours. Professional experience internship is required.

State University of New York at Morrisville

School of Business, Department of Hospitality Technology

Program Enrollment: 170
Institutional Enrollment: 2843
Degrees Awarded: Associate of Applied Science
Degree Categories: Food Service Administration; Hotel-Restaurant Management; Travel-Tourism; Hospitality Management; Casino Management; Certificate in Casino Management

Institutional Accreditation: Middle States Association of Colleges and Schools; all curricula registered with the New York State Department of Education.
Contact: Dr. Joan Johnson, Professor, School of Business, Charlton Hall 114, State University of New York College of Agriculture and Technology, Morrisville, NY 13408; phone (315) 684-6017; Fax(315) 684-6225

Institution Description

Morrisville is a unit of the State University of New York and a Think Pad University. All Hospitality Technology majors are provided with a laptop computer to facilitate learning, communication and research.

Students have on-campus housing options. Full and part-time study is available. Hospitality Technology majors earn the Associate in Applied Science Degree.

Program Description

SUNY Morrisville offers associate programs in Food Service Administration, Restaurant Management, Institutional Food Management, Travel-Tourism and Hospitality Management, and Casino Management.

Special Features

Facilities include technology-based classrooms, lounges, laboratories and laptop cafes. In addition, a quantity food production lab, student-operated restaurant, student-operated travel agency, and a computer/technology laboratory serve the needs of the majors. Several courses are national certification courses and many graduates continue their studies to complete a bachelor's degree.

Financial Aid and Scholarships

The financial aid program includes part-time employment, loans, grants and scholarships. There are various competitive scholarships offered as well.

Admissions

Most programs require a minimum 2.0 average and a high school diploma. Some require specific units of defined math and science. Contact (800) 258-0111.

Approximate Tuition and Fees

Tuition and fees are $3,740 per year. Room and board is $5,440 per year.

Graduation Requirements

To graduate, a degree candidate must complete all specific coursework within the program chosen to meet the minimum total number of semester hours required for the appropriate degree. The Associate of Applied Science degree requires 20 hours of general education course work. Students in the travel-tourism, foodservice, hotel-restaurant management and Casino management curricula are required to complete a cooperative employment experience prior to graduation.

Tadmor Hotel School

All levels of Hotel Management and Hotel Operations

Institutional Enrollment: 750
Degrees Awarded: Hotel Management Diploma, Higher Hotel Management Diploma; Certificate
Degree Category: Operations and Management
Emphases & Specialization: Comprehensive & Advanced Hotel Management, Hotel Business Management, Food Service Management; all levels of Culinary Arts; all levels of Hotel operations

Program Accreditation: Israeli Ministry of Labour; Israweli Ministry of Tourism; Bar-Ilan U.; Rupin Institute; articulations with many universities in Europe and the United States
Contact: S. Nadir, Director, Tadmor Hotel School, 38 Basel St. Herzeliya, Israel, 46660, phone: (972) 9-9547480; fax: (972) 9-9547490; e-mail: HOPX@ibm.net

Institution Description

Tadmor is a state funded Hebrew Speaking institute of learning, situated 10km North of Tel-Aviv. The school combines a teaching wing with a 60 room commercial hotel which is also used for practice and learning.

Program Description

Tadmor is Israel's largest hotel school and operates numerous hospitality education programs. Programs vary in length from 5 months entry level practical courses to 2 year 2,000 hour academic programs leading towards BA, BSC and BBA degrees in a number of well known universities. The school holds numerous articulation agreements with universities in Israel and abroad. Many of the courses, notably the comprehensive Hotel Management Course start 3-4 times a year. Academic courses begin in the Fall and Spring semesters.

Special Features

Tadmor is located in the heart of a most desirable residential and tourist area; .5 km from the beach, and from shopping centers. The school comprises teaching and training wings; modern kitchen facilities, and a commercial teaching hotel in which students train and work. Studies are conducted in Hebrew. English language courses are now being planned. Practical courses are conducted 5 days a week from 08:00-14:00. Academic studies are conducted 3 times a week in the afternoon and evening. Various enrichment courses are offered in the evenings.

Financial Aid and Scholarships

Many of Tadmor's larger courses are government subsidized. Several scholarships for academic students are available. The school also operates a subsidized residential facility for students with cheap modes lodgings. Students are further offered subsidized meals in the modern school dining facility.

Tuition Rates

Tuition rates vary course and duration. Tuition for the 2 year comprehensive course in 1998 was approximately $2,500 for the whole course. Academic course rates in 98 were approximately $4,000 PA.

Admissions and Graduation Requirements

Admission and graduation requirements vary for different courses. Academic course requirements further vary by the university in which students wish to complete their degree. Applicants for practical courses should inquire by letter or phone at the school offices. Academic applicants should direct inquiries to the head of academic studies.

Taylor's College, School of Hotel Management

Diploma in Hotel Management, Higher Diploma in Hotel Management, Diploma in Tourism Management, Higher Diploma in Tourism Management

Program Enrollment: 170
Institutional Enrollment: 170
Degrees Awarded: Diploma in Hotel Management (Brevet de Technicien Hotellerie), Higher Diploma in Hotel Management (Brevet de Technicien Superieur), Diploma in Tourism Management (Brevet de Technicien Tourisme) and Higher Diploma in Tourism Management (Brevet de Technicien Superieur Tourisme) - Awarded by Academie de Grenoble, an educational division of the Ministry of Education in France.
Emphases/Specializations: Hotel Trade, Restaurant Trade, Rooms, Division, Food & Beverage, Cuisine
Institutional Accreditation: The Ecole Hoteliere Thonon les Bains de l'Academie de Grenoble is an educational division of the Ministry of Education in France.

Program Description

Both the diploma and Higher Diploma in Hotel Management and the Diploma and Higher Diploma in Tourism Management are two years in duration. All four programs involve study and industrial training. Credits obtained can be transferred to universities in the United Kingdom, United States, Australia and France.

Special Features

Taylor's provides the opportunity to learn French hospitality as well as Eastern hospitality. In the Tourism programs Diploma students will visit a regional destination while Higher Diploma students will visit a regional and an international destination where they will be given an opportunity to have a first hand experience on the varied approaches applied in the Tourism industry.

Admissions

GCE 'O' Level, High School qualification for the Diploma programs GCE 'A' Level, Pre-University qualification for the Higher Diploma programs

Approximate Tuition and Fees

Diploma in Hotel Management (Fees for 1 academic year): Enrollment Fee: US $100, Tuition Fee 1st Term - US $1,440, 2nd Term - US $1,440, 3rd Term - US $965, Laboratory Fee (yearly) - US $235. Higher Diploma in Hotel Management (Fees for 1 academic year): Enrollment Fee: US $100, Tuition Fee 1st Term - US $1,600, 2nd Term - US $1,600, 3rd Term - US $1,450, Laboratory Fee (yearly) - US $305 Diploma in Tourism Management (Fees for 1 academic year): Enrollment Fee- US $100, Tuition Fee 1st Term - US $950, 2nd Term - US $950, 3rd Term - US $540, Laboratory Fee (yearly) - US $132 Higher Diploma in Tourism Management (Fees for 1 academic year): Enrolment Fee - US $100, Tuition Fee 1st Term - US $1000, 2nd Term - US $1000, 3rd Term - US $645, Laboratory Fee- US $132

Graduation Requirements

Must successfully complete 66 weeks of study and 24 weeks of practical training. Maximum grade are 520 marks, minimum passing marks are 260.

Tidewater Community College

Hospitality Management Program

Program Enrollment: 80
Institutional Enrollment:18,500
Degree Awarded: The Associate in Applied Science Degree (AAS),The Certificate, and The Career Studies Certificate.
Degree Categories: Hospitality Management
Specializations: Food Service Management and Lodging Management

Institutional Accreditation: Commission on Colleges of the Southern Association of Colleges and Schools; State Council of Higher Education for Virginia
Contact: Peter Kane, F.M.P., Program Director Hospitality Management, Tidewater Community College, Virginia Beach Campus, 1700 College Crescent, Virginia Beach, VA 23456; phone (757) 321-7173; fax (757) 468-3077; E-mail: tckanep@tc.cc.va.us

Institution Description

Tidewater Community College, part of the Virginia Community College System, serves the South Hampton Roads communities of Chesapeake, Norfolk, Portsmouth and Virginia Beach. TCC is a comprehensive, public, two-year institution with campus locations in the four city service area.

Program Description

The Hospitality Management Program at TCC Virginia Beach Campus is designed to provide the knowledge essential to a successful career in the rapidly expanding hospitality industry. The curriculum is a blend of professional, technical and liberal arts courses which enables graduates for entry-level management careers.

Special Features

TCC's Hospitality Management Program is located in Virginia Beach, Virginia. A major east coast tourist destination with 2.5 million annual visitors and 11,000 hotel rooms. This location allows students to study and work in a thriving hospitality area.

Financial Aid

Two departmental scholarships are available; one from the Virginia Beach Restaurant Association-$300 per year; and one from the Tidewater Branch of the International Food Service Executives Association-based on need. Other financial aid is available from federal, state and local sources.

Admissions

Students who have a high school diploma or the equivalent are eligible for admission to Tidewater Community College. To be admitted as a curricular student, one must: submit a completed official Application for Admissions, complete Student Assessment Program placement testing, and submit official transcripts.

Tuition and Fees

Tuition for state residents is $53.50 per credit approximately $1605 per year; for nonresidents $167.20 per credit approximately $5016 per year. Room and board is not available on campus. Textbooks typically cost $600.

Specialization Area

Hotel and Lodging Management, Restaurant and Food Service Management.

Graduation Requirements

Graduation requires the completion of 65 semester hours, which includes 18 hours of general education, 4 semester hours of computer applications, and 43 hours of hospitality and related courses. The career studies and certificate programs can be completed in two semesters. The Associate in applied science degree requires four semesters of full-time study.

Tompkins Cortland Community College

Hotel and Restaurant Management, Travel and Tourism

Program Enrollment: 80
Institutional Enrollment: 2,150 FTE, 4,000 headcount
Degrees Awarded: Associate In Applied Science Degree
Degree Categories: Hotel and Restaurant Management; Travel and Tourism
Emphasis/Specializations: N/A
Program Accreditation: N/A
Institutional Accreditation: Commission of Higher Education of the Middle States Association of Colleges and Secondary Schools

Contact: John N. Martindale, Professor, Hotel and Restaurant Management, Tompkins Cortland Community College, PO Box 139 170 North St., Dryden, NY 13053-0139; phone (607) 844-8211; fax (607) 844-9665; E-mail: martinj@sunytccc.edu; Web site: www.tc3.edu

Institution Description

Public (local/state) two-year community college, operating under the supervision of the State University of New York, offering associate degrees and certificates in the fields of allied health, business, hospitality, liberal arts, public service, and science and technology. Off-campus programs offered in Cortland, Ithaca, and Owego, NY.

Program Description

The Hotel and Restaurant Management degree prepares students for management positions in restaurants, hotels, and other hospitality related facilities. Students learn a broad range of skills to prepare for the climb up the management ladder. Travel and Tourism students learn job-oriented skills that relate directly to the travel industry.

Special Features

The Hotel and Restaurant Management degree is offered on the Internet. All students gain valuable work experience through internships and CoOp programs.

Financial Aid and Scholarships

Financial assistance is available to Tompkins Cortland students through a combination of private grants and federal and state programs.

Admissions

Tompkins Cortland is an open admission institution. Students admitted to a degree program will be academically assessed before registration. Applicants with a regular high school diploma or general equivalency diploma will be offered admission to the College.

Tuition & Fees

	Per Credit Hour	Per Semester
In-State:	$95.00	$1,250.00
Out-of State:	$190.00	$2,250.00
Acceptance Deposit: $50.00		
Student Association Fee: $4.35		$65.00
Student Accident Insurance: $13.00		

Specialization Area

Hotel and Lodging Mgmt., Restaurant & Food service Management, Travel and Tourism Mgmt.

Graduation Requirements

Hotel and Restaurant Management graduation requires a minimum of 67 credits which includes 24 credits in HRMG. Travel and Tourism graduation requires a minimum of 64 credits which includes 15 credits in TOUR.

Trocaire College

Hospitality Management Program

Program Enrollment: 25
Institutional Enrollment: 800
Degree Awarded: Associate of Applied Science
Emphasis/Specialization: Hospitality Management
Institutional Accreditation: Middle States Association of Colleges and Schools
Contact: Melissa Dallas, J.D., Director, Hospitality Management Program, Trocaire College, 360 Choate Avenue, Buffalo, NY 14220; phone: (716) 827-2503; fax: (716) 828-6107

Institutional Description

Trocaire College is a private, two-year liberal arts college established by the Buffalo Regional Community of the Sisters of Mercy in 1958. The College, located in South Buffalo, offers over 25 Associate Degree and Certification programs. Trocaire College is known for its teaching excellence, individualized instruction, concern for student learning, and community outreach.

Program Description

The Hospitality Management Program at Trocaire College began in 1995 and is continuing to grow. The curriculum focuses on the development of professional skills and knowledge, and includes a strong liberal arts component. Upon completion of the program, students may begin a hospitality career in an entry-level position, or may transfer to a four-year institution. Articulation agreements are currently in place with Niagara University, Canisius College, and Paul Smith's College.

Special Features

Upon graduation, students will be certified in CARE (Controlling Alcohol Risks Effectively), ServSafe, and HOTS II (Hospitality Strategy and Simulation). Each student is required to complete 400 hours of industry work experience.

Financial Aid and Scholarships

The Financial Aid Office at Trocaire College works closely with students to help them in their quest for financial aid. Currently, 100% of Hospitality Management Program students receive financial aid in the form of grants and scholarships.

Admissions

Candidates must have a high school degree or its equivalent. Demonstration of acceptable college-level competencies in writing, mathematics, and science on either the college-administered assessment tests or the SAT/ACT test must be proven, although this requirement is waived for those with a bachelor's degree or higher. The college accepts both full-time and part-time students at the beginning of fall, spring, or summer term.

Tuition and Fees

Full-time annual tuition: $7,150. Approximate annual fees: $115.

Graduation Requirements

Graduates complete 70 semester hours of study including hospitality, business, and liberal arts courses. A minimum grade point average of 2.0 on a 4.0 scale is required for graduation. As well, students must receive a 2.0 or better in each of their hospitality and business classes.

The University of Akron

Hospitality Management

Program Enrollment: 175
Institutional Enrollment: 24,000
Degrees Awarded: Associate (2+2 programs also available), Certificate
Degree Categories: Applied Business in Hospitality Management
Emphasis/Specializations: Associate in Culinary Arts, Hotel/Motel Management, Hospitality, Marketing & Sales, Restaurant Management; Certificate in Culinary Arts, Hotel/Motel Management, Restaurant Management

Institutional Accreditation: Association of Collegiate Business Schools and Programs, North Central Association of Colleges and Secondary Schools
Contact: Mr. Lawrence Gilpatric, CEC, CCE, CHA, FMP, Coordinator, Hospitality Management Department, The Community and Technical College, The University of Akron, Akron, OH 44325-7907; phone (330) 972-5393, fax (330) 972-5525, E-mail: gilpatr@uakron.edu.

Institution Description

The University of Community and Technical College is one of seven degree-granting colleges. Associate degrees are offered in 30 technical fields. The programs may be pursued on a full or part-time basis available days or evenings. Our programs allow for easy continuation to four-year bachelor's degrees.

Program Description

For over 25 years, the Hospitality Management Program has successfully trained hospitality students into personnel and recognized industry leaders. The student staffed Crystal Room Restaurant serves as practical application learning analogue for the academic program. By working in the front and back of the house, students apply the theory learned in the classroom.

Special Features

Our program offers small laboratory classes and individualized training. Faculty certifications: Our ice-carving teams are 3 times NICA collegiate champs.

Financial Aid and Scholarships

Information regarding grants and scholarships may be obtained from the Financial Aid Office at (330) 972-7032. Opportunities are available based on financial need, academics, and industry experience.

Admissions

The University of Akron is a state university with an open admissions policy. If under 21, you are required to submit your high school transcripts and ACT/SAT scores. If under 25, high school transcripts or GED scores must be submitted. Transfer students must submit all college transcripts. Applications fee: $25.00.

Tuition & Fees

In-state: Tuition and Fees $3,486, Room and Board $4,120-4,990. Out-of-state: Tuition and Fees $8,686.50, Room and Board $4,120-4,990. The tuition and fees are based on 13-16 credit hours. Laboratory fees for some courses. Fees are subject to change without notice.

Specialization Area

Hotel & Lodging Management, Restaurant Management, Culinary Arts

Graduation Requirements

Graduation requires the successful completion of 68 semester hours, which includes general education requirements, with an overall grade point average no less than 2.0.

University of Maine at Augusta

Hotel/Restaurant/Tourism Management Program

College: University College of Bangor
Program Enrollment: 15
Institutional Enrollment: 6,000; undergraduate: 6,000
Degree Awarded: Associate of Science in Hotel/Restaurant/Tourism Management
Degree Category: Associate Degree in Hotel/Restaurant/Tourism Management
Institutional Accreditation: New England Association of Schools and Colleges, Inc./Commission on Institutions of Higher Education (NEASC-CIHE)
Contact: F. Richard King, Chairperson, Hotel/Restaurant/Tourism Management Program, 210 Texas Avenue, Bangor, Maine 04401-4367; phone (207) 581-6212

Institution Description

University College of Bangor is one of the three campuses of University of Maine at Augusta. The University of Maine at Augusta, one of seven institutions governed by the Trustees of the University of Maine System, is a single institution, geographically dispersed, delivering student support services, and educational programs and work force training both through traditional and interactive telecommunication/telecomputer instruction at multiple campuses, centers, and distance learning sites throughout the state in selected associate, baccalaureate, and master's degrees, individually and cooperatively with other public and private institutions of higher learning.

Program Description

The Hotel/Restaurant/Tourism Management Program is designed for persons with well-focused career goals in the hospitality industry and emphasizes management skills. The curriculum is academically challenging, combining courses which develop increased management skills stressing financial and resource management with specialized courses related to the hospitality industry.

Special Features

Graduates are required to complete an internship in a facet of the hospitality industry, providing them an opportunity to gain valuable on-the-job experience.

Financial Aid and Scholarships

A wide variety of financial aid packages and scholarships are available to qualifying students.

Tuition and Fees

In-State: $2,700 per year; Out-of-State: $7,200 per year. Dormitory Housing is available at the University of Maine in Orono, Maine. Other Fees: $100

Admissions

University College of Bangor encourages all persons interested in pursuing a college education to apply for admission. Applicants must have a high school diploma or its equivalent. Those students with weaknesses in reading, English or mathematics are offered special assistance through the Developmental Studies Division. Special instruction in small group settings is designed to allow each student to progress at his or her own pace. Students requiring preparatory work may require an additional semester to complete all degree requirements.

Graduation Requirements

Graduates complete 60 credit hours including liberal arts, management and hospitality courses. Students also complete a 3-hour mandatory internship. A minimum grade point average of 2.0 on a 4.0 scale is required for graduation.

Volunteer State Community College

Hospitality Management; Culinary Arts

Program Enrollment: 45 in Hospitality Management; 75 in Culinary Arts
Institutional Enrollment: 7,000
Degrees Awarded: Associate of Applied Science; Certificate
Degree Categories: Associate of Applied Science in General Business Administration with a concentration in Hospitality Management; Certificate in Hospitality Management; Institutional Certificates in Hospitality Management; Associate of Applied Science in General Technology with a concentration in Culinary Arts.
Emphases/ Specializations: Hotel Management; Restaurant and Food Service Management; Culinary Arts-Chef's Apprenticeship
Institutional Accreditation: Southern Association of Colleges and Schools
Contact: Mary Nunaley, Coordinator, Hospitality Management, or Dr. John Espey, Dean, Business Division, Volunteer State Community College, Nashville Pike, Gallatin, TN 37066; phone (615) 452-8600; fax (615) 230-3326

Institution Description

Volunteer State Community College (Vol State), is an accredited, public, two year college. The college is located 20 miles from Nashville in Gallatin, Tennessee and serves a 12 county area. Vol State offers more than 30 university-transfer and career-education programs and a variety of technical and institutional certificate programs. The college is a Tennessee Board of Regents institution.

Program Description

Vol State's Hospitality Management Program builds on a solid foundation of business course offerings such as accounting and marketing. Course offerings in the HM Program include many food and beverage and rooms division courses. Cooperative work experience courses are also available.

Special Features

The Culinary Arts Program has a special agreement with the Opryland Hotel Culinary Institute to provide over 6,000 hours of hands-on training for the chef's apprentices. This program is A.C.F. Accredited and leads to the AAS degree.

Financial Aid and Scholarships

Vol State's Financial Aid Office is available to assist in making educational goals attainable. Financial aid programs include: loans, scholarships and work-study.

Tuition and Fees

In-state: full-time is $568 per semester; part-time is $50 per semester hour; out-of-state: full-time is $2196 a semester; part-time is $192.00 per semester hour; other fees: application fee is $10.

Admissions

An open admissions policy is in effect. All persons admitted must complete an application and have transcripts of all previous education sent directly to the college. Placement tests may be required prior to enrollment. Admission to the Culinary Arts Program is very competitive and additional selection criteria are used.

Graduation Requirements

The AAS degree with a concentration in Hospitality Management requires completion of 66 credit hours of which 33 credit hours are business and hospitality management courses. The AAS degree with a concentration in Culinary Arts requires completion of 73 credit hours of which 49 credit hours are culinary arts and hospitality management courses.

Wake Technical Community College

Hospitality Management

Program Enrollment: 84
Institutional Enrollment: 16,123
Degree Awarded: Associate of Applied Science
Degree Categories: Hotel and Restaurant Management, Culinary Technology
Institutional Accreditation: Southern Association of Schools and College

Institution Description

One of North Carolina's largest two-year colleges, Wake Technical Community College offers 80 associate degree, certificate and diploma programs, with a university transfer option. Quality instruction, the convenience of day and evening classes, low tuition and strong local job market make Wake Tech "The Smart Choice" for college.

Program Description

The two-year comprehensive associate degree programs provide a rich educational foundation for entry into the hospitality industry and upon which to build a rewarding professional career.

Special Features

A Hospitality Center opened during the 1996-97 academic year, with hotel rooms, a restaurant and six kitchens. Management and culinary students may co-op in France.

Financial Aid and Scholarships

Student financial aid consists of various loans, grants and work-study positions.

Tuition and Fees

Tuition and fees per semester are estimated to be $278.25 for North Carolina residents and $2,257.50 for out-of-state students.

Admissions

Wake Technical Community College follows an open door policy. The minimum requirement for acceptance is high school or GED diploma. Applicants are tested for math and English skills to determine placement into appropriate courses.

Graduation Requirements

An AAS degree in Hotel and Restaurant Management or Culinary Technology requires a minimum of 70 and 76 semester credit hours, respectively.

Washtenaw Community College

Culinary and Hospitality Management Program

Program Enrollment: 11,000
Degrees Awarded: Associate; Certificate
Degree Categories: Associate in Culinary Arts Technology; Hotel Restaurant Management Technology; Certificate in Food Production Specialist (one year)
Institution Accreditation: State of Michigan Department of Education; North Central Association of Colleges and Secondary Schools

Contact: Don L. Garret, Department Chair, Culinary and Hospitality Management Program, Washtenaw Community College, 4800 E. Huron River Dr., Ann Arbor, MI 48106; phone (313) 973-3584

Institution Description

Washtenaw Community College (WCC) is a community-based college providing open access to its instructional programs and services to persons of all ages and backgrounds. As a comprehensive community college, it provides occupational education, general education, the first two years of a four-year college program, developmental education and community service programs. The college's close liaison with area employers, agencies and groups makes it an integral part of the daily life of the communities it serves. The social purpose of the college is to help people in the Washtenaw County area achieve, through education, their life goals.

Program Description

The Hospitality Career Program involves hands-on training in the kitchen and in the Artist Gallery Restaurant, a working campus restaurant. The associate degree programs also include extern experiences at off-campus food and lodging establishments. Programs are designed for either full-time or part-time students and also for those students wishing to go on to four-year hospitality programs. WCC has an articulation agreement with Grand Valley State College and Eastern Michigan University.

Special Features

The Culinary and Hospitality Program owns and operates a full-service restaurant open to the public, with a daily changing menu. Students not only receive hands-on instruction, but are given an equal amount of time devoted to managerial skills with emphasis placed on problem-solving in the hospitality industry.

Financial Aid and Scholarships

WCC maintains a fully staffed financial aid office. The bulk of financial aid awards are made to students in July and August, prior to the beginning of the fall semester. There are numerous scholarships available to students. Department scholarships are also awarded each year by the Hospitality Program.

Approximate Tuition and Fees

In-district tuition is $52.00 per credit hour; out-of-district is $77 per credit hour; and out-of-state is $98 per credit hour.

Admissions

Admission to credit studies at WCC is open to all persons 18 years of age or older, high school graduates, those who have passed the GED examination, and transfer students.

Graduation Requirements

Graduation requires the completion of 65-71 credit hours of instruction. Students must also have completed a minimum of 300 hours of field experience. A 2.0 GPA is required for graduation.

Waukesha County Technical College

Hospitality & Tourism Management, Culinary Management, Culinary Arts, ACF Apprenticeship

Program Enrollment: Hospitality & Tourism Management - 101; Culinary Management - 29; Culinary Arts - 22; ACF Culinary Apprenticeship - 21.
Institutional Enrollment: 6,000
Degrees Awarded: Associate of Applied Science; Diploma; Certificate
Degree Categories: Associate in Hospitality & Tourism Management; Associate in Culinary Management; Diploma in Culinary Arts; Certificate in ACF Culinary Apprenticeship
Program Accreditation: Wisconsin Technical College System; American Culinary Federation Educational InstituteAccrediting Commission
Institutional Accreditation: North Central Association of Colleges and Secondary Schools
Contact: Timothy J. Graham, Associate Dean, Center for Hospitality Management and Culinary Arts Studies, Waukesha County Technical College, 800 Main St.,Pewaukee, WI 53072; phone (414) 691-5322

Institution Description
Waukesha County Technical College (WCTC) is a publicly funded technical college in the Wisconsin Technical College System. WCTC presently offers 52 programs earning either an Associate of Applied Science degree or a vocational diploma. In addition, WCTC assists business and industry by developing tailored training programs that are company *specific* and by addressing changing needs to stay competitive.

Program Description
Programs are competency-based with credit transferability to the University of Wisconsin-Stout and other baccalaureate institutions at home and abroad. Lab facilities include a front desk, computer lab, dining room, kitchen and bar lab areas. Strong curriculum emphasis on sales/marketing, cost controls, accounting, critical life skills, leadership and management skills.

Special Features
Faculty are formally educated in their area of specialty instruction with a minimum of 12 years occupational industry experience and are certified through the Educational Institute of the American Hotel & Motel Association and the American Culinary Federation.

Financial Aid and Scholarships
Numerous financial aid opportunities exist along with over 20 scholarship programs related to the hospitality industry.

Admissions
WCTC has an open admissions policy. High school course work in business,finance and home economics is recommended.

Approximate Tuition and Fees
Hospitality Management Program: tuition, books and supplies—$6,423.40. Culinary Management Program: tuition, books and supplies—$7,332.40; Culinary Arts Program: tuition, books and supplies—$3,511.15. ACF Culinary Apprenticeship Program: tuition and fees—approximately $250 per semester.

Graduation Requirements
70 credits required for graduation from the Hospitality & Tourism Management Program; 72 credits required for graduation from the Culinary Management Program; 31 credits required for graduation from the Culinary Arts Program; and 20.5 credits required for graduation from the ACF Culinary Apprenticeship Program.

Westchester Community College

Restaurant Management Program

Program Enrollment: 80
Institutional Enrollment: 11,000
Degree Awarded: Associate of Applied Science
Degree Category: Restaurant Management
Emphases/Specializations: Food Service Administration; Culinary Arts; Business Management
Program Accreditation: State Department of Education
Institutional Accreditation: Middle States Association of Colleges & Secondary Schools
Contact: Daryl Nosek, Curriculum Chairperson, Restaurant Management, 75 Grasslands Road, Valhalla, New York 10595; phone: 914-785-6551 or 785-6765

Institution Description

Westchester Community College is affiliated with the State University of New York (SUNY). WCC enrolls more than 11,000 full-time and part-time credit students annually and a number of noncredit students. Students pursuing restaurant management are candidates for the AAS degree. A variety of certificate programs for career training and advancement is available.

Program Description

The Restaurant Management curriculum leads to careers - not only in restaurants, but also in commercial, industrial and institutional feeding establishments. Graduates of the Restaurant Management curriculum are initially employed in middle-management positions, such as assistants to managers, supervisors of food production and service. Coursework includes culinary arts, business management, an approved work experience, and liberal arts.

Special Features

Students receive hands-on experience in food preparation, quantity, culinary techniques and dining room service. WCC is a partner school with the Educational Foundation of the National Restaurant Association.

Financial Aid and Scholarships

Financial aid and scholarships are available. All financial aid is based on enrollment status, satisfactory academic progress and satisfactory attendance.

Approximate Tuition and Fees

Westchester Community College, because of its substantial support from the State University of New York and Westchester County, is able to maintain relatively modest tuition and fees. Full-time (12 credit hours or more per semester); resident (per semester) $1175; nonresident (per semester) $2937.50. Part-time (fewer than 12 credit hours per semester); resident (percredit) $98; nonresident (per semester) $245.

Admissions

Admission to Westchester Community College is open to applicants who meet one of the following criteria:

1. possess a high school diploma
2. possess a high school equivalency diploma
3. be admitted under the Early Admissions Program
4. be 18 years of age or older and not have attended high school formally for at least one year.

Contact the Office of Admissions (914) 785-6735 to determine eligibility.

Graduation Requirements

Requirements for the Associate of Applied Science degree include the completion of 65 credits and a cumulative GPA of 2.0. Candidates for the associate degree must pass two semesters of physical education. Certificate courses are available in various areas of foodservice training.

Westmoreland County Community College

Hospitality Programs

Program Enrollment: 129
Institutional Enrollment: 5,770
Degree Awarded: Associate in Applied Science Degree and Certificate
Degree Category: Applied Science
Degree Specializations: Baking and Pastry; Culinary Arts (apprenticeship and non-apprenticeship options); Dietetic Technician; Dining Room Management; Food Service Management; Hotel/Motel Management; Travel and Tourism
Program Accreditation: American Culinary Federation Educational Institute Accrediting Commission
Institutional Accreditation: Middle States Association of Colleges and Schools, Pennsylvania State Department of Education
Contact: Mary B. Zappone, Professor of Hospitality Programs, Westmoreland County Community College, Youngwood, PA 15697; (724) 925-4016; fax: (724) 925-4293

Institution Description

Westmoreland County Community College (WCCC) is a two-year college located in southwestern Pennsylvania offering associate degree, diplomas and certificates. The curriculum encompasses 45 majors in allied health, business, communications, hospitality, human services and the technologies. A university transfer program enables students to transfer to most colleges and universities.

Program Description

WCCC offers full-and part-time study in seven hospitality programs. The culinary arts program features a three-year apprenticeship option combining course work with 6,000 hours of supervised practice at approved facilities, and a two-year non-apprenticeship option combining classroom/food laboratory experiences in WCCC's culinary arts complex and a 150-hour internship.

Special Features

WCCC culinary arts graduates are employed across the U.S. and win national awards. One alumnus captained the U.S. Culinary Olympics team, winning several medals.

Financial Aid and Scholarships

Aid in the form of grants, loans, college work study and scholarships is available to students meeting award criteria through the WCCC Financial Aid Office.

Tuition and Fees

In-State
US$1,440 per year (Westmoreland County residents; US$2,820 per year (non-Westmoreland County, Pennsylvania residents). Out-of-state: US$4,200.

Admissions

WCCC maintains an open door policy; high school graduates and GED holders are granted admission to the college. The hospitality programs have no special admission criteria. All students must take a placement test before beginning classes.

Graduation Requirements

Students enrolled in degree programs must successfully complete 18 credits of general education courses and 42-50 credits of major courses. Chef apprentices must also complete a 6,000 hour supervised practice. Non-apprenticeship students must complete a 150-hour internship. Students enrolled in certificate programs must successfully complete 14-16 credits of major courses.

William Rainey Harper College

Hospitality Management Program

Program Enrollment: 140 students
Institutional Enrollment: 25,000
Degrees Awarded: Associates of Applied Science, Certificate of Completion
Degree Categories: A.A.S. Hospitality; Certificates in Culinary Arts, Baking, Hotel or Hospitality
Emphasis/Specializations: A.A.S. Foodservice or Hotel
Program Accreditation: Cooperative programs and certificates available jointly with the Retailer's Bakery Association, The Education Foundation of the National Restaurant Association and the Educational Institute of the American Hotel & Motel Association
Institutional Accreditation: North Central Association of Colleges and Secondary Schools
Contact: Patrick J. Beach, Professor, Hospitality Management, 1200 W. Algonquin Road, Palatine, IL 60067; phone (847) 925-6874, fax (847) 925-6031; E-mail: pbeach@harper.cc.il.us

Institution Description

Large, suburban Chicago, commuting, comprehensive community college with over 100 programs.

Program Description

25-year-old program in northwest Chicago suburbs with many alumni and exception institutional and business support.

Special Features

Curriculum offers internships, experienced faculty, student clubs and exceptional placements.

Financial Aid

College offers a superb financial aid office including loans, work studies, need and performance based scholarships.

Admissions

We have an open admissions policy.

Tuition and Fees

In-district: Approximately $2,000 year
Out-of-district: Approximately $4,000 year
Room and board: Not-Available
Other Fees: Nominal

Specialization Areas

Hotel & Lodging Management, Restaurant and Foodservice Management, Culinary Arts

Graduation Requirements

Degrees require 62 semester hours (Two years) and certificates require 21-32 hours (about 1 year full time study. Work experience required.

York County Technical College

Culinary Arts and Hospitality Management

Program Enrollment: 20 Hospitality Management; 40 Culinary Arts
Institutional Enrollment: 659
Degrees Awarded: Associate of Applied Science Degree; Certificate
Degree Categories: Associate of Applied Science Degree in (1) Culinary Arts and (2) Hospitality Management; Certificate in Food Service Specialist
Institutional Accreditation: New England Association of Schools and Colleges (fully accredited)
Industry Affiliations: Maine Innkeepers Association; Maine Restaurant Association; New England Innkeepers Association; American Culinary Federation; American Hotel/Motel Association; Council Hotel, Restaurant, Institutional Education
Contact: Norman J. Hebert CHE, Chairperson, Hospitality Management/Culinary Arts Department, York County Technical College, 112 College Drive, Wells, ME 04090; phone: 207-646-9282 x213; E-mail ynhebert@yctc.net; fax: 207-646-9675

Institutional Description

York County Technical College (YCTC) is located on the Southern Coast of Maine in Wells. The newest technical college of the state-wide Maine Technical College System. Established in 1994 YCTC currently offers seven (7) degree programs and four (4) certificate programs in a state of the art educational facility.

Program Description

YCTC offers two, Associate of Applied Science degrees: one in Culinary Arts the other in Hospitality Management with emphasis in hotel and restaurant management. YCTC also offers a one (1) year certificate program as a Food Service Specialist. Utilizing the many local hospitality and food service establishments as a positive learning environment.

Special Features

All programs have been designed through the DACUM process using local industry leaders. Advisory committees work closely with students to ensure professional growth and career opportunities.

Financial Aid and Scholarships

YCTC offers financial assistance to students with needs in numerous forms. Federal, state, and institutional grants, scholarships, are funded through charitable gifts, federal work study and loans.

Admissions Policy

YCTC maintains a "rolling admissions" policy allowing candidates to apply an be considered for acceptance throughout the year. Assessment testing is required for each student prior to being matriculated, in English and math for level assessment. A high school diploma or GED certificate are required.

Graduation Requirements

Graduation requires the successful completion of all technical and general education courses. In addition to successfully completing an extensive externship at a approved location, and be current with all financial obligations.

Youngstown State University

The Hotel, Restaurant, and Event Management Program
Associate Baccalaureate College of Health and Human Services

Program Enrollment: 110
Institutional Enrollment: 12,500
Degrees Awarded: Associate and Bachelor
Degree Categories: Associate of Applied Science in Hospitality Management, Bachelor of Science in Applied Science in Hospitality Management
Emphases/Specializations: Lodging Administration, Food and Beverage Management, Event Management

Institutional Accreditation: North Central Association of Schools and Colleges
Contact: Robert C. Campbell, Associate Professor - Human Ecology Coordinator, Hotel, Restaurant, and Event Management, State University, Youngstown, OH 44555; phone (330)742-3338/3344; fax (330)742-2309; Hotelprof@aol.com

Institution Description

Youngstown State University is a dynamic, urban university with substantial housing for resident students. The Hotel, Restaurant & Event Management program is one of the fastest growing programs on campus, stressing on-the-job application to classroom experiences. The program takes advantage of its ideal location, halfway between New York City and Chicago, by emphasizing hotel administration. The Northeast Ohio setting offers much in the way of experience, entertainment, and career opportunities.

Program Description

The associate-degree program offers a well-rounded industry education. All coursework completed in the associate-degree program transfers to the bachelor-degree program. Assistance is provided in finding paid internships and for placement of graduates. The program features an active student organization, the Hospitality Management Society.

Special Features

Faculty recognize the value of work experience subsequent and/or concurrent with study in Hospitality Management. Graduation credit is given with approval of a faculty committee. Students have an option of completing both the associate's and/ or bachelor's degree program without loss of credit. The Hotel, Restaurant and Event Management program is developing smooth articulation for their students.

Admissions

Youngstown State University is an open admission university.

Graduation Requirements

The AAS program requires 99 quarter hours; the BS in AS program requires 186 quarter hours.

Baccalaureate Degree-Granting Programs

Please note: All listings are correct at time of publication based on information submitted by each school.

American Hospitality Management College

Hotel and Restaurant Management

Program Enrollment: 226
Institutional Enrollment: 226
Degree Awarded: Associate of Sciences; Diploma; Certificate; Bachelor of Hospitality Management
Degree Categories: Hotel and Restaurant Management
Emphasis/Specialization: Foodservice Management; Food and Beverage Management; Bar and beverage Management; Hotel and Lodging Management; Human Resources Management ; Mixology and Bartending Practice; Prevention Service and Risk Management: Marketing and Feasility Study
Institutional Accreditation: Full College's Professional Management Development Program Partners agreement with the Educational Foundation of the National Restaurant Associate of U.S.A.
Contact: David Wen-Wei Chou, MHM, Professor and Director, Department of Hotel and Restaurant Management, American Hospitality Management College, 300 Hanko Rd. Sec4, Taichung, Tawan 404, phone (886)4-2328119; fax (886)4-2328093, Email: AHMCUSER@msll.hinet.net

Institution Description

Since 1995, AHMC has been devolping programs of professional study and creative concepts of training, especially designed for Chinese students who are interested in Hotel and Restaurant management. AHMC is located n the heart of Taiwan, only 15 minutes from Taichung airport. AHMC is famous for its progressive quality programs and super facilities. Our bartender training facility is the best in China and a dedicated faculty and staff offer a wealth of credentials. Costs are among the lowest and training quality is among the highest in the whole china.

Program Description

The curriculum is two years or sixteen months of intense study and practice. AHMC offers two paid internship of two months. Our hospitality management program prepares students for management careers. Students may specialize in hotel, restaurant, bar, or club management business. Our program is well structured so that students may enter the profession or transfer to a four-year instuition such as Johnson & Wales and Lynn Universities in the United States. Certainly, our credits can be transferred to numerous professional universities in the U.S.A. and the U.K.

Special Features

The program began as a partnership with the United States National Restaurant Association (NRA), and that vital link thrives today. The best from two continents—AMHC's combination of China and American education. Our student orginization "hospitality entrepreneurs" is active in many ongoing community projects. Cooperative education and internships are available to all students.

Financial Aid and Scholarships

Financial aid is available to all eligible full-time students. Contact our financial aid office for details.

Approximate Tuition and Fees

Tuition per semester (18 weeks) was US$1,695 in 1999/2000. Courses commence every spring and fall in February and September.

Admissions

AHMC has an open admissions policy. Applicants for the A.S. degree course must have completed high-school or have succesfully passed a college placement test or equivalent examination. In addition, they must be at least 16 years of age, and full of enthusiasm.

Graduation Requirements

The AS degree in Hotel and Restaurant Management requires completion of 99 credit hours. Required courses in general studies, hospitality management and specific area of study must be completed prior to receiving the Associate of Science degree. A minimum cumulative grade point average of 2.0 is also required, AHMC will accept transfer credits in equivalent work from other educational instuitions provided the grade achieved was a C or better.

Appalachian State University

Hospitality and Tourism Management Program

College: John A. Walker College of Business
Program Enrollment: 130
Degree Awarded: Bachelor of Science
Degree Category: Business Administration
Emphases/Specializations: Students can structure their curricula to develop an area of emphasis in either hospitality or tourism management.
Program Accreditation: American Assembly of Collegiate Schools of Business (graduate and undergraduate)
Institutional Accreditation: Southern Association of Colleges and Schools; North Carolina Department of Public Instruction
Contact: Dr. Michael Evans, Hospitality and Tourism Management Program, College of Business, Appalachian State University, Boone, NC 28608; phone (828)262-6222. E-mail: Evansmr@appstate.edu

Institution Description
Appalachian State University (ASU), part of the University of North Carolina system, is a comprehensive university offering 130 academic majors at the baccalaureate level and over 70 academic majors at the master's and intermediate levels.

Program Description
Hospitality & Tourism Management is part of the Management Department of the College of Business. In addition to courses in hospitality and tourism, students complete a core of business subjects. Students learn contemporary service management concepts and applications in a business school setting.

Special Features
The university is located in the North Carolina "High Country", a well established regional resort and tourism destination. The University owns and operates the Broyhill Inn and Conference Center and students have an opportunity to complete several lab experiences in three separate management courses. The University also has lodging facilitities in New York City and Washington, D.C. These facilities can be used for internship housing or special field trips to these destinations.

Financial Aid and Scholarships
ASU offers many scholarships, loans, grants and work opportunities for qualified students.

Admissions
Students must be admitted to the College of Business after completing 60 semester hours of coursework including seven specified introductory business courses with a 2.5 GPA.

Graduation Requirements
Students must complete a minimum of 122 semester hours. This includes 21 semester hours of business core courses and 30 semester hours of hospitality and tourism management courses. An internship and work experience practicum are also required.

Arkansas Tech University

Hospitality Administration

College: Systems Science
Program Enrollment: 65
Institutional Enrollment: Undergraduate 4,500; Graduate 200
Degree Awarded: Bachelor of Science
Degree Category: Hospitality Administration
Institutional Accreditation: North Central Association of Colleges and Schools; National Council for Accreditation of Teacher Education

Contact: Morgan W. Geddie, Ed.D., Hospitality Administration, Department of Parks, Recreation and Hospitality Administration, Williamson Hall, Arkansas Tech University, Russellville, AR 72801, phone (501)968-0607, fax (501)968-0600

Institution Description

Arkansas Tech University (ATU) is a state-supported institution offering majors within its schools of systems science, business, education, liberal and fine arts, and physical and life sciences. The spacious campus is located on the northern edge of the city of Russellville, a growing community of approximately 25,000 ideally situated between the mountains of the Ozark National Forest and the Ouachita National Forest. It is midway between Fort Smith to the west and the state's capital Little Rock to the east on interstate highway 40. The Arkansas River forms 36,600 acre Lake Dardanelle with 315 miles of shoreline behind a lock and dam located just southwest of the city. Fishing, hunting, boating, and hiking are sports that are easily accessible.

Program Description

Hospitality Administration is located in a department with Parks and Recreation. This combination emphasizes tourism opportunities as a basis for food, lodging, travel, and other leisure-related businesses in the private sector as well as those in the public sector such as the state park and national forest systems.

Students who graduate from the Hospitality Administration program receive a solid business base as well as traditional liberal studies, both of which are enhanced by the technical hospitality administration subjects. Students take such professional courses as introduction to hospitality management, lodging operations, sanitation, food production, quantity food production, meetings and convention management, legal aspects of hospitality administration, resort management, personnel management, beverage management, hospitality financial analysis, dining services management, facilities management and design, menu analysis and purchasing, travel and tourism, and hospitality marketing. An internship is required. Computer technology is used in almost every major course.

Special Features

ATU features small classes averaging 22 students and an opportunity for individual attention. Students are assisted in obtaining internships in many hotels, restaurants and resort areas. Leadership is encouraged by student involvement in campus, community, state, and national organizations. Students benefit from opportunities to volunteer with class projects. The Hospitality Society is open to all majors. Junior and senior honor students are invited to become members of Eta Sigma Delta, an international hospitality honorary fraternity. Students are encouraged to participate in group trips to the International Hotel, Motel and Restaurant trade show in New York City and the National Restaurant Association trade show in Chicago. Fundraising activities by the Hospitality Society help students defray some of their traveling expenses.

Financial Aid and Scholarships

The university makes financial aid, scholarships, grants, loans and part-time employment available to qualified students.

Admission

Students must be high school graduates and participate in the ACT or SAT program. The university accepts transfer of similar courses completed at other accredited institutions with approval by the registrar. In the hospitality administration major, up to ten elective credit hours can be accepted for courses that are not similar.

Tuition and Fees

In-State $2,016; Out-of-State $4,032; Room and Board $2,664; Other Fees $110

Specialization Areas

Hotel and Lodging Management, Restaurant and Foodservice Management

Graduation Requirements:

Graduation requires the successful completion of 124 semester hours with a minimum GPA of 2.0. Required courses include 37 hours in general education, 24 hours in business and professional courses, 53 hours of in hospital-

Ashland University

Hotel/Restaurant Management Program

College: School of Business Administration and Economics
Program Enrollment: 50
Institutional Enrollment: 5,800 total (undergraduate and graduate); 2,000 on-campus undergraduate
Degree Awarded: Bachelor of Science
Degree Category: Business Administration
Emphasis/Specializations: Hotel and Restaurant Management
Institutional Accreditation: Association of Collegiate Business Schools and Programs; North Central Association of Colleges and Schools; National Council for the Accreditation of Teacher Education
Contact: Mr. Terry Rumker, Director Hotel & Restaurant Management Program, Ashland University, Ashland, OH 44805; phone (419) 289-5698; fax (419) 289-5910

Institution Description

A private, liberal arts institution with a strong academic program, Ashland University (AU) offers 84 majors within five schools. In addition, the university's class size, dedicated faculty and built-in academic flexibility all exist to meet the needs of the individual student. This "Accent on the Individual" remains an important factor in Ashland's reputation of academic excellence.

Program Description

Ashland University is the only business school in the state of Ohio accredited by the Association of Collegiate Business Schools and Programs (ACBSP). AU's Hotel/ Restaurant Management Program focuses on the management perspective of the hospitality industry. An important aspect of the curriculum is the requirement that each student must work two summers in the hospitality field, giving students the opportunity to apply what is learned in the classroom.

Special Features

All faculty have extensive past and current industry experience to provide students with practical expertise and insight to the hospitality field. Students gain first-hand experience through the university's nationally recognized foodservice operation. In addition, the Accent Room, a public restaurant operated by the university, is one of the hotel/restaurant "classrooms."

Financial Aid and Scholarships

AU maintains a fully staffed financial aid office offering financial assistance awarded on the basis of outstanding scholarship, accomplishments, talents and/or financial need.

Approximate Tuition and Fees

Total of $19,366 for tuition, fees, room and board (1998-99).

Admissions

Applicants must have graduated from a high school accredited by a regional accrediting agency or by a state department of education and have a record indicating a likelihood of success at AU. The quality of the academic record is shown by an applicant's grades, class standing and schedule of courses taken.

Graduation Requirements

Graduation requires the completion of 128 semester hours, which includes 42 hours of business-related courses and 30 hours of study in hotel and restaurant management, as well as two summers of work experience in the hospitality field.

Auburn University

Hotel and Restaurant Management

College: School of Human Sciences
Program Enrollment: 126
Institutional Enrollment: 19,142 undergraduate; 2,633 graduate
Degree Awarded: Bachelor of Science
Degree Category: Hotel and Restaurant Management
Emphases/Specializations: Hotel Management or Restaurant Management
Institutional Accreditation: Southern Association of Colleges and Schools
Contact: Cheng-i Wei, Department Head, Department of Nutrition, Food Science, School of Human Sciences, Auburn University, Auburn, AL 36849-5605; phone (334) 844-4261; fax (334) 844-3268

Institution Description

Auburn University is a comprehensive, land-grant university committed to the pursuit of excellence through teaching, research and extension. Auburn offers 130 baccalaureate degree programs, 60 master's degree programs, and the doctorate in 40 areas.

Program Description

The Hotel and Restaurant Management (HRMT) curriculum combines liberal arts studies, general business courses, and a modern approach to hospitality management education to prepare graduates for responsible positions in fine hotels, restaurants and clubs. Auburn places a strong emphasis on understanding and managing the art and science of world-class service. Our students also learn a balanced approach to managing both people and profits, as well as their responsibilities to society.

Special Features

The HRMT Program features two annual career fairs—one held on the Auburn campus, the other in Atlanta, in conjunction with several other hospitality programs. Auburn HRMT interns may be found from Beverly Hills to the U.S. Virgin Islands, from Chicago to Disney World, and points in between. The faculty is comprised of both full-time professionals and adjunct instructors from the hospitality industry. HRMT majors automatically earn a minor in business. Auburn alumni are known around the world for their spirit and loyalty.

Financial Aid and Scholarships

Financial aid is available to students who demonstrate need. University, school, and departmental scholarships, grants, loans and part-time employment are also available.

Approximate Tuition and Fees

Tuition is $920 per quarter for state residents; $2,760 per quarter for nonresidents.

Admissions

Entrance requirements to Auburn University and the HRMT program are based primarily on high school records, scores on the ACT or the SAT, and transcripts from other colleges or universities attended.

Graduation Requirements

Graduation requires the completion of 201 quarter hours, which includes 61 hours of liberal education, 38 hours of business and, 58 hours of hospitality management. Students are required to gain 400 hours of general work experience in the industry prior to their junior year, and complete a structured 400-hour internship prior to graduation. Auburn requires all transfer work to be C or above.

Australian International Hotel School

Hospitality Management Program

Program Enrollment: Current enrollment of 230 anticipated to rise to a maximum of 360 by 2003
Institutional Enrollment: As above
Degree Awarded: Bachelor of Business (Hotel Management)
Degree Category: Hospitality Management
Program Accreditation: The Bachelor of Business (Hotel Management) is conferred jointly by the Australian International Hotel School and RMIT University, in affiliation with the School of Hotel Administration, Cornell University. The degree is also accredited by the Australian Capital Territory Accreditation Agency
Institutional Accreditation: The Australian International Hotel School is a statutory authority of the Australian Capital Territory established by the Hotel School Act 1996
Contact: Professor Michael V. Conlin, Director and Dean, Australian International Hotel School, PO Box E243, Kingston, Canberra, ACT 2604, Australia; phone 61.2.6234.4400; fax 61.2.6234.4545; e-mail: <michael.conlin@aihs.edu.au>; web page <http://www.sha.cornell.edu/aihs/

Institutional Description

The Australian International Hotel School (AIHS) is a not for profit, specialized and self-contained tertiary institution which is a statutory authority of the ACT Government established by the Hotel School Act 1996. The AIHS has two strategic alliances with the School of Hotel Administration, Cornell University, USA and RMIT University, Melbourne, Australia.

Program Description

The Bachelor of Business (Hotel Management) is a four year degree program delivered in an accelerated mode over three years. All studies are full time throughout the nine term program. The AIHS recognizes prior learning and grants advanced standing where appropriate. The curriculum, which has been developed by the Cornell Hotel School and accredited by RMIT University, includes general education subjects, generic business administration subjects, generic hospitality management subjects, specialized hospitality management electives, and three structured practical experiences.

Special Features

The AIHS owns and commercially operates the heritage Hotel Kurrajong, situated in Australia's Federal Triangle in Canberra. The Hotel won the 1996 Australian Hotel Association National Award for Best Hotel Accommodation. Students undertake a structured internship in the award winning Hotel as part of the program. The facility also includes residency for up to 120 students as well as excellent teaching, computing, and library facilities.

Tuition and Fees

Total tuition and fees for the entire program are Aus$39,925 for national students and Aus$47,575 for international students. Tuition and fees can be paid monthly, by term, or annually. The AIHS offers a range of residence and board plans. Residence and board are available for Aus$2,800 on average per term. As of December 31, 1998, the Australian dollar was worth US$.61.

Admissions

The AIHS admits students on a range of criteria including academic ability, leadership potential, and commitment to the hospitality industry. AIHS students generally fall into the top 30% of their academic population. Applications must include a completed application form, letters of reference, and standardized test scores or equivalents. Applicants whose first language is not English must submit TOEFL scores of 580 or equivalent or an IELTS score of 6.5 overall or equivalent. All applicants will be interviewed by AIHS faculty in persons or by phone.

Graduation Requirements

To graduate, students must pass 30 academic subjects, the Hotel Kurrajong Internship, the Operational Externship, and the Management Externship. Students must also have conversational ability in a language other than English and this can be obtained through two elective subjects which can form part of the above requirement.

Ball State University

Food Management

Program Enrollment: 40 plus
Institution Enrollment: 18,026 undergraduate 2,304 graduate
Degrees Awarded: Bachelor of Science; Associate; Masters
Degree Categories: Food Management; Dietetic Technology; Dietetics, Dietetic Internship
Emphases/Specialization: Foodservice Management
Program Accreditation: Indiana State Board of Vocational and Technical Education; American Assembly of Collegiate Schools of Business
Institutional Accreditation: North Central Association of Colleges and Schools; Indiana Commission on Higher Education
Contact: Lois A. Altman, Associate Professor, Food Management, Department of Family and Consumer Sciences, Ball State University, Muncie, IN 47306: phone: (765) 285-5931; fax (765) 285-2314

Institutional Description

Ball State is a state-funded, comprehensive university with accredited programs in teacher education, business, the sciences, humanities, exercise physiology, nursing, music and other programs. Ball State offers more than 120 undergraduate degree programs, 50 master's degree programs and 30 doctoral degree programs.

Program Description

Ball State's Food Management Program features a strong liberal arts component, business coursework, and specific foodservice management and foodservice skills courses. Students pursue specific coursework in Human Resources, Quantity Foods, Food, Beverage and Labor Cost Control and Menu Planning.

Special Features

The Program features extensive practicum experience, including internships. A student-run restaurant, quantity foods kitchen, and extensive microcomputer availability are hall marks of our program.

Financial Aid and Scholarships

Ball State University has an extensive financial aid program with a large staff of counselors. Some grants are based on need, while others are based on merit.

Approximate Tuition and Fees

Tuition for Indiana residents is $2,464 per year; nonresidents pay $5,872 per year. Room and board costs $3,168 per year.

Admissions

Ball State students have typically graduated in the top half of their high school class, and possess SAT scores (combined) of 800 or above (or ACT scores of 18 or above). To be admitted to the Food Management Program, the student must have a GPA of 2.0 or above.

Graduation Requirements

The bachelor of science degree specifies 126 semester hours, of which 42 hours are general studies, 45 are Food Management hours, 16 are college core courses, and the rest are electives. A sophomore practicum, or senior internship and 500 hours of foodservice work experience are also required.

Ben-Gurion University of the Negev

Hotel and Tourism Management

College: The School of Management
Program Enrollment: 180
Institutional Enrollment: 8,500 undergraduate; 4,500 graduate
Degree Awarded: Bachelor of Arts
Degree Category: Hotel and Tourism Management
Institutional Accreditation: Council for Higher Education, Government of Israel

Contact: Prof. Arie Reichel, Director, Dept. Of Hotel and Tourism Management, Ben-Gurion University of the Negeve, P.O. Box 653, Beer Sheva 84105, Israel; phone (972) 7-647-2193; fax (972) 7-647-2920

Institution Description

Founded in 1964, Ben-Gurion University of the Negev includes four degree-granting faculties and a School of Management in Beer Sheva, the capital of Israel's Negev Desert region. A diverse group of scholars and scientists, together with renowned visiting lecturers from Israel and abroad, bring a continuous input of fresh ideas and the latest methods to the University. The relatively low student-to-faculty-ratio allows for a personal rather than an institutionalized approach to learning.

Program Description

The B.A. in Hotel and Tourism Management is a three year degree program combining business management courses and specialized hospitality and tourism management courses and specialized hospitality and tourism management courses. The language of study is Hebrew, and in addition to English, students must complete one year of a modern foreign language. Also, students complete a minimum of 1,200 hours of supervised on-the-job experience, as part of the degree requirements.

Special Features

The program was prepared with the help of experts from Israel's Ministry of Tourism, industry professionals and academic specialists, thus answering the needs of the industry while training professionals with management skills for a wide variety of career choices. The supervised internship, an integral part of the program, offers students an opportunity to receive practical, first-hand experience in the hospitality field.

Financial Aid and Scholarships

Financial aid is available from a variety of university, government, Jewish Agency and private sources. The Student Authority, which functions within the framework of the Ministry of Immigrant Absorption, sometimes grants financial aid to students who are new immigrants to Israel. In addition, several hospitality industry scholarships are available based on academic achievement.

Admissions

Admission is selective, and decisions are made by a faculty committee based on the applicant's prior academic records, college and entrance exams (Israeli psychometric exam or SAT exam) and the results of a required personal interview.

Approximate Tuition and Fees

Tuition is determined annually by the Council for Higher Education for all Israeli institutions of higher education. An initial payment is required prior to the commencement of the term for which the students is registered, and the balance of the tuition can be paid in convenient installments. Current tuition is approximately $3,000 a year.

Specialization Area

Hotel & Lodging Management, Travel & Tourism Management

Graduation Requirements

Graduation requires the successful completion of 125 credit hours and 1,200 hours of practical experience. The program is 3 years in duration.

Bethune-Cookman College

Hospitality Management Program

Program Enrollment: 100
Institutional Enrollment: 2,500
Degree Awarded: Bachelor of Science
Degree Category: Hospitality Management
Emphasis/Specializations: Balanced exposure to food, lodging, travel and entertainment service management; Business School Core
Institutional Accreditation: Southern Association of Colleges and Schools; Florida State Department of Education; Accreditation Commission on Programs In Hospitality Administration (ACPHA)

Contact: Ernest P. Boger, CHA,FMP, CHE, Director, Hospitality Management Degree Program Division of Business, Bethune-Cookman College, 640 Dr. Mary McLeod Bethune Blvd., Daytona Beach, FL 32114;e-mail address: bogere@cookman.edu; phone: (904) 255-1401, ext. 355; fax: (904) 257-5960

Institution Description

Bethune-Cookman College is a career-oriented, church-related, liberal arts, coeducational and residential institution. It is the sixth largest of 43 colleges affiliated with the United Negro College fund, and is located in the Atlantic Coast city of Daytona Beach, Florida, which has a metropolitan area population of over 160,000.

Program Description

The program is designed primarily to prepare graduates for entry-level management positions. A threephase internship oriented educational program has been developed as part of the Hospitality Management Program curriculum. This plan requires students to alternate periods of class attendance with three periods of summer work experience in approved hospitality industries.

Special Features

The Hospitality Management Program features faculty who possess several years of professional work experience in the hospitality industry as personnel managers, restaurant owners and general managers. All hold appropriate advanced degrees and professional certification. The campus is located within the concentrated Florida hospitality environment, one hour from the Disney complex, the Kennedy-NASA Space Center and St. Augustine-the oldest settlement in the United States.

The Division of Business has a 50,000 sq.ft.-3 story atrium style building which incorporates an entire floor dedicated to hospitality training activities. These include front office and accounting labs, a teaching and production kitchen and sample branded guest rooms.

Financial Aid and Scholarships

Ninety percent of B-CC students receive financial aid and/or scholarships. Upon appropriate application, a financial package is arranged for each student. This includes Federal, state and private sector (hospitality industry) funds.

Approximate Tuition and Fees

$236.65 per semester credit hour. $2,711 residence hall fee per semester.

Admissions

Satisfactory completion of an accredited four-year high school course or its equivalent (GED). Presentation of the SAT or the ACT scores are required as part of the admission requirement.

Transfers: any applicant with an acceptable average earned at an accredited college and with a transcript statement to the college that they are in good standing and eligible for return.

Graduation Requirements

All majors must complete a hands-on work experience (internship) of at least 1,000 clock hours, spread over three summers. An oral and written evaluation of this experience is required. Coursework requirements are: 40 credit hours, general studies; 25 credit hours, business core; 60 credit hours, hospitality concentration; and six credit hours, free electives.

Bilkent University

Tourism and Hotel Management

Program Enrollment: 1,836
Institutional Enrollment: 3,348 undergraduate; 650 graduate
Degree Awarded: Bachelor of Science
Degree Category: Tourism and Hotel Management

Contact: Kamer Rodoplu, Director, School of Tourism and Hotel Management, Bilkent University, 06533 Ankara, Turkey; phone: (90-312) 266-4297; fax: (90-312) 266-4607; e-mail: rodoplu@bilkent.edu.tr

Institutional Development

Bilkent University was founded on October 20, 1984, by Ihsan Dogramaci through a resolution of the foundations, which he had earlier established. The establishment of this private university was later approved by an act of Parliament. The aim was to create a center of excellence in higher education and research. The name "Bilkent" exemplifies the founder's aim, since it is an acronym of "bilim kenti," Turkish for "city of learning and science." The university attracts students from 30 different countries and has an inter-nationally renowned academic staff. The University attracts students from 30 different countries and has an inter-nationally renowned academic staff. The university's campus is about eight miles from the civic center and is connected by regular bus service to the city. To create a friendly, self-contained community conducive to a productive academic life, Bilkent's academic buildings and cafeterias are located on campus within easy walking distance of each other.

Program Description

Bilkent University's dedication to excellence is exemplified by the development of its well-regarded School of Tourism and Hotel Management, which offers both an associate and bachelor's degree program. The Bilkent School of Tourism and Hotel Management is working dedicatedly toward fulfilling the needs of the international hospitality management industry. Although the school considers itself young, it continues to establish a reputation for itself internationally, and is increasingly popular with students of university age. The school is particularly progressive in its approach toward management and hospitality, and toward satisfying the needs which the tourism industry generates. An internationally experienced faculty, coupled with an excellently designed curriculum, enhances the quality of education provided. Creativity and innovation are the keys to Bilkent University's School of Tourism and Hotel Management, and the idea that knowledge is power is reiterated both among faculty and to students on a daily basis.

Special Features

Hotel and Restaurant business, food science and travel industry are the school's primary areas of concern. The desire that students have practical and theoretical courseware preparation in these areas results in students being able to find jobs within the international tourism market later. In addition to regular laboratories, the Bilkent Hotel provides students with the means to run a hotel on a daily basis while concentrating on problem-solving, business operations, management and feedback. Industrial training courses are guided by the school so that students may complete internships that provide real-life experience within the hospitality industry. The school maintains mutually beneficial relations with industry, so that students receive excellent on-the-job training, followed later by job offers. The advisory process in this way is provided both by faculty members and industry representatives.

Financial Aid and Scholarships

Bilkent University is a nonprofit institution supported by endowments from its foundations. Students may be eligible for a tuition subsidy from the foundations . Other scholarships, provided by industry are also available.

Approximate Tuition and Fees

Tuition and fees: For international students: US$5,000.

Admissions

To begin undergraduate studies at Bilkent, all applicants to the School of Tourism and Hotel Management must take the two-stage examination administered by the national Student Selection and Placement Center. Applicants who successfully pass these examinations are admitted to the program. International applicants must take the Foreign Students' Entrance Examination in English administered by the aforementioned center. These examinations are held in Ankara, Turkey, as well as in many other Turkish and international cities.

Graduation Requirements

Students with a cumulative GPA of 2.0 or higher on completion of all the required courses are entitled to receive the bachelor's degree.

Bowling Green State University

Hospitality Management Program

College: Business Administration
Program Enrollment: 75
Institutional Enrollment: 15,300 undergraduate; 2,000 graduate
Degree Awarded: Bachelor of Science
Degree Category: Business Administration
Emphasis/Specialization: Hospitality Management
Program Accreditation: American Assembly of Collegiate Schools of Business
Institutional Accreditation: North Central Association of Colleges and Schools
Contact: Kenneth Crocker, Ph.D., Director, Hospitality Management Program, College of Business Administration, Bowling Green State University, Bowling Green, OH 43403; Phone (419) 372-8713/2025; Fax (419) 372-2770

Institutional Description

Bowling Green State University (BGSU) is a state-funded, comprehensive university with nationally recognized programs in the sciences, business, education, humanities, music and health care systems. BGSU presently offers 170 undergraduate degree programs, 75 master's degree programs and doctoral degrees in more than 40 specialty areas.

Program Description

BGSU's Hospitality Management Program (HMP) builds on a solid foundation of liberal education, professional business education and practical work experience. Students pursue specialized hospitality industry study in human resource management, law, finance, marketing, business policy and food management. In addition, students complete at least 800 hours of practical work experience.

Special Features

The HMP makes extensive use of the case method of study, maintains active student professional and social organizations, and provides placement and internship assistance. Elective tracks are available in Recreation, Travel and Tourism, Sales and Marketing; Foreign Languages and Culture, Human Resources, and Restaurant and Institutional Food Service Management.

Financial Aid and Scholarships

The University maintains a fully staffed financial aid office and the HMP offers several scholarships based on both academic achievement and industry experience.

Approximate Tuition and Fees

Per academic year (full-time students): instructional/general fees, $4,000; room and board, $2,900. Nonresident surcharge per academic year, $3,664.

Admissions

Admission to the HMP is selective and based on meeting minimum GPA requirements on a series of preprofessional courses including accounting, economics, and statistics. Freshmen are admitted to the program as "pre" majors; however, formal matriculation occurs in the junior year after admission criteria are met.

Graduation Requirements

Graduation requires the completion of 122 semester hours, which includes 44 hours of general education, 24 hours of preprofessional study, 27 hours of required courses in business administration, 18 hours of study in hospitality management, and at least 800 clock hours of hospitality work experience.

Brigham Young University — Hawaii

Hospitality and Tourism Management

College: School of Business
Program Enrollment: Approx. 125
Institutional Enrollment: 2,000 undergraduate
Degrees Awarded: Bachelor of Science; Associate of Science
Degree Categories: Hospitality and Tourism Management with choice of Hospitality or Tourism track; Travel Management Associate Degree; Hospitality and Tourism minor
Institutional Accreditation: Western Association of Schools and Colleges
Contact: John E. Taylor, Chairman, Marriott Center for Hospitality Management, School of Business, Brigham Young University-Hawaii, Laie, HI 96762-1123; phone (808) 293-3594

Institution Description

Brigham Young University — Hawaii (BYUH) is sponsored by the Church of Jesus Christ of Latter-day Saints and is a four-year liberal liberal arts institution emphasizing strong general education and carefully selected career programs. The school was established in 1955 and is situated in Laie on the windward shore of Oahu, 38 miles from Honolulu and is a part of Brigham Young University, Provo, Utah.

Program Description

The Hospitality and Tourism Management Programs at BYUH offer students who come from over 60 countries the opportunity to train for careers in hospitality, tourism, and travel management. (The programs benefit from a close relationship with the adjacent Polynesian Cultural Center, the number one paid tourist attraction in Hawaii.

Special Feature

Students participate in an integrated, entrepreneurial business care, and benefit from a multi-cultural, diverse student body.

Financial Aid and Scholarships

Scholarship opportunities are available for qualified students. In addition, many students at the school work part time at either the school or the Polynesian Cultural Center.

Approximate Tuition and Fees

$1,110 per semester for LDS Church members, $1,664 for non-LDS Church members. Room and board $2,030 per semester.

Admissions

BYUH does not discriminate against students. Students are required to observe an honor code which includes abstinence from tobacco, alcohol and harmful drugs. Students are expected to observe the highest Christian ideals in their everyday lives.

Graduation Requirements

Students must complete 128 semester hours of credit with a minimum 2.0 grade point average. This includes approximately 60 hours of general education courses, 34 hours of business fundamental core classes, and 27 hours of study in their major area of emphasis. An internship and/or work experience is expected (but not mandatory) of every student.

California State Polytechnic University, Pomona

Hotel and Restaurant Management

College: School of Hotel and Restaurant Management
Program Enrollment: 500
Institutional Enrollment: 17,800
Degree Awarded: Bachelor of Science
Degree Category: Hotel and Restaurant Management
Emphases/Specializations: Food and Beverage Management; Hotel Management

Institutional Accreditation: Western Association of Schools and Colleges; California State Commission For Teacher Preparation
Contact: James F. Burke, Dean, School of Hotel and Restaurant Management, California State Polytechnic University, Pomona, 3801 West Temple Avenue, Pomona, CA 91768; phone: (909) 869-2275

Institution Description

California State Polytechnic University (CSPU) Pomona is a state-assisted, polytechnic university with nationally recognized programs in business, engineering, environmental design (architecture), agriculture, science, arts and hospitality management. CSPU presently offers 61 undergraduate and graduate degree granting programs.

Program Description

CPSU's Hotel and Restaurant Program is based on a solid foundation of general education, business administration and hospital management courses which emphasize hands-on food and beverage operations management,hotel and restaurant computer applications and critical hospitality management analysis. An 800-hour practical work experience is required for graduation.

Special Features

The James and Carol Collins Center for Hospitality Management features: a student-run, 125-seat public table service restaurant; research in energy management, foodservice equipment, foodservice emissions control and food evaluation, and hotel and computer laboratory facilities.

Financial Aid and Scholarships

The university's financial aid office directs students in securing financial assistance. The Hotel and Restaurant Program also offers scholarships based on a variety of criteria. Total program scholarships for 1998-99 was $60,000.

Approximate Tuition and Fees

All students must pay a $55 application fee. California resident fees: 0-6 units, $416 per quarter; 6.1 units or more, $638 per quarter. Nonresident tuition: $164 per quarter unit. Room and board is approximately $1,650 per quarter.

Admissions

An applicant must be a high school graduate; have a qualifiable eligibility index (combination of high school GPA and score on either the ACT or SAT); and have completed the courses in the comprehensive pattern of college preparatory subject requirements with grades of C or better.

Graduation Requirements

200-quarter units credit required. Credit breakdown: 28 business credits; 88 hotel and restaurant management credits; and 84 general education credits. An 800-hour work experience (400 hours in residence) is also required.

California State University, Long Beach

Hospitality Foodservice and Hotel Management

Program Enrollment: 25
Institutional Enrollment: 28,600
Degrees Awarded: Bachelor of Science
Degree Categories: Hospitality Foodservice & Hotel Management
Institutional Accreditations: Western Association of Schools and Colleges

Contact: Lee Blecher, Program Director, Hospitality Foodservice & Hotel Management, Department of Family and Consumer Sciences, 1250 Bellflower Blvd., Long Beach, CA 90840-0501, Phone(562)985-4484/4493, fax (562) 985-4414

Institution Description

California State University, Long Beach (CSULB) is a comprehensive public university with a 50-year tradition for challenging academic programs and attention to students' needs. Sitting just three miles from the Pacific Ocean and its array of beaches, CSULB is a vibrant campus that stretches across 322 beautifully landscaped acres.

Program Description

The program in Hospitality Foodservice and Hotel Management is designed to prepare students with the necessary background and expertise for entry level management positions in the restaurant, foodservice, and lodging industries. The program provides a broad-based foundation in both academic and professional courses and includes hands-on practical experience.

Special Features

The Hospitality Foodservice and Hotel Management program is housed in the Family and Consumer Sciences Building featuring foodservice labs/kitchens, state-of-the-art computer facilities, banquet and meeting rooms. Students enjoy the option to participate in various extracurricular activities plus have many opportunities for work experience and job placement in the surrounding geographical area.

Financial Aid and Scholarships

Many opportunities for financial aid, general scholarships and fellowships are available through the Office of Financial Aid. A wide range of additional scholarships are available at the Department for Hospitality Foodservice and Hotel Management majors.

Approximate Tuition and Fees

Tuition and fees for in-state residents are $1768 (full-time) and $1138 (part-time) per academic year. Tuition for out-of-state students is $246/unit.

Admissions

Admission into the program (major code: 3-1011) is based on university requirements which include meeting an eligibility index derived from a combination of standard entrance exam scores and/or high school grades, and taking required college preparatory courses. Freshman, transfer, returning, and international students are all encouraged to apply. On-line information: www.csulb.edu

Graduation Requirements

To receive the bachelor of science degree, students must complete 129 semester units which includes major and general education requirements. As part of the program, students are required to complete 800 hours of work experience plus an internship.

Canisius College

Statler Hotel Management Program

College: Richard J. Wehle School of Business
Program Enrollment: 45
Institutional Enrollment: 4,790 (undergraduate: 3,320; graduate: 1,470)
Degree Awarded: Bachelor of Science
Degree Category: Hotel Management
Program Accreditation: The International Association for Management Education (AACSB)
Institutional Accreditation: Middle States Association of Colleges and Schools
Contact: Paul Beals, Ph. D., Director, Statler Hotel Management Program, Canisius College, 2001 Main Street, Buffalo, NY 14208; phone: (800) 685-9808 or (716) 888-3270; fax: (716) 888-3211; web site: www.canisius.edu/swiss; e-mail: bealsp@canisius.edu

Institution Description

Founded in 1870, Canisius College is one of the oldest of the 28 Jesuit colleges and universities in the U.S. Canisius is a member of a select group of institutions identified as among the best values in undergraduate education in three separate guides, including *Barron's Best Buys in College Education*. While maintaining the personal attention that has become a Canisius trademark, the College offers over 40 academic majors in its four divisions: The College of Arts and Sciences, the Richard J. Wehle School of Business, the School of Education and Human Services, and the Graduate Division.

Program Description

The Statler Hotel Management Program is a department of the School of Business, which is accredited by the International Association for Management Education (AACSB). The quality standards of the AACSB ensure a thorough, contemporary education in business while also requiring a liberal arts component. The Statler Program builds on the strength of this core curriculum with courses specific to the industry in the areas of human resources management, marketing, finance, strategy and operations management. Students gain a detailed firsthand knowledge of the industry's day-to-day realities through frequent contacts with industry guest speakers, summer placements, their European work experience, and the examples of current practices and problems the faculty brings to the classroom.

Special Features

A distinctive feature of the Statler Program is the European study-and-work experience, whereby students take their required operational courses at Switzerland's world renowned Centre International de Glion. The Statler Program is the *only* undergraduate hotel management program in North America to incorporate European study as an integral component of its curriculum.

Financial Aid and Scholarships

Some 80 percent of the students studying at Canisius receive financial aid. In addition to financial aid available from the College, separate scholarships are available to hotel management students through the financial support of the Statler Foundation.

Tuition and Fees

In-State: $14,200. Out-of-State: $14,200. Room and Board: $6,100. Fees: $382.

Admissions

Candidates for admission are evaluated based on their secondary school performance, their scores on either the SAT or ACT examination, and their promise for success in the hospitality industry. Students who have attended associate-degree programs in hotel and restaurant management and who seek a business complement to their technical training are especially encouraged to apply.

Graduation Requirements

The bachelor of science degree is awarded on completion of 126 credit hours, including courses in the liberal arts, the core business curriculum, and both required and elective courses in hotel management.

Central Michigan University

Hospitality Services Administration/Foodservice Administration

College: Business Administration/Education & Human Services

Program Enrollment: 315 majors

Institutional Enrollment: 15,200 undergraduate; 1,800 graduate

Degree Awarded: Bachelor of Science in Business Administration/Bachelor of Science; Bachelor of Applied Arts

Degree Category: Hospitality Services Administration/ Foodservice Administration

Emphasis/Specialization: Hospitality Services Administration, Hospitality Information Systems, Gaming & Entertainment Management, Foodservice Administration, Dietetics

Program Accreditation: American Assembly of Collegiate Schools of Business

Institutional Accreditation: North Central Association of Colleges and Schools

Contact: Yvette N. J. Green, Director, Hospitality Services Administration, 100 Smith Hall, Central Michigan University, Mt. Pleasant, MI 48859; phone (517) 774-7355; fax (517) 774-7406; email: yvette.green@cmich.edu; or Wesley Luckhardt, Program Director, Foodservice Administration, 205 Wightman Hall, Central Michigan University, Mt. Pleasant, MI 48859; phone (517) 774-5591; fax (517) 774-2435; email: 34yvqug@cmuvm.csv.cmich.edu

Institutional Description

Central Michigan University (CMU) is a residential campus in the center of the state of Michigan. The emphasis at CMU is on quality education in a personalized atmosphere. CMU is a member of the Mid-Atlantic Conference for all athletic events.

Program Description

Students in Hospitality Services Administration (HSA) may concentration in hospitality management, hospitality information systems, or gaming & entertainment management. In addition, students complete a full-time, 400-hour internship. Students in Foodservice Administration (FSA) or Dietetics may concentrate in applied nutrition. Applied knowledge in a variety of laboratory settings is used. Student organizations are active. Placement after graduation from all programs is excellent.

Financial Aid and Scholarships

The university maintains a fully staffed financial aid office and the Hospitality Services Administration/ Foodservice Administration programs offer several scholarships based on both academic achievement and need.

Admissions

Admission to the HSA program is based on meeting a 2.5/4.0 GPA requirement in a series of pre-professional business courses. Admission to the FSA program is the same as admission to the university. No special requirements are stipulated.

Approximate Tuition and Fees

In-state: $3,065 per year (based on 31 credits), plus $470 in fees; out-of-state: $7,960 per year (based on 31 credits), plus $470 in fees. Room and board: $4,176 per year.

Specialization Area

Hotel & Lodging Management
Restaurant & Foodservice Management
Travel & Tourism Management

Graduation Requirements

For both programs, graduation requires the completion of 124 semester hours, 30-33 hours of which are general education. The HSA program requires: 24 hours of pre-professional core courses; 27 hours of required courses in business administration; and 36 hours of study in Hospitality Services Administration, including a 400-hour internship. The Foodservice Administration program requires 47 hours in Foodservice and 20-30 hours in a minor area of study.

Central Missouri State University

Hotel and Restaurant Administration

College: College of Education and Human Services
Program Enrollment: 100
Institutional Enrollment: 9,136 undergraduate 2,222 graduate
Degrees Awarded: Bachelor of Science
Degree Categories: Hotel and Restaurant Administration
Emphases/Specializations: Minors available through other departments in areas such as tourism, recreation, marketing and modern languages

Institutional Accreditation- North Central Association of Colleges and Schools
Contact: Department Chair, Department of Human Environmental Sciences, Central Missouri State University, Warrensburg, MO 64093; phone 660)543-4362; fax (660)543-8295

Institution Descriptions

Central Missouri State University, founded in 1871, is located 50 miles southeast of Kansas City. The university's four colleges provide outstanding undergraduate and graduate programs to meet students' needs in applied sciences and technology, business and economics, arts and sciences, and education and human services. Students may earn associate, bachelor's, master's or education specialist degrees in more than 150 areas of study. Central's 17 to 1 student-faculty ratio allows for personalized instruction and individualized education.

Program Description

The program prepares students for entry-level management positions; hence it is management oriented rather than skill oriented. Approximately a third of the core program consists of business courses. Subject matter courses provide a broad background for management decisions. No minor is required, but is available in related areas.

Special Features

A 350-hour internship is scheduled between the junior and senior year. An active student organization provides additional opportunities for professional business networking.

Financial Aid and Scholarships

Central offers more than $3 million in merit-based scholarships and awards to students each year. The university also administers more than $31 million in financial aid annually in grants, loans and student employment.

Admissions

Central admits students from accredited high schools who graduate in the upper two-thirds of their graduating class, achieve a 20 to 36 ACT composite score, and complete the high school core curriculum. Other applicants are reviewed on an individual basis. All admitted students will be assessed for the purpose of placement in courses which will provide an appropriate challenge for their level of preparedness and enhance their opportunity for success. Students in good standing from other colleges and universities may apply and transfer with appropriate credentials.

Tuition and Fees

1998-99 fees are approximately $91 per credit hour for in-state undergraduates and $182 per credit hour for out-of-state undergraduates. Room and board is approximately $1,985 per semester.

Specialization Area

Hotel & Lodging Mgmt.; Restaurant & Foodservice Mgmt.

Graduation Requirements

To graduate a student must earn a total of 124 semester credit hours. The program requires 68 semester hours of major core, 48 semester hours of University studies, and 11 semester hours of free electives. A five-semester-hour internship is part of the core requirement.

The Chinese University of Hong Kong

Bachelor of Business Administration Program in Hotel Management

Faculty: Faculty of Business Administration
School: School of Hotel Management
Program Enrollment: 150
Institutional Enrollment: 9,500 undergraduate; 2,900 postgraduate
Degree Awarded: Bachelor Degree
Degree Category: Bachelor of Business Administration Program in Hotel Management
Emphases/Specialization: Hotel, tourism and other service industries in Hong Kong and Asia.
Institutional Accreditation: The Chinese University of Hong Kong has full autonomy to accredit all degree programs as agreed between PRC and Hong Kong SAR. The Faculty of Business Administration has also accepted the invitation to become the first pilot business school in Asia to take part in the AACSB-IAME accreditation exercise in 1998/99.
Contact: Prof. Kam-hon Lee, Acting Director, School of Hotel Management, Faculty of Business Administration, Shatin, Hong Kong SAR. Tel: 852 2609 7776; Fax: 852 2603 5917; email:

Institution Description

The Chinese University of Hong Kong is a comprehensive research university. The aim of the Faculty of Business Administration is international standard business education of the highest quality. The basic objective of the School of Hotel Management is to offer an integrated business program using the hospitality industry as a laboratory.

Program Description

The program is industry-driven in nature. It delivers an integrated business education in the context of the hotel and tourism industries with a view to bringing up talents who can make investment decisions and run business operations in the hotel, tourism and other service industries in Hong Kong and Asia.

Special Features

Students are required to complete 2 courses on field-work and internship. A mentor system will be adopted during and after the study period.

Financial Aid and Scholarships

The University and the Faculty of Business Administration offer a variety of scholarships and financial aids.

Tuition and Fees

Approx. US$ 5433.- (HK$ 42,100) for 98-99 academic year, in 2 installments.

Admissions

Hong Kong Certificate of Education Examination and Advanced Level Examination results, or other qualification recognized by the University. For details, please contact the Admission Section (Tel: 852 2609-8947) or http://www.cuhk.edu.hk/adm

Graduation Requirements

Students are required to take a minimum of 99 units to earn a BBA degree in Hotel Management in which 72 units should be in the major program. Internship and group project are also required.

Cornell University

Hotel Administration

College: School of Hotel Administration
Program Enrollment: 850 undergraduate; 110 graduate
Institutional Enrollment: 12,950 undergraduate; 5,500 graduate
Degrees Awarded: Bachelor of Science; Master of Management in Hospitality; Master of Science; Doctor of Philosophy
Degree Categories: Hotel Administration
Emphases/Specializations: Operations Management, Human Resource Management, Financial Management, Information Systems, Food and Beverage Management, Marketing, Property Asset Management, Entrepreneurship
Program Accreditation: Middle States Association of Colleges and Schools
Contact: Mrs. Cheri Farrell, Director of Student Services, School of Hotel Administration, Cornell University, Statler Hall, Ithaca, NY 14853; phone (607) 255-6376; fax (607) 255-4179; http:/hotelschool.cornell.edu/mmh/

Institution Description

Located in the Finger Lakes Region of upstate New York, Cornell University, the largest school in the Ivy League, comprises 13 colleges and schools that offer instruction in virtually every field. Its numerous interdisciplinary programs provide wide ranging opportunities for study that cut across traditional department boundaries. Members of the current faculty have been awarded numerous Nobel Prizes, Pulitzer Prizes, MacArthur Fellowships, and more.

Program Description

The first of its kind, the School of Hotel Administration at Cornell University has a tradition of academic excellence dating back to 1922. It is distinctive for the breadth of its curriculum, the size and credentials of its faculty, the diversity of its student body, and the splendor of its facilities.

Special Features

Statler hall includes classrooms, laboratories, the school's library (the largest of its kind, with a collection numbering over 25,000 volumes), and an extensive computer center. Adjacent to Statler Hall is the 150-room Statler Hotel and J. Willard Marriott Executive Education Center, a full-service hotel and state-of-the-art management training facility for the hospitality industry.

Financial Aid and Scholarships

Undergraduate financial aid at Cornell University, including the School of Hotel Administration, is awarded solely on the basis of financial need. Financial aid packages generally include loans, employment and grants. Ensuring adequate financial aid for its students is a priority of the School.

Approximate Tuition and Fees

Tuition & fees: $21,914; room and board, $7,110; books and other expenses, $1,925.

Admissions

Admission to the undergraduate program is selective, and decisions are made by a faculty committee based on the applicant's educational goals, prior academic record, college entrance tests (either the SAT or ACT), relevant work experience in the hospitality industry, extracurricular activities, recommendations, and the results of a required personal interview.

Graduation Requirements

Undergraduate students must complete eight terms in residence, or the requirement designated for transfer students; complete the prescribed course curriculum and attain a cumulative GPA of at least 2.0; achieve a GPA of at least 2.0 in the final semester; qualify in one language other than English; complete the university's physical education requirement, usually during the first year of residence (including a swim test); and complete two units of practice credit (work in the industry) before registering for the senior year.

The Culinary Institute of America (CIA)

Bachelor's Degree Program

Program Enrollment: 150 students total admitted annually to the bachelor's degree programs
Institutional Enrollment: 2,150
Degrees Awarded: Bachelor of Professional Studies
Degree Categories: Culinary Arts Management, Baking and Pastry Arts Management
Emphases/Specializations: Cooking, Baking, and Foodservice; Foodservice Management, Marketing, Human Resources, Communications, and Finance
Program Accreditation: New York State Department of Education
Institutional Accreditation: Accrediting Commission of Career Schools and Technology (ACCSCT); Candidate for Accreditation Status, Commission on Higher Education (Middle States Association of Colleges and Schools)

AMERICA'S CENTER FOR CULINARY EDUCATION SINCE 1946

Contact: Doug Thompson, Vice President of Enrollment Planning, The Culinary Institute of America, 433 Albany Post Road, Hyde Park, NY 12538-1499; phone 914-452-9430 or 1-800CULINARY; e-mail: Admissions@culinary.edu; Web site: www.ciachef.edu

Institution Description
An independent, not-for-profit institution of higher education committed to providing the world's best professional culinary arts and science education; degree and continuing education programs provide students with the opportunity to acquire the general knowledge and practical skills they need to build successful careers in an ever-changing foodservice and hospitality industry.

Program Description
Hands-on teaching of cooking and baking in the college's 38 professional kitchens and bakeshops; invaluable experience in the college's four fine-dining public restaurants on campus; and managerial and creative courses in areas such as marketing, communications, foreign languages, computers in the food business, and history and culture.

Special Features
An 18-week paid externship off campus; sixteen entry dates a year for culinary arts and eight entry dates a year for baking and pastry arts; a wine and food seminar in California's wine country.

Financial Aid and Scholarships
A variety of federal, state, and CIA aid for those who qualify, including Federal Pell Grants, Federal SEOGs, college work-study, Federal Perkins Loans, parent loans, Veterans Administration educational benefits, vocational rehabilitation grants, and emergency student loans.

Admission
The Admissions Committee seeks candidates who have demonstrated a commitment to a culinary career and have the personal initiative, confidence, and motivation to succeed. The basic requirements are successful completion of a secondary school education or its equivalent and some experience in the foodservice and hospitality industry. Applicants are evaluated on overall performance, the type of program taken, academics, and leadership ability.

Tuition and Fees
Tuition is $15,400 a year for freshman and sophomore years and $10,800 for junior and senior years; residence hall rates average about $3,000 a year; fees for supplies, student activities, and practical exams average $725 per year for freshman and sophomore years and $425 for junior and senior years; one-time fees include application ($30), enrollment ($100), externship ($350), wine and food seminar in California ($3,440), and associate and bachelor's degree graduations ($220 each).

Specialization Area
Restaurant & Foodservice Management; Culinary Arts

Graduation Requirements
Successful completion of the entire course of study: eight on-campus semesters of 15 weeks each (approximately 3,295 hours), one 18- to 21-week semester of an approved externship (600 hours), and one six-week intersession seminar (120 hours); completion of 132 credits, maintaining a grade point average of at least 2.00.

Davis & Elkins College

Hospitality & Tourism Management

Program Enrollment: 50
Institutional Enrollment: 700 undergaduates
Degree Awarded: Bachelor of Arts
Degree Category: Hospitality and Tourism Management
Emphases/Specializations: Hospitality Management; Recreation Management and Tourism.

Institutional Accreditation: North Central Association of Colleges and Secondary Schools
Contact: Michael J. McCorkle, Department of Hospitality & Tourism Management, Allen Hall #204, Davis & Elkins College, Elkins WV 26241; Telephone: 304-637-1802; Fax: 304- 637-1809

Institution Description

Davis & Elkins College is a private liberal arts and science institution affiliated with the Presbyterian Church. It is located on a beautiful 170 acre campus in the heart of the Mid-Atlantic ski country, three hours from south of Pittsburgh and four hours west of Washington, D.C. The college was founded by two U.S. Senators in 1904 and takes great pride in its heritage and in offering a value-oriented undergraduate education in a small-college environment.

Program Description

The Hospitality and Tourism Management program is now in its second decade and has capitalized on the many tourist and outdoor recreation opportunities in the Potomac Highlands region of West Virginia. The program is strongly rooted in the liberal arts curriculum and requires approximately 52 semester hours of major courses. Experiential learning opportunities are available in the campus-located Graceland Inn and Conference Center, nearby ski resorts and other hospitality businesses.

Special Features

Graceland Inn is a recently restored, 100-year old, Victorian stone mansion formerly belonging to Senator Davis, now operating as an inn and restaurant. The Inn has 13 guest rooms in 16,000 square feet and in 1996, received National Historic Landmark status. The Allen Hall Conference Center houses 26 guest rooms and meeting space for accommodating parties of 100 persons.

Financial Aid and Scholarships

The College Financial aid office makes available numerous opportunities for entering students.

Admissions

Students should be ranked in the upper 50% of their high school class.

Approximate Tuition and Fees

1998-1999: tuition and fees $11,700; room and board $5,080.

Specialities

Hotel and lodging management; Restaurant and foodservice management; Travel and Tourism management

Graduation Requirements:

Successful completion of 124 semester hours which includes: 56 hours in general and liberal arts and sciences; 52 hours of hospitality, tourism and business management courses and other various electives.

Delaware State University

Hospitality Management

Program Enrollment: 55
Institutional Enrollment: 3,390
Degree Awarded: Bachelor of Science
Institutional Accreditation: Middle States Association of College and Secondary Schools; Delaware State Board of Education; American Chemistry Society; National League for Nursing; Council on Social Work Education; National Council for Accreditation of Teacher Education; Accreditation Commission for Programs in Hospitality Administration
Contact: Anne W. Smith, Coordinator, Hospitality Management, School of Management, Delaware State University, 1200 North Dupont Highway, Dover, Delaware 19901-2277, e-mail address: awsmith@dsc.edu , phone:(302)-739-4971, fax:(302)-739-1551

Institution Description

Delaware State University is located in Kent County Delaware, 45 miles south of Wilmington on the Delmarva Peninsula. It is a progressive liberal arts institution committed to academic excellence and intellectual competence. From its 1890 beginnings as a land grant institution, Delaware State University has developed into a 400-acre complex with numerous modern buildings and various university programs to support its mission.

Program Description

The Hospitality Management program was established in 1988 with the support of the federal Department of Education's Title III funds. The mission of the program strives to prepare students to become management professionals who possess the hospitality, entrepreneurial, and mangerial skills and competencies necessary to make positive contributions to the hospitality industry, including enhancing operational efficiency and effectiveness— and the financial viability— of organizations in the hospitality industry. The curriculum offers a balance between courses in general education, business administration and hospitality management which includes two required internships.

Special Features

The Hospitality Management program is housed in a newly constructed $17 million dollar building with the state of the art computer laboratories, distant learning technology, food service production kitchen and dining room laboratories. The program is supported by an active industry advisory council of local, regional and national industry representatives.

Financial Aid and Scholarships

Financial Assistance at the University is available through scholarships, grants, loans and part-time employment opportunities.

Tuition and Fees

Tuition (In-State $1,407 per semester total for year $2,814.
Student Activity fee $80.00 per semester total for year $160.00.
Tuition (Out-of State) $3,281 per semester and for the year $6,562.
Room $1,345 per semester total for year $2,690
Board $1,000 per semester total for year 2,000
Residential Fee $220.00 per semester and for year $440.00.

Admissions

Applicants seeking admission to the university should complete and submit their applications with all supporting documents by June 1, for fall semester admission and December 1, for spring semester admission.

Graduation Requirements

Requirements for the Bachelor of Science degree include 124 credit hours;. 48 hours of general education courses, 42 hours of business administration courses, 34 hours of hospitality management courses, and two required internships. A minimum overall grade point average of 2.00 (C) grade.

Domino Carlton Tivoli International Hotel And Business Management School (DCT)

Hotel Management Diploma Program, Culinary Arts Certificate; A.A. in General Business Adm.

Program Enrollment: 275
Degrees Awarded: Diploma in International Hotel Management; Diploma in Hotel Management; Diploma in Food and Beverage Management; Graduate Entry Diploma in Hotel Management
Degree Category: Hotel Management; Culinary Arts; General Business

Contact: Walter Spaltenstein, Director, Carlton Tivoli International Hotel Management Career Centre, Haldenstrasse 57, CH-6002 Lucerne, Switzerland; phone 41-41-4180707; fax 41-41-4109754

Institution Description

Established in 1992, the DCT Hotel Management Career centre is part of a large, privately owned Swiss company that specializes in the hospitality sector. The centre is a residential college specialising in hotel management. Because of its commitment to excellence, DCT is rapidly gaining a reputation as one of the finest Swiss hospitality management institutions. It has an outstanding location and resources, as well as top-quality faculty, all of which ensures a first-class hospitality education. The quality of DCT's programs have been recognised by government offices in several European countries, and by professional associations in the United States. DCT is accredited through the Association of Collegiate Business Schools and Programmes and by CHRIE.

Program Description

DCT's programs are structured so that theoretical and practical learning are both balanced and interrelated. These two main components are complemented by periods of experimental learning in hotels where the nexus and interdependence of skills and hands-on competencies; as well as creative and analytical thinking and problem-solving, can be made operational. DCT's modular program places emphasis on both the practical skills necessary for graduates to succeed in the hospitality industry and on management skills which will ensure that successful students are not only competent practitioners, capable of dealing with real-life problems and acting creatively in many situations, but are also thinking and caring people, able to plan effectively, analyse clearly and make judgements related to finances and people's welfare and comfort.

Special Features

Industrial internships are co-ordinated through DCT's Career Planning and Placement Office, and students are guaranteed placement in leading Swiss hotels. Career guidance and job placement throughout the graduates' career is also organised through this organization. Classes are small, using the most up-to-date equipment, and student learning is enhanced by using the parent organisation's facilities for pre-Industry training.

Approximate Tuition and Fees

Tuition per term (11weeks) is SFr 8,400 board and lodging per term is SFr 1,500. Courses commence every quarter in January, April, July and October.

Admissions

Applicants for the Associate Degree/Diploma courses must have completed high school or have successfully passed on equivalent examination. In addition, they must be at least 18 years of age and have a minimum TOEFL score of 500. Applicants for the Graduate Entry Diploma course must have a recognised bachelor's degree and a TOEFL score of at least 550. For GE-S program, a Diploma from an accredited college or university.

Graduation Requirements

Graduation requires an aggregate grade of C or above in academic and operational units, and successful completion of the industrial internship periods in Swiss hotels. DCT is an educational partner with Florida International University for a joint Diploma-Bachelor of Science Degree in International Hospitality Management on our Luzern campus.

Drexel University

Hotel and Restaurant/Culinary Arts Management

College: Nesbitt College of Design Arts
Program Enrollment: 200
Institutional Enrollment: 9,500 undergraduate; 3,000 graduate
Degree Awarded: Bachelor of Science
Degree Category: Hotel, Restaurant and Institutional Management, Culinary Arts Management
Emphasis/Specialization: Hospitality Management in Foodservice and Lodging, Culinary Arts Management
Institutional Accreditation: Middle States Association of Colleges and Schools; American Assembly of Collegiate Schools of Business
Contact: John Canterino, Ph.D., CHA, Chair, Hotel and Restaurant Management, Nesbitt College of Design Arts, 13-503, Drexel University, Philadelphia, PA, 19104; phone (215) 895-4923; fax (215) 895-4917

Institution Description

Drexel University is a private, nonsectarian, coeducational school. It operates one of the largest mandatory cooperative education programs in the nation, and was the first school to require all students to own a personal computer. The six colleges offer undergraduate and graduate degrees in humanities and social sciences, design arts, business, engineering, information science and science.

Program Description

Drexel's Hotel, Restaurant and Institutional Management (HRIM) Program is composed of subject area sequences in science, liberal arts, behavioral sciences, communication and hospitality management. Our graduates have developed competency in computer applications and, having studied several aspects of design, are able to see hospitality in a design and cultural perspective. They also receive a minor in business as well as credit for the first year of foundation courses toward an MBA.

Special Features

The HRIM program includes courses in interiors, architecture, and graphics and publishing, as they relate to the hospitality industry. Student professional organizations interact regularly with the regional industry. A 14,000-square-foot state-of-the-art commercial foodservice facility with two kitchens, two dining rooms, a lounge, a computer laboratory and a food and wine *les Dame d'Escoffier* library is provided.

Financial Aid and Scholarships

The office of financial aid administers a variety of scholarships, grants, loans and work-study opportunities. Many competitive scholarships are available through the HRIM department head.

Admissions

Admission to the freshman HRIM class is highly selective, requiring graduation from an approved secondary school, in a well-rounded college preparatory or academic program. The academic GPA and SAT scores are assessed individually, and the ability and promise of each applicant are considered to be important.

Graduation Requirements

Graduation requires a minimum of 180 credits, which includes 69 credits in general education, 34 credits in business administration, 58 credits in HRIM Department requirements, and 19 credits in unrestricted electives. Nine months of full-time employment in the hospitality industry are required of each student to satisfy the mandatory cooperative education experience.

East Carolina University

Hospitality Management Program

College: School of Human Environmental Sciences
Program Enrollment: 150
Institutional Enrollment: 14,800 undergraduate; 3,150 graduate
Degree awarded: Bachelor of Science
Degree Category: Hospitality Management
Emphasis/Specialization: Hospitality Management
Institutional Accreditation: Southern Association of Colleges and Schools

Contact: Dori Finley, PhD, Chair, Department of Nutrition and Hospitality Management, School of Human Environmental Sciences, East Carolina University, Greenville, NC 27858-4353; phone (252) 328-6917; fax (252)328-4276, e-mail FinleyD@mail.ecu.edu.

Institution Description

East Carolina University, a constituent of the consolidated University of North Carolina, is the third largest university in the state. A wide range of undergraduate programs are available in 150 areas. Graduate programs leading toward master's and doctoral degrees are available. The university has facilities for both residential and commuter students.

Program Description

The Hospitality Management Program has been developed to prepare managers for the foodservice and lodging industries. The bachelor's degree program includes general education courses, specialized courses in foodservice and lodging management, and a minor in business administration. A self-paced management level internship is required.

Special Features

A state-of-the-art computer lab and a wide variety of opportunities for internships are available. Qualified students can complete the BS and MBA in 5 years.

Financial Aid and Scholarships

Scholarships are available from the American Hotel Foundation, Red Lobster, ARAMARK, NC Tourism Education Foundation, and other organizations. A financial aid office is available to assist students.

Admissions

Admission to the university requires: graduation from an accredited secondary school; 20 units of secondary credits including English (four units), mathematics (three units), science (two units) and social studies (two units); and satisfactory scores on the SAT.

Tuition and Fees

Full time tuition (12 or more hours) for in-state residents: $916 per semester; out-of-state residents $4480 per semester. Dormitory room: $1140 per semester. Meal plan: $1055 per semester.

Specialization Area

Hotel & Lodging Mgmt., Restaurant & Foodservice Mgmt.

Graduation Requirements

A total of 126 semester hours are required for the Hospitality Management degree. These credits include 44 hours of general education and 24 hours in a business administration minor. The remaining hours consist of courses in the program and an internship.

East Stroudsburg University of Pennsylvania

Hotel, Restaurant, & Tourism Management

College: Professional Studies
Program Enrollment: 210
Institutional Enrollment: 4,950 undergraduate; 650
Degree Awarded: Bachelor of Science
Degree Category: Hotel, Restaurant, & Tourism Management
Emphases/Specializations: Hotel & Lodging Management; Food and Beverage Management; Tourism Management
Institutional Accreditation: Middle States Association of Colleges and Schools
Contact: Albert J. Moranville, Chairperson, Hotel, Restaurant & Tourism management Department, East Stroudsburg University, East Stroudsburg, PA 18301; phone (570) 422-3511, Fax: (570) 422-3777

Institution Description
East Stroudsburg University (ESU), one of 14 state universities in Pennsylvania, has nationally recognized programs in hospitality management, education, physical education and computer science. Located in Pennsylvania's Pocono Mountain resort area, ESU is only 90 miles from Philadelphia and 75 miles from New York City.

Program Description
The Hospitality Management Program at ESU offers three concentrations: general hotel management, food and beverage management and tourism management. It incorporates a strong liberal arts base and has a supervised internship at the senior level. With a program of excellence, ESU graduates students who show special accomplishments in people skills. The faculty, in addition to its strong academic credentials, has extensive experience in hospitality management.

Special Features
Involvement with the hospitality industry is emphasized. An active hospitality management advisory board assures input from industry leaders. The student organizations in hospitality management are among the largest and most active on campus. The Hospitality Management Club, the student charter chapter of the Hotel Sales and Marketing Association, and Eta Sigma Delta direct their activities to develop professionalism in students.

Financial Aid and Scholarships
ESU has a fully staffed office of financial aid. In addition, the Hospitality Management Department receives fourteen $1,000 scholarships awarded by local hospitality organizations. The department also participates in the American Hotel Foundation Scholarship Program, the Educational Foundation of the National Restaurant Association Scholarship Program and the Statler Scholarship Program. Local hotels also sponsor a bonus/scholarship program that is open to students who wish to work part time, allowing them to receive $1000 per year toward tuition.

Admissions
The Hospitality Management Department is a limited enrollment department, selecting applicants who have SAT scores and high school averages at the upper level. Transfer students must have a minimum 2.5 GPA and schedule a personal interview. Students who major in hospitality management must maintain a 2.5 GPA to graduate from the program.

Tuition and Fees
Total annual cost including tuition, room and board, and applicable fees is $7,188.00 for in-state residents, and $14,544.00 for out-of-state residents.

Specialization Area
Hotel & Lodging Mgmt., Restaurant & Foodservice Mgmt., Travel & Tourism Mgmt.

Graduation Requirements
Total of 129 credits: 50 credits in general education and 69 credits in major and core-required subjects, which includes a 9-12 credit senior-level internship.

Eastern Illinois University

Hospitality Services (Proposed change to Hospitality Management under review)

College: Lumpkin College of Business and Applied Sciences
Program Enrollment: 80
Institutional Enrollment: Undergraduate 10,174; Graduate 1,561
Degrees Awarded: Bachelor of Science
Degree Category: Family and Consumer Sciences
Emphases/Specializations: Hotel and Lodging Management
Program Accreditation: American Association of Family and Consumer Sciences (AAFCS); American Dietetic Association (ADA)
Institutional Accreditation: North Central Association of Colleges and Schools
Contact: Dr. Loretta P. Prater, Chairperson, School of Family and Consumer Sciences, Klehm Hall, Eastern Illinois University, Charleston, IL 61920; Phone: (217) 581-6076; Fax: (217) 581-6090; E-Mail: cflpp@eiu.edu; Website: http://www.eiu.edu/~famsci/welcome.htm

Institution Description
Established in 1895, Eastern Illinois University offers superior yet accessible undergraduate and graduate education. Students learn the methods and outcomes of free inquiry in the arts, sciences, humanities and professions guided by a faculty known for its commitment to teaching, research/creative activity, and service. The University community strives to create an educational and cultural environment in which students refine their abilities to reason and to communicate clearly so as to become responsible citizens in a diverse world. EIU is conveniently located two hours west of Indianapolis, two-and-a-half hours east of St. Louis and three-and-a-half hours south of Chicago.

Program Description
The Hospitality Services program provides development of a broad base in foodservice management; hotel services, operation and administration; and business concepts, as well as appropriate technical skills. A Family and Consumer Sciences degree with a concentration in Hospitality Services provides preparation for middle-management positions in restaurants, hotels, and a variety of business and institutional settings.

Special Features
Students graduating in Family and Consumer Sciences with a concentration in Hospitality Services also receives a minor in Business Administration. For more information, see our website (address above).

Financial Aid and Scholarships
The office of Financial Aid administers a variety of programs to help students with expenses incurred while pursuing an education. Numerous scholarships are awarded annually with values ranging from $300 to $5,000.

Admissions
Freshman admission requirement is based on ranking in high school and score on ACT or SAT. There are also certain high school preparatory classes required for university admission.

Tuition and Fees
In-State 1997-98 full-time $1,615.80 per semester
Out-of-State full-time $3,803.80 per semester
Room and Board University room and board options range from $1,836 - $2,948 per semester.

Specialization Areas
Hotel and Lodging Management

Graduation Requirements
The curriculum requires the completion of 120 semester hours, which includes 40 to 48 hours of general education depending on foreign language, 24 hours of business, 18 hours of family and consumer sciences and 34 hours of hospitality courses. A grade point average of at least 2.0 on a 4.0 scale is required for graduation.

Eastern Michigan University

Hotel and Restaurant Management

College: Health and Human Services
Program Enrollment: 120 undergraduates; 20 graduates
Institutional Enrollment: 24,000; Undergraduate: 19,000; Graduate: 5,000
Degrees Awarded: Bachelor's Degree, Master's of Science Degree
Degree Categories: Hotel and Restaurant Management
Emphases/Specializations: Hotel and Restaurant Management

Institutional Accreditation: North Central Association of Colleges and Secondary Schools
Contact: Giri Jogaratnam, PhD, Coordinator, Hotel and Restaurant Management, Eastern Michigan University, 206 Roosevelt Hall, Ypsilanti, MI 48197; phone: 734-487-1226; fax: 734-484-0575

Institution Description

As one of the state's four regional universities, Eastern dates back to 1849 when it trained teachers for the public schools. Now a multipurpose university with five colleges, it offers over 180 fields of study. Today's students include residential and commuter students, both full-time and part-time, from traditional college age to mature adults returning to complete their college education. Additional information available at WWW.EMICH.EDU

Program Description

Eastern offers a balanced program of study that integrates the principles of hotel and restaurant management with the physical and social sciences and business. The program is designed to give students varied options that best serve their individual needs. The program has built-in opportunities to operate and manage a student-run restaurant and assume leadership roles. Faculty has extensive industry experience and offer personalized advising based on a low student to faculty ratio.

Special Features

Two 600-hour co-operative education work experiences are required and students are assisted in finding jobs both on and off campus. In addition, a senior internship as a management trainee provides students with supervised managerial experience. The student Hospitality Management Club provides leadership opportunities and regularly organizes trips to industry trade shows. Undergraduate Catalog available at WWW.EMICH.EDU

Financial Aid and Scholarships

Students have access to academic scholarships, grants, work study, and loans. The Office of Financial Aid provides details on which of these programs students may qualify for each year. Scholarships from various hotel and restaurant professional associations are also available to students.

Admissions

High School Diploma with SAT/ACT scores for students under 21 years of age. Transfer students from either two-year community colleges or from other four-year institutions can expect many courses to transfer. Contact the program coordinator with course descriptions and syllabi for details.

Tuition and Fees

In-State: $100 per credit hour
Out-of-State: $265 per credit hour
Room and Board: $1400
Other Fees: $75

Specialization Areas

Hotel and Lodging Management; Restaurant and Foodservice Management

Graduation Requirements

Complete required courses totaling at least 124 credit hours and maintain a Grade Point Average (GPA) of 2.0 or higher. Must also complete the two 600-hour co-operative work experiences and the senior internship hours.

Ecole Hoteliere de Lausanne

International Hospitality Management Program

Program Enrollment: 1,000
Institutional Enrollment: 1,200
Degrees Awarded: Bachelor of Science
Degree Category: International Hospitality Management
Emphases/Specializations: Hospitality Management
Program Accreditation: New England Association of Schools and Colleges (USA)
Institutional Accreditation: University of Applied Sciences (Switzerland)

Contact: Ms. Antoinette Bruegger, Director of Admissions, Ecole hoteliere de Lausanne, Le Chalet-a-Gobet, CH- 1000 Lausanne 25, Switzerland, tel. (41 21) 785 1111, fax (41 21) 784-1407. Email: admission@ehl.ch

Institution Description

The first hotel school in the world, the Ecole Hoteliere de Lausanne remains among the most highly-respected. Our rigorous curriculum focuses on acquiring both business skills and operating practices. Our record of success is excellent: EHL graduates can be found managing top-class enterprises in 100+ countries worldwide.

Program Description

Our 4-year bachelor's degree program, offered in English or French, concentrates on every aspect of the modern hospitality industry: culinary, service and supervisory techniques, as well as finance, marketing, human resources, engineering, strategic planning and foreign languages. Students work on group consulting projects and an individual dissertation.

Special Features

The 4-year program includes two 1-semester internships. EHL helps place students literally all over the world.

Financial Aid Scholarships

Thanks to government grants, fee reductions are accorded to Swiss citizens. For students from other countries, please consult our Admissions Office.

Admissions

Entrance requirements include: successful secondary education, excellent command of English (or French), 2-month preliminary internship, entrance examination.

Tuition and Fees

All students- average tuition $6,900/semester; room/board $5,400/semester; other fees $2,200/semester (No fees are payable during the two year internship semesters).

Specialization Area

Hotel & Lodging Mgmt.

Graduation Requirements

The degree is awarded to students successfully completing the four years of study, including two semesters spent in industry internships.

Endicott College

Hospitality Division

College: Liberal & Professional Arts
Program Enrollment: 110
Institutional Enrollment: Undergraduate- 1230; Graduate - 100
Degrees Awarded: Bachelor of Science
Degree Categories: Hotel/Restaurant/Travel Administration: International Programme for Hospitality Studies

Institutional Accreditation: New England Association of Schools & Colleges
Contact: Edward P. Doherty, Associate Dean, Endicott College, Hotel, Rest. & Travel Administration, 376 Hale St., Beverly, MA 01915, phone: (508) 927-0585

Institution Description

Endicott College is a four-year coeducational independent college located 20 miles North of Boston, Massachusetts. Well known for its required internship programs, the college is situated on a beautiful 200-acre oceanfront campus. Over 90% of the 1230 students reside on campus. A new $10,000,000 Sports Science and Fitness Center will open in the Fall of 1999.

Program Description

The Hospitality Division offers two Bachelor Degree granting programs; the Hotel, Restaurant and Travel Administration and the International Programme for Hospitality Studies. Our programs are designed to give the student options that best serve their individual professional goals. Whether a student is interested in managing a hotel, food services operation or a club, working in the tourism industry or meeting planning, Endicott's innovative and challenging Hospitality and Culinary curricula is designed to give the student professional knowledge and skills while also instilling an educational foundation with breadth.

Special Features

Internships and international opportunities are central to the educational experience within the Hospitality Division. Students participate in professionally oriented internships during their four year program either in three January internships and a semester long internship or for two semester long internships.

International opportunities include studying at the world class Les Roches Hotel Management School in Crans-Montana, Switzerland, participating in a four week London internship or doing a semester long internship in Europe.

Financial Aid and Scholarships

Endicott Grants are provided by the College based on financial need and merit. Seventy-five percent of Endicott students receive some form of financial aid. Over eight million dollars are disbursed annually of which 3.7 million dollars are in the form of Endicott scholarships and grants.

Admissions

Qualified applicants are notified within three or four weeks. Minimum requirements include an official secondary school transcript, a letter of recommendation, essays and SAT or ACT scores. TOEFL scores are required for international students.

Tuition & Fees (1998/99)

In/Out of State Tuition: $13,475
Traditional Housing: $5,008
Traditional Board: $2,147
Fees: $546

Graduation Requirements

Students in the Bachelor of Science degree programs are required to complete 128 credits in the professional and liberal arts.

Escuela Universitaria de Hostelería y Turismo Hotel-Escuela de Sant Pol de Mar / Barcelona

Hotel, Restaurant and Tourism Administration

College: Hotel, Restaurant and Tourism Adm.
Program Enrollment: 180
Degree Awarded: (1) Diplomatura de Turismo (Spanish 3-year Baccalaureate degree), (2) Hotel Administration and H.A.Post degree (Universitat de Girona Diploma, (3) EURHODIP in Management.
Degree Category: Diplomatura in Tourism, Post-Graduate Degree in Hotel Management or CulinaryArts. EURHODIP in Management or Practical in F&B.
Institutional Acreditations: Spanish Government, Universitat de Girona, EURHODIP (Program Accreditation European Hotel Schools) and EFAH (European Foundation od Accreditation of Hotel Schools)
Contact: Mr. Ramon Serra, Manager Director, EUHT StPOL, Ctra. N-II s/n 08395 Sant Pol de Mar / Barcelona (Spain); phone: 34-93 760 0051 Fax: 34-93 760 0985

ESCUELA UNIVERSITARIA DE HOSTELERÍA Y TURISMO
HOTEL-ESCUELA DE SANT POL DE MAR / BARCELONA

Universitat de Girona

Institutional Description

Founded in 1966, The EUHT StPOL is located 45 km. from Barcelona, Spain, next to the Costa Brava, on the Mediterranean Coast. It is the first and oldest Hotel-School in Spain where both the students and faculty members serve the Hotel Gran Sol's guests (the School's full service Hotel).

Program Description

(1) Tourism: 840 lecture hours in each of the 3 years
(2) Hotel Adm.: (1) + 160 lecture hours + 660 practice hours in each of the 3 years (practice in restaurant, front desk and kitchen)
(3) Post-Graduate Degree in H.Adm.: 1 year—440 lecture hous and 440 practice hours.
(4) Post-Graduate Degree in Culinary Arts: 1 year—300 lecture hours and 900 practice hours.

Special Features

The School has 3 computer labs, a library, a video room, a kitchen anphitheather, a wine -sensorial room, three kithchens and two restaurants. A 44-room full service hotel open 365 days a year with tennis court and swimming pool.

Financial Aid and Scholarships

Ask at the Spanish Ambassy or Consulate for Spanish Government aid. The School makes available financial aid plans both officially and privately.

Approximate Tuition and Fees

Tuition per school year

Tourism:	505.000 ptas
Hotel Adm.:	1.534.000 ptas
Post Degree in Hot.Adm.:	1.534.000 ptas
Post Degree in Culinary Arts:	1.550.000 ptas

The School offers meal plan and residence.

Admissions

Interviews are required. The "selectividad" (Spanish University admission test) is required for Tourism and Hotel Administration, unless the candidate has a previous Diplomature or Bachelor in A. or S. Post-Graduate Degree candidates need a Bachelor in A. or S. or Diplomature (Hotel Adm.) or Cooking School Diploma (Culinary Arts).

Graduation Requirements

Graduation requires a successful completion of the theorethical classes and practice, both in-school and in outside companies, as well as the final project.
Tourism Students need a minimum of 360 practice hours in the industry.
Hotel Administration students need a completion of 2 months practice in the industry after the second and third year (apart from the practice in the School's Hotel).

Fairleigh Dickinson University

School of Hotel, Restaurant and Tourism Management

College: New College of General and Continuing Studies
Program Enrollment: 250
Institutional Enrollment: 6,000 undergraduate, 4,000 graduate
Degrees Awarded: Bachelor of Science, Bachelor of Arts in General Studies (Adult Learners), Master of Science in Hospitality Management Studies
Degree Categories: Bachelor in Hotel, Restaurant and Tourism Management; Master in Hospitality Management Studies
Emphases/Specialization: Hotel, Restaurant and Tourism Management areas.
Institutional Accreditation: Middle States Association of Colleges and Schools
Contact: Richard J. Wisch, ed., Director, School of Hotel, Restaurant and Tourism Management, Fairleigh Dickinson University, 1000 River Road, Teaneck, NJ 07666; phone: (201) 692-7271

Institution Description
Fairleigh Dickinson University (FDU) is represented by four units-two in New Jersey, one in Banbury (Wroxton) and one in Tel-Avi Israel. The Teaneck-Hackensack Campus is 10 minutes from Manhattan. Florham-Madison is the former Vanderbilt Estate. Hospitality courses are offered on all campuses.

Program Description
FDU offers a four-year, 129-credit baccalaureate degree program in hotel, restaurant and tourism management. Twelve hundred hours of supervised internships are required. A special adult oriented BA in General Studies with a Specialization in Hospitality (120 credits) is also offered. Two-year transfer students receive liberal credit for courses taken elsewhere.

Professional development is emphasized in a series of courses and extra-curricular activities and projects. Sophomore semester in Wroxton, England is offered. Senior Seminar in Switzerland is required. School has two affiliated hospitality training properties. The 5-diamond Hilton Short Hills and Hamilton Park Executive Conference Center adjacent to Madison, NJ Campus. Unique faculty has extensive management experience in the hospitality industry and instruction emphasizes building management know how.

Financial Aid and Scholarships
Numerous industry and private scholarships are available.

Approximate Tuition and Fees
New or re-admitted full-time students are subject to the new tuition rate of $6,995.00 per semester. All other students are subject to the following per-credit charges:
$454.00 per credit Undergraduate
$522.00 per credit Graduate

Admissions
FDU considers a student's total academic profile when granting admission to the university. All BS candidates are asked to submit an official copy of their SAT or ACT scores along with the application. It is recommended that a student have at least 16 academic units of high school study, including four years of English, at least two years of math, one year of science with a lab, two social sciences and four academic electives. BA in General Studies with a Specialization in Hospitality does not require SAT or ACT scores. Most transfer credits accepted. Life experience credits.

Graduation Requirements
One hundred and twenty-nine credits are required for graduation. Fifty one are in the major and related general education courses. A supervised internship involving 1200 hours of internship training, over three summers, is generally required.

Ferris State University

Food Service/Hospitality Management

College: College of Business
Program Enrollment: 70 associate; 36 bachelor
Institutional Enrollment: 10,00 undergraduate; 110 graduate
Degrees Awarded: Associate of Applied Science; Bachelor of Science
Degree Categories: Associate in Food Service Management; Bachelor in Hospitality Management
Institutional Accreditation: North Central Association of Colleges and Schools
Contact: Anthony Agbeh, Program Director, Ferris State University, Food Service/Hospitality Management, 106 West Commons, 1316 Cramer Circle, Big Rapids, MI 49307-2736; phone (616) 592-2382

Institution Description

The campus is located on the southern edge of Big Rapids, a city with a population of approximately 26,000, including students. It is about 60 miles north of Grand Rapids. The 1993 fall enrollment was 11,000 students. Ferris is an open admissions college. It has 255 academic buildings and 48 housing units on more than 600 acres. Educational offerings are conducted through the Colleges of Allied Health, Arts and Science, Business, Education, Pharmacy, Technology and Optometry.

Program Description

The Hospitality Management Program prepares students for supervisory or midmanagement positions in hospitality industries, with emphasis on hospitality management, marketing and business disciplines. Likewise, the Food Service Management Program prepares graduates for supervisory or midmanagement positions in the food service industry, combining practical and theoretical studies directed specifically to food service in all categories.

Special Features

The program emphasizes hands-on experience through cooperative education. An emphasis is placed on the specialization of developing management skills. A hotel and conference center are located on campus and enhance the program. The capstone course of the Food Service program manages and operates a restaurant. Hospitality Policies and Issues, the Hospitality capstone course, discusses topics relating to the industry through readings, projects, workshops, seminars, etc. The program has active national Advisory Board.

Financial Aid and Scholarships

The university maintains a fully staffed financial aid office, and the Hospitality Management Program offers several scholarships based on both academic achievement and industry experience.

Approximate Tuition and Fees

Tuition and fees: $1,611 per semester for in-state residents; $3,263 per semester for non-residents. Room and board: $1,961.50 per semester.

Admissions

Ferris State University, in keeping with its tradition, is able to admit most mature, serious-minded applicants because of its diverse curricula offerings. This should not be interpreted to mean that any applicant may be admitted to a chosen program. Admission to a particular program depends on the applicant's qualifications for the program.

Graduation Requirements

Overall 2.0 grade point average; College of Business, 2.0 GPA; Food Service/Hospitality Management, 2.0 GPA.

The Florida State University

Hospitality Management

College: College of Business
Program Enrollment: 175 upper division
Institutional Enrollment:
Undergraduate 22,600
Graduate 5,903
Degree Awarded: Bachelor of Science
Degree Category: Hospitality Administration
Emphases/Specializations: Professional Golf Management, Resort and Condominium Management, Management Information Systems, Senior Services Management, European Summer Study

Program Accreditation: American Assembly of Collegiate Schools of Business, The Professional Golfers' Association of America
Institutional Accreditation: Southern Association of Colleges and Schools
Contact: Joseph J. West, Ph.D., Chairman, Department of Hospitality Administration, College of Business, Florida State University, One Champions Way, Suite 4100, Tallahassee, FL 32306-2541; phone 850.644.4787; fax 850.644.5565

Institutional Description

The Florida State University is a Research 1, public, fully accredited, coeducational institution. We recognize that a superior faculty and a student body motivated to achieve are the basis of a quality education. Located in the state capital and in close proximity to some of the most beautiful beaches in the country, students have access to countless activities.

Program Description

Liberal studies, business courses, professional courses and work experience provide an excellent preparation for a career in management. Small classes in the department enable students to develop their full potential in a personal, nurturing environment. Each departmental classroom possesses complete audio-visual presentation equipment and software including internet access.

Special Features

The program continues to attain a 100 percent placement for graduates. FSU's College of Business is consistently ranked as one of the nations top fifty by US News and World Report.

Financial Aid and Scholarships

Financial aid and scholarships are available to certified majors based upon need, academic achievement and industry work experience.

Admissions

Admission to FSU is highly competitive. The program is upper division (juniors/seniors) in the College of Business. Admission is based upon completing 55 credits (including economics, accounting, calculus and business statistics) with a G.P.A. of 2.30.

Tuition and Fees

In-State $66.26 per credit hour
Out-of-State $263.48 per credit hour
Room and Board $4,706 per year

Graduation Requirements

Graduation requires 120 semester hours, the last 30 in residence at FSU. These hours include 36 in liberal studies, 33 in business core and 27 in hospitality. 1000 hours of satisfactory, verifiable industry work experience is also required.

Fort Lewis College

Tourism and Resort Management

College: School of Business Administration
Program Enrollment: 100
Institutional Enrollment: 4,400 undergraduate
Degree Awarded: Bachelor of Arts of Business Administration
Degrees Category: Tourism and Resort Management
Emphases/Specializations: Hotel and Lodging Management; Travel and Tourism Management
Program Accreditation: American Assembly of Collegiate Schools of Business (AACSB)
Institutional Accreditation: North Central Association of Colleges and Schools
Contact: Dr. Roy Cook, Associate Dean, School of Business Administration, Fort Lewis College, 1000 Rim Dr., Durango, CO 81301; phone (970) 2477550; fax (970) 247-7623

Institution Description

Fort Lewis College sits on a mesa overlooking the City of Durango and the 13,000-foot peaks of the La Plata Mountains. On campus, you'll find a relaxed but exciting atmosphere, where students and faculty easily mingle. Making friends will be easy; classes are small and the many student activities on campus provide ample opportunity to get involved.

Program Description

The Tourism and Resort Management option focuses on the career opportunities in the service sector with a special emphasis on tourism and resort management. The use of analytical tools and techniques for decision making, the development of the capacity for critical thought and leadership, and the ability to work with others is emphasized in classes and through internship work experiences.

Special Features

The college operates on a trimester system, allowing students who attend full-time, year-round classes to graduate in as few as 2 2/3 years.

Financial Aid and Scholarships

About 69 percent of the students enrolled at Fort Lewis receive some form of financial assistance for their educations. For more information about financial aid, call toll-free: (800) 233-6731.

Approximate Tuition and Fees

In-state tuition is $819 per trimester; out-of-state, $3969.

Admissions

Fort Lewis College selects for admission those applicants who appear to be best qualified to benefit from and contribute to the educational environment of the college. Prospective students must be either a high school graduate or must have successfully passed the GED test. All freshmen applicants must have the results of their ACT or SAT examination sent to Fort Lewis prior to registration. Transfer applicants are expected to have a cumulative scholastic average of C and be in good standing at college and universities previously attended. Students may apply for admission to Fort Lewis College any time after completion of their junior year of high school.

Graduation Requirements

A student who majors in one of the bachelor of arts degree programs in the School of Business Administration must successfully complete a minimum of 128 credits. In addition to a common body of working knowledge, a student must also complete 16 hours specifically focused on tourism and resort management.

Galway-Mayo Institute of Technology

Program: BA in Hotel and Catering Management; National Diploma in Hotel and Catering Management (Full-time); National Diploma in Hotel and Catering Management (Block-release); National Certificate in Hotel Accommodation and Languages; National Certificate of the NTCB: Professional Cookery; Advanced Kitchen Programmes; Retail Butchery; Supervision of Restaurant Service Operations; Supervision of Bar Service Operations; Hospitality Skills; Advanced Restaurant Service Skills and Bar Service.

College: School of Hotel and Catering Studies

Institutional Enrollment: Undergraduate 1200

Degree Awarded: BA in Hotel and Catering Management;

Degree Categories: Business Administration

Contact: Secretary, School of Hotel and Catering Studies, Galway-Mayo Institute of Technology, Dublin Road, Galway, Ireland. Telephone: +353-91-770555 x2236; Fax No: +353-91-758411; e-mail: liam.hanratty@gmit.ie

Institution Description

The school is one of Ireland's leading hotel schools, offering a wide range of courses in the Hotel, Catering and wider Hospitality industries and comprises two departments. The Department of Hotel and Catering Management concentrates on courses for future managers at all levels – from department head of a small unit to general management of a large hotel or group, whilst the Department of Hotel and Catering Operations offers courses in Professional Cookery, Retail Butchery, Food and Beverage Supervision, Restaurant Operations, Bar Operations, Accommodation Services and Hospitality Skills.

Special Features

All programs involve periods of Industrial attachment

Admissions

Admissions to Courses in BA in Hotel and Catering Management, National Diploma in Hotel and Catering Management (Full-time) and National Certificate in Hotel Accommodation and Languages in the Department of Hotel and Catering Management is through the CAO/CAS National System. Interviews are carried out for the National Diploma in Hotel and Catering Management (Block-Release).

Admission to courses in the Department of Hotel and Catering Operations is through CERT, CERT House, Amiens Street, Dublin 1, Ireland. Telephone: +353-1-855 6555

Tuition & Fees

In-State: Details available from college

Out-of-State: Registrar, Mr Tony Quinlan

Room and Board: telephone: +353-91-770555 x2327

Specialization Area

Hotel and Lodging Management

Restaurant & Foodservice Management

Culinary Arts

The George Washington University

International Institute of Tourism Studies

Institutional Enrollment: 5,000 undergraduate; 14,000 graduate

Degrees Awarded: Bachelor of Business Administration, concentration in Tourism and Hospitality Management; Bachelor of Business Administration/Master of Tourism Administration (5-year program).

Emphases/Specializations: Tourism and Hospitality Management; Individualized Program in Sport Management.

Institutional Accreditation: Middle Atlantic Association of Colleges of Business Administration; Assembly of Collegiate Schools of Business.

Contact: Sheryl Spivack, Coordinator, BBA Degree in Tourism/Hospitality; Dr. Lisa Delpy, Individualized Program in Sport Management. The George Washington University, School of Business Administration and Public Management, 817 23rd Street NW, Washington, DC 20052; phone (202) 994-6281; fax (202) 994-1420; e-mail: iits@gwis.circ.gwu.edu; URL: http://www.gwu.edu/~iits

Institution Description

Founded in 1821, George Washington University (GWU) is a private, nonsectarian, coeducational institution located in the Foggy Bottom district of the nation's capital. GWU has nationally and internationally recognized programs in the sciences, medicine, education, government and business administration, law, and public and international affairs. GWU offers 75 undergraduate degree majors and 34 graduate and professional degree programs.

Program Description

GWU's Tourism and Hospitality BBA program is directed toward understanding and analyzing the forces shaping the tourism and hospitality industry worldwide. The program of study emphasizes the industry's organizational structure, service systems, communication and transportation linkages, legal and regulatory environment, financial aspects, and operational requirements, with an international emphasis on strategic management and marketing approaches. The undergraduate program prepares students for entry-level positions with hotels and resorts; restaurants and food service operations; visitor and convention bureaus; them parks and recreation centers; tour operators, travel management firms, and event sponsors and producers. The five-year dual BBA/MTA program is designed to prepare students for a specialized endeavor in the tourism and hospitality field. Students in the dual program are required to gain at least 500 hours of work experience in the tourism and hospitality industry if they do not have equivalent previous experience.

Special Features

The Tourism and Hospitality Management Program is closely linked to world tourism development through the GWU/World Tourism Organization International Institute of Tourism Studies. Major research emphasis is on policy analysis through the Tourism Policy Forum. GWU's location in Washington, D.C. Provides unique opportunities to obtain practical experience with and exposure to the major tourism and hospitality organizations and associations.

Financial Aid and Scholarships

GWU maintains a financial aid office on campus. There are a variety of financial aid programs available, including loans, scholarships, fellowships, assistantships and work-study.

Approximate Tuition and Fees

Tuition for full-time undergraduate study for the 1996/97 academic year is $19,065. Part-time and non-degree students are charged $625 per credit hour. Registration and student center fees are additional. Some courses may also have additional laboratory or materials fees.

Admissions

The Tourism Administration Program seeks students with strong academic potential, high motivation, and aptitude to do quality work. The school requires acceptable test scores on the SAT/ACT. An interview and/or letter of reference may be required.

Graduation Requirements

At least 120 semester hours are required for successful completion of an undergraduate degree.

Georgia Southern University

Hotel and Restaurant Management

College: Health and Professional Studies
Program Enrollment: 120
Institutional Enrollment: 13, 950
Degree Awarded: Bachelor of Science
Degree Category: Hotel and Restaurant Management
Emphases/Specialization's: None
Program Accreditation: None

Institutional Accreditation: Southern Association of Colleges and Schools,
Contact: Dr. H. Leslie Furr, Director, Hotel and Restaurant Management Program, Georgia Southern University, PO Box 8034, Statesboro, GA, 30460-8034, Phone: 912-681-5617; Fax: 912-681-0276; e-mail: lfurr@gsvms2.cc.gasou.edu

Institution Description

Georgia Southern University, a unit of the University System of Georgia, was founded in 1906 and became a regional university in 1990. The 634-acre campus is located in Statesboro, 50 miles northwest of historic Savannah and 200 miles southeast of Atlanta. The university is within convenient driving distance of Hilton Head Island and Georgia's Golden Isles.

Program Description

The Hotel and Restaurant Management (HRM) program blends management theory and communication skills with a practical "hands-on" approach to introduce leadership and problem solving skills to fledgling hospitality managers.

The HRM curriculum is designed to expose students to a variety of hospitality and tourism industry career opportunities including lodging, restaurant, convention-service and private-club management. Students in the HRM program operate a 50-seat "restaurant/lab" and a commercial kitchen each semester. The program also requires each HRM graduate to complete a semester-long paid internship with an approved hospitality or tourism industry business.

Financial Aid and Scholarships

The University maintains a financial aid office open to all qualified students. The Hotel and Restaurant Management Program also distributes a $2,000 scholarship each year based on academic achievement, service and financial need.

Admissions

Admission to GSU requires graduation from an approved high school, completion of a college preparatory curriculum, and a satisfactory SAT score (480 verbal, 440 math) or ACT score (21 verbal, 19 math). Admission requirements to the HRM Program are identical to the University's requirements.

Tuition and Fees

In state full-time tuition is $1,174.50 per semester
Out of state full-time tuition is $3,784.50 per semester

Specialization Areas

Hotel and Lodging Management
Restaurant & Foodservice Management

Graduation Requirements

Graduation requires the completion of 126 semester hours:
48 Hours Core Curriculum, (required of all students);
18 Hours — Courses Appropriate to the HRM Major;
39 Hours Major Course Requirements (which includes a 12 hour internship requirement); and 21 Hours of Non-major requirements and Electives.

Georgia State University

School of Hospitality Administration

College: J. Mack Robinson College of Business
Program Enrollment: 250 undergraduate; 30 graduate
Institutional Enrollment: 22,800 undergraduate; 6,800 graduate
Degree Awarded: Master of Business Administration
Concentration Category: Hospitality Administration
Institutional Accreditation: Southern Association of Colleges and Schools
Contact: Michael M. Lefever, Director, School of Hospitality Administration, J. Mack Robinson College of Business, Georgia State University, University Plaza, Atlanta, GA 30303-3083, phone: (404) 651-3512, fax: (404) 651-3670

Institution Description

Georgia State University is a public urban research university located in downtown Atlanta. It is the second largest among 78 accredited institutions of higher education in the state. In an average semester, over 2,000 course selections are scheduled between 7 a.m. and 10 p.m., providing one of the most flexible academic time schedules for the working student. Fifty-three percent of the students work full-time and 25 percent work part-time.

Program Description

The program introduces students to management and administrative careers in the following industry segments: lodging; commercial and institutional food service; fair and trade show management; meeting planning; private club management; and tourism.

Special Features

The diversified curriculum is designed to expose students to varied hospitality and tourism industry career opportunities. A required work study component encourages students to diversify their career perspectives. The school offers the most extensive listing of courses in fair and trade show management in the United States.

Financial Aid and Scholarships

The School of Hospitality Administration distributes scholarships and stipends in amounts ranging from $100 to $1,500, based on academic achievement, service and financial need. Graduate students are encouraged to apply for Research Assistant positions, which grant a tuition waiver.

Approximate Tuition and Fees

Matriculation for Georgia residents is $101.00 per semester hour. Nonresident matriculation and tuition is $360.00 per semester hour.

Admissions

Consideration is given to the applicant's academic record, scores on the Graduate Management Admission Test (GMAT), educational background and objectives, experience in business or government and professional activities.

Graduation Requirements:

The Master of Business Administration degree is awarded upon completion of a prescribed program ranging from 39 to 60 semester hours of credit, depending on the academic background of students and on options selected by the students.

Glasgow Caledonian University

BA (Hons) Hospitality Management

Faculty: Faculty of Business
Program Enrollment: 300
Institutional Enrollment: 11,000; Undergraduate: 10,000, Graduate: 1000
Degrees Awarded: BA/BA (Hons) Hospitality Management
Degree Categories: N/A
Emphasis Specializations: HRM and quality management, entrepreneurship,distribution technologies, branding and internationalization.

Program Accreditation: Exemption from HCIMA examinations
Institutional Accreditation: N/A
Contact: Mr Ken Waddell, Programme Leader, Department of Hospitality, Tourism and Leisure Management, Glasgow Caledonian University, 1 Park Drive, Glasgow, G3 6LP, UK. tel 041 337 4321, fax 041 337 4000, email K.A.Waddell@gcal.ac.uk

Institution Description

Glasgow Caledonian University is committed to excellence in learning and teaching at undergraduate, postgraduate and professional levels. The Department of Hospitality, Tourism and Leisure Management is one of the largest providers of academic and commercial research and consultancy services in the UK.

Program Description

The programme seeks to develop management skills and knowledge appropriate to the hospitality industry. Emphasis is placed upon the development of operational and functional management areas across the sector.

Special Features

The program is based on contemporary management issues and is delivered by a young and research active team of academics. Students are able to study associated modules from out Tourism, International Travel and Leisure Management degrees.

Financial Aid and Scholarships

N/A

Admissions

This program operates by entry into year one or direct entry into years two and three. Entry to year two requires a relevant certificate. Entry to year three requires a relevant diploma or associate degree. The Department will consider applications to years two and three from students with non-standard entry qualifications.

Tuition and Fees

University fees for undergraduates is currently £6500.

Specialization Area

N/A

Graduation Requirements

The program requires students to pass six modules of study per academic year.

Golden Gate University

Hotel Restaurant and Tourism Management

College: School of Technology and Industry
Program Enrollment: 120
Institutional Enrollment: 4,000; Undergraduates; 5,500
Degrees Awarded: Bachelor of Science
Degree Categories: Hotel, Restaurant and Tourism Management
Emphases/Specializations: Hotel Management; Restaurant Management; Tourism Management.
Institutional Accreditation: Western Association of Schools and Colleges
Contact: John T. Self, Ph.D., Department Chair, Hotel, Restaurant and Tourism Management, Golden Gate University, 536 Mission Street, San Francisco, CA, 94105; Phone (415) 442-7802; Fax (415) 442-7049

Institutional Description

Founded in 1853, Golden Gate University is the fourth oldest and fifth largest private university in California. Its mission is to prepare students for successful careers in professional fields through programs of exceptional quality that integrate theory with practical experience.

Program Description

The HRTM department offers the finest internships available and an advisory board of Industry leaders available for mentoring. The program is located within the school of Industry and Technology and teaches the full range of managerial skills with a practical industry orientation. All faculty are practitioners in the field.

Special Features

The HRTM program emphasizes working closely with each student on their career advising and placement needs, which is exemplified by a placement rate exceeding 96 percent.

Financial Aid and Scholarships

GGU has extensive financial assistance programs available for students. In addition, the HRTM Program offers several scholarships based on academic achievement, financial need and hospitality industry experience.

Approximate Tuition and Fees

Tuition for both in-state and out-of-state undergraduate classes is $1,059 per course.

Admissions

Admission to Golden Gate University is based on evidence of a student's ability to benefit from its educational programs. Such evidence typically includes the official academic record at other institutions, scores on any required tests and stated educational objectives. TOEFL results and proof of financial support required for international students.

Graduation Requirements

The Bachelor of Science requires the completion of 123 hours. In addition, an internship of 220 hours in the hospitality industry is required.

Grand Valley State University

Department of Hospitality & Tourism Management

College: Division of Mathematics & Science
Program Enrollment: 150
Institutional Enrollment: 16,500 combined
Degrees Awarded: Bachelor of Science or Bachelor of Arts
Degree Categories: Hospitality & Tourism Management
Emphases/Specialization: Food Service Mgmt., Lodging Mgmt., Tourism Mgmt. (Students also may put together a different emphasis of their own with prior advisor and program director approval. Examples of other emphases include Computer Applications, Facilities Mgmt., Health Care, Human Resource Mgmt., Meeting/Conventions Mgmt, Resorts Mgmt., and Clubs Mgmt.)
Institutional Accreditation: North Central Association of Colleges and Schools.
Contact: Richard R. King, Director, Department of Hospitality & Tourism Management, Grand Valley State University, Allendale, Michigan 49401-9403; Phone (616) 895-3118; fax (616) 895-3115; e-mail kingr@gvsu.edu; Internet http//www4.gvsu.edu/~htm/index.htm

Institution Description
GVSU is a public, comprehensive institution which provides educational services to west Michigan. It offers liberal arts and professional education for its students, contributes to the advancement of knowledge, applies that knowledge to societal needs, assists the state in its development, and enriches the cultural life of the citizens of the region.

Program Description
The HTM program prepares students for management positions and leadership roles in the field. It was established in 1977 in response to the need in the region for educational support and aid in preparing qualified managers in the profession. The industry's diversity and rapid expansion provide excellent career opportunities for our graduates.

Special Features
The program is administered and taught by professionals with successful backgrounds in both academia and industry. The program combines directed field experience with a comprehensive interdisciplinary curriculum consisting of courses in the arts and science, business, and hospitality and tourism.

Financial Aid and Scholarships
Over 70% of Grand Valley students qualify for some form of financial aid, including scholarships, grants-in-aid, long-term loans, and student employment.

Admissions
GVSU welcomes qualified students to submit their applications. Admission decisions are selective based on the secondary school record, grades earned, as well as courses selected, the personal data submitted on the application, and ACT or SAT results. The HTM program maintains articulation agreements with several two-year schools which permits the transfer of work completed toward the associate degree in a hospitality- or tourism-related major.

Specialization Area
Hotel & Lodging Mgmt., Restaurant & Foodservice Mgmt., Travel and Tourism Mgmt.

Graduation Requirements
Students must complete a 28-29 credit core of eight courses specifically designed for hospitality and tourism majors, a 12-credit business cognate, and 15-credit in an HTM emphasis area. Students must complete a series of field experience requirements (7-credits) in their area of emphasis. The requirements consists of orientation, work experience, and senior-level management internship. Additional course work required for graduation includes the GVSU General Education and basic skill requirements.

Griffith University

Bachelor of Hotel Management

College: School of Tourism and Hotel Management
Program Enrollment: 450 students (enrolled in Bachelor of Hotel Management)
Institutional Enrollment: Undergraduate 18,126; Graduate: 3,000
Degrees Awarded: Bachelor of Hotel Management; Bachelor of Business in Restaurant and Catering Management; Bachelor of Business in Tourism Management; Bachelor of Business in Club Management; Master of Hospitality Management; Master of Tourism Management
Degree Categories: Tourism and Hospitality Management
Emphases/Specializations: Hotel, Restaurant and Catering , Tourism and Club
Program Accreditation: HCIMA
Institutional Accreditation: State Government of Queensland, Australia
Contact: Dr Beverley Sparks, Head of School of Tourism & Hotel Management, PMB 50, Gold Coast Mail Centre, Qld 9726 Australia

Institution Description

Griffith University is a six campus university located in the South East corner of the State of Queensland, Australia. The University, long noted for its teacher education and innovative programs in both its undergraduate and graduate curricula. The School of Tourism and Hotel Management is located on the Gold Coast (approximately 70 klms South of the Brisbane Campus). The Gold Coast is a national and international tourist destination.

Program Description

Griffith's Tourism and Hospitality Management programs is based on a solid academic foundation consisting of university core components, courses required for a minor in Business Administration with subjects in operations management and administration, computer applications and marketing in addition to hospitality and tourism internships.

Special Features

THM degrees provide five different emphasis areas from which to choose, Tourism, Hotel, Club and Restaurant and Catering Management.

Financial Aid and Scholarships

Both the university financial aid office and private industry make available numerous opportunities for students with scholarships and prizes offered based on academic achievement.

Admissions

Based on academic achievement in formal education or on experience and other achievements. Applications are made through the Queensland Tertiary Admissions Centre.

Tuition and Fees

Undergraduate (HECS) 0$3356-$5593 per year for a full time student, can be paid upfront or deferred.

Graduation Requirements

Graduation requires the successful completion of a combination of subjects totally 240 credit points and includes over 600 hours of industry experience.

Haaga Institute Polytechnic

Hotel, Restaurant and Tourism Management

Program Enrollment: 520 full time, 150 part time; 40 graduate (University of Helsinki)
Institutional Enrollment: 2500
Degrees Awarded: Bachelor; Master of Science
Degree Category: Hotel, Restaurant and Tourism Management
Program Accreditation: HCIMA Hotel Catering and Institutional Management Association, and EFAH European Foundation for the Accreditation of Hotelschool Programmes
Institutional Accreditation: Finnish Ministry of Education
Contact: Mr. Antti Halli, President, or Mr. Teemu Kokko, Vice President, Haaga Institute, School of Hotel, Restaurant and Tourism Management, Pajuniityntie 11, 00320, Helsinki, Finland; phone 358 9 580 7888; fax 358 9 580 78 387; e-mail teemu.kokko@haaga.fi

Institution Description

Haaga Institute is a private, state-subsidized institute with a nationally recognized Bachelor program in hotel, restaurant and tourism management. A Master of Science degree program in hotel and restaurant management is carried out jointly by the Helsinki School of Economics, the University of Helsinki and the Haaga Institute. In addition, the Department of Continuing Education provides supplementary training and education, including MBA and Bachelor of HRTM programs based on part-time studies through distance learning, for persons at different supervisory and managerial levels.

Program Description

Haaga Institute's Bachelor of Hotel, Restaurant and Tourism Management consists of professional business education and practical work experience. Students pursue hospitality industry study in human resource management, tourism, marketing, accounting and finance, law, languages, hotel services, and food and beverage management. In addition, students complete 1,500 hours of practical work experience. The Bachelor program is offered both in Finnish and in English.

Special Features

HRTM students receive hands-on practical experience at the Institute's training hotel—Hotel Haaga—a 120-room establishment with four restaurants and excellent conference facilities.

Financial Aid and Scholarships

There are no tuition fees as the institution is subsidized by the state. Material costs are approx. FIM 1,000 per year.

Admissions

Admission to the Bachelor Program is selective. The completion of a 12-year general education course (A level) and good health are required. Applicants get points for school reports, work experience, personal interview and admission examination. Applications are due in March. Mature and overseas applicants are welcome.

Graduation Requirements

Graduation requires completion of three and a half to four years of fulltime study, which equals 140 credits (one credit equals one week/40 hours of full-time studies.)

Specialization Area

- Hotel and Restaurant Management
- Food Production Management
- Travel and Tourism Management

The Hong Kong Polytechnic University

Hotel and Tourism Management

Program Enrollment: 940
Institutional Enrollment: 13,790 undergraduate; 850 postgraduate
Degree Awarded: Master of Science / Postgraduate Diploma; Bachelor of Arts with Honors; Higher Diploma
Degree Categories: Hotel and Catering Management; Hotel Management; Tourism Management

Institutional Accreditation: The Hong Kong Polytechnic University Accreditation
Contact: Dr. Ray Pine, Head, Department of Hotel & Tourism Management, The Hong Kong Polytechnic University, Hung Hom, Kowloon, Hong Kong, Phone: (852) 2766 6383; Fax: (852) 2362 9362 or (852) 2362 6422

Institutional Description

Founded in 1972, Hong Kong Polytechnic is a large, city-centre institution offering a range of courses, mainly at the degree and postgraduate levels in disciplines such as applied science, textiles, business and management, communication, construction, engineering, and health and health and social studies.

Program Descriptions

The courses are at a management level and are designed to meet the educational requirements of future managers and executives. The philosophy of the department is to provide an education that is both intellectually sound and directly relevant to the hospitality industry.

Special Features

All courses contain an integrated internship so that graduates always study within a related framework. The department has exceptionally well-equipped operational facilities.

Financial Aid and Scholarships

General Polytechnic bursaries and scholarships are available through allocation and competition. Several industry-funded scholarships are awarded through the department as well.

Approximate Tuition and Fees

Approximate tuition and fee: US$5,400 per year (98/99) (In-state)

Admissions

Demand for places in the program is very high, and most successful applicants hold a minimum of one Hong Kong Advanced Level subject (equivalent to the U.K.'s "A" level).

Graduation Requirements

Bachelor degrees are three and four-year integrated programs.

Hotel Institute Montreux (HIM)

Hotel Management

Program Enrollment: 200
Institutional Enrollment: 200
Degrees Awarded: Diploma; Bachelor of Science Degree in Association with the University of South Carolina.
Degree Categories: Hotel Management (three years)
Emphases/Specializations: Hotel Management
Program Accreditation: Educational Institute of American Hotel and Motel Association,
Institutional Accreditation: New England Association of Schools and Colleges Inc. (NEASC), Swiss Hotel Schools Association (ASEH), European Foundation for Accreditation of Hotel School Programmes (EFAH).

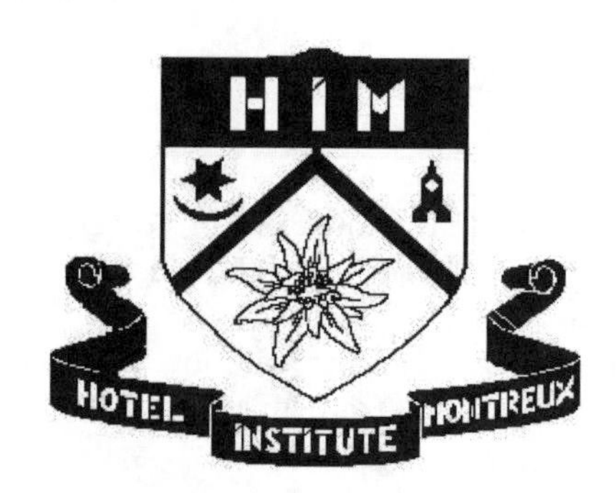

Contact: E.P.O. Dandrieux, Director, Hotel Institute Montreux, 15 Avenue des Alpes, 1820 Montreux, Switzerland; phone ++41 21 963-7404; fax ++41 21 963-8016; e-mail Web page http://www.him.ch

Institution Description
Hotel Institute Montreux (HIM) is an English-speaking hotel management institution situated in Montreux, Switzerland, one hour by train from Geneva airport. In principle, all programs are residential, but non-residential students are accepted. HIM's three year Hotel Management Program is the major program.

Program Description
JOINT DEGREE PROGRAM: HIM offers a 3-year Bachelor's Degree in association with the University of South Carolina, consisting of 2.5 years in Switzerland (including two internships), and two semesters at University of South Carolina on Hilton Head Island. The graduate receives the HIM and AH&MA Diplomas, and a Bachelor of Science from USC.

Special Features
The practical workload is predominant in the first year. Swiss or American trained faculty, specialized kitchens, dining rooms, library, computer lab and classrooms offer an ideal working environment.

Financial Aid and Scholarships
As with all Swiss hotel institutes, HIM does not offer scholarships. Students are permitted to settle fees on an instalment basis.

Admissions
All of HIM's programs require a high school education as well as an excellent command of the English language. Students come from over 30 countries. HIM has representatives in most of these countries who interview students and screen admissions for HIM.

Tuition and Fees
In-state $10,000
Out-of-State $10,000
Room and Board $3,000
Other Fees $2,000 deposit for books, uniform, insurance, etc.

Specialization Area
Hotel & Lodging Management

Graduation Requirements
All subjects are obligatory. Continuous assessment takes the form of progress tests or quizzes, and final exams are required in all subjects. Maximum grades are 100 percent, minimum passing grades are 70 percent overall. A maximum of two failures in minor subjects is allowed.

Hotelschool The Hague, International Institute of Hospitality Management

Hotel and Business Administration

Degrees Awarded: Bachelor of Hotel Administration
Degree Categories: Hotel and Business Administration
Emphases/Specializations: International Hotel and Restaurant Management; Institutional Management; Travel and Tourism Management; Conference Management

Contact: Dr. Ewout The. Cassee, President of the Board of Directors, Hotelschool The Hague, Institute of Hospitality Management, 2 Brusselselaan, 2587 AH The Hague, The Netherlands; Phone (31) 703512481; Fax (31) 70-3512155; Internet: http://www.hdh.nl

Institution Description

The school was founded in 1929 by the Dutch hotel employer's organization. The school is a private foundation, but is subsidized by the Dutch government. Besides the four-year degree course taught in Dutch and English, the school offers a one-year diploma course, a one-month executive program of hospitality management, and an advanced management course in English.

Program Description

The course is divided into periods of each 8 weeks. The students work in small groups, the teacher being their coach. Much is being done by using Internet and e-mail. Each student has his own personal laptop. The four-year program is a balance between theory and practice. Much attention is paid to foreign languages and management skills. Two periods of industrial placement are included in the program. At least one of these trainee periods is spent abroad. (Europe, United States, Far East, South America, etc.)

Special Features

The first year, students live together in the Students Hostel. This is an important part of the study; they learn how to live together, work together, and study together 24 hours a day. The school operates like an actual hotel/restaurant, with four restaurants and three kitchens. In the language laboratory the students learn at least three foreign languages.

Financial Aid and Scholarships

For Dutch students, the governmental system of study finance is applicable. Some scholarships are available for international students. EC students get a refund of the tuition fee.

Admissions

Due to the large number of applicants, the Hotelschool The Hague applies a strict admission standard. Candidates must have: International Baccalaureate/Grammarschool (GCE-A level) or any other qualifications at the university level, and a good command of the English language (all candidates will have to pass an entry test). For subjects such as accounting and economics, there are no formal admission requirements, although a basic knowledge of these subjects is strongly recommended. Due to a limited number of places, we have admission interviews with applicants in various European countries. Applicants are required to satisfy the admission panel with regard to their suitability for the course in terms of motivation, attitude, and enthusiasm for a career in international hotel management.

Howard University

Hospitality Management

Program Enrollment: 100
Institutional Enrollment: 9,565 undergraduate; 2,940 graduate
Degree Awarded: Bachelor of Business Administration—Hospitality Management
Degree Category: Bachelor of Business Administration—Hospitality Management
Institutional Accreditation: Middle States Association of Schools and Colleges; American Assembly of Collegiate Schools of Business
Contact: Dr. Andrew E. Raschid, Director, Director, Hospitality Management Program, School of Business, Howard University, 2600 Sixth St., NW, Washington, DC 20059; phone (202) 806-1535; fax (202) 797-6393; e-mail: ARASCHID@HOWARD.EDU

Institutional Description
Founded in 1867, Howard University is a coeducational, private institution of higher learning located in the nation's capital, Washington, D.C. Howard consists of 18 schools and colleges, offers programs in a variety of disciplines, including baccalaureate and graduate programs in liberal arts and sciences. The university also offers degrees in various professional programs and in health sciences.

Program Description
The Hospitality Management program is housed in the Management Department, School of Business. The clear and vital mission of the program is to prepare graduates for entry-level management positions. The program integrates a variety of university courses in the humanities, social science, the science disciplines and combines a strong business administration curriculum with the specifics of the hospitality industry. The Howard University Hotel, located on campus, serves as a training facility for hospitality students. Other training opportunities are available from numerous hospitality facilities in Washington, DC and throughout the United States.

Financial Aid and Scholarships
There are a variety of financial aid programs, including scholarships, loans, grants, part-time employment, and work study opportunities.

Approximate Tuition and Fees
Tuition for full-time students is US$8,105 annually. There is a one-time application fee of $25.

Admissions
Students must be graduates of accredited high schools with acceptable high school records and SAT or ACT scores.

Graduation Requirements
Each candidate for the degree must complete a total of 128 credit hours as follows: 55 general education requirements; 46 business core requirements; and 27 hospitality management requirements.

Special Features
The Hospitality Management internship allows students to acquire outstanding hands-on experience, and provide monitored, coordinated and structured management development sequence. The HUHMA student organization is highly active in local hospitality activities.

Indian Institute of Hotel Management

Run by the Taj Group of Hotels, India

Program Enrollment: 60
Degree Category: Hotel Management
Contact: Mr. Ramesh Takulia, Principal, Indian Institute of Hotel Management, Rauza Bagh, AURANGABAD PIN-431 001. Maharashtra, INDIA; phone: 0091-240-381104, 381113; fax: 0091-240-38112; e-mail: iihmtaj@bom4.vsnl.net.in

Institution Description

The Indian Institute of Hotel Management, located in Aurangbad, a State of Maharashtra, under the aegis of Maulana Azad Educational Trust, has been modelled on the lines of some of the leading Hotel Management Institutions of the world and has a hotel of the Taj Group attached to it to provide on-the-job training as a part of the course curriculum. The Indian Institute of Hotel Management is run with the expertise of the Taj Group of Hotels. The students come from all over the country and live on campus, as this is a residential course.

Program Description

The curriculum is so designed that at the end of 3-years, the students can take up junior managerial positions and it will facilitate earlier progression to more senior roles. The program includes theory sessions in classrooms, practical training in well-equipped labs and on-the-job training in the attached hotel of the Taj Group. For practical training, the Institute has various training kitchens, training restaurants, front office lab, housekeeping lab, and computer lab, in addition to a well equipped, self-learning center. The 3-year program includes accommodation management; food & beverage management; strategic management; human resources management; sales and marketing management; computers; hotel engineering and system management; general management and administration; hotel accounting & financial management, and computers.

Special Features

As an integral part of the program and the course design, the hotel operated by the Taj Group of Hotels, is managed primarily by the students, who work in all operation areas covering all shifts of work.

Approximate Tuition and Fees

Tuition is US $750; lab and welfare fees US $360; and room and board fees US $720 per year.

Admissions

Those who have passed the 12 years of schooling (A-levels) or passed an equivalent examination with a minimum of 50% marks in aggregate. The admissions are open to students up to 22 years of age, relaxable up to 24 years of age for those who have work experience of a minimum of two years in the hospitality industry. On the basis of written examination, group discussions and personal interviews are conducted in different cities in India.

Graduation Requirements

The students who successfully complete the eon-the-job training, project and assignment work, and pass the examinations conducted at the end of each year are awarded a Baccalaureate Degree by the University of Huddersfield, United Kingdom.

Indiana University of Pennsylvania

Hotel, Restaurant, and Institutional Management

College: College of Health and Human Services
Program Enrollment: 275
Institutional Enrollment: 13,000 undergraduate; 1,398 graduate
Degree Awarded: Bachelor of Science
Degree Categories: Hotel, Restaurant, and Institutional Management
Emphases/Specializations: Restaurant and Food service Management; Lodging Management
Institutional Accreditation: Middle States Association of Colleges and Schools; National Council for Accreditation of Teacher Education
Program Accreditation: Accreditation Commission for Programs in Hospitality Administration (ACPHA)
Contact: Jeffrey A. Miller, Chairperson, Department of HRIM, Ackerman Hall, Indiana University of Pennsylvania, Indiana, PA 15705; Phone (724) 357-4440

Institution Description

Located 50 miles northeast of Pittsburgh, Indiana University of Pennsylvania (IUP) is Pennsylvania's fifth largest university. It includes six colleges and two schools and offers graduate programs in professional and applied areas as well as five programs at the doctoral level. More than 100 majors are available within 45 academic departments.

Program Description

IUP's Hospitality Management Program began over three decades ago and has developed into the Bachelor of Science in Hotel, Restaurant, and Institutional Management (HRIM). Students gain a strong business backgwournd, take general HRIM courses, concentrate in hotel management or restaurant and food service, and complete a 900-hour work experience/internship.

Special Features

IUP is one of 300 colleges and universities included in this yar's edition of *Barron's Best Buys in College Education.* IUP offers HRIM students a faculty with an array of industry experience, state-of-the-art food production and service operation, modern classroom and computer facilities, and one of Pennsylvania's largest internship programs.

Financial Aid and Scholarships

More than 80 percent of IUP students currently receive financial assistance in the form of student employment, loans, grants or scholarships.

Approximate Tuition and Fees

In-state tuition is $2,954 per year; out-of-state, $7,352 per yar. Room and board costs are $2,982 per year. Annual fees amount to $585.

Admissions

Admission to IUP is determined by the applicant's high school record, scores from the Scholastic Aptitude Test (SAT) or American College Test (ACT), recommendations from high school guidance counselors, an evaluation of extracurricular activities, and any other information helpful in judging the applicant's ability to successfully complete the academic program.

Graduation Requirements

Graduation requires 124 credit hours, which includes 54 credits from liberal studies and 60 credits within the major. A 900-hour work experience and internship is also required.

International College of Hotel Management

International Hotel Management

College: Swiss Hotel Association
Program Enrollment:300
Institutional Enrollment:300
Degrees Awarded: Bachelor of International Hotel Management
Degree Category: International Hotel Management
Diploma Category: Diplôme Culinaire d'Hotelier of Le Cordon Bleu; Swiss Hotel Association Diploma of International Hotel Management
Certificate Category: Certificate IV in Hospitality (International Hotel Operations)
Emphases/Specializations: Food & Beverage; Front Office and Housekeeping Departments; Wine Studies; Information Technology Management for Hospitality Businesses

Institutional Accreditation: Commonwealth Register of Institutions and Courses for Overseas Students
Contact: Gerald J Lipman, Chief Executive, ICHM, GPO Box 249, Adelaide 5001, South Australia; Telephone (08) 8223 6039; Facsimile (08) 8224 0984; E-mail: glipman@ichm.com.au; http://www.ichm.cm.au

Institution Description
The International College of Hotel Management (ICHM) is the Asia-Pacific Basin campus of the Swiss Hotel Association (SHA) and the only hotel management school in the world to incorporate Diplôme Culinaire d'Hotelier of Le Cordon Bleu. The training facilities and on-campus accommodation incorporates the very best in international student housing.

Program Description
A 3-year Bachelor of International Hotel Management, inclusive of 3-year Swiss Hotel Association Diploma. Final 30-week Degree program can be undertaken on campus or through distance learning (both paper based and on-line)

Special Features
Each of the first three years consists of 20 weeks of on-campus study and 20 weeks of practical experience (Stage) in a hotel or other hospitality establishment.

Financial Aid and Scholarships
ICHM provides a number of entry scholarships for both Australian and overseas applicants.

Admissions
Applicants are required to be 17 years and completed Year 12 within Australia, or the equivalent in overseas countries, US High School Certificate. The required level of fluency in English is IELTS 6.5 (TOEFL 575). Degree entrants must have completed a suitable 3-year hospitality course.

Tuition & Fees
A$19,500 per year (1999) which includes board and lodgings for 20-22 weeks, tuition and exams, student learning materials and texts and professional uniforms. The fees also include full medical and accident insurance cover for students who are not Australian residents.

Specialization Area
Hospitality; international hotel management; Cordon Bleu; food & beverage; wine studies; tourism development and management; gastronomy

Graduation Requirements
To graduate with the SHA Diploma, students must have completed three 20-week semesters on campus; minimum of 1400 hours Stage and second language competency. To graduate with Degree, students must have Diploma (or equivalent) and pass 8 subjects in the 30-week period (or longer if taken part-time/distance mode)

International Hotel Management Institute, Lucerne (IMI)

Hotel and Tourism Management

College: College of Hotel Management
Program Enrollment: 380
Degree Awarded: Bachelor of Arts in International Hotel and Tourism Management, Higher Diploma and Postgraduate Diploma in Hotel and Tourism Management
Degree Category: Hotel, Catering and Tourism Management
Program Accreditation: Manchester Metropolitan University, England
Institutional Accreditation: Department of Education of the state of Nidwalden, Switzerland.
Contact: Admissions Department, IMI Kestanienbaum, Seeacherweg 1, CH - 6047 Kastanienbaum, Switzerland; phone: + 41 41 340 12 66; fax: +41 41 340 12 82; e-mail: registrar@imi-luzern.ch; http://www.imi-luzern.ch

Institution Description

Established in 1990 by three experienced hotel management school operators. The International Hotel Management Institute, Lucerne is already one of the best known of many English speaking hotel management schools in Switzerland. The curriculum combines modern management techniques with traditional Swiss "hotelier." It is a co-educational school with an International group of students.

Program Description

The institute offers a comprehensive broadly based program which can also be taken in one year modules e.g. Food and Beverage Management or Accommodation Services Management. Degree holders may proceed to several universities in USA, UK, Europe, Australia and New Zealand where they may complete a Masters degree in one further year.

Special Features

The high staff student ratio ensures individual attention. Paid internships are provided by the institute. The staff are all highly qualified professionals. In addition to its full-time staff, IMI has many visiting professors from around the world.

Financial Aid and Scholarships

Fees may be paid in installments.

Approximate Tuition and Fees

The fee is all inclusive and consists of tuition and full board in a good quality hotel (some single rooms available). Each room has a television and a refrigerator. Books and medical insurance are not included. Diploma Fee is approximately US$12,500, and the Degree and Postgraduate fee is approximately US$14,000.

Admissions

The Admissions Dept. Expects applicants to have the basic qualifications for university entry in their own country, and are also influenced by recommendations from former teachers. Mature students otherwise not qualified are considered on their merits.

Graduation Requirements

The full program requires 4 academic years (the first 3 lasting five months and the last one lasting six months) in addition to the student completing at least 12 months internship. Year one requires 600 hours of practical theory classes including a language (French or German). Year two requires 520 hours. Year three requires 500 hours consisting of lectures, case studies and projects, and Year four requires 280.

Iowa State University

Hotel, Restaurant, and Institution Management

College: Family And Consumer Sciences
Program Enrollment: 275 undergraduate; 20 graduate
Institutional Enrollment: 20,000 Undergraduate; 4,000 graduate
Degrees Awarded: Bachelor of Science; Master of Science; Doctor of Philosophy
Degree Categories: Hotel, Restaurant, and Institution Management
Emphases/Specializations: None
Program Accreditation: Accreditation Commission for Programs in Hospitality Administration (ACPHA)
Institutional Accreditation: North Central Association of Colleges and Schools
Contact: Mary B. Gregoire, PhD, Department ChairHotel, Restaurant, and Institution Management11 MacKay Hall, Iowa State University, Ames, IA 50011-1120; phone 515/294-1730; fax 515/294-8551; e-mail mgregoir@iastate.edu

Institution Description

Iowa State University (ISU) is a public, land-grant university with nationally recognized programs in agriculture, engineering, education, family and consumer sciences, business, and the sciences. ISU enjoys a strong residence hall system, which houses approximately 9,000 students, and an excellent Greek system with 32 fraternities and 16 sororities.

Program Description

The Hotel, Restaurant, and Institution Management (HRIM) undergraduate program is planned to provide a balanced curriculum of general education, business, HRIM professional, and elective courses. Instruction includes both theoretical and hands-on experiences. Master's and doctorate programs are flexible and allow an emphasis in either hotel, restaurant, or foodservice systems management.

Special Features

Students receive hands-on experiences in the program's Tearoom and other food and lodging facilities. All faculty have industry experience; tenured/tenure-track faculty have earned doctorates.

Financial Aid and Scholarships

ISU's financial aid office maintains scholarship and work-study programs. HRIM and the Family And Consumer Sciences College offer numerous scholarships.

Admissions

Upper-half high school rank or an ACT score of at least 24; 2.0 cumulative GPA for transfer students. High school courses should include: English (4 yr); algebra/geometry (3 yr); science (3 yr), including two of the following: biology, chemistry and physics (3 yr); social science (studies) (2 yr) with US history (1 yr) and US government (1 semester).

Tuition and Fees

In-state tuition — $1,333; out-of-state tuition — $4,472; Room and board (1997-98) — $3,958/yr double occupancy, full board plan

Specialization Area

Hotel and Lodging Management, Restaurant and Foodservice Management

Graduation Requirements

Graduation requirements for the Bachelor of Science degree include successful completion of 128.5 semester credits.

James Madison University

Hospitality & Tourism Management Program

Program Enrollment: 150
Institutional Enrollment: 14,000
Degrees Awarded: Bachelor of Business Administration (BBA)
Degree Categories: Hospitality & Tourism Management Program
Emphasis/Specializations: Food & Beverage Management; Lodging Management; Meeting Planning & Events Management; Tourism & Entertainment Management
Program Accreditation: American Assembly of Collegiate Schools of Business (AACSB)
Institutional Accreditation: Southern Association of Colleges and Schools
Contact: Dr. Reg Foucar-Szocki, Director, JW Marriott Professor of Hospitality Management, James Madison University, College of Business, MSC 0205, Harrisonburg, VA 22807, Phone (540) 568-3224, Fax (540) 568-2754, Website: http://www.jmu.edu

Institution Description
Established in 1908, James Madison University (JMU) is a comprehensive university, which offers a wide range of undergraduate and graduate programs in liberal arts, fine arts, the sciences, business, education, communications, and nursing. Several national publications have cited JMU as one of the best universities in the United States for undergraduates. JMU is also listed in several guides to America's most prestigious colleges and universities.

Program Description
The Hospitality program at JMU is about helping each student become the very best hospitality professional possible. A dedicated faculty working with a dynamic advisory board strives to make JMU the premier BBA program in hospitality management. A solid foundation in General Education is complemented with the basics in business and given a hospitality twist to develop tomorrow's leader who not only understands the functional areas of business and is able to apply this understanding to the industry.

Special Features
Building on JMU's strength as one of the finest undergraduate universities in the nation, the HTM Program places the highest priority on working one-on-one with students in HTM courses and laboratories, professional and career advising, placement in internships, and career planning and placement.

Financial Aid & Scholarships
The JMU financial aid office makes available numerous opportunities, and the HTM Program offers several scholarships based on both academic achievement and hospitality industry experience.

Admissions
Admission to JMU is highly competitive. The Admissions Committee is most interested in: the quality of the applicant's high school program of study, performance on the SAT. Recommendations provided by the applicant's counselors and teachers. The depth of involvement in extracurricular activities which indicate leadership, organizational and problem-solving skills.

Tuition & Fees
In-State - $4,256; Out-of-State - $9,256; Room & Board - $5,008

Specialization Areas
Food & Beverage Management; Lodging Management; Meeting Planning & Events Management; Tourism & Entertainment Management

Graduation Requirements
Graduation requires the successful completion of 120 semester hours and includes:
40 hours of General Education; 40 hours of College of Business courses; 24 hours of Hospitality courses
16 hours of electives selected in consultation with student's advisor.

Johnson & Wales University

College of Culinary Arts/The Hospitality College

Program Enrollment: 4,601 in College of Culinary Arts; 2,733 in The Hospitality College; at campuses in Rhode Island, South Carolina, Florida, Virginia*, and Colorado*
Institutional Enrollment: 11,599
Degrees Awarded: Certificate; Associate in Applied Science; Associate in Science; Bachelor of Science; Master of Business Administration; Master of Arts; Doctor of Education (Ed.D.)
Degree Categories: (see Associate Degrees section for associate degrees offered) Baking & Pastry Arts; Culinary Arts; Culinary Nutrition; Food Marketing; Food Service Entrepreneurship; Food Service Management; Hospitality Management; Hospitality Sales & Meeting Management; Hotel Restaurant/Institutional Management; International Hotel & Tourism Management; Sports/Entertainment/Event Management; Travel-Tourism Management; Travel-Tourism Marketing
Institutional Accreditation: Johnson & Wales University is accredited by the New England Association of Schools and Colleges, Inc., and is accredited as a senior college by the Accrediting Council for Independent Colleges and Schools. In addition, the hospitality programs at the Providence, R.I. campus are accredited by the Accreditation Commission for Programs in Hospitality Administration.

Contact: Ms. Caroline A. Cooper, Dean, The Hospitality College; Chef Jean-Michel Vienne, Dean, College of Culinary Arts; Johnson & Wales University, 8 Abbott Park Place, Providence, RI 02903; phone Dean Cooper (401) 598-1475; Dean Vienne (401) 598-1130; South Carolina campus (800) 868-1522; Florida campus (800) 232-2433; Virginia campus (800) 277-2433; Colorado campus (970) 476-2993

Institutional Description

Johnson & Wales is a private, coeducational institution offering practical career education in food service, hospitality, business and technology. J&W's associate, bachelor's and graduate degree programs prepare students to enter the work world. Technology and graduate programs are offered at the Providence campus only.

Program Description

J&W hospitality and culinary programs offer an opportunity for students to combine academics with hands-on training in one of the University's three hotel/food service properties. Students take courses in their major during their first year. A four-day school week allows students to put academics into practice on the long weekends.

Special Features

Johnson & Wales University's upside down curriculum and hands-on training facilities allow students to gain experience in their fields before graduation. Corporate partners, including American Express Travel, Radisson and Marriott, also give students experience. J&W boasts a 98% graduate employment rate within 60 days of graduation.

Financial Aid and Scholarships

J&W has a fully staffed financial aid and planning office to assist qualified students in meeting educational expenses by putting a financial aid package together for them. J&W awarded over $25 million in institutional aid to students at all campuses last year.

Approximate Tuition and Fees

Undergraduate tuition for the culinary program at J&W's Providence, R.I. campus for 1999-2000 is $15,840; hospitality program $13,824. Room & Board ranges from $5,829 to $7,050; general and orientation fees are $525 and $140, respectively. Tuition varies at other campuses and in the Alan Shawn Feinstein Graduate School. J&W's Guaranteed Tuition Plan freezes tuition at the first year enrollment rates.

Admissions

Admission to J&W requires a high school diploma or its equivalent. Although not required, the University encourages applicants to submit SAT or ACT test scores. An applicant's motivation and interest in succeeding in a chosen field are also given strong consideration.

Graduation Requirements

Degree candidates must successfully complete the required number of courses and/or term hours as prescribed in the various curricula with a minimum average of 2.0. All students graduating with an associate degree are eligible to continue on to a four-year degree program.

**Culinary Arts program only.*

Johnson State College

Hospitality & Tourism Management

College: Business/Economics
Program Enrollment: 100
Institutional Enrollment: 1,591
Degree Awarded: Bachelor of Arts
Degree Category: Hospitality & Tourism Management
Program Accreditation: none
Institutional Accreditation: New England Association of Schools and Colleges
Contact: Reed Fisher; Hospitality & Tourism Management; Johnson State College; 337 College Hill; Johnson, VT 05656; 802-635-1301 (phone); 802-635-1248 (fax); fisherr@badger.jsc.vsc.edu (e-mail); www.jsc.vsc.edu (web site)

Institutional Description

Established in 1828, Johnson State College is a rural, coeducational institution located just minutes north of the Stowe resort area in north-central Vermont. The mission of the College is to provide a learning community characterized by active engagement in teaching and learning, by high standards of academic work and human relations, and by seriousness of purpose. We endeavor to provide our students with the skills, knowledge, and understanding which are the basis of productive employment.

Program Description

The Hospitality & Tourism Management program has been completely redesigned to meet the changing needs of the industry. The program combines course work with extensive field trips and internships in order to fully integrate academics with industry experience. Beginning with the freshman year, over 900 hours of experiential learning are woven throughout the student's four years of study. Areas of specialization include: lodging and resort management, food and beverage management, and tourism management.

Special Features

The HTM program has developed a state-of-the-art technology lab. The HTM lab provides the latest in property management systems, restaurant management systems, menu design software, lodging and restaurant simulation software, and access to the Internet. Our Hospitality Association is an extremely active student organization. The HA plans a trip to the International Hotel Show in New York City every fall semester as well as a spring semester tour of a variety of hospitality properties. The HTM program also sponsors a Career Fair for the JSC student body.

Financial Aid and Scholarships

Financial aid at Johnson State College consists of grants or scholarships, self-help in the form of low-interest loans, and college employment in the Federal Work Study Program. Specific HTM scholarships may also be available.

Tuition and Fees

Tuition for the 1998/1999 academic year is $3,924 for in-state residents, $9,192 for out-of-state residents, and $5,904 for NEBHE (a New England Regional student program) eligible residents. Room, board, and additional fees are approximately $3,050 per semester.

Admissions

No formula is used to determine who is admitted to Johnson State College. Admission counselors consider a range of information about each individual candidate and carefully evaluate each student's academic preparation as reflected by transcripts, course selection, letters of recommendation, SAT or ACT scores, and class rank. They also look closely at personal qualities such as motivation, ambition, and individualism as demonstrated through involvement in extracurricular activities and community service.

Graduation Requirements

Graduation requires the successful completion of 120 semester hours and includes: 40 hours from the General Education Core Curriculum; 61 hours of HTM courses; and 19 hours of electives selected in consultation with the student's advisor.

Specialization Area

Hotel and Lodging Management; Restaurant and Food Service Management; Travel and Tourism Management

Kansas State University

Hotel and Restaurant Management

College: Human Ecology
Program Enrollment: 185
Institutional Enrollment: 17,500 undergraduate and 3,000 graduate
Degrees Awarded: Bachelor of Science
Degree Categories: Hotel and Restaurant Management
Emphases/Specializations: Generalist Program in Foodservice and Lodging Management
Program Accreditation: Accreditation Commission for Programs in Hospitality Administration
Institutional Accreditation: North Central Association of Colleges and Schools
Contact: Patrick Pesci, Director, Hotel and Restaurant Management Program, 103 Justin Hall, Kansas State University, Manhattan KS 66506-1404; phone (785) 532-2210; fax (785) 532-5522; e-mail pesci@humec.ksu.edu; http://www.ksu.edu/humec/hrimd/hrimd.htm

Institution Description

Kansas State University (KSU), one of the first land-grant institutions, is comprised of nine colleges and offers more than 200 undergraduate majors and options and advanced degrees in 107 areas. Faculty at KSU are dedicated to excellence in teaching, student advising, research, extension education and scholarly achievement.

Program Description

The Hotel and Restaurant Management (HRM) Program provides students with a broad liberal education, an understanding of business administration, a solid foundation of professional hotel and foodservice courses, and hands-on experience in the hospitality industry. A 400-hour field experience for academic credit is required.

Special Features

Extensive hands-on experience in commercial and quantity food production, practicums in hotels and restaurants, and applications of foodservice and hotel management computer software.

Financial Aid and Scholarships

Financial aid is available. Scholarship support is available from hospitality organizations, professional associations, members of the hotel and restaurant industry, and the KSU Foundation.

Admissions

Students meeting Kansas high school graduation requirements can enter the HRM Program. Other prospective students must take the ACT or have a 2.0 GPA from another university. Work experience in the hospitality industry, cultural experiences, and travel are encouraged.

Tuition and Fees

In-State Tuition - $68.05/credit hour; Out-of-State Tuition- $283/credit hour; Campus fees - $64 for first credit hour, $17/credit hour up to 12 hours; total of $251 for 12 or more credit hours

Specialization Area

Hotel and Lodging Management; Restaurant and Foodservice Management

Graduation Requirements

Graduation requires completion of 120 semester hours, including 54-55 hours of general education, 15 hours of business courses (minor in business), 14-15 hours of electives, six hours of support courses in human ecology, 43 hours in hotel and restaurant management, and 800 hours of hotel and restaurant work experience.

Kent State University

Hospitality Food Service Management

College: Fine and Professional Arts
Program Enrollment: 75
Institutional Enrollment: 26,350; undergraduate; 4,750 graduate
Degree Awarded: Bachelor of Science
Emphases/Specialization: Food Service Management; Restaurant Management
Institutional Accreditation: North Central Association of Colleges and Schools
Contact: Jeannie Sneed, PhD, RD, Director and Associate Professor, Hospitality Food Service Management, P.O. Box 5190, Kent, OH 44242-0001; phone (330) 672-2197; fax (330) 672-2194; jsneed@kent.edu

Institution Description

Kent State University is dedicated to providing a superior university education, to advancing significant research and creative activities, and to furthering the fulfillment of societal goals. The oldest state university in Northeast Ohio, Kent reflects the advantages of the vital cultural and commercial region in which its eight campuses are located. Kent offers an extensive array of associate's, baccalaureate, master's, and doctoral degrees.

Program Description

The baccalaureate degree program in Hospitality Food Service Management (HFSM) at Kent State University prepares graduates for management careers in food service and related areas. Liberal, technical, and professional education, with an emphasis on business management, integrates theory with practical application to prepare students for future career demands.

Special Features

The HFSM program has a close working relationship with Kent Food Services, is guided by an industry advisory board, and has many industry ties that provide internship opportunities and 100% job placement.

Financial Aid and Scholarships

Kent's Financial Aid Office provides assistance for students seeking funding to support their college education. The HFSM program offers 3-4 annual scholarships and two scholarships for students to participate in the Salute to Excellence. There also are scholarship opportunities in the School.

Admissions

The HFSM program has a pre-professional and a professional phase. The preprofessional phase consists of the first two years and emphasizes basic food production and management. Students admitted into the professional phase have completed four HFSM courses; attained the first aid certificate, CPR certificate, and the Ohio Certified Manager status; and documented the completion of at least 400 hours of food service work experience.

Tuition and Fees

In-state: $4,660 per year; out-of-state: $9,320; room and board: $4,210 to $5,062 per year; some course fees are required

Graduation Requirements

Students are required to complete a total of 121 semesters hours for graduation, with an overall grade point average of 2.0 and a 2.25 in the major. A semester long industry internship is required.

Leeds Metropolitan University

School of Tourism and Hospitality Management

Program Enrollment: 1,200
Institutional Enrollment: 15,000
Degrees Awarded: MSc Hospitality Management; BA (Hons) International Hospitality Business Management; BA (Hons) Events Management; BA (Hons) International Tourism Management; BSc (Hons) Licensed Retail Management; BA (Hons) Service Sector Management; BA (Hons) Retailing. All courses run on a full-time or part-time basis for a period of two, three or four years; these are available by a distance learning mode of study.
Degree Categories: MRes/MPhil or PhD research degrees may be obtained after successful completion of written theses on selected related topics in Hospitality Management, Events Management Tourism Management and Services Management. Students may study full-time or part-time between two and five years

Contact: Vicky Harris, Head of School for Tourism & Hospitality Management, Leeds Metropolitan University, Calverley Street, Leeds LS1 3HE; phone 44 113 2835937; fax 44 113 2833111; email V.Harris@lmu.ac.uk

Institutional Description

Leeds Metropolitan University has a history which goes back over 100 years, to the nineteenth century colleges from which it grew. Today it is one of Britain's largest universities, with an enviable graduate employment record. In a recent student survey, Leeds was voted the most popular University city in the United Kingdom.

Program Description

All the courses in the School of Tourism and Hospitality Management are integrated within a modular framework. Mature and non-standard entry students can apply for accreditation of prior learning.

Programs can be studied by distance learning and Continuing Professional Development plays a large part in the work of the School, providing courses for industry, graduates and students. In addition to its undergraduate provision, the School also offers opportunities for studying for Masters by Research (MA/MSc), MPhil and PhD degrees in a wide range of topics. Students registering for any of these receive an opportunity to complete a University Award (Post Graduate Certificate in Research Methodology before undertaking their project.

Special Features

Both the BA (Hons) International Hospitality Business Management and BA (Hons) International Tourism Management courses prepare students for management careers in a multi-cultural and international industry. This is achieved by instilling an awareness and sensitivity to cultural diversity through the exploration of other cultures and the opportunity to study languages.

The BA (Hons) Events Management offers students an exciting exploration into the world of events management, opening the doors to management careers in this vibrant and rapidly expanding international market. Students are actively encouraged to take advantage of our many exchange programmes.

The BA (Hons) Hospitality Business Management degree, top-up programme, can be studied by distance learning mode of study and is ideal for Managers working in the industry who have studied up to diploma level.

Financial Aid and Scholarship

A variety of financial aid programmes are available, including loans and scholarships.

Approximate Tuition and Fees

Approximately £5,500-£6,500 per year. Approximate cost of accommodation, food etc is £3,000-£4,000 pa.

Admissions

Courses are very up-to-date and offer our students maximum flexibility and choice in modes of study, entry and exit points and special electives. We offer a two semester start, in September through UCAS and in February by direct application to Central Admissions at the University. For distance learning awards enrollment can be at any time.

We are keen to articulate students from Community Colleges into our degree programmes and have many agreements with institutions overseas to make the admissions process very simple.

Graduation Requirements

Graduation requires the successful completion of all applicable course modules.

Swiss Hotel Association Hotel Management School *Les Roches*

Bachelor of Science (Honours) in International Hospitality Management, Swiss Hotel Association Hotel Management Diploma (3-years), Associate Diploma Program(1-year)

Program Enrollment: 900
Institutional Enrollment: 1000
Degrees Awarded: Bachelor of Science(Honours), Swiss Hotel Association Diploma, Associate of Science, Post Graduate Diploma.
Emphases/Specializations: International Hospitality Management, Hotel Management, Culinary Arts, F & B Operations.
Program Accreditation: Swiss Hotel Association.
Institutional Accreditation: New England Association of Schools and Colleges (NEASC), Swiss Hotel Association, State (Canton) of Valais.
Contact: Admissions Office, Les Roches, CH-3975 Bluche-Crans-Montana, Valais Switzerland Tel:(+41) 27 485 96 00, Fax: (+41) 27 485 96 15; e-mail: admin.roches@roches.vsnet.ch

Institution Description
Les Roches Hotel Management School is located in the small village of Bluche. In the center of the Valaisan Alps at an altitude of 4,200 feet, Bluche is less than two miles from the international ski resort of Crans-Montana. Students live in chalet-style accommodation, with modern, comfortable living quarters. A quality working environment together with extensive study and information technology network offer each student the best conditions for the successful completion of their studies.

Program Description
The "International Hospitality Industry Management Programme" offered in Bluche has been designed in collaboration Swiss, English and American industry and educational partners. It reflects our willingness to draw on the expertise of each partner in specific areas of education. Students completing this program will receive state of the art courses in culinary arts corresponding to the Swiss Hotel Association standards combined with the best college level management courses from the United Kingdom and the United States. The program is international through its design, course content and faculty experience and nationality, and student body which is drawn from some seventy countries.

Special Features
The program is run over a period of four years for Bachelor of Science (Honours) degree, three for the Swiss Hotel Association Hotel Management Diploma and two for the Associate Degree in Food and Beverage Operations. Each year of the first three years are divided into two 21-week semesters spent alternatively on campus and practising within the industry on paid (if accomplished in Switzerland) internships. The fourth year is based on two 16 week sessions spent on campus.

Financial Aid and Scholarships
All inquiries should be sent in writing to the School Board at the above address.

Admissions
The admission decisions are given taking into account the international origins of our applicants. Determining factors which are taken into consideration are the candidate's successful completion of high school, SAT scores, high school recommendation and personal interview results with one of our accredited agents.

Tuition and Fees
Tuition, room, board and books, per annum is approximately US$15,000

Marywood University

Program-Hotel and Restaurant Management

College: Business and Managerial Science Programs
Program Enrollment: Undergraduate
Institution Enrollment: Undergraduate 1758; Graduate 1168
Degrees Awarded-Bachelor of Business Administration (BBA)
Degree Categories: Hotel and Restaurant Management
Emphases/Specializations: Hospitality Management
Program Accreditation: Middle States Association of Colleges and Schools, Candidate for Accreditation by the Association of Collegiate Business Schools & Programs (ACBSP)
Institution Accreditation: Commission on Higher Education, Middle States Association of Colleges and Schools, Pennsylvania Department of Education.
Contact: S. P. Dagher, Ph.D., Executive Director & Chairman, Business & Managerial Science Programs or Charles Lipinski, D.B.A., Coordinator Hotel & Restaurant Management Program, Marywood University, 2300

Adams Ave., Scranton, PA 18509-1598; Phone (570) 348-6274 or (800) 346-5014; FAX (570) 961-4762

Institution Description

Located in Pennsylvania's picturesque Pocono Mountain Region, Marywood University is a comprehensive, coeducational Catholic university that offers the educational qualities you need to succeed. On the scenic spacious 160-acre campus, students enjoy small classes, close interaction with knowledgeable professors, fine facilities and plenty of opportunities of hands-on involvement.

Program Description

The Hotel and Restaurant Management Program is a multidisciplinary field of study that prepares students for management, marketing and operations positions in the expanding, service-oriented hospitality (foods, accommodations, tourism) industry. The curriculum builds on a broad foundation of liberal arts, business and hospitality courses, as well as practical work experience.

Special Features

The learning experiences offered at Marywood University range from classroom lectures and seminars to consultations and field trips. All graduates receive career placement through the Office of Career Planning and Placement.

Financial Aid and Scholarships

Marywood University is committed to quality education at an affordable cost. The University offers a comprehensive program of financial aid, including federal, state and University awarded scholarships and grants, to assist students in meeting educational costs.

Admissions

There are no special admission requirements to the program. Admission to the Hotel/Restaurant Management Program is identical to that outline in the undergraduate catalog.

Tuition and Fees

Annual tuition for 1998-99 is $14,208; annual room and board $6,200.

Specialization Area

Hotel & Lodging Mgmt.; Restaurant & Food Service Mgmt.

Graduation Requirements

A minimum of 128 semester hours are required to graduate.

Michigan State University

The School of Hospitality Business

College: The Eli Broad College of Business; The Eli Broad Graduate School of Management
Program Enrollment: 605 undergraduate, 14 graduate
Institutional Enrollment: 33,420 undergraduate; 7,838 grad uate
Degrees Awarded: Bachelor of Arts in Business Administration; Master of Business Administration; Master of Science in Foodservice Management
Degree Categories: Bachelor in Hospitality Business; Master in Hospitality Business or Foodservice Management
Program Accreditation: American Assembly of Collegiate Schools of Business

Institutional Accreditation: Association of American Universities
Contact: Ronald F. Cichy, PhD, CHA, CHE, Director, *The* School of Hospitality Business, 231 Eppley Center, Michigan State University, East Lansing, MI 48824-1121; phone (517) 353-9211; FAX (517) 432-1170

Institution Description
As a pioneer land-grant institution and a respected research and teaching university, Michigan State University (MSU) is committed to leadership and developing knowledge. MSU strives to discover practical uses for theoretical knowledge. In fostering both research and its applications, MSU continues to be a catalyst for positive intellectual, social and technological change.

Program Description
The mission of *The* School of Hospitality Business at MSU is to be the leader in hospitality business education through teaching, research, and service. Our curriculum is unique because it combines integrated studies requirements with business core courses and hospitality business major courses.

Special Features
As the top-ranked business college-based school in the world, *The* School offers an exceptionally well-crafted curriculum taught by innovative professors. The faculty includes leading textbook authors, sought-after consultants, and respected researchers. All of their teaching and research efforts focus on addressing today's and tomorrow's hospitality business challenges.

Financial Aid and Scholarships
MSU offers a comprehensive financial assistance program, including both scholarships that reward academic excellence and financial aid programs based on need.

Approximate Tuition and Fees
In-state tuition for a full-time undergraduate is approximately $5,100 per year.

Admissions
Admission to *The* School of Hospitality Business is selective and based on meeting minimum overall GPA and GPA requirements in a series of business core courses including accounting, economics, mathematics and computer science. Freshmen are admitted to the program as "pre-majors"; formal matriculation occurs in the junior year after admission criteria are met.

Graduation Requirements
Graduation requires the completion of 120 semester hours which include 27 credits of general education, 18 credits of pre-College of Business courses, 24 credits of College of Business core courses, 39 credits of hospitality business major courses, and 8 elective credits. A minimum of 800 hospitality internship hours is also required.

Morehead State University

Hotel, Restaurant and Institutional Management

College: College of Science and Technology, Department of Human Sciences
Program Enrollment: 46
Institutional Enrollment: 7,200 undergraduate; 100 graduate
Degree Awarded: Bachelor of Science
Emphases/Specializations: Hotel, Restaurant and Institutional Management
Institutional Accreditation: Southern Association of Colleges and Schools
Contact: Marilyn Sampley, Chair, Department of Human Sciences, UPO 889, Morehead State University, Morehead, KY 40351; Phone (606) 783-2966; FAX (606) 783-5007

Institution Description

Morehead State University is a state-funded, Coeducational institution with a full-time teaching faculty of 323. The university offers 96 undergraduate degree programs, two certificate programs and 10 preprofessional programs of study.

Program Description

Morehead State University's Hotel, Restaurant and Institutional Management (HRIM) Program includes courses in all aspects of hotel management and food service administration. Managerial skills are developed through accounting, economics, marketing, and management and computer management. Students must complete six semester hours of hands-on practical work experience and must choose a minor in business.

Special Features

The HRIM Program has its own food service laboratory-a completely equipped food processing and preparation facility directed by students enrolled in the program.

Financial Aid and Scholarships

The university maintains a fully staffed financial aid office and scholarships are available through the office of admissions.

Tuition and Fees

Kentucky residents tuition: $1,075 per semester; resident hall housing: $783.00. Meals are purchased wither on a pay-as-you-go basis or in advance through a Dining Club. A student health service fee is consolidated with tuition and is a mandatory fee.

Admissions

There are no special admission requirements to the program. Admission to the HRIM Program is identical to that outlined in the undergraduate catalog.

Graduation Requirements

Graduation requires the completion of 128 semester hours, which includes 48 hours of general education, 30 hours of required courses in business administration, 36 hours in hospitality management, and six semester hours of hospitality work experience.

Morgan State University

Hospitality Management Program

Program Enrollment: 100
Institution Enrollment: 6,000 Undergraduate; 400 Graduate
Degree Category: Hospitality Management
Institutional Accreditation: Middle States Association of Colleges and Schools, American Assembly of Collegiate Schools of Business
Contact: Charles F. Monagan, Ph.D., Director, Hospitality Management Program, 1700 East Cold Spring Lane, Baltimore, MD 21251, Phone (443) 885-4454; Fax (410) 319-4034; E-mail: Cmonagan@morgan.edu

Institution Description

Founded in 1867, Morgan State University (MSU) is a comprehensive university located in the City of Baltimore, Maryland. The campus is situated within a residential area and has a suburban feeling; minutes away from the attractions of Baltimore's Inner Harbor and Fell's Point. A public urban university, Morgan State offers over 40 different baccalaureate degree programs. Graduate programs offer students advanced degrees in selected disciplines.

Program Description

The Hospitality Management Program is designed to prepare students for management positions in the hospitality industry. It is housed in the Department of Business Administration, School of Business and Management. The program integrates a variety of university courses in humanities, the science disciplines and combines a strong business management curriculum with the specifics of the hospitality industry. It is recommended that students complete a minimum of 800 hours of supervised on-the-job experience. The Greater Baltimore Community is an exciting and unique place to major in Hospitality Management. Majors have opportunities to work and learn from managers of leading corporations in all segments of the hospitality industry.

Special Features

The 800 hours of work experience program offers students an opportunity to receive practical, hand-on experience in the hospitality industry. Active student organizations provide additional opportunities for professional and business networking. Placement assistance is provided.

Financial Aid and Scholarships

MSU administers a comprehensive financial aid program, such as loans, grants, scholarships and career related student work programs. In addition, scholarships are available from the hospitality industry and associations.

Approximate Tuition and Fees

All students must pay $25 application fee. Maryland residents' tuition: $1853 per semester; non residents $4405 per semester; Room and Board $2648.

Admission

The Hospitality Management Program follows general university admission requirements, which include a minimum of 2.0 GPA from high school or from other post-secondary institutions.

Graduation Requirements

The Hospitality Management Degree requires 130 semester hours, which include 67 hours of general education requirements, 33 hours in business and 30 hours in the hospitality management. At least 800 hours of work experience in the industry is recommended.

Mount Mary College

Hotel and Restaurant Management

Program Enrollment: 20
Institution Enrollment: 1,500
Degree Awarded: Bachelor of Arts
Degree Categories: Hotel and Restaurant Management
Institutional Accreditation: North Central Association of Colleges, State of Wisconsin
Contact: Marlene L. Larson, CHE, Director, Hotel and Restaurant Management, Mount Mary College, 2900 North Menomonee River Pkwy., Milwaukee, WI 53222; phone (414) 258-4810, ext.404; fax (414) 2561205; e-mail: larsonm@mtmary.edu

Institutional Description

Mount Mary is a Catholic women's liberal arts college. Students may select from 30 professional areas of study or combine areas of concentration to tailor their own major. Mount Mary is large enough for diversity and challenge, small enough for friendly attention. Opportunities abound for the development of self-confidence and leadership

Program Description

Hotel and Restaurant Management is an interdisciplinary four-year program. The program emphasizes management principles and practices. The curriculum is designed to provide students with concepts, cognitive and technical skills, and the experience and know-how necessary to successfully fulfill people's need for lodging, food, recreation and entertainment away from home.

Special Features

The program features junior and senior internships in major hotel chains; an advisory board of experienced hoteliers; a student hospitality association; and faculty with experience in both teaching and industry. The program results in a bachelors degree in hotel and restaurant management and business administration. Certification is available to members of both sex is they have a bachelors degree from another college or university.

Financial Aid and Scholarships

Financial awards include entrance and in-course scholarships, bursaries, prizes and awards of merit. A financial aid officer is available on campus. Students are paid by employers during co-operative education work terms in this program.

Approximate Tuition and Fees

Full-time tuition, $15,900 per year; $330 per credit hour. Depending on the room type and meal plan selected, on-campus room and board ranges from $2010-$3,194 per year.

Admissions

Admission is based on high school diploma or equivalent; 2.30 GPA based on a 4.00 point scale; and SAT or ACT test scores. In addition transfer students or nonimmigrant alien students may be admitted based on specific requirements. Placement tests for math and English competency are given on campus.

Graduation Requirements

A student must complete satisfactorily 128 credits; fulfill all core curriculum requirements; maintain a cumulative 2.3 GPA; complete at a minimum the last 32 semester credit hours at Mount Mary College. HRM majors must complete all class requirements and internships with a minimum 2.5 GPA.

New Mexico State University

Hotel, Restaurant & Tourism Management

College: Agriculture and Home Economics
Program Enrollment:310
Institutional Enrollment: 15,100 undergraduate; 2,500 graduate
Degrees Awarded: Bachelor of Science
Degree Category: Hotel, Restaurant and Tourism Management
Emphases/Specializations: Hotel Operations; Food and Beverage Operations; Tourism Services; Convention, Meeting Planning and Special Events Administration
Institutional Accreditation: North Central Association of Colleges and Secondary Schools
Contact: Deborah Breiter, Associate Professor and Interim Department Head, Department of Hotel, Restaurant and Tourism Management, New Mexico State University, Box 30003 MSC 3HRTM, Las Cruces, NM 88003; phone (505) 646-2227; fax (505) 646-8100; e-mail: dbreiter@nmsu.edu

Institution Description

New Mexico State University, established in 1888, serves a student body of over 15,515. It has a faculty of 670 (faculty / student ratio is 1 to 18.8) and a staff of 2,000. One of the Southwest's major research universities, NMSU ranks 60th among the top 100 public universities receiving federal funding for research and development and holds $300 million in research contracts. NMSU is a member of the Hispanic Association of Colleges and Universities and is also a recognized minority institution. Featured in 1999 Student Guide to America's Best College Buys.

Program Description

The Department of Hotel, Restaurant and Tourism Management at NMSU is designed to prepare students with an excellent foundation in hotel, restaurant and food service operations in the context of the broad tourism sector as well as general education. The curriculum design allows the student to continue at the senior level with general hospitality education or to concentrate in a particular area such as hotels operations, restaurants and food service operations or tourism management. Students can tailor make the final year of their program with their advisor.

Special Features

Career Fair with national hospitality firms in attendance, trips to major industry trade shows throughout the country, and field trips to major hospitality properties are only a few of the professional activities. Faculty all have doctoral degrees and a depth of professional industry experience. Hospitality and Tourism Student Association. International Foodservice Executive Association.

Financial Aid and Scholarships

The College of Agriculture and Home Economics has more than $100,000 available in scholarships every year, giving majors in the college an excellent chance for scholarship support at NMSU. Endowed scholarships are available through some of New Mexico's most prominent businesses, organizations and individuals.

Approximate Tuition and Fees

Tuition for New Mexico residents is $1,173 per semester; for nonresidents, $3,825 per semester.

Admissions

Formal application accompanied by a $15 admission fee. An official transcript of the student's high school credits. Graduation from an accredited state or approved high school or academy with a 2.0 GPA, and ACT score of at least 19. The program encourages transfer students.

Graduation Requirements

Bachelor of Science in Hotel, Restaurant and Tourism: general education of 43 credit hours. Sixty hours or 20 courses to be taken in the field of student's major interest. Free electives sufficient to bring the total number of credits to a minimum of 128 semester credits. Of this total, at least 55 semester credits must be in upper-division courses. A 2.0 minimum GPA must be maintained. Students must complete internship and work experience requirement.

New York City Technical College

Hospitality Management

Program Enrollment: 800
Institutional Enrollment: 11,000
Degrees Awarded: Bachelor of Technology; Associate of Applied Science
Degree Category: Hospitality Management
Institutional Accreditation: Middle States Association of Colleges and Schools; Accreditation Commission for Programs in Hospitality Administration; New York State Board of Regents

Contact: Dr. Patricia S. Bartholomew, Chair, Hospitality Management Department, New York City Technical College, 300 Jay St., Namm 220, Brooklyn, New York 11201; phone (718) 260-5630; fax (718)260-5997

Institution Description

New York City Technical College (City Tech), part of the City University of New York system, is a national and international leader in technical education. City Tech offers a dazzling spectrum of career education opportunities. Approximately 10,000 students choose from over 40 programs in engineering, business and communications technologies, health and natural sciences, and the liberal arts.

Program Description

Located in the international center of hospitality and cuisine, City Tech's programs in hospitality management offer unparalleled involvement with the world's greatest hotel keepers, chefs, managers and organizations. The department offers two programs, one leading to the associate degree, the other to the bachelor degree.

Special Features

City Tech's Hospitality Management (HM) Department, the oldest in New York City, enjoys an international reputation. Students have opportunities to study abroad and to serve apprenticeships at leading European hotels and four-star restaurants. Small classes lead to close contact with our expert faculty. There is a strong commitment to community service and the department offers numerous opportunities for students to volunteer their time to enrich the community.

Financial Aid and Scholarships

NYC Tech offers a full range of state and federal financial aid. Merit scholarships are also awarded to outstanding students.

Approximate Tuition and Fees

Tuition for full-time students who are state residents is $1,600 per semester; for full-time, non resident students, $3,275 per semester. Tuition for part-time students who are state residents is $135 per credit; for part-time, nonresident students, $285 per credit.

Admissions

Applicant must be a high school graduate or hold a General Equivalency Diploma (GED). Prospective students must file an official application one semester in advance.

Graduation Requirements

Students must meet the basic admissions requirements to the City University of New York and the proficiency standards for upper division study. All students are initially admitted to the associate degree program; students may then apply for the bachelor degree if they meet certain requirements. The bachelor degree requires the completion of 120 credits.

New York University

Center for Hospitality, Tourism, and Travel Administration

College: School of Continuing and Professional Studies
Program Enrollment: 150
Institution Enrollment: 38,000 in degree programs
Degree Awarded: Bachelor of Science in Hotel and Tourism Administration; Bachelor of Science in Recreation and Leisure Studies
Degree Category: Hotel and Tourism Management; Recreation and Leisure Management
Emphases/Specializations: Hotel and Resort Operations Analysis; Tourism Planning and Management; Hospitality and Tourism Planning and Management; Hospitality and Tourism Information Technology; Sports Management and Marketing, Recreation
Institutional Accreditation: New York University is a member of the Association of Universities and is accredited by the Middle States Association of Colleges and Schools

NEW YORK UNIVERSITY
Center for Hospitality, Tourism and Travel Administration

Contact: Sharr Prohaska, Program Director, Center for Hospitality, Tourism and Travel Administration, New York University, 48 Cooper Square, New York, NY 10003; phone: (212) 998-9109; fax: (212) 995-4676; e-mail: chtta.scps.@nyu.edu

Institution Description

New York University (NYU) is the largest, private institution of higher learning in the United States, enrolling students from all 50 states and from 120 countries. Classes are conveniently located in New York City, one of the greatest hotel and tourist centers in the world.

Program Description

The Bachelor's program offers two degree programs, a Bachelor's degree in Hotel and Tourism Management and a Bachelor's degree in Recreation and Leisure Studies. Each degree provides individualized education and training that draws on the extensive resources of both the university and New York City. Concentration areas focus on hotel and resort operations analysis, tourism planning, conference and event management, information technology, sports management and marketing, and recreation leadership. Cooperative education is a key aspect of the program. The program is committed to developing industry professionals who have the analytical and problem solving skills necessary to succeed in the industry. The program is recognized by the World Tourism Organization.

Special Features

The program draws on New York City's wealth of hotels, tourism business, and sports organizations and their personnel to prepare students for careers in diverse aspects of these industries. The center's advisory board is comprised of world-renowned industry leaders. Through internships, cooperative programs, professional development programs, lecture series, and conferences, we offer our students opportunities to network with acclaimed industry leaders. Our motto: "The city is our laboratory...the industry is our faculty...and our students are the future of the profession" defines our commitment to quality education.

Financial Aid and Scholarships

Scholarships, grants, loans and part-time employment are available based on financial need, academic achievement and availability of funds.

Approximate Tuition and Fees

For full-time students (12-18 points) the cost per term is approximately $11,000, not including fees, housing, or registration. For students enrolled part-time, tuition per point, per term is $620. (1998-99)

Admissions

Admissions to the Bachelor's degree is selective. Applicants must have a high-school degree, and recommendations from guidance counselors, teachers, and others. All freshmen applicants are required to submit official results of either the SAT or the ACT exams. International applicants whose native language Is not English must take the TOEFL exam, plus additional testing.

Graduation Requirements

The Bachelor of Science degree requires 128 credits, of which 60 are in the liberal arts. Hospitality and tourism coursework requires 68 credits, including financial management, human resources, information technology, tourism and hospitality law and hotel facilities operations. Students perform at least 300 hours in cooperative work experience, which also earns academic credit.

Niagara University

Institute of Travel, Hotel and Restaurant Administration

Program Enrollment: 210
Institutional Enrollment: Undergraduate: 2300; Graduate: 750
Degrees Awarded: Bachelor of Science; Master of Business Administration
Degree Categories: Hotel and Restaurant Administration; Travel and Tourism Administration
Emphases/Specializations: Hotel and Restaurant Administration, Travel and Tourism, Food Service Administration, Financial Management, Marketing, Hospitality and Gerontology, Recreation and Leisure.
Program Accreditation: Accreditation Commission for Programs in Hospitality Administration
Institutional Accreditation: Niagara University holds memberships in the American Council on Education and the Commission on Independent Schools and Colleges. It is accredited by the Middle States Association of Schools and Colleges.
Contact: Carl D. Riegel, Ed.D., Professor and Director, Institute of Travel, Hotel and Restaurant Administration, Niagara University, NY 14109-2012; Phone: 716-286-8270; Fax: 716-286-8277

Institution Description

Niagara University, founded in 1856, is a private liberal arts university following the Vincentian tradition. The university consists of five academic colleges and offers over 50 undergraduate and numerous graduate degrees. It is located in western New York just minutes from Niagara Falls, 20 minutes from Buffalo and 90 minutes from exciting Toronto.

Program Description

The Institute, established in 1968, prepares students for careers in hospitality and tourism enterprises. The curriculum combines a strong grounding in the liberal arts with a core of courses in business and administration. Students pursue specialized study in either Tourism or Hospitality Administration and then use electives to add an area of emphasis. There is a work experience requirement and students are strongly encouraged to take advantage of the many cooperative education opportunities.

Special Features

The program offers study abroad experiences, extensive cooperative education opportunities, an honors program, small classes, numerous professional organizations and outstanding placement assistance.

Financial Aid and Scholarships

In addition to federal and state aid, Niagara University provides grants to students based on both need and merit. Furthermore many Institute students receive generous assistance from private foundations and organizations. In total, about 90% of Niagara's students receive financial aid in one form or another.

Admissions

Admission is based on previous academic performance, SAT or ACT test scores, references and a writing sample. Although the Institute makes admission decisions, prospective students should apply to the University Admissions Office. Favorable decisions are based upon evidence that applicants will be able to successfully complete their program of study.

Tuition and Fees

Annual tuition for the 1998-99 academic year is $12,886 and additional fees average $450. For students choosing to live in the residence halls, room and board is $6,078.

Specialization Areas

Hotel and Lodging Mgmt., Travel and Tourism Mgmt. and Restaurant and Foodservice Mgmt

Graduation Requirements

Graduation requires the successful completion of 123 semester hours of which 60 are in general education and 63 are in the major. In addition Institute students must complete a minimum of 800 clock hours of approved work experience. Some areas of emphasis may require more academic credits or additional internships.

Nicholls State University

Chef John Folse Culinary Institute

Program Enrollment: 150
Institutional Enrollment: 7,300
Degrees Awarded: Bachelor of Science, Associate of Science
Degree Categories: Culinary Arts
Emphasis/Specializations: Product preparation and development; culinary operations, Culinary education
Institutional Accreditation: Southern Association of Colleges and Schools

Contact: Dr. Jerald Chesser, CEC, CCE, Dean, Chef John Folse, Culinary Institute, Nicholls State University, P.O. Box 2099, Thibodaux, LA, 70310, USA; phone (504) 449- 7100; fax (5040 449-7089

Institution Description

Nestled deep in the heart of Cajun and Creole Country, between New Orleans and Baton Rouge, Nicholls State University is located in Thibodaux, Louisiana. The area is rich in cultural heritage and is known for its hospitality and fine cuisine. NSU students receive Excellence in Education with a Personal Touch!

Program Description

The Chef John Folse Culinary Institute is an academic college at Nicholls State University dedicated to the culinary arts. The Institute's Bachelor of Science degree program includes classical culinary arts, culinary operations, product development, and Louisiana's culinary heritage. The 125-hour curriculum stresses development of critical thinking, conceptual knowledge, and technical skills.

Admissions

Admission to the University will be granted to individuals who have achieved one of the following criteria: minimum grade point average of 2.0 on a 4.0 scale on core courses; OR minimum ACT composite score of 19; OR graduation in the upper 25 percentile of the high school class. Admission to the Bachelor of Science Degree program in culinary arts is limited to those with a 2.5 GPA on a 4.0 scale and a minimum ACT composite score of 19.

Tuition & Fees

Approximate tuition and fees for one year (not including summer semester) are: in-state $2388, out-of-state $4980. Additional fees include a $250 fee per culinary laboratory course, approved uniform set, $290 and approved knife kit, $309.

Specialization Area

Culinary Arts

Special Features

The Institute's faculty hold both professional and academic credentials. Students learn in state-of-the-art kitchens and classrooms. The Institute provides opportunity for exposure to the rich culinary traditions of the region and the world through its visiting chefs program and externship program.

Graduation Requirements

Completion of either the 125 hour Bachelor of Science or 66 hour Associate of Science degree program with an overall 2.0 (C) GPA. Grade of C or better in the following: all Culinary Arts Courses: English 101, 102; and Math 102, 214.

Financial Aid and Scholarships

Culinary arts majors are eligible to apply for Carl Perkins grants (AS only) and a number of other types of financial aid. The Institute offers a limited number of competitive scholarships to first-time freshmen. Interested individuals are encouraged to contact the NSU Financial Aid Office.

Norfolk State University

Hospitality Management

Program Enrollment: 65
Institutional Enrollment: 7,500
Degree Awarded: Bachelor of Science
Degree Category: Hospitality Management
Program Accreditation: Accreditation Commission for Programs in Hospitality Administration
Institutional Accreditation: Southern Association of Colleges and Schools; American Assembly of Collegiate Schools of Business; National Council for Accreditation for Teacher Education
Contact: Lawrence E. Epplein, Interim Program Coordinator, Hospitality Management Program, Norfolk State University, 2401 Corprew Avenue, Norfolk, Virginia 23504; phone (757)683-8782; fax (757)683-9534

Institution Description

Norfolk State University is an urban, state-supported comprehensive university with programs in business and entrepreneurship, education, arts and letters, social sciences, social work, technology and health related professions and sciences. NUS offers associate, baccalaureate, masters and doctoral degrees. It is a member of the Tidewater Consortium which allows students to take courses and any of five area colleges and universities.

Program Description

The Hospitality Management program is located in the School of Business and Entrepreneurship and seeks to educate and train students through the use of theory-based instruction and practical leadership to assume roles in a challenging and changing global hospitality environment.

Admissions

Applicants must have graduated from an accredited high school with minimum 2.0 grade point average or have successfully completed the GED tests. SAT or ACT scores must be submitted.

Tuition & Fees

In-State $3,335
Out-of-State $7,540
Room and Board $4,992

Graduation Requirements

Graduation requires completion of 120 semester hours, which includes 66 hours of general education and non-major courses, 51 hours in hospitality management and 3 hours of general electives. An 800 hour management internship is a requirement for four hours of credit in work experience classes.

North Carolina Central University

Hospitality and Tourism Administration

College: College of Arts and Sciences
Program Enrollment: 30
Institutional Enrollment: 4700
Undergraduate: 1,000 graduate
Degree Awarded: Bachelor of Science in Hospitality and Tourism Administration
Degree Categories: Hospitality and Tourism
Emphases/Specialization: Food service, Lodging, Travel and Tourism
Program Accreditation: N/A
Institutional Accreditation: Commission on Colleges of the Southern Association of Colleges and Schools
Contact: Dr. Beverly A. Bryant, Director, Hospitality and Tourism Administration Program, North Carolina Central University, 1810 Fayetteville St, P.O. Box 20024, Durham, NC 27707; phone (919) 560-6235, fax (919) 220-5455

Institution Description

North Carolina Central University, a state-supported liberal arts institution chartered in 1909 as a private institution, opened to students on July 10, 1910. As a comprehensive university it offers a wide range of programs at the bachelor and master's levels, and at the first professional level in law. The university and programs are accredited by several accrediting bodies.

Program Description

The Hospitality and Tourism Administration Program: The program is designed to provide students with a common body of knowledge in hospitality administration and to prepare them for leadership and entrepreneurial roles and management careers. This program requires 1000 hours of work experience and prepares students for mobility across various sections of the industry.

Special Features

The program draws from the resources of the hospitality industry, various departments and supports and encourages students with career advising, planning and internships. The faculty holds terminal degrees and has vast professional experience.

Financial Aid and Scholarships

Financial assistance is available to qualified students. Through the university, the department offers a limited number of competitive scholarships to students who meet the criteria.

Approximate Tuition and Fees

In-state, full-time: undergraduate housing and boarding is $4,675 per year, non-boarding is $1,039.75 year; out-of-state, full time: undergraduate housing and boarding is $11,014 per year, non-boarding is $9,180 per year. In-state part-time: undergraduate $439 per year (0-5 semester hours), $809 per year (6-9 semester hours), $882 per year (6-11 semester hours; out of state, part-time: undergraduate $1330 per year (05 semester hours, $3,482 per year (6-9 semester hours), $3,555 per year (6-11 semester hours). Other fees: In addition to the University's tuition, board and fees, the Hospitality and Tourism majors will incur additional expenses. These costs are estimated (but not limited to) as follows: books, school supplies $700, transportation to and from local work experience and internship sites (variable) liability insurance; and student membership dues $70/year.

Admissions

Admission requirements, in addition to NCCU's specific requirements include 4 course units in English, 3 in mathematics, 3 in science, and 2 in social studies. Freshmen may be required to take various tests as part of their orientation and follow-up procedures. A minimum of 950 (combined) on SAT is required of all entering freshmen.

Graduation Requirements

Graduation requires passing all course work in the four year plan (128) credit hours; maintaining a cumulative grade point average of 2.0 or better and 3.0 in Hospitality Courses, Internships; passing the Hospitality and Tourism Competency Exit Examination; and holding professional memberships.

North Dakota State University

Hotel, Motel, Restaurant Management

College: Human Development and Education
Program Enrollment: 80
Institutional Enrollment:
Undergraduate: 9,000
Graduate: 800
Degrees Awarded: Bachelor of Science
Degree Categories: Hotel, Motel, Restaurant Management
Emphases/Specializations: Business Administration
Program Accreditation: North Central Association of Colleges and Schools

Contact: Mort Sarabakhsh, PhD, CHA, Director, Hotel, Motel, Restaurant Management Program, Food and Nutrition Department, College of Human Development and Education, North Dakota State University, Fargo, ND 58105; phone (701) 231-7356 or (701) 231-7474; fax (701) 231-7174; e-mail: sarabakhsh@plains.nodak.edu

Institution Description

North Dakota State University (NDSU) is a land-grant university which has approximately 9,800 students enrolled in eight fully accredited colleges. Students enrolled in the Hotel, Motel, Restaurant Management (HMRM) Program have a unique opportunity to enroll in classes at three different colleges: North Dakota State University, Moorhead State University and Concordia College, all situated within a few miles of each other.

Program Description

North Dakota State University's Hotel, Motel, Restaurant Management Program offers an excellent opportunity for students who are interested in receiving a four-year degree in hospitality management. The program begins with a solid foundation in general education coursework followed by management and hospitality-related courses, such as beverage operations management, computer science, introduction to hospitality management, tourism and travel management, hospitality law, food sanitation, catering and others. A minor in business administration is required with this major.

Special Features

Students in the HMRM Program are able to join the International Food Service Executives Association (IFSEA) student chapter.

Financial Aid and Scholarships

The financial aid office makes available grants, loans, scholarships and employment opportunities. In addition, scholarships are available through the Department of Food and Nutrition.

Admissions

Graduation from high school with a minimum of 13 academic units, which includes at least 4 units of English, 3 units of mathematics, 3 units of lab sciences plus 3 units of social studies related courses. Completion of ACT 21 or higher, or SAT is required. Completion of the NDSU Application for Admission, supporting credentials, plus a nonrefundable application fee of $25 is required.

Tuition & Fees

Tuition for the HMRM Program is $112.17 per semester credit hour for in-state residents; $118.38 for Minnesota residents; $161.42 for South Dakota, Alaska, Colorado, Hawaii, Idaho, Montana, New Mexico, Oregon, Utah and Wyoming residents, as well as Saskatchewan and Manitoba, Canada residents. Tuition and fees is $276.50 per credit hour, up to a maximum of $3,153.00 per semester (12 credits or more), for international students and students from other states not listed above.

Specialization Area

Hotel and food service management with emphasis on business operation.

Graduation Requirements

The Bachelor of Science degree in HMRM requires a minimum of 127 semester credit hours, which includes 55 credits of professional requirements, 39 credits of general education, 9 credits of human development core, and 21 credits of business administration (minor). Students are also required to take 4 semester credit hours as part of the professional requirements practicum or internship.

Northeastern State University

Meetings and Destinations Management

Program Enrollment: 150
Institutional Enrollment: 8,000
Degree Awarded: Bachelor of Business Administration
Degree Category: Meetings and Destinations Management
Emphasis/Specializations: Meeting and Convention Management; Tourist Destination Development and Management
Program Accreditation: Accreditation Commission for Programs in Hospitality Administration, Professional Convention Management Association
Institutional Accreditation: North Central Association of Colleges and Secondary Schools
Contact: Dr. Penny Dotson, Department chair, Marketing and Meetings and Destination Management, Northeastern State University, College of Business, Tahlequah, OK 74464-2399, phone: 918-456-5511 Ext. 3086, fax: 918-458-2193, dotson@cherokee.nsuok.edu, http://www.nsuok.edu/academic/depts/mdm/index.html

Institution Description

NSU is the second oldest institution of higher education west of the Mississippi. It is located in Tahlequah, Oklahoma, the national capital of the Cherokee Nation. The university is surrounded by several lakes, the Ozark mountains, and the Illinois River, all of which offer year-round recreational activities.

Program Description

The Meetings and Destination Management program is oriented toward three areas: knowledge and skills which relate to the chosen field of study; marketing and management of travel and tourism services; and development of interpersonal communications skills through active participation in industry activities.

Special Features

Students intern 1,000 working hours, accumulated in three separate segments. Student organizations include the Professional Convention Management Association and Meeting Planners International . An exchange program is available for class credit and work experience in Mexico. Courses are offered through distance learning and traditional classes.

Financial Aid and Scholarships

Pell Grants, Supplemental Educational Opportunity Grants, college work-study, institutional employment, Perkins Loans and scholarships.

Approximate Tuition and Fees

Freshman and sophomore classes; $59.15 per credit hour for Oklahoma residents; $137.65 per credit hour for nonresidents. Junior and senior classes: $60.15 per credit hour for residents; $147.15 per credit hour for nonresidents.

Admissions

Applicants must graduate from an accredited high school, have participated the American College Testing Program (ACT), and satisfy at least one of the following: maintained a four-year high school GPA of 3.0 or higher on a 4.0 scale; ranked scholastically among the upper one-half of their graduating class; or attained a minimum composite score of 20 on the enhanced ACT, plus high school course requirements to enter college.

Graduation Requirements

To graduate, students must have earned 124 semester credit hours with a cumulative GPA of at least 2.0 (2.5 in the major field of study). The major consists of 36 hours, including six hours of intern credit; the required business core contains 39 hours; the remainder include general education credits and elective courses.

Ohio University

Food Service Management and Dietetics

College: College of Health and Human Service
Program Enrollment: 150 students
Institutional Enrollment: Undergraduate - 16,271 students; Graduate – 2,872 students
Degrees Awarded: Bachelor of Science in Human and Consumer Sciences
Degree Categories: Food Service Management & Dietetics
Emphases/Specializations: Dietetics/ Nutrition with Science

Program Accreditation: ADA Approved
Institutional Accreditation: North Central Association of Colleges and Secondary Schools, American Association of Family and Consumer Sciences
Contact: Annette Graham, Ph.D., Food Service Management, Coordinator, Ohio University, School of Human and Consumer Sciences, 108 Tupper Hall, Athens, OH 45701-2979, Phone: (740) 593-0700, Fax: (740) 593-0289, e-mail: grahama@ohio.edu

---

Institution Description

Founded in 1804, Ohio University is a Research II residential institution located in the rolling hills of southeast Ohio. Among our students are people from all 50 states and more that 100 countries. Ohio University offers 314 undergraduate majors, 49 master's programs and 32 doctoral degree programs.

Program Description

The Food Service Management and Dietetics program prepares students for careers in the management and supervision of hotels, motels, restaurants, institutional foodservice and dietetics.

Special Features

The undergraduate program emphasizes hands – on experience through labs, field experience and practicum. Opportunities as a foodservice student manager are available. Students also complete a business minor that is built into the program.

Financial Aid and Scholarships

Ohio University financial aid office in conjunction with federal and state governments and private and civic organizations, offers a variety of scholarships, grants, loans and part-time employment.

Admissions

Admission to Ohio University is selective and is based upon high performance, aptitude test scores (ACT or SAT), and overall achievement. Transfer applicants must have completed 30 quarter hours of transferable credit from an accredited institution with a minimum of a 2.5 cumulative GPA on a 4.) scale.

Tuition and Fees

Tuition (based on 11-20 credits) for state residents is $1,510; per quarter; for nonresidents, $3,177 per quarter. Room (double occupancy) is $835 per quarter; board (20 meals), $860 per quarter. Admission application filing fee is $30. Note: These rates are subject to change.

Specialization Area

Restaurant & Foodservice Mgmt.

Graduation Requirements

Students must have a minimum cumulative GPA of 2.0 (C) and complete a minimum of 192 credit hours at Ohio University. Students must earn at least a 2.0 (C) in each course that is a major requirement for the foodservice management major.

Oklahoma State University

School of Hotel and Restaurant Administration

College: College of Human Environmental Sciences
Program Enrollment: 187 undergraduate; 35 graduate
Institutional Enrollment: 20,0000 undergraduate; 4,300 graduate
Degrees Awarded: Bachelor of Science; Master of Science
Degree Categories: Hotel Administration and Restaurant Management
Emphasis/Specialization: Hotel, Restaurant, and Tourism
Institutional Accreditation: North Central Association of Colleges and Schools
Program Accreditation: Accreditation on Commission for Programs in Hospitality Administration (ACPHA)

Contact: Patrick J. Moreo, Ed.D., CHA, Professor and Director, School of Hotel and Restaurant Administration, Oklahoma State University, 210 Human Environmental Sciences West, Stillwater, OK 74078-6173; phone (405) 744-6713; fax (405) 744-6299; e-mail: wellsme@okstate.edu; Internet: www.okstate.edu/hes/hrad/hrad.html

Institution Description

A land-grant institution, Oklahoma State University (OSU) is a large, comprehensive university. Its size does not minimize the amount of personal attention to which each student is entitled. The individual is more than just a number in this university. OSU is nationally recognized for its coeducational residence halls, outstanding Allied Arts Program and well-balanced social activities. The Student Guide to America's 100 Best College Buys in 1999 says the nation's best college value is Oklahoma State University.

Program Description

The School of Hotel and Restaurant Administration at OSU is one of the oldest and most highly recognized of its kind in the nation. The school combines academic theories with industry application in both controlled educational situations and area businesses.

Special Features

An additional 22,500-square foot hospitality industry educational facility was opened in 1990, featuring formal service and multiunit foodservice and hotel front office training laboratories.

Financial Aid and Scholarships

The program receives continued strong financial support from the Oklahoma Restaurant Association, alumni, friends, and industry. Scholarship and grants vary in dollar value and selection criteria. Tuition fee waiver scholarships are available for out-of-state students meeting specific criteria. This scholarship will allow out-of-state students to pay in-state tuition rates. Information is available through High School and College Relations, 210 Student Union.

Approximate Tuition and Fees

Tuition and fees (based on 14 credit hours) for in-state residents are $1,100 per semester; non-Oklahoma residents; $2,975 per semester. University housing is available for $$2,200 per semester. Textbooks and supplies are approximately $415 per semester.

Admissions

Students must satisfy one of the following requirements; 1) achieve a four-year high school grade point average of 3.0 or higher on a 4.0 grading scale and rank scholastically among the top one-third of their graduating class or 2) attain a composite score of 21 or higher on the enhanced ACT or a 900 or higher on the SAT.

Getting the Job

Students in this program are highly recruited for management positions with national and international companies. Seniors that actively interview usually have at least three job offers prior to graduation. OSU alumni are well respected in the restaurant industry and include the vice president of the famous 21 Club in New York City, the executive vice-president of the Oklahoma Restaurant Association, and the owner of Harry Starker's in Kansas City. Other alumni are well respected in the lodging industry and include the CEO and president of Universal Studios, president of American General Hospitality, Inc., and senior vice-president of Sheraton Hotels.

Graduation Requirements

Complete 124 total hours with a cumulative 2.0 GPA overall and a 2.5 GPA in major requirements. Graduate degrees require a minimum of a 3.0 GPA in all coursework and research.

Oxford Brookes University

Hotel and Restaurant Management

Program Enrollment: 140
Institutional Enrollment: Undergraduate-12,000
Graduate 1,200
Degrees Awarded: Bachelor of Science (with Honours); Bachelor of Arts (with Honours)
Degrees Categories: Hotel and Restaurant Management; Hospitality Management Studies
Emphases/Specializations:
Program Accreditation: Hotel and Catering International Management Association

Institutional Accreditation: Oxford Brookes University
Contact: Mr. Donald Sloan and Ms Nina Downie, Undergraduate Program Directors, School of Hotel and Restaurant Management, Oxford Brookes University, Gipsy Lane, Headington, Oxford, OX3 0BP; phone +44 (0) 1865 483801; fax +44 (0) 1865 483878; email: admin@hrm.brookes.ac.uk; website: http://www.brookes.ac.uk/schools/harm

Institution Description

Established in 1865, Oxford Brookes is a coeducational, state-aided university operated by its own board of governors. Brookes offers a wide range of undergraduate and graduate programs in the sciences, business, education, communications and nursing. The School is recognised as an Area of Outstanding Quality.

Program Description

Students complete a period of Supervised Work Experience in industry. They have the opportunity of a period of study in the United States on an exchange basis. Operations and business management is supported by studies in financial management, marketing and human resources management. Students complete an individual project investigation.

Special Features

Brookes offers opportunities for study in a city with a long history of academic excellence. The School's training restaurant has undergone major industry supported refurbishment.

Financial Aid and Scholarships

For European Community students a tuition fee, currently $1,548 per annum, is payable. A number of national governments make scholarships available for selected students.

Admissions

Admission to Brookes is highly competitive. Admission is based upon attainment at high school or in post-high school programs, with evidence of motivation towards the hospitality industry. Entry with credit based on prior qualifications and/or experience may result in the overall period of study being reduced.

Tuition & Fees

In-State: $1,548 per year
Out-of-State: $1,548 per year for EC, $9,754 per year for non-EC
Room and Board: according to choice
Other Fees

Specialization Area

Hotel & Lodging Mgmt
Restaurant & Foodservice Mgmt

Graduation Requirements

Completion of 24 modules, including compulsory units. For honours, this must include an individual project. Interested applicants should request current details.

Paul Smith's College of Arts & Science The College of the Adirondacks

Hospitality Management and Culinary Arts

Program Enrollment: 400
Institutional Enrollment: 800
Degrees Awarded: Bachelor of Science, Bachelor of Professional Studies, Associate in Applied Sciences
Degree Categories: Culinary Arts and Service Management; Culinary Arts; Culinary Arts/Baking; Hotel, Resort & Tourism Management; Hotel and Restaurant Management; Tourism Management
Emphasis/Specialization: Management, Leadership, Culinary, Baking
Program Accreditation: American Culinary Federation Accrediting Commission
Institutional Accreditation: New York State Department of Education; Middle States Association of Colleges and Schools

Contact: Professor Paul Sorgule, CCE, AAC, Assistant Dean, Hospitality/Culinary, P.O. Box 265, Paul Smith's College Paul Smiths, New York 12970; (518) 327-6215; (518) 327-6369 FAX; e-mail: sorgulp@paulsmiths.edu; College Web Page: www.paulsmiths.edu

Institution Description
Paul Smith's Colege is a residential campus located in the heart of the Adirondack Mountain Olympic Region. It is situated on the northern shore of the Lower St. Regis Lake on the site of the original Paul Smith's Hotel. Surrounding this waterfront site are 14,000 acres of college-owned forests and lakes.

Program Description
Paul Smith's is one of the oldest two-year colleges of hospitality management in the U.S. And one of the newest and most innovative four-year institutions offering degrees in hospitality and culinary arts. The college enjoys an outstanding reputation in the industry as proven by over 14,000 graduates. Paul Smith's prides itself in the experiential emphasis of all of its programs that include internship and externship semesters.

Special Features
There are six state-of-the-art kitchens on the campus, a high-tech computer classroom, full scale retail bakery, a 92 room hotel used for training, and plans for a training restaurant and food technology laboratory in it's Statler Hospitality Center. Students in the college hotel are trained on the Springer-Miller Property Management System.

The college offers internship options in its hotel, in the Burgundy Region of France, and on-campus in its full-scale bakery. Students enjoy more than 300 choice properties for externship throughout the United States.

Financial Aid and Scholarships
Paul Smith's College maintains a full-time financial aid office prepared to assist parents, as well as prospective and enrolled students with information concerning the various avenues through which they may receive assistance in meeting the cost of an education. In addition, scholarships are available from the industry and private individuals.

Approximate Tuition and Fees
Tuition is $12,500 per year, room and board is approximately $6,000 per year, and lab fees between $450 and $800 per semester. Books, tools, and uniforms are extra.

Admissions
Admission to Paul Smith's College os based on academic ability and aptitude as well as character, related work experience and extracurricular activities. SAT or ACT test scores are required.

Transfer students are very welcome from institutions offering similar degrees. AAS and AOS two-year degree graduates can bridge into baccalaureate programs with relative ease.

Graduation Requirements
Cumulative Grade Point Average of 2.0; complete minimum credit hours for degree; college core liberal arts to include English, Math, and Social Sciences.

Other
14:1 students to faculty ratio. Laboratory classes carry a cap of 15 and most lecture classes accommodate less than 25. Paul Smith's has a 99% placement rate.

Pennsylvania College of Technology

Hospitality

Program Enrollment: 150
Institutional Enrollment: 4,850
Degrees Awarded: Associate of Applied Science, Bachelors of Arts
Degree Categories: Food and Hospitality Management, AAS; Culinary Arts, AAS, BS; Baking and Pastry Arts, AAS; Dietary Manager Technology, AAS
Program Accreditation: American Culinary Federation Educational Institute Accrediting Commission (CA,BK) CAHM (FH)
Institutional Accreditation: Middle States Association of Colleges and Secondary Schools
Contact: Mr. William C. Butler, Dean School of Hospitality, One College Avenue, Williamsport, PA 17701; phone: 570-327-4505,fax: 1-570-327-4503, e-mail bbutler@pct.edu

Institution Description

As a Penn State affiliate, Penn College is realizing its full potential as Pennsylvania's premier technical college. Continuing in a tradition of excellence, Penn College is a strong force in higher education in Pennsylvania, offering certificate, associate and baccalaureate degree programs. Students from around the state, the nation, and the world are enjoying the benefits of state-of-the-art programs in traditional and emerging technologies.

Program Description

This program prepares the students in fine product preparation and presentation. Extensive practical experience with the variety of cuisine and techniques is available through hands-on instruction. The program is fully accredited by the American Culinary Federation Educational Institute Accrediting Commission. Food and Hospitality Management – This program includes academic classroom study and practical laboratory work in business and personnel management, food preparation and supervision, and related subjects. Guest speakers, field trips and directed community field work experiences expand students' learning opportunities. Baking and Pastry Arts – This program prepares the student to produce a full range of baked goods and pastries, classical and contemporary. Extensive practical hands-on experience is enhanced by classroom instruction. The program is fully accredited by the American Culinary Federation Educational Institute Accrediting Commission. Dietary Manager Technology – This program prepares students to perform as a key link between Dieticians and cooks in health care and institutional facilities. It combines culinary skills with strong theoretical and clinical education in nutrition.

Special Features

Students have an opportunity to become Junior Members of the American Culinary Federation, West Branch Chapter, which enables them to become certified in various levels within the organization. Students participate in food show competitions, end-of-the-semester projects and culinary salons throughout the area. Other opportunities are available including: The Visiting Chef Series, California Winery Association Events, the NRA Salute to Excellence, The Kentucky Derby, The Breeder's Cup and Hunt Country Vineyard's Weekend Open House, and assisting on "You're the Chef", our syndicated PBS series.

Financial Aid and Scholarships

Recognizing that the cost of education is often greater than the student and his/her family can afford without help, the Financial Aid Office helps students obtain financial assistance through Grants and Scholarships (College and School possibilities), Loans, College Work Study Programs, Veteran's Benefits, Vocational Rehabilitation Sponsorship and part-time employment.

Admission

Committed to serving the educational needs of students from all walks of life, Pennsylvania College of Technology operates under an "open door" admissions policy and is open to anyone with a high school diploma or its equivalent. An adult who does not have a high school diploma or its equivalent may be admitted as a "special student." Acceptance to some programs of study, including baccalaureate degree programs, is based upon the applicant's meeting the requirement including necessary academic skills and prerequisites of the specific program of study. The College reserves the right to deny admission or readmission to any student if, in the opinion of College authorities, his/her admission is not in the best interest of the student or the College. Equal opportunity for admission is offered without regard to age, sex, handicap, race, religion, creed, national origin, veteran status, or political affiliation. The College will provide opportunities to develop the basic skills necessary to enroll in degree and certificate courses to those who demonstrate such needs of the College's placement tests.

Tuition and Fees

APPLICATION FEE– applicants for status as full-time students in degree or certificate programs must include a non-refundable application fee with their Admissions Application. You are required to pay this non-refundable fee only once (unless you are enrolling after more that two years). IN-STATE STUDENTS: Tuition and fees will total approximately $7,000 per year in 1998-99.* OUT-OF-STATE STUDENTS; tuition and fees will total approximately $8,300 per year in 1998-99. * The College reserves the right to change tuition and other fees as required.

Plattsburgh State University of New York

Hotel, Restaurant and Tourism Management

Program Enrollment: 175
Institutional Enrollment: 5,500 undergraduate; 800 graduate
Degree Awarded: Bachelor of Science BaSnce
Degree Category: Hotel, Restaurant, and Tourism Management
Institutional Accreditation: Middle States Association of Colleges and Secondary Schools; Board of Regents
Contact: Marilyn Chase, Chair, Hotel, Restaurant & Tourism Management, School of Business and Economics, Plattsburgh State University of New York,101 Broad Street, Plattsburgh, NY 12901; phone (518) 564-2164

Institution Description

Plattsburgh State offers nearly 60 major fields of study, complemented by a wide variety of minors and study options. Our major programs encompass arts and sciences, business and economics, and professional studies. The city of Plattsburgh is located in the northeast corner of the state, on the shore of Lake Champlain just each of the Adirondack Park.

Program Description

The Hotel, Restaurant and Tourism Management (HRT) program is designed to prepare students for successful management careers in the hospitality industry. The primary purpose of the program is to educate students in hospitality management and prepare graduates to meet the challenges of the 21st century. This aim is accomplished through a well-balanced curriculum; dedicated faculty, small class size, and off-campus activities, all designed to enhance the student's opportunity for success.

Special Features

Ranked ninth of one hundred best college buys in the northeast according to Money Magazine based on delivery of the highest quality education for the tuition and fees charged. The on-campus chapters of International Foodservice Executive Association and the Eta Sigma Delta International Hospitality Honor Society strengthens the ties between academics and the hospitality industry.

Financial Aid and Scholarships

The Financial Aid Office at Plattsburgh administers programs designed to assist students in securing the financial resources needed to pay for college. During the past six years, Plattsburgh has awarded more than $1.2 million in private financial assistance to students. Information about scholarships and financial aid may be obtained by writing the Financial Aid or Admissions Offices, SUNY Plattsburgh, Kehoe Bldg., Plattsburgh, NY 12901; phone (518) 564-2072.

Approximate Tuition and Fees

Resident tuition is approximately $2,650 per year; non-New York State residents pay $8,300 per year. Mandatory student fees total $437 per year for a full-time student. These costs are subject to change.

Admissions

Admission to the College is competitive and based on the academic and personal qualifications of the applicant. A substantial percent of the HRT students usually enroll as transfers from two-year programs. A 2.7 GPA is required on prior college work. Articulation agreements exist to facilitate transfer from many of the two-year programs in New York State.

Graduation Requirements

The HRT Program requires 120 semester credits, including 60 credits in liberal arts with 42 credits in general education, 45 credits in hotel, restaurant and tourism management and/or food and nutrition courses, 21 credit business minor, and 15 credits in free electives. Additional requirements include 800 hours of approved hospitality industry-related work experience.

Prince of Songkla University, Phuket Campus,Thailand

Hotel and Tourism Management

Program Enrollment: 150
Institutional Enrollment: 272 Certificate; 11,946 Undergraduate; 1,921 Graduate; 38 Postgraduate
Degrees Awarded: Bachelor of Business Administration (Hotel Management)
Degree Categories: Bachelor of Arts; Bachelor of Business Administration
Emphases/Specializations: Hotel Management; Tourism Management
Program Accreditation: Ministry of University Affairs
Institutional Accreditation: Government of Thailand
Contact: Manat Chaisawat, Director/Associate Professor, Faculty of Hotel and Tourism Management, Prince of Songkla University, Phuket Campus, 80 Moo 1 Vichit Songkram Rd., Amphur Kathu, Phuket, Thailand, 83120. Phone (66-76) 202556-7; fax (66-76) 202558; e-mail h&t@ratree.psu.ac.th or cmanat@ratree.psu.ac.th

Institution Description
Prince of Songkla University was established in 1967 to increase opportunities for tertiary education in South Thailand and to support the development of the region. The university was planned as a multi-campus institution which now has five educational sites.

Program Description
The Faculty of Hotel and Tourism Management was set up in 1992. Phuket was chosen as the site for the new faculty because this area has become a major destination for the international tourism industry and allows for intern training in many of the area's five star hotels.

Special Features
All courses are taught in English and the Faculty is strongly involved in the issues facing international tourism.. The new campus features a 33 room luxury hotel, a computer laboratory and proximity to one of Thailand's major international tourism destinations.

Financial Aid and Scholarships
While Thai applicants are eligible for tuition waivers there are at present no financial aid programs available for international students.

Admissions
Admission to the Faculty of Hotel and Tourism Management depends upon graduation from secondary school, a TOEFL score of 500 and above and recommendations from advisers or supervisors about the potential student's previous work or study.

Tuition & Fees
International students: Tuition US $2,000 per annum; room and board US $ 2,500 per annum.

Specialization Area
Hotel and Lodging Management

Graduation Requirements
Students are expected to successfully complete 144 units of course work, over 4 years, for the Bachelor Degree, in addition to 500 (1st and 2nd years) and 600 (3rd and 4th years) hours of internship every year, in a hotel operation, during the semester breaks. Students may leave the program with a Certificate of Food and Beverage after successful completion of the second year and a Certificate of Hotel Management after the third year.

Purdue University

Restaurant, Hotel, Institutional, and Tourism Management (RHIT)

College: School of Consumer and Family Science
Program Enrollment: 550
Institutional Enrollment: 30,159 undergraduate; 6,719 graduate
Degrees Awarded: Bachelor of Science; Master of Science; Doctor of Philosophy; Associate of Applied Science
Degree Categories: Restaurant, Hotel, Institutional, and Tourism Management
Emphases/Specializations: Lodging, Foodservice, and Tourism (attention can also focus on club management and contract foodservice)
Program Accreditation: Accreditation Commission for Programs in Hospitality Administration (ACPHA)
Institutional Accreditation: North Central Association of Colleges and Schools

Contact: Raphael R. Kavanaugh, Ed.D., CHA, FMP, Head, Department of Restaurant, Hotel, Institutional, and Tourism Management, Purdue University, 1266 Stone Hall, West Lafayette, IN 47907-w1266; phone (765) 494-4643; fax (765) 494-0327; e-mail brubakerm@cfs.purdue.edu; website http://www.cfs.purdue.edu/RHIT/

Institutional Description

Description: Located in the heart of the Midwest, Purdue was founded in 1869 as a land-grant university. As one of the 25 largest schools in the nation, its alumni include Nobel Prize winners, astronauts, three U.S. Secretaries of Agriculture, literary figures, and college and corporate presidents. Purdue offers students infinite social and cultural events as well as some of the best athletic facilities in the Big Ten. This beautifully landscaped campus is located in a major metropolitan center 125 miles southeast of Chicago and 65 miles northwest of Indianapolis.

Program Description

Ranked among the top ten hospitality programs in the nation, RHIT offers students a choice of three specializations. In addition to the specification and core requirements, there is a solid base of general education courses, as well as electives. Six Areas of Concentration outside RHIT have been developed in Information Systems, Finance, Human Resources, International Business, Marketing/Sales, and Transportation.

Special Features

The RHIT Computer Resource Center integrates the latest computer technology into classroom usage. The RHIT Café and restaurant kitchens provide a state-of-the-art training facility for students, as well as public dining, in which students gain hands-on and management experience. RHIT students develop industry networks through unique interaction with the RHIT Advisory Board and the annual RHIT Career Day. The RHIT Recruiting Center provides internship opportunities and coordinates interviewing and job placement for RHIT students.

Financial Aid and Scholarships

Purdue University's Office of Financial Aid provides students with information on many sources of financial assistance. In addition, over $60,000 in merit scholarships and financial assistance are awarded annually to students within the RHIT Department.

Admissions

Admission to Purdue is dependent on class rank in high school, probability of success, grade average, trends in achievement, strength of college preparatory program, and ACT or SAT scores. Transfer students should have a 2.0 GPA. Articulation agreements for transfer credits have been established with several hospitality two-year programs.

Approximate Tuition and Fee

In-state tuition is $3,564 per year; out-of-state tuition is $11,784 per year.

Specialization Area

Hotel & Lodging Mgmt., Restaurant & Foodservice Mgmt., and Travel
Tourism Mgmt.

Graduation Requirements

130 hours which include 45 hours general education 50 hours RHIT core courses, 17-22 hours specialization courses, and 13-21 hours electives. A minimum of 300-hour industry internship experience is required.

Queen Margaret College

Department of Business and Consumer Studies

Program Enrollment: 300
Institutional Enrollment: 3,000 undergraduate; 100 graduate
Degree Awarded: Bachelor of Arts; Post-Graduate Diploma, Msc
Degree Categories: Hospitality and Tourism Management; International Hospitality Management; Tourism Management
Emphases/Specializations: Tourism and Leisure Management; Entrepreneurial Management; Enterprise and Innovation; Language; Hospitality Practice and Operations
Institutional Accreditation: Hotel, Catering and Institutional Management Association
Contact: David Kirk, Head, Department of Business and Consumer Studies, Queen Margaret College, Clerwood Terrace, Edinburgh, Scotland EH12 8TS; phone +44 (0) 1 31-317 3000; fax +44 (0) 1 31-317 3777; e-mail: d.kirk@mail.qmced.ac.uk

Institutional Description

Queen Margaret College is a University level institution funded by the Scottish Higher Education Funding Council. QMC has been in existence since 1875, moving to its present site in 1970. The campus is situated four miles from Edinburgh and is 25 acres in size. Facilities include a swimming pool, squash courts, tennis courts, gymnasium and student union.

Program Description

The Department of Business and Consumer Studies is primarily oriented toward a business and management studies education base. The thrust of the proposed new semester-based, modular degree is in the area of enterprise and innovation as it applied to hospitality and tourist-related areas. Each course has a 22 week period of industrial placement in industry. The course is either 3 years (BA) or 4 years (BA Honours) in length.

Special Features

Exchange programs are arranged with similar courses in North America and continental Europe. The Department of Hospitality and Tourism Management is developing a high level of case-study input into its courses and moving toward nontraditional methods of student assessment. Student can elect to specialize in hospitality and tourism.

Financial Aid and Scholarships

Scholarships are available to students from the UK and European Union.

Admissions

Admission to the department's courses is based on minimum academic performance levels at school, as well as exceptional entry for mature and highly motivated students without the necessary qualifications. The postgraduate courses require a first degree qualification as a minimum, although an exceptional entry can be given without this qualification, but with considerable industrial experience.

Rochester Institute of Technology

School of Food, Hotel and Travel Management

College: Applied Science and Technology
Program Enrollment: 300 undergraduate; 68 graduate
Institutional Enrollment: 11,864 undergraduate; 2,153 graduate
Degrees Awarded: Bachelor of Science; Master of Science
Degree Categories: Bachelor's in Food, Hotel and Travel Management; Master's in Hospitality/Tourism Management and Service Management
Emphases/Specializations: Hotel/Resort Management; Food Management; Travel Management; Dietetics; Food and Marketing Distribution
Institutional Accreditation: Middle States Association of Colleges and Schools
Contact Name: Francis M. Domoy, Ph.D., Chair, Rochester Institute of Technology, School of Food, Hotel and Travel Management,14 Lomb Memorial Drive, Rochester, NY 14623; phone: (716)475-2867 or (716)475-5576; fax: (716)475-5099; e-mail: FMDISM@RIT.edu

Institution Description

Rochester Institute of Technology (RIT) is a composite of seven colleges: applied science and technology, business, engineering, imaging arts and sciences, liberal arts, science, and National Technical Institute for the Deaf.

Program Description

RIT's School of Food, Hotel and Travel Management is a very comprehensive set of programs in every aspect of the hospitality and tourism industry. Food management, corporate travel planning, meeting management, hotel/resort management, nutritional programming, risk and yield management, tourism management and property management highlight the major areas of employment that the diversified curriculum is targeted to fill.

Special Features

Cooperative education; American Airlines SABRE Lab; dedicated computer lab; National Advisory Board; and state-of-the-art Henry's Restaurant

Financial Aid and Scholarships

The institute's financial aid office assists eligible students in securing scholarships, loans, and part-time employment through the college work-study program academic achievement.

Admissions

Students in the School of Food, Hotel and Travel Management are accepted directly into the program in their freshman year, or as transfers from two-year colleges within the United States and from various international institutions.
academic records, college and entrance exams (Israeli psychometric exam or SAT exam) and the results of a required personal interview.

Tuition and Fees

Undergraduate tuition is $16,710 per year. Room and Board $6,625

Graduation Requirements

Upon graduation, the student will have completed 180 quarter hours, which included 58 credits of liberal arts, 12 credits in business management, 24 credits of science-related subjects, and 82 credits in the hospitality discipline. A 1,600-hour cooperative work experience is also required.

Schiller International University

International School of Tourism and Hospitality Management (I.S.T.H.M.)

College: International School of Tourism and Hospitality Management (I.S.T.H.M.)
Program Enrollment: 176 undergraduates; 32 graduates
Institutional Enrollment:934 undergraduate; 254 graduate
Degrees Awarded: Associate of Science; Bachelor of Business Administration: Master of Business Administration; Master of Arts; Diploma
Degree Categories: International Hotel and Tourism Management
Emphases/Specializations: International residence and foreign languages, international internships
Program Accreditation: Accreditation: Accrediting Council for independent Colleges and Schools; Hotel, Catering and Institutional Management Association (London) Travel and Tourism (London)
Contact: Wilfried Iskat, PhD, CHA, FMP, FHCIMA, Dean, international School of Tourism and Hospitality Management , 453 Edgewater Drive, Dunedin, FL 34698; phone (727)736-5082; fax: (727) 736-6263; tollfree (USA only) 1(800) 336-4133; email: ISTHM@msn.com or wilfred_iskat@schiller.edu.

Institution Description

Founded in 1964, and with students from more than 100 nations enrolled, SIU offers the opportunity for an American education in an international setting with English as the language of instruction at all eight campuses in six countries: Tampa Bay Area, Florida, USA; Central London, England; Paris and Strausbourg, France; Heidelberg, Germany; Engelberg and Leysin, Switzerland; and Madrid, Spain. Students are encouraged to transfer freely between SIU's

Program Description

The program is designed primarily to prepare graduates for entry-level management positions. A threephase internship oriented educational program has been developed as part of the Hospitality Management Program curriculum. This plan requires students to alternate periods of class attendance with three periods of summer work experience in approved hospitality industries.

Special Features

SIU offers the four-year Bachelor of Business Administration degree in Hospitality Management and in International Tourism Management. Both programs combine a full range of professionally focused courses, plus courses in international business administration, general education, and language. Special Hotel Management Term Abroad Programs are also available at the campuses in the Tampa Bay Area in Florida, USA and in Engelberg, Switzerland (near Lucerne), and in Strasbourg, France. Each of these focuses on the special hotel, restaurant, and tourism management aspects of the respective countries.

Financial Aid and Scholarships

Schiller offers both scholarships and work-study opportunities and participates in government-sponsored loan programs.

Approximate Tuition and Fees

No in-state-out-of-state differentials, but the fee structure applies to the Florida and European campuses. 1999-2000 undergraduate per academic year: Florida, US$12,400; Europe, US$13,400. Room and board: Florida US$5,200; Europe, US$8,700. other fees: US$390.

Admissions

For undergraduate degrees and diplomas: successful completion of 12 years of formal education. Students need an advanced knowledge of English, but those with a good intermediate knowledge can take a course in English as a Foreign Language while beginning work on their degree. Others can enroll initially at one of our English language institutes.

Graduation Requirements

Bachelor's degrees: 124 semester credit hours, including the requirements for the related associate degree (see that section), plus upper-level courses in hotel tourism management, business administration and economics, and courses in social science.

SENAC – CET - Center of Studies in Tourism and Hotel Management

Superior Course in Hotel Administration / Superior Course in Tourism Technology / Bachelor Course in Hotel Management

Program Enrollment: 270
Institutional Enrollment: 780
Degrees Awarded: Associate and Bachelor
Degree Categories: Hotel Management
Emphases / Specializations – none

Program Accreditation: Brazilian Ministry of Education
Contact: Luiz Gonzaga Godoi Trigo, Director, Av. Francisco Matarazzo, 249, 05001-150, São Paulo – SP – Brazil, Tel: (55) (11) 263-2511, Fax: (55) (11) 864-4597, e-mail: cet@sp.senac.br

Institution Description

The Center of studies in Tourism and Hotel Management (CET) is an Institution maintained by Senac. It offers Undergraduate and graduate programs, continuing education and extention courses, international seminars and work training programs for the hotel, tourism and catering industries. CET offers its students the opportunity to practice skills at internships in our Model Hotel Schools.

Program Description

The Superior Course in Hotel Administration available in São Paulo, Águas de São Pedro and Campos do Jordão, provides opportunities to students who want to become professional in this field and able to perform middle management positions. The Superior Course In Tourism technology is starting this year in Águas de São Pedro. The Bachelor Course in Hotel Management is offered only in the capital and prepares students for leading positions.

Special Features

Superior Course in Hotel Administration – Food and Beverage laboratory/Housekeeping lab/internship at the hotel school. Superior Course in Tourism Technology – Computer lab applied to tourism/ Professional Practice at the hotel school. Bachelor Course in Hotel Management – Cooking lab/Computer Lab applied to the industry/Housekeeping lab.

Financial Aid and Scholarships

SENAC offers limited financial aid, based on the student's financial situation and scholatic achievement. This student will be developing a research in the field.

Admissions

Students applicants with a high school diploma will be admitted according to their ranking as determined by scholastic aptitude exams.

Specialization Area

Hotel and Lodging Management and Travel & Tourism Management

Graduation Requirements

In order to graduate the student must successfully pass all course requirements and complete a 450 hour externship in the field or hospitality institution of his choice.

Siena Heights University

Hospitality Management (HOS)

Program Enrollment: 55
Institutional Enrollment: 2,200 undergraduate; 155 graduate
Degree Awarded: Bachelor of Arts
Degree Category: Hotel and Hospitality Management
Institutional Accreditation: North Central Association of Colleges

Contact: Marilee Purse, HOS Program Coordinator, Business and Management Division, Siena Heights University, 1247 East Siena Heights Drive, Adrian, MI 49221; phone: (517) 264-7635; fax: (517) 264-7731

Institution Description

Siena Heights is a Catholic Liberal Arts college founded in 1919 by its current sponsors, the Adrian Dominican Sisters. We offer 6 graduate and 34 undergraduate programs. Seven programs, including HOS, are housed in the Business and Management Division. Residential, commuter, nontraditional and international students are welcome.

Program Description

Rooted in the liberal arts tradition, HOS emphasizes both hands-on experience and general management skill development. Graduates are not only prepared for first line management but long term personal and professional growth as well.

Special Features

Small classes model and emphasize the personal touch vital to success. Experiential learning includes co-ops and internships. Both graduation placement and career planning are strengths.

Financial Aid and Scholarships

Along with state and federal aid, we offer 16 different need based academic scholarship programs, including three HRIM Competitive Scholarship awarded annually.

Approximate Tuition and Fees

Tuition: $11,000; Room and Board: $4,000; Other Fees: $75-$100.

Admissions

Our open admissions considers grades, recommendations, participation in school or work, and test scores (ACT or SAT, and TOEFL for international applicants). Transfer students need a 2.0 cumulative GPA. Both traditional and nontraditional students are welcome.

Graduation Requirements

This four-year degree requires 120 semester credits with 50 credits in the major, 28 in HRIM and 22 in Business. Beyond the major and general education, 40 credits remain for academic minors (Spanish, Communications, for example). Transfers must complete 30 credits minimum, 18 in HOS at Siena Heights.

South Dakota State University

Hotel and Foodservice Management

College: Family and Consumer Sciences
Program Enrollment: 80
Institutional Enrollment: 7,800 undergraduate: 1,250 graduate
Degree Awarded: Bachelor of Science
Degree Category: Hotel and Foodservice Management
Institutional Accreditation: North Central Association of Colleges and Schools

Contact: Dr. Ruth Krause, Assistant Professor, Hotel and Foodservice Management, Department of Nutrition, Food Science and Hospitality, Box 2275A, Brookings, SD 57007; Phone: (605) 688-5150; fax: (605) 688-5603

Institution Description

South Dakota State University (SDSU) is a state-funded, land-grant institution established in 1881. SDSU is the largest university in the state offering approximately 200 majors, minors and options in eight colleges. Located in the eastern South Dakota city of Brookings, SDSU provides an excellent setting for students desiring a high quality education. SDSU is extremely proud of its reputation for academic advising and emphasis on the needs and goals of the individual student.

Program Description

SDSU's Hotel and Foodservice Management Program (HFM) provides a firm foundation in either lodging or foodservice management supported by a strong background in business. On-the-job experience for college credit strengthens the academic program. Academic requirements consist of five components: liberal arts, college core studies, business courses, HFM courses, and electives selected according to student interests.

Special Features

HFM students have a minor in Business Administration included in their curriculum, can earn a minor in Economics with the addition of one Economics course, and can graduate with emphases in both the lodging and foodservice areas with appropriate selection of elective courses.

Financial Aid and Scholarships

The College of Family and Consumer Sciences offers more than $150,000 in scholarships to qualified students each year. Scholarships specifically for HFM students are provided by the South Dakota Innkeepers Association, the South Dakota Retailers Association, ARAMARK, and other hospitality-related organizations. Additional financial assistance is available through the university's financial aid office.

Approximate Tuition and Fees

{Based on 16 credits per semester} In-State Tuition: $899; Out-of-State Tuition: $2,860; Other University fees: $617; On-campus Room and Board $1,365; Books and Supplies; $350.

Admissions

Admission to SDSU is open to all academically qualified students. Admission of high school students or recently graduated high school students is based on the high school transcript and ACT composite score. Transfer students are considered for admission based on their college and high school transcripts. For details contact the Office of Admissions, South Dakota State University, Box 2201, Brookings, SD 57557-0649, or call (605)-688-4121. E-mail: sdsuadms@adm.sdstate.edu.

Graduation Requirements

Graduation requires the successful completion of 128 semester credit hours and includes: 42 hours of liberal studies courses, 6 hours of College core courses, 49 of HFM courses, 24 hours of business and economics courses, and 7 hours of electives.

Southern Cross University

Tourism/Hospitality Management

College: School of Tourism and Hospitality Management
Program Enrollment: 1000
Institutional Enrollment: 10,000
Degrees Awarded: Bachelor of Business in Tourism, Bachelor of Business in Hotel and Catering Management
Degree Categories: Tourism Management, Hotel and Catering Management and Hospitality Management
Emphases/Specializations: Hotel and Resort Management, Convention and Event Management, Tourism Marketing and Planning, International Tourism Management, Gaming and Club Management, Hotel and Catering Management.
Program Accreditation: Winner of New South Wales Award for Excellence in Tourism - Industry Education category, 1997 and 1998. Finalist in 1997 and 1998 in the Australian Tourism Awards – Industry Education category.
Institutional Accreditation: N/A
Contact: Professor Gary Prosser, Head, School of Tourism and Hospitality Management, Southern Cross University, PO Box 157, Lismore, NSW, 2480, Australia. Ph: +61 26620 3354, Fax +61 26622 2208

Institutional Description
Southern Cross University is a government regulated and funded university with an unequivocal commitment to excellence. Located on the beautiful East Coast of northern New South Wales, there are campuses in Lismore, Coffs Harbour and Sydney. Southern Cross University is the South Pacific's largest provider of university level tourism education.

Program Description
The courses are three years full-time, which includes 24 weeks structured work experience in the hotel/tourism industry with an option to study one semester overseas. The courses may be studied on-campus or by distance education, provide management skills in a variety of tourism-related fields, and allow specialization in specific areas.

Special Features
Students may elect to participate in one semester of full-time study at one of three international exchange partner universities in the United Kingdom, USA or the Netherlands.

Financial Aid and Scholarships
The Australian Government provides financial assistance to international students through a range of scholarship programs.

Admissions
To satisfy admission requirements of entry to undergraduate courses students must have completed an appropriate educational qualification deemed at least equivalent to matriculation in Australia (minimum score of USA: SAT 970) and have met the University's English language requirements.

Tuition and Fees
Tuition fees are $11,000 per annum for the undergraduate program.

Specialization Area
Travel and Tourism Management.

Graduation Requirements
Graduates have to successfully complete 24 units. All students are required to complete 16 core units and eight elective units including at least one minor elective stream, which allows students the flexibility to specialize within the course. All students must complete a six-month work experience placement within the Tourism and Hospitality industries.

Southern Illinois University-Carbondale

Hotel, Restaurant and Travel Administration

College: College of Agriculture
Program Enrollment: 160
Institutional Enrollment: 19,000; undergraduate; 4,000 graduate
Degree Awarded: Bachelor of Science
Degree Category: Food and Nutrition
Emphases/Specializations: Hotel, Restaurant and Travel Administration
Institutional Accreditation: North Central Association of Colleges and Schools
Contact: Dr. Trish Welch, Professor, HRTA, c/o Food and Nutrition, Room 209, Quigley Hall, SIU, 4317, Carbondale, IL 62901; phone (618) 453-5193 or (618) 536-2157; fax (618) 453-7517

Institution Description

Southern Illinois University-Carbondale (SIUC), situated in an enviable scenic location, is a comprehensive, public university with a thoughtful approach to the blending of old wisdom and new knowledge, as well as comprehensive student services from admissions to placement. Resources include an open-stack library, state-of-the-art computer laboratories and local businesses as classrooms.

Program Description

The Hotel, Restaurant and Travel Administration (HRTA) Program provides students with a comprehensive range of general education requirements, core business courses and HRTA courses. The emphasis of the program is to develop management capability through interdisciplinary exposure, analytical problem-solving and case-study analysis. The program combines management theory with practical application to meet the challenges of a career in the hospitality industry.

Special Features

The HRTA Program, which provides placement assistance, seeks to match internship experiences with students' professional interests. In a cooperative effort with the university, students are responsible for the operation of a faculty dining room. They also work with the Touch of Nature Lodge & Conference Center.

Financial Aid and Scholarships

Program scholarships are supported by contributions from industry, special interest groups and professional organizations. These awards complement the university's extensive scholarship pool; over $80,000 in scholarships are given out by the university each year.

Approximate Tuition and Fees

In-state tuition and fees are $3,821 per year, out-of-state tuition and fees, $6,602 per year.

Admissions

Applicants for admission must submit ACT scores if they are less than 21 years of age. Freshmen may immediately enter the HRTA Program. Up to 60 hours of transfer credit will be accepted from community colleges.

Graduation Requirements

Graduation requires the completion of 120 semester hours, which includes 46 hours of general education, 65 hours within the specialization, and nine hours of electives. Two preplanned internships are part of the required coursework.

Southern Oregon University (SOU)

Hotel, Restaurant and Resort Management Option

College: School of Business
Program Enrollment: New Program
Institutional Enrollment: 4,364 undergraduate, 362 graduate
Degrees Awarded: Bachelor of Arts or Science in Business Administration, Master of Business Administration Degree Categories: hotel, restaurant, and resort management option
Emphases/Specializations: Hotel Management; Restaurant and Food Service Management
Institutional Accreditation: Northwest Association of Schools and Colleges
Contact: Dr. Suad Cox, Director, Hotel, Restaurant, and Resort Management Program, School of Business, Southern Oregon University, Ashland, OR 97520; phone (541) 552-8202

Institution and Description

SOU's mission is to provide quality education in liberal arts and professional programs. The college's approximately 4,726 students are able to pursue coursework in 36 different degree programs. The college occupies a 175-acre campus with 15 academic buildings, 14 resident halls, a 280-,000-volume library and a new state-of-the-art Computing Services Building.

Program Description

The Hotel, Restaurant and Resort Management (HRRM) program is part of the School of Business Administration. The liberal arts and sciences, and business subjects form a solid foundation upon which to build the specialization in hospitality management. This specialization consists of a core of hospitality courses which provide a comprehensive hospitality management education. Cooperative and education internship placements totaling 800 hours of practical work experience are also included. The mission of the program is to provide theoretical and practical educational opportunities which lead to middle and upper-level management positions in hotels, restaurants, in a variety of business and institutional settings.

Special Features

The HRRM program builds on the fundamental foundation of a School of Business Management degree through an integrated approach. It places a strong emphasis on providing students with small class environment, close one-to-one interactions with faculty, and access to a developed international study/work-abroad network.

Financial Aid and Scholarships

A full range of financial aid programs are available to students. Students are also eligible for any number of business and HRRM Scholarships.

Approximate Tuition and Fees

Tuition for residents is $3,147; for out-of-state students $8,847; Room and board is $4,200.

Admissions

Enter freshmen are required to have completed 14 units (1 unit=1 year) of college preparatory subjects in English (4) math (3), science (2), social sciences (3), and one foreign language (2). Students also need to have a high school grade point average of 2.75 or a SAT of 1010.

Graduation Requirements

Graduation requires completion of 180 quarter credits, which includes 60 hours of liberal arts and sciences, 16 hours of lower-division business coursework, 28 hours of upper-division business core courses, and 28 hours in HRRM core courses and internships. The balance of credits are electives and choice of minor.

Southern Vermont College

Hospitality/Resort Management Program

Program Enrollment: 20
Institution Enrollment: 700
Degrees Awarded: Associate Degree; Bachelor Degree
Degree Categories: Associate of Science Degree in Hospitality/Resort Management; Bachelor of Science; Degree in Hospitality/Resort Management
Emphasis/Specializations: Minor concentrations available in Accounting, Business, Child Development, Communications, Corporate Security, Criminal Justice, English, Environmental Studies, Gerontology, History, Human Services, Management, Marketing, Natural Resources, Psychology, and Visual Arts. Individualized degree programs are also available.
Institutional Accreditation: New England Association of Schools and Colleges
Contact: Bobbi Gabrenya, Director of Admissions, Southern Vermont College, 982 Foothills Road, Bennington, VT 05201; phone 802-447-6304 or 800-378-2782; fax 802-447-4695; e-mail: admis@svc.edu

Institution Description

Southern Vermont College is a small, private, liberal arts college in historic Old Bennington, Vermont. The College offers 11 associate and 15 bachelor degree programs which emphasize a career-oriented, liberal arts curriculum. On the base of Mount Anthony in the southwest corner of Vermont, Southern Vermont College is home to the scenic Green Mountains, ponds, meadows, and forests. Only 1 hour from Albany, NY, and 3-1/2 hours from New York City, Montreal, and Boston, the area is noted as prime ski country and home to many performing arts groups.

Program Description

The Program Coordinator, William "Scotty" Gray, brings a wealth of experience to the Hospitality/Resort Management Program. Scotty, an author and consultant, believes in flexibility and "hands-on" learning. In addition to a wide variety of internships, courses offered include: Front Office & Guest Services Management; Kitchen Management and Food Production; Beverage Management & Wine Appreciation; business management courses; accounting courses; Public Relations; and Human Resources Management.

Admissions

To formally apply to the College, a student must submit the following: a completed application form and a $25 application fee; an official high school transcript or GED; an essay; two letters of recommendation; and SAT, ACT, or College placement test scores. Admissions are on a rolling basis; however, applicants for the fall semester are encouraged to submit their application by March.

Graduation Requirements

Associate Degree: 24 credits in program requirements; 24 credits in general core courses; 12 credits in electives, for a total of 60 credits. Six Forum (cultural) credits are also required to graduate.

Bachelor Degree: 54 credits in program requirements; 48 credits in general core courses; 18 credits in electives; for a total of 120 credits. Twelve Forum (cultural) credits are also required to graduate. work experience (400 hours in residence) is also required.

Southwest Missouri State University

Hospitality and Restaurant Administration

College: Health and Human Services
Program Enrollment: 350
Institutional Enrollment: 16,500
Degree Awarded: Bachelor of Science
Degree Category: Hospitality and Restaurant Administration
Institutional Accreditation: North Central Association of Colleges and Schools; National Council for Accreditation of Teacher Education

Contact: Hank Huitt, Director, Hospitality and Restaurant Administration Southwest Missouri State University, 901 South National Ave., Springfield, Missouri 65804; phone 417/836-4908, fax 417/836-7673, e-mail HankHuitt@mail.smsu.edu

Institution Description

Southwest Missouri State University is a metropolitan university serving a unique combination of urban and rural environments, whose single purpose is to develop educated persons. The university is committed to the creation of a teaching and learning environment which maximizes the student's opportunity to become such a person.

Program Description

The Hospitality and Restaurant Administration program at SMSU is committed to excellence in education. The student will receive a combination of theory and practical educational experience to prepare the graduate for entry-level management, sales, personnel and accounting positions with hotels, resorts, restaurants, clubs, theme parks and other hospitality related businesses.

Special Features

The program is located in a major tourism area which offers excellent opportunities for students to gain valuable experience in the industry while attending college. In addition, the faculty is made up of professors who have both academic and professional skills to guide students in the areas of study necessary to succeed in the hospitality careers.

Financial Aid and Scholarships

Several scholarships are available for hospitality majors based on academic achievement and industry experience.

Approximate Tuition and Fees

Tuition for state residents if $1,068; for nonresidents, $2,245. Room and board is $1,455. Books typically cost $250.

Admissions

Tests accepted for admission purposes are: ACT, SAT, PSAT, and SCAT. Students must be graduates of accredited high schools or have successfully completed the GED exam.

Specialization Area

Hotel and Lodging Management Restaurant and Foodservice Management

Graduation Requirements

Graduation requires the completion of 126 semester hours, which includes 47 hours of general education, 67 hours in hospitality and consumer studies, and 12 hours of general electives. Two work experience classes are included for eight hours credit.

St. Johns University, New York

Restaurant, Travel and Tourism

College: St. Vincent's College
Program Enrollment: 103
Institutional Enrollment: 13,000 undergraduate, 5,000 graduate
Degrees Awarded: Bachelor of Science
Degree Categories: Hospitality Management
Emphases/Specification: Hotel Management, Restaurant Management, Travel and Tourism Management
Institution Accreditation: Middle States Association of Colleges and Schools

Contact: Dr. Francis . Brown, CHA, FMP, Director, Hospitality Management Program, St. John's University, 376 Bent Hall, 8000 Utopia Parkway, Jamaica, NY. 11439-0001; phone(718) 990-6137; fax (718) 990-1882; e-mail brownf@stjohns.edu

Institutional Description

St. John's University, founded in 1870, is the largest catholic university in the United States. The main campus is located in Hillcrest, Queens, New York City. We are committed to academic excellence and respect for the rights and dignity of every person through compassion and zeal for service.

Program Description

In 1996 the university established the Division of Hotel, Restaurant, Travel and Tourism with the goal of providing students with the competencies recognized as fundamental for positions in the hospitality field. These competencies include accounting & finance, computer operations, facilities management, hotel & restaurant management, human & organizational behavior, marketing & sales and purchasing & cost controls.

Special Features

Small classes. Study abroad programs, in Hungry, Ireland, Italy, and Japan. Internships and lifetime placement assistance. transfer students are welcome.

Financial Aid and Scholarships

St. John's University awards over $100 million dollars in federal, state, university and extended financial aid in funds each year.

Admissions

St. Johns welcomes students whose aptitude and demonstrated academic achievement in high school gave evidence of their ability to successfully complete various university programs.

Approximate Tuition and Fees

tuition for the 1998-1999 academic year is $6,600 per semester for 12 to 18 credits; general fees are $215 per semester. Room and board for the 1999-2000 academic year is expected to be $4,300 per semester.

Specialization Areas

Hotel and Lodging Management, Restaurant and Foodservice Management, Travel and Tourism Management

Graduation Requirements

Graduation requires a total of 126 semester credit hours. Half of the course units are in the liberal arts and sciences; the remainder are in hotel, restaurant, travel and tourism management as well as general business administration.

Saint Louis University

Hospitality Management

College: College of Education and Human Services
Institutional Enrollment: 11,000
Degree Awarded: Bachelor of Science
Degree Category: Hospitality Management
Institutional Accreditation: North Central Association of Colleges and Secondary Schools.
Contact: Dr. Anne V.S. Ledbetter, Director Hospitality Management, School for Professional Studies, DuBourg Hall Room 17, 221 N. Grand Boulevard, St. Louis, MO 63103, (314) 977-2330. Fax (314) 977-2333.

Institution Description

Saint Louis University is a Catholic, Jesuit institution dedicated to providing excellence in teaching, research, health care and community service. Established in 1818, the University was the first institution of higher education founded west of the Mississippi River. Today, the University educates 11,000 students on its three campuses and offers a myriad of undergraduate, graduate, and professional degree programs in 13 colleges and schools.

Program Description

Hospitality Management is offered in the School for Professional Studies which was founded in 1996. The school is specifically designed for the student seeking a Bachelor of Science degree while working. The program builds on a solid liberal arts foundation with a hospitality management core and includes courses in professional studies.

Special Features

The School for Professional Studies offers weekly courses during the evening and on Saturday mornings, in an eight-week format for five terms per year. The program is specifically designed for the working adult. The university's location is in a major metropolitan area, which provides excellent hospitality industry opportunities.

Financial Aid and Scholarships

Saint Louis University has a variety of financial aid programs available including loans, scholarships and grants. Each year industry-related scholarship and grants are available.

Admissions

Admission criteria: (1) 22 years or older, (2) at least three years of work experience or the equivalent, (3) high school diploma or composite GED score of at least 225, (4) successful pre-admission interview with an academic advisor to review informal transcripts, and (5) transfer minimum cumulative grade point average of 2.0. The student may be required to complete a writing assessment.

Tuition and Fees

Tuition is $325 per credit hour with most courses offered for three credit hours. No distinction is made between resident and non-resident tuition. A one-time $25 application fee is applicable.

Graduation Requirements

Graduation requires the completion of 120 credit hours for the BS degree. Course work accepts as a transfer equivalent from accredited institutions will be evaluated on a course by course basis. The degree is composed of 60 credit hours of general education, 42 credit hours ın hospitality and organizational studies and 18 credit hours of general electives.

Saint Thomas University

Tourism and Hospitality Management

Program Enrollment: 125
Institutional Enrollment: 1,700 undergraduate; 900 graduate and law
Degree Awarded: Bachelor of Business Administration
Degree Categories: Tourism and Hospitality Management
Emphases/Specializations: Travel and Tourism Management; Hotel and Hospitality Management
Institutional Accreditation: Southern Association of Colleges and Schools
Contact: Paul-Michael Klein, Departmental Program Coordinator, Tourism/Hospitality Management, St. Thomas University, 16400 NW 32nd Ave., Miami, FL 33054; phone Admissions 1-800-367-9010; fax (305) 628-6504

Institution Description

Situated on a 140-acre campus located midway between Miami and Ft. Lauderdale, St. Thomas University is a Catholic university for students of all faiths, dedicated to excellence in education. The University enrolls some 2,600 students in our undergraduate, graduate programs and our law school. While classes are generally small, we seek a diverse student body and currently enroll students from 32 different states and 65 countries. A comprehensive financial aid program includes both need-based and noneed scholarships. Intercollegiate and intramural sports, in addition to over 30 clubs and activities, contribute to an active extracurricular program for our students.

Program Description

The Department of Tourism and Hospitality Management offers a careeroriented curriculum, offering courses designed to give students an overall view of the industry with particular emphasis on management and sales and marketing, with a strong background in liberal arts. Practical experience is gained through a required internship and the Campus Hospitality Service.

Special Features

The Greater Miami/South Florida/Caribbean Basin provides a wealth of laboratory internship opportunities, as does the international scope of the student body, faculty and local culture.

Financial Aid and Scholarships

Financial aid and scholarships are available from the university, as well as state and federal programs. Eighty percent of our students are on some form of aid and inquiries should be directed to the Financial Aid Office.

Approximate Tuition and Fees

Tuition $12,000, on-campus room and board; $4,200 fees.

Admissions

Students must submit high school transcripts, SAT or ACT score, a written essay and letters of recommendation. The major emphasis is placed on the school transcripts. St. Thomas generally enrolls C+ to B+ students.

Graduation Requirements

All graduates are required to maintain an overall 2.0 GPA for graduation. Each candidate must complete 57 credits of general education requirements.

State University of New York College of Technology at Delhi

BBA in Hospitality Management

Program: BBA in Hospitality Management
Program Enrollment: 65
Institutional Enrollment: 2,100
Degrees Awarded: Bachelor of Business Administration
Degree Categories: Bachelor of Business Administration in Hospitality Management with concentrations in Hotel & Resort Management, Restaurant Management, and Travel & Tourism Management
Emphases/Specializations: Associate, Diploma Certificate
Program Accreditation: Middle States Association of Secondary Schools andColleges, A.S.T.A. Travel School
Contact: Rosalie Higgins, Department Chair and Professor, SUNY-Delhi, Delhi, NY 13753; phone: (607) 746-4402; fax: (607) 746-4769

Institution Description

Established in 1913, the College of Technology at Delhi offers Baccalaureate and Associate Degrees in a residential setting. A unit of the State University of New York, it is a leader in technical education.

Program Description

Building on a foundation of 50 years of hospitality education, Delhi's new Bachelor of Business Administration Degree prepares graduates for management positions in the industry. Study abroad is available and professional internship is required.

Special Features

Delhi's state-of-the-art Alumni Hall Hospitality Center houses a hospitality lobby, housekeeping laboratories, banquet and catering facilities, beverage laboratory, AAA Travel Branch Office, and a student restaurant. Delhi maintains strong industry relationship through three leading hospitality travel associations. Delhi's over 3,500 successful hospitality management alumni provide curriculum advisement and employment assistance.

Financial Aid and Scholarships

The college financial aid office, hospitality industry, and various associations offer financial aid and scholarships to deserving students.

Admissions

Students applying for enrollment as freshmen must be graduates of an accredited secondary school or have an equivalent education. The following high school course distribution is recommended: 4 units of English, 3 units of social science and at least 4 units of math and science (with a minimum of 2 units in each of those areas). An Admissions Committee will review applications for transfer students. A 2.3 cumulative grade point average is recommended. An interview is also recommended. Previous study in hospitality is not required for transfer students. Students with an associate's degree in liberal arts, business and related areas are encouraged to apply.

Tuition & Fees

In-State $3,400; Out-of-State $5,000; Room and Board $5,300; Other Fees $1,000±

Specialization Area

Hotel & Lodging Mgmt., Restaurant & Foodservice Mgmt., Travel & Tourism Mgmt.

Graduation Requirements

Graduation requires 128 credit hours. General education, 43 hours; hospitality management core, 28 hours; business management core, 21 hours; specialization core, 36 hours. Professional experience internship is required.

State University of New York - Oneonta

Food Service & Restaurant Administration

College: Department of Human Ecology
Program Enrollment: 40
Institutional Enrollment: 4,800 Undergraduate; 730 Graduate
Degrees Awarded: Bachelor of Science
Degree Categories: Food Service & Restaurant Administration
Program Accreditation: American Association of Family and Consumer Sciences
Institutional Accreditation: Middle States Association of Colleges and Secondary Schools, American Chemical Society, American Association of University Women, New York State Education Department
Contact: Dr. Loraine L. Tyler, Chiar/Professor, Human Ecology Department State University of New York College at Oneonta, Oneonta, NY 13820-4015; Phone: (607) 436-2705; fax: (607) 436-2051

Institution Description

The State University of New York was established in 1948 and Oneonta joined with other existing campuses to form what has become one of the largest university systems in the country. The College is comprehensive, multi-purpose institution offering numerous programs in the liberal arts and sciences, as well as in selected preprofessional fields.

Program Description

The Food Service & Restaurant Administration major provides students with a substantial academic background in foodservice management, business, food science, nutrition and liberal arts courses. Students develop leadership and professional skills, two keys to success in this field. Classes are generally small in size and students have numerous opportunities to interact with faculty and fellow students to explore individual interests.

Special Features

All classes are instructed by faculty members who hold graduate degrees in their areas of specialization. Each student is assigned a faculty member as Academic Advisor. The faculty and administration are devoted to quality education and to helping students achieve their potential. Foods labs and a computer lab further student's experiential knowledge base.

Financial Aid and Scholarships

The college financial aid office makes available numerous opportunities, and the Human Ecology Department offers scholarships based on both academic achievement and leadership potential.

Admissions

The Admissions Committee is most interested in: (1) the quality of the applicant's high school program of study; (2) performance on the SAT; (3) recommendations provided by the applicant's counselors and teachers; and (4) the depth of involvement in extracurricular activities which indicate leadership, organizational and problem-solving skills. Transfer students are welcome.

Tuition & Fees

In-State $3,400 per year; Out of State: $8,300 per year; Room and Board: $5,175 per year; Other Fees: $455 per year College fees.

Graduate Requirements

Graduation requires the successful completion of 122 semester hours and include 60 hours of liberal studies courses; 12 hours of Department of Economics and Business courses; 37 hours of Foods and Nutrition courses; and 12 hours of electives selected in consultation with the student's advisor.

Stephen F. Austin State University

Hospitality Administration

College: College of Education
Program Enrollment: 85
Institutional Enrollment: 12,500 undergraduate; 1,400 graduate
Degrees Awarded: Bachelor of Science
Degree Categories: Hospitality Administration
Institutional Accreditation: Southern Association of Colleges and Schools

Contact: Department of Human Sciences, Stephen F. Austin State University, P.O. Box 13014 - SFA Station, Nacogdoches, TX 75962-3014, Phone: (409) 468-4502; Fax (409) 468-2140

Institutional Description

Stephen F. Austin is a comprehensive, state-supported regional university. The university is a student-oriented institution that offers excellence in both academic and student-life programs in a residential setting unique among the state's comprehensive institutions. SFA is located in Nacogdoches, the oldest city in Texas.

Program Description

The Hospitality Administration Program prepares students for management positions in the hospitality industry. The program is broad in scope and combines academic theories with industry application in both educational situations and area businesses.

Special Features

SFA takes great pride in being able to provide small classes and an opportunity for individual attention. Students are encouraged and assisted in obtaining internships.

Financial Aid and Scholarships

SFA maintains a fully staffed financial aid office. Additional scholarships are available through the Alumni Association to qualified students.

Admissions

Admission criteria include rank in high school class, SAT/ACT scores, and high school academic core requirements. Requests for applications concerning admission should be directed to the Office of Admissions, P.O. Box 13051 SFA Station, Nacogdoches, TX 75962-3051; phone (409) 468-2504; fax (409) 468-1117.

Tuition and Fees

Registration fees at SFA are established by legislative enactment. Other expenses are determined within statutory limitation by the university's Board of Regents.

Graduation Requirements

Graduation requires the completion of 130 semester hours, which includes 45 hours of general education, 18 hours of required courses in human sciences, 36 hours in hospitality courses, 18 hours in general business, and 12 hours of electives. A minimum of 42 hours of residence work is required; at least 36 hours must be advanced.

Sullivan College

National Center for Hospitality Studies

Program Enrollment: 401
Institutional Enrollment: 3,002
Degrees Awarded: Bachelor of Science; Associate of Science; Diploma
Degree Categories: Bachelor of Science degree in: Hospitality Management; Associate of Science degrees in: Culinary Arts; Baking and Pastry Arts; Professional Catering; Hotel Restaurant Management; Travel and Tourism; Dual degrees in: Culinary Arts and Hotel/Restaurant Management; Culinary Arts and Baking and Pastry Arts; Diplomas in: Professional Cook; Professional Baker; and Travel and Tourism
Program Accreditation: American Culinary Federation Educational Institute Accrediting Commission
Institutional Accreditation: The Commission on Colleges of the Southern Association of Colleges and Schools

Contact: Greg Cawthon, Director of Admissions, Sullivan College, 3101 Bardstown Road, P.O. Box 33-308, Louisville, KY 40232; phone (502) 456-6505 or (800) 844-1354; fax (502) 456-0040; www.sullivan.edu; email: admissions@sullivan.edu

Institution Description

Sullivan College is a private, master's degree granting institution offering 33 certificate, diploma and degree programs on a spacious suburban campus in Louisville, KY. College housing is available for students age 21 and younger who live outside the Louisville area

Program Description

Eleven degree and diploma programs are offered by Sullivan College's National Center for Hospitality Studies in state-of-the-art facilities. Seven teaching kitchens, an off-site retail bakery, an on-campus gourmet restaurant, an on-line Worldspan airline reservations system, modern computer labs, and highly experienced, credentialed, award-winning faculty are among the many benefits of Sullivan College.

Special Features

Lifetime, nationwide job placement assistance; national companies recruit on campus; retail bakery and on-campus gourmet restaurant provide practicum experiences.

Financial Aid and Scholarships

All federal financial aid programs are available to students who qualify. State and institutional grants and scholarships are also available and are based on need and/or ability.

Admissions

Normal admissions require that the student have: a high school diploma or GED, successful completion of an aptitude analysis, and a personal career interview with a member of the admissions staff. A tour of the facilities is highly recommended.

Specialization Areas

Hotel and Lodging Management; Restaurant and Foodservice Management; Professional Catering; Travel and Tourism; Culinary Arts; and Baking and Pastry Arts.

Graduation Requirements

Graduates must maintain a 2.0 (C) average over the course of their diploma or degree program. Culinary Arts, Professional Catering, and Hotel/Restaurant Management majors participate in a unique 400-hour on/off campus practicum as part of their program.

Svenska Handelshögskolan

Swedish School of Economics and Business Administration

Program Enrollment: (Only in Vasa) 25 Bachelor of Tourism Administration (BTA); 20 Master of Tourism Management (MTM); 10 MSc (econ.)
Institutional Enrollment: in Vasa 450 Graduate; 16 Postgraduate; in Helsinki-1,500 Graduate; 69 Post-graduate
Degree Categories: BTA, MTM, MSc (econ.), Doctorate of Economics
Contact: MSc (econ.) and Doctorate of Economics, Professor Lars-Johan Lindqvist, Ph. D., phone: +358-6-3533 712; BTA and MTM: Director of Program, MSc Jan Koskinen; P.O.BOX 287, FIN 65101 VASA, FINLAND; phone: +358-6-3533 704; fax: +358-6-3533 702

Institution Description

Svenska Handelshögskolan, SHH, (Swedish School of Economics and Business Administration) is the oldest Business School in Scandinavia. The school was founded in 1909, and it gives education in two locations, in Helsinki, the capital of Finland, and since 1980 also in Vasa.

Program Description

The main programs are Master of Science in Economics, Doctorate of Economics and Tourism as specialty.

Special Features

After graduating from BTA, students can transfer to MTM, and after graduating from MTM, students can apply for the right to continue MSc (econ.).

Approximate Tuition and Fees

SHH is owned by the Finnish Government and the MSc and Doctorate education are free of charge. The BTA and MTM programs are meant for students with a vocational education and minimum of three years of working experience. The tuition for the BTA program is FIM 9,000, and for the MTM program FIM 10,000.

Syracuse University

Restaurant and Food service Management

College: College for Human Development
Program Enrollment: 65
Institutional Enrollment: 12,000 undergraduate; 4,000 graduate
Degree Awarded: Bachelor of Science
Degree Category: Restaurant and Food service Management
Program Accreditation: American Assembly of Collegiate Schools of Business
Institutional Accreditation: New York State Board of Regents; Middle States Association of Colleges and Schools; Association of American Universities

Contact: Norm Faiola, Ph.D., Chairperson, Restaurant and Food service Management, Department of Nutrition and Food service Management, College for Human Development, Syracuse University, 034 Slocum Hall, Syracuse, NY 13244-1250; phone (315) 443-238

Institution Description

Founded in 1870, Syracuse University is a nationally recognized private university with a full-time enrollment of 16,000 and a part-time enrollment of 4,000. Syracuse is organized into 21 major academic units, including architecture, engineering, law, and nursing, as well as the prestigious Maxwell School of Citizenship and Public Affairs and the Newhouse School of Public Communications. The College for Human Development, which sponsors the Restaurant and Food service Management degree, has been offering food and nutrition courses since 1917.

Program Description

The restaurant and food service management bachelor's degree combines a food service core with requirements in management and the liberal arts. An independent study degree program is also offered.

Special Features

The restaurant and food service management degree is designed to qualify students for management positions in all aspects of the Hospitality industry.

Financial Aid and Scholarships

Depending on whether they are part or full time, students enrolled in Syracuse's independent study degree programs are eligible for the same institutional and government aid as traditional campus or evening college students.

Admissions

Admission is selective and based on an autobiographical essay, written recommendations, and evaluation of transcripts of prior college work, if any. High school graduates are eligible, as are students with associate degrees from other institutions, if their GPA is at least 2.0.

Graduation Requirements

Graduation requires completion of 124 credits , with a minimum average of GPA of 2.0. Of these, a minimum 30 credits must be completed at Syracuse. The curriculum consists of 50 credits in nutrition and food service management, 18 credits in management, 45 credits in the liberal arts and 11 credits of electives. A practical work experience component, coordinated through the college, is required.

Tennessee State University

Hospitality & Tourism Administration

Institutional Enrollment: 8,750
Degrees Awarded: Bachelor of Science
Degree Categories: Hospitality and Tourism Management
Emphases/Specializations: Lodging and Restaurant Administration, Tourism Administration
Program Accreditation: Eligible to apply in 2000
Institutional Accreditation: Southern Association of Colleges and Schools

Contact: Wayne C. Guyette, Head, Department of Hospitality & Tourism Administration, Tennessee State University, 3500 John Merritt Boulevard, Nashville, Tennessee 37209-1561, 615/963-5631 [VOICE], 615/963-5709 [FAX], wguyette@picard.tnstate.edu [E-Mail Address]

Institution Description

Tennessee State University, an 1890 land grant institution founded in 1912, is a major state-supported, urban and comprehensive university governed by the Tennessee Board of Regents. Located in Nashville, the state capitol, the community is known internationally as "Music City USA."

Program Description

Initiated in 1991, the Hospitality & Tourism Administration (HTA) curriculum helps students develop their technical, operational, managerial and analytical skills through extensive study and practical experience. In cooperation with The Tennessee Hospitality Education Council, a 227 room hotel—equipped with restaurant and meeting facilities—has been secured for the program which provides our HTA majors with opportunities for "real world" application of theoretical management principles.

Special Features

Our business-oriented program targets operational/practical skills through its courses, a 1,200 hour internship, extensive industry consulting projects and computer application instruction.

Financial Aid and Scholarships

TSU offers a very comprehensive financial assistance program, including scholarships, loans, grants and employment. Approximately 80% of freshmen receive some type of financial assistance.

Admissions

In-state and out-of-state residents entering as a freshman must pass the High School Proficiency Exam and have either a high school GPA of 2.50 or better or an Enhanced ACT Assessment score of at least 19. All students entering the HTA Program as juniors, must have a 2.6 GPA and have completed 600 hours of supervised work experience/internship.

Tuition & Fees

In-State: $958.00 (full-time/semester)
Out-Of-State: $3,126.00 (full-time/semester)
Room and Board: $1,015 (single room); $675.00 (19 meals)
Other Fees: $56.00

Specialization Area

Lodging Administration, Restaurant Administration, Tourism Administration, Culinary Arts Administration

Graduation Requirements

Graduation requires the successful completion of 133 semester hours, which includes 34 hours of general education courses; 15 hours of general elective courses; 9 hours of School of Business courses; 54 hours of HTA courses; and, 21 hours of HTA specialty electives.

Texas Tech University

Restaurant, Hotel and Institutional Management

College: College of Human Sciences
Program Enrollment: 425
Institutional Enrollment: 22,000 undergraduate; 3,400 graduate
Degree Awarded: Bachelor of Science
Degree Category: Restaurant, Hotel and Institutional Management
Program Accreditation: Accreditation Commission for Programs in Hospitality Administration (ACPHA)
Institutional Accreditation: Southern Association of Colleges and Schools

Contact: Lynn Huffman, Ph.D., Chair, Education, Nutrition and Restaurant/Hotel Management, Texas Tech University, P.O. Box 41162, Lubbock, TX 79409-1162; phone (806) 742-3068; fax (806) 742-3042; Internet: www.ns.ttu.edu/dept/enrhm/rhim

Institution Description

Texas Tech is one of the state's four major comprehensive universities and academically the most diverse. The university provides students with a range of programs and the opportunity for a liberal education. Texas Tech is located in Lubbock, a sun belt city with a population of over 200,000.

Program Description

The restaurant, Hotel, and Institutional Management (RHIM) Program offers a multidisciplinary approach to hospitality education. The curriculum is designed to prepare the student to meet both current and future hospitality needs. The program emphasizes problem-solving and creativity, in addition to practical laboratory experiences. The RHIM program is accredited by the Accreditation Commission for Programs in Hospitality Administration, a specialized accrediting body.

Special Features

Practical management experience is gained through diverse laboratory experiences ranging from hotel operations to a student-run restaurant to modern computer facilities. Over 40 companies each semester come to campus to recruit RHIM students. Placement rate is excellent, with 90% employed before graduation.

Financial Aid and Scholarships

Texas Tech maintains a fully staffed financial aid office. The RHIM Program offers several competitive scholarships to students.

Admissions

Requests for applications or questions concerning admission should be directed to: Admissions Office, Texas Tech University, Lubbock, TX 79409; phone (806) 742-3661, or online at www.texastech.edu.

Graduation Requirements

Graduation requires the completion of 134 semester hours, which includes 41 hours of general education, 19 hours of support courses, 59 hours in RHIM core courses and 15 hours of electives.

Tiffin University

Hospitality Management

Program Enrollment: 65
Institutional Enrollment: 1700
Degrees Awarded: Bachelor of Business Administration Degree
Degree Categories: Hospitality Management
Emphases/Specializations: Hospitality Management
Institutional Accreditation: North Central Association of Colleges and Schools, Accredited by the Association of Collegiate Business Schools & Programs

Contact: Tim Schultz, Dean, School of Business 155 Miami Street, Tiffin, Ohio 44883, 800-YOUOHIO, 419-443-5002

Institution Description

Tiffin University is an independent college that is in its second century of preparing its students for places in business, criminal justice, and graduate school. Tiffin University extends will beyond the classroom. Involvement in student activities, such as the Hospitality Club, International Student Association, Student Government, Fellowship of Christian Athletes, and Intramural Sports, helps in forming new friendships and affords students the opportunity to pursue their current interests and find new ones.

Program Description

Tiffin University's Hospitality Management curriculum prepares students for a career in this expanding field through practical hands-on experience. In addition, students must fulfill a hospitality internship.

Special Features

Federal programs determine the financial need from the information submitted by students and parents on the Free Application for Federal Student Aid (FAFSA). Scholarships available: Valedictorian/Salutatorian Scholarship, Trustees Scholarship, President's Scholarship, Dean's Scholarship, and many more.

Admissions

Ideally, a student's high school transcript must show credit for the following: four units of English, three units of Mathematics, Science, Social Studies, and academic or commercial subjects. Applicants are admitted based on University's evaluation of their potential to benefit from higher education and likelihood of success at the college level.

Tuition and Fees

In-State: $9870 tuition fee per year
Out-of-State: $9870 tuition fee per year
Residence Housing per year: $2750-Single, $2350-Other

Specialization Area

none

Graduation Requirements

The Tiffin University General Education Program consists of four components: the integrated core curriculum (61 Semester Hours), an enriched major area of study (51-54 Semester Hours), the open electives (18 Semester Hours), and the Co-Curricular Program (2 Units).

Transylvania University

Hotel, Restaurant and Tourism Administration

College: Transylvania University
Program Enrollment: 20
Institutional Enrollment: 1000
Degrees Awarded: Bachelor of Arts in Business Administration
Degree Categories: Baccalaureate
Emphases/Specializations: Hotel, Restaurant and Tourism Administration
Program Accreditation: None
Institutional Accreditation: Commission on Colleges of The Southern Association of Colleges and Schools

Contact: Michael R. Pepper, Chairman, Division of Business and Economics, Transylvania University, 300 N. Broadway, Lexington, KY 40508; phone (606) 233-8249; fax (606) 233-8797; E-Mail: mpepper@mail.transy.edu

Institution Description

Transylvania University, founded in 1780, is a private coeducational liberal arts college located three blocks from downtown Lexington. The campus blends the benefits of living in a small college community with access to the cultural and recreational advantages that only a large city can offer.

Program Description

Hotel, Restaurant and Tourism Administration offers a unique combination: excellent career preparation, business management and liberal arts education. A combination of practical skills preparation and theoretical development prepare students to function optimally in the management and people-intensive hospitality industry. Students plan and conduct dinners in the foods laboratory and dining facility on campus.

Special Features

Two summer practicums are required; internships are offered and senior projects are available. Class size does not exceed 30 with fewer than 10 in HRT courses.

Financial Aid and Scholarships

William T. Young scholars program for a full four-year scholarship; National Restaurant Association; Transylvania-designated scholarship for $4,000.

Admissions

Completed application form, high school transcript, scores on SAT and/or ACT, and two recommendations as specified on the application form.

Tuition & Fees

$13,930, Room & Board $19,100

Graduation Requirements

At least 36 courses, including distribution requirements in general education and requirements of an approved major pattern, and at least a C average.

United States International University

Hotel, Restaurant and Tourism Management

College: College of Business Administration
Program Enrollment: 75
Institutional Enrollment: 2,600
Degree Awarded: Bachelor of Science
Degree Categories: Hotel and Restaurant Management or Tourism Management
Institutional Accreditation: Western Association of Schools and Colleges

Contact: Dr. John R. Walker, Professor and Director, Hotel, Restaurant and Tourism Management, United States International University, 10455 Pomerado Road, San Diego, CA 92131; phone (619) 635-4627; FAX (619) 635-4528

Institution Description

United States International University (USIU), founded in 1952, is a private, non-profit university. At USIU, the approach to education has been fundamentally changed to emphasize the results rather than the process of education. Our graduates leave USIU with the skills and knowledge to live, work and lead in the 21st century. Students can attend USIU's main campus, located in San Diego, California, or its international campuses in Nairobi, Kenya and Mexico City. Students come to USIU from 83 countries, creating a multicultural enviroru-nent that is a daily part of campus life. Approximately 65% of the student body comes from the United States. USIU features small classes (15-20 student average) and an internationally renowned faculty, 93% of whom have doctoral degrees.

Program Description

Students in the HRTM programs at USIU take general education and business courses designed to provide a broad base of knowledge and skills relative to the business world. In addition, students take a number of specific courses in one or two majors: hotel and restaurant management or tourism management. Work experiences and internships are not only a requirement for graduation, but they provide a practical balance to the academic studies.

Special Features

Recognized as America's finest city, San Diego is the perfect place to study hotel, restaurant and tourism management. A wonderful climate and a plethora of Southern California attractions are linked to thousands of thriving tourism businesses. World class hotels, theme parks, cruise ships and other attractions provide plenty of employment opportunities. USIU students gain a competitive advantage through the many internships offered by these types of organizations. More than 90% of the students receive job offers upon graduation. Additionally, students may enroll at the beginning of any quarter and may accelerate their program to finish in three and one-half years.

Financial Aid and Scholarships

All students entering USIU with a high school GPA of 3.0 or higher automatically qualify to receive a merit scholarship. Overall, approximately 81 percent of the undergraduate American citizens and eligible noncitizens attending USIU take advantage of financial aid programs to help meet educational costs. While the average amount of assistance received annually is $8,000, many students receive over $10,000 in assistance each year.

Approximate Tuition and Fees

Tuition per quarter unit of study at USIU is $290. A fulltime student who completes 16 units of study per quarter would pay $12,000 in tuition per academic year.

Admissions

USIU seeks to enroll students who demonstrate leadership potential and who show evidence of intellectual ability and creativity. Adn-Lission to USIU is based on a high school and/or transfer GPA of at least 2.5; satisfactory SAT or ACT score is required for domestic freshmen. The office of admissions reviews applications on a rolling admission basis. Intemafional students require a minimum TOEFL score of 550, or may be conditionally admitted into the University and transition into their academic program upon successful completion of our ESL program.

Graduation Requirements

A minimum of 186 academic (quarter hour) units with at least a C average, and the meeting of course and residency requirements of at least 45 academic units. A 1,000-work experience and a management internship are also required for graduation.

Universidad de las Americas-Puebla

Hotel & Restaurant Management Program

College: College of Business
Program Enrollment: 290
Institutional Enrollment: 5,900 undergraduate; 500 graduate
Degree Awarded: Bachelor of Hotel & Restaurant Management
Degree Categories: Hotel & Restaurant Management
Emphases/Specializations: Hospitality Management; Restaurant Management
Institutional Accreditation: Southern Association of Colleges and Schools
Contact: Alfonso R. Rocha, Ph.D., Department Head, Department of Hotel and Restaurant Management, P.O. Box 100, Santa Catarina Cholula, Puebla, Mexico 72820; phone: (22) 29-20-59; fax: (22) 29-24-04

Institution Description

The Universidad de las Americas-Puebla (UDLAP) is a Mexican institution of superior education and research in a creative, multicultural and multilingual environment. As a comprehensive university, UDLAP offers a wide range of undergraduate programs in business, education, communications, humanities, business administration, science and engineering. UDLAP is also listed in several guides as America's most prestigious colleges and universities.

Program Description

UDLAP's Hotel & Restaurant Management Program builds on a solid academic foundation consisting of different courses: (1) Hotel Management courses; (2) Restaurant Management courses; (3) Administration courses; (4) Languages courses; (5) General studies courses; (6) Accounting courses; (7) Quantitative courses; (8) Computation courses; (9) Legal area courses; (10) Economy and Financial courses; (11) Optional courses; and (12) Thesis.

Special Features

This University has a small hotel with eighteen rooms and a lodge which are used for professional practices by the students. The Hotel and Restaurant Management Program places the highest priority on working with the students in a Food and Beverage Laboratory and a bar which are also used for professional practices.

Financial Aid and Scholarships

The University financial aid office makes available numerous opportunities and the Hotel & Restaurant Management Program offers several scholarships.

Admissions

Admission to UDLAP is highly competitive. The admissions committee is most interested in: (1) the results of the admission examination which are extremely important. To pass this examination is essential for the formal admission in the Institution. (2) There is another examination that is presented when the student has been accepted in the University.

Tuition and Fees

Mexican and overseas students: US$2,500 per semester. Room and board: US$625 - $670 per semester.

Specialization Area

Hotel & Lodging Management

Graduation Requirements

This nine-semester Program requires the completion of 302 units. A 1000-hour work experience and internship and a professional examination (final project) are also required.s and choice of minor.

The University of Alabama

Restaurant and Hospitality Management

College: College of Human Environmental Sciences
Program Enrollment: 190
Institutional Enrollment: 20,000 undergraduate; 3,000 graduate
Degree Awarded: Bachelor of Science
Degree Category: Human Environmental Sciences
Emphases/Specializations: Restaurant Management; Hotel Management; Meetings and Convention Management
Institutional Accreditation: Southern Association of Colleges and Schools

Contact: Olivia W. Kendrick, Human Nutrition and Hospitality Management, The University of Alabama, Box 870158, Tuscaloosa, AL 35487-0158

Institution Description

The University of Alabama is the state's capstone institution of education and a renowned center of education in the Southeast. As a comprehensive, residential university, it offers more than 140 academic areas with over 330 accredited undergraduate and graduate degree programs.

Program Description

The Restaurant and Hospitality Management (RHM) Program offers a variety of courses designed to develop the skills and abilities required for a successful career in hospitality management. Students may select from one of three options within the program: restaurant management, hotel management, and meetings and convention management. A 1,000-hour hospitality management practicum is required.

Special Features

During the junior year, students operate and manage the J.J. Doster Café, a 1,800-square-foot dining area with a seating capacity of 100. The cafe is open to the public for lunch and serves an average of 200 patron daily.

Financial Aid and Scholarships

Several scholarships are offered by the Human Nutrition and Hospitality Management department. In addition, the university and the College of Human Environmental Sciences offer a variety of scholarships and financial aid.

Approximate Tuition and Fees

In-state tuition is $1,034 per semester; out-of-state tuition is $2,583 per semester.

Admissions

Admission to the freshman class of The University of Alabama results from a satisfactory evaluation of a student's high school academic record and ACT or SAT test scores. The university admits transfer students who have a C average or above on all college work attempted.

Graduation Requirements

Graduation requires the completion of 128 semester hours, which includes a 52-hour university core curriculum, 26 hours of professional courses, a minor in a complementary area, and 9-11 hours of electives.
A 1,000-hour practicum in hospitality management is required.

The University of Calgary

World Tourism Education and Research Centre

Colleges: Faculty of Management, Faculty of General Studies
Program Enrollments: 100 Tourism and Hospitality Management, 240 Leisure, Tourism and Society
Institutional Enrollment: 18,000 undergraduate; 2,500 graduate
Degrees Awarded: Bachelor of Commerce (BComm); Bachelor of Arts (BA)
Degree Categories: Tourism and Hospitality Management; Leisure, Tourism and Society
Program Accreditation: World Tourism Organization; American Assembly of Collegiate Schools of Business

Contact: Mr. Lorn Sheehan, Tourism and Hospitality Management, Faculty of Management, The University of Calgary, Calgary, Alberta, Canada, T2N 1N4; phone (403)220-8310, or Dr. Dianne Draper, Leisure, Tourism and Society, Department of Geography, The University of Calgary, Calgary, Alberta, Canada, T2N 1N4; phone (403)220-5596

Institution Description
Conceived in 1945 and established as a fully separate institution in 1966, the University of Calgary is a coeducational, nondenominational, public institution. The campus is located in the City of Calgary at the foot of the Rocky Mountains. The University of Calgary was the site of sport venues during the 1988 Olympic Winter Games, and in 1989 was designated a World Tourism Education and Research Centre by the World Tourism Organization, a United Nations affiliate.

Program Description
The BComm Tourism and Hospitality Management program integrates general management concepts and professional knowledge required by the tourism and hospitality industry. The BA Leisure, Tourism and Society program is intended to integrate theories and research methodologies with their practical applications in the fields of leisure, recreation and tourism from a multidisciplinary perspective.

Special Features
The BComm Tourism program offers an optional Cooperative Education component. There are three student organizations: Tourism Association of Students in Commerce; Tourism Studies Association; and TTRA International Student Chapter. Several noncredit programs are also available for industry practitioners.

Financial Aid and Scholarships
The Student Awards are Financial Aid Office administers numerous scholarships and awards, and assists students seeking financial assistance. Specific awards and scholarships are exclusively available to tourism students in their final year of study.

Approximate Tuition and Fees
Canadian students: US $2497 per year; international students; US $4739 per year; room and board: US $5000 per year.

Admissions
Admission to the University of Calgary (for both programs) requires a high school matriculation minimum average of 71 percent Alberta Residents and 76 percent for all other applicants. The BComm Tourism program requires a minimum grade point average of 2.7 (on a 4.0 scale) for admission after completion of the premanagement program (years one and two).

Graduation Requirements
Both programs take a total of four years of full-time study to complete (with May through August off). The Cooperative Education option extends the BComm Tourism program to five years. A copy of the calendar may be obtained by contacting, the University of Calgary Bookstore; phone (403)220-5937.

University of Central Florida

Hospitality Management

Program Enrollment: 350
Institutional Enrollment: 25,000 undergraduate; 5,200 graduate
Degree Awarded: Bachelor of Science in Business Administration with specialization in Hospitality Management; MBA with specialization in Hospitality Management; PhD in Hospitality Management
Degree Category: Business, Hospitality Management
Emphases/Specializations: Accommodation Management; Foodservice Management; Tourism Management; Convention and Conference Management; Time Share Management

Program Accreditation: American Assembly of Collegiate Schools of Business; Accreditation Commission for Programs in Hospitality Administration
Institutional Accreditation: Southern Association of Colleges and Schools
Contact: Taylor Ellis, PhD, Interim Chair, Department of Hospitality Management, College of Business Administration, University of Central Florida, Orlando, FL 32816-1400; phone (407) 823-2188; fax (407) 823-5696

Institution Description

The University of Central Florida is a comprehensive urban university located in Orlando and is one of ten state universities in the State. The University offers bachelor, master and doctoral level degrees in five colleges with 60 different academic majors. Besides its emphasis on Hospitality Management, the university has established a national presence in computerized simulation and training, artificial intelligence in engineering, and the fine arts. The university is located on a 1,445 acre campus in the northeastern section of the city and students have easy access to all the attractions of the Greater Central Florida area. There are over 50 buildings, a new student union, and residential housing available for students. UCF has both intercollegiate and intramural athletics and a wide variety of other activities available for its students. In addition to the main campus, the University offers undergraduate and graduate coursework at its Cocoa and Daytona Beach Campuses.

Program Description

Orlando is a remarkable and unique place to major in Hospitality Management. Majors have the opportunity to work with and learn from the top managers of some of the leading organizations in all major segments of the hospitality industry. The major combines practical work experience with a newly redesigned academic curriculum that was developed in collaboration with industry leaders. Students, like all College of Business students, experience the innovative and nationally acclaimed BE 2000 educational curriculum in which they develop competency in teamwork, communication, creativity and adapting to and managing change. Hospitality Management students can also pursue their specific interests in convention and meetings management, foodservice operations, lodging and motel/hotel management, Time Share, and travel and tourism by taking specialized coursework in these areas.

Special Features

Study abroad programs are available in cooperation with a number of schools across the world. Student exchange opportunities are also available to any student meeting the equivalent of the Associate of Arts degree program requirements for College of Business admission. The department houses the Dick Pope, Sr. Institute for Tourism Studies, modern computer and foodservice teaching labs, and offers co-op and internships opportunities in the more than 400 hotels, 1,400 restaurants and 50 theme parks located in the Greater Orlando area.

Financial Aid and Scholarships

There are a number of industry-funded scholarships totaling more than $60,000 per year available to hospitality management majors. In addition, there are numerous university scholarships and community financial aid programs available.

Approximate Tuition and Fees

In-state undergraduate tuition is $64.32 per credit hour. Out-of-state tuition is $261.34 per credit hour. Fees are approximately $200 per semester. On campus room and board is an additional $2,200–$2,800 per semester.

Admissions

Admission to UCF and the program is limited and based on meeting both minimum GPA and SAT or ACT scores. Students whose native language is not English must submit a minimum TOEFL score of 550.

Graduation Requirements

One hundred and twenty credits, approximately half of which are in the liberal arts/general education areas and the remainder in business administration and hospitality management courses are required for graduation. The State of Florida requires students to pass the College Level Academic Skills Test (CLAST) and satisfy the Gorden Rule writing requirement.

University Center "Cesar Ritz"

The International College of Hospitality Administration

Program Enrollment: (ICHA) 150
Institutional Enrollment: (Washington State University) 19,035 undergraduate; 2,818 graduate
Degree Awarded: Bachelor of Arts
Degree Category: International Hospitality Management
Institutional Accreditation: WSU program: American Assembly of Collegiate Schools of Business (AACSB), one of 110 fully accredited business schools out of 1,200 institutions in the USA, ICHA: Department of Education, State of Valais, Switzerland (Fachhochschule)
Contact: WSU Program: Dr. William H. Samenfink, Program Director of WSU at ICHA; Swiss Higher Diploma: John Antonakis, SHD Program Director at ICHA; Post Graduate Programs: Cristina Norton, PG-Program Director at ICHA; International College of Hospitality Administration, Englisch Gruss-Strasse 43, CH-3900 Brig, Switzerland; Phone (+41) 27 924 20 50; Fax (+41) 27 924 20 55; email:hoco.admissions@ritz.vsnet.ch, homepage: www.icha.ch

Institutional Description

ICHA is an academic partnership between WSU and hotelconsult "Cesar Ritz" Colleges, Switzerland. The degree program is offered and managed by WSU at their Swiss Campus. ICHA also hosts tow other programs: the Swiss Higher Diploma and a Post Graduate Program, both under the responsibility of hotelconsult "Cesar Ritz" Colleges who operate the University Center 'Cesar Ritz'.

Program Description

The Washington State University BA degree, offered at the Swiss campus, ICHA, Brig, is a unique program. It combines the strength of US hospitality in the field of business administration and modern hospitality management with the professionalism and art of European hospitality education. It consists of two components: a Swiss Higher Diploma in Hotel Management and a Bachelor's Degree in Hotel and Restaurant Administration, preparing students for a truly international career. An internship of 22 weeks in Switzerland or abroad adds additional value to the unique program. The accelerated degree program consists of three trimesters (1 year January to December). In order to qualify for the WSU program, students must successfully complete the ICHA Swiss Higher Diploma (2 years) with a GPA of 2.5.

Students who are enrolled in hospitality degree programs at other universities may join ICHA for a semester abroad program, to gain Swiss and international experience. The one year Post Graduate Diploma Program is available to applicants who have already completed a university degree in fields other than hotel management and wish to enter the hospitality industry. A 22 week industry training is part of the program. Graduates of the PGD Program may complete the M.S. degree in one additional semester.

Special Features

The ICHA/WSU partnership provides students with a dynamic, forward thinking, truly international environment. Graduates join the extensive HOTELCONSULT alumni organization. Students may receive the BA in Hotel & Restaurant Administration from the WSU College of Business and Economics, and are entitled to all rights and priveleges of a WSU alumni.

Financial Aid and Scholarships

American students (transfers from WSU or other US programs) should investigate the possibility of loans from federal/state aid programs.

The University of Commerce and Law

Tourism Management and Administration

Program Enrollment: 430
Institutional Enrollment: 9000
Undergraduate: 6500
Graduate: 2500
Degree Awarded: Bachelors Degree and Masters Degree
Degree Categories: Economics; Business Administration; International Trade; Tourism Administration and Management; Law
Program Accreditation: The Minister of National Education
Institutional Accreditation: The Minister of National Education

Contact: Christopher Lazarski, Ph.D. Director, Office for International Contacts, WSHiP, ul. Chlodna 9, 00-891 Warsaw, Poland; phone: (4822) 669-4252; fax: (4822) 639-8539; e-mail: krzysztof.lazarski@wship.edu.pl

Institution Description

The University of Commerce and Law(WSHiP) was established in 1993, originally as an undergraduate college and since 1996 as a university. The Undergraduate School lasts three years (six semesters). In the first three semesters, the students follow a common curriculum. In the last three semesters, they major in one of the following areas: (1)general economics; (2)business administration; (3)banking; (4)finance and accounting; (5)tourism and recreation; (6)business law; (7)marketing; (8)business translation/interpreting. The Graduate School lasts two years (four semesters) and offers the following majors: (1)business management; and (2)foreign trade.

Program Description

WSHiP follows its own schedule and curricula which comprise the following subjects: macro-economics; micro-economics; mathematics; statistics; finance and accounting; marketing; law; trade management; foreign trade; administration and management; computer science; social sciences; foreign languages. Students are also obliged to complete a relevant internship.

Special Features

WSHiP provides a dual educational system linking studies with practice. It enables the graduates of post-secondary Hotel and Tourism Management schools to continue their education and obtain BA and MA degrees. WSHiP provides its own textbooks and other materials adapted to its curricula.

Tuition and Fees

US$ 1200 per year (can be paid in monthly installments). Admission fee: US$ 180. WSHiP operations costs are covered by tuition and admission fees.

Admission

WSHiP does not set entrance examination. The candidates should submit an application form, the General Certificate of Education (and BA Diploma for the candidates to the Graduate School), and other required documents.

Graduation Requirements

A WSHiP student is obliged to take examinations or obtain "pass" marks in accordance with the rules and regulations of the studies in each semester. Graduation requires successful passing of all the examinations, completion of the required courses and relevant internships and defense of the Bachelor or Master's thesis.

University of Delaware

Hotel & Restaurant Management Program

College: College of Human Resources, Education and Public Policy
Program Enrollment: 350
Institutional Enrollment: Undergraduate: 15,300; Graduate: 3,000
Degree Awarded: Bachelor of Science
Degree Category: Hotel, Restaurant and Institutional Management
Institutional Accreditation: Middles States Association of Colleges and Secondary Schools
Contact: Paul E. Wise, Chair and Professor, Hotel, Restaurant and Institutional Management, The University of Delaware, Amy Rextrew House, 321 S. College Avenue, Newark, DE, 19716; phone (302) 831-6077; fax (302) 831-6395; paul.wise@mvs.udel.edu (e-mail); www.udel.edu/HRIM (web)

Institution Description

A private University with public support, the University of Delaware is a Land-Grant, Sea-Grant, Space-Grant and Urban-Grant institution established in 1833. Recently, the University was honored as a national model for its exemplary campus-wide technology network planning, management and accessibility. There are six undergraduate and seven graduate colleges offering over 120 majors, 87 minors and 1,500 courses.

Program Description

The HRIM program is a four-year major with a curriculum based in liberal arts, business and specialized courses in technical applications for the hotel and restaurant industries. The curriculum provides both a practical and theoretical education. The Hospitality program offers the Vita Nova restaurant, a student-operated laboratory featuring a 65-seat dining room, exhibition and demonstration kitchen with state-of-the-art video and satellite capabilities. Students are linked to hospitality leaders who provide placement assistance and with peers through the Hospitality and Student Mentor Systems.

Special Features

Students have the opportunity to study abroad through a joint degree agreement with Swiss School of Hotel and Tourism Management (SSH) in Chur, Switzerland. HRIM also offers a 4+1 program, in conjunction with the College of Business and Economics, that enables students to complete their undergraduate work and obtain an MBA in five years of study.

Financial Aid and Scholarships

The University of Delaware awards more than $53 million annual in aid. Corporations donate more than $30,000 per year specifically for HRIM student scholarships.

Admissions

Admission to the HRIM Program is selective. Applications are evaluated on the depth of college preparatory course, grades earned in academic courses, grade index, test scores, and class rank, if available.

Tuition & Fees

In-state $4,250
Out-of-State $12,250
Room and Board $4,952
Other Fees $400

Specialization Area

Hotel & Lodging Management
Restaurant & Foodservice Management

Graduation Requirements

A Bachelor of Science degree in the College of Human Resources, Education and Public Policy requires 120 semester academic credits. This includes 37 credits in general education, 25 credits in business and economics, 18 credits of human resources, and 50 credits in HRIM and electives. A documented and paid work requirement of 800 hours must be completed by the senior year.

University of Denver

College: Business Administration
Program Enrollment: 200
Institutional Enrollment: 4,000 undergraduate; 2,500 graduate
Degree Awarded: Bachelor of Science in Business Administration
Degree Category: Business Administration
Program Accreditation: American Assembly of Collegiate Schools of Business
Institutional Accreditation: North Central Association of Colleges and Schools

Contact: Robert O'Halloran, Director, School of Hotel, Restaurant and Tourism Management, University of Denver, CO 80208; phone: (303) 871 4268

Institution Description

The University of Denver, recognized both nationally and internationally for its academic excellence, is a medium-sized, private university in a metropolitan setting. The university is a comprehensive university with a variety of programs at the undergraduate and graduate level. The university is scaled to human size where the student is important, the classes small and faculty attention available.

Program Description

The School of Hotel, Restaurant and Tourism Management is part of the Daniels College of Business. The liberal arts and sciences and business subject cores form a firm foundation upon which to build the specialization consists of a core of courses that provide a general hospitality management education and electives which allow for specific specialization. There is also a major in resort and club management which is built upon the hospitality core courses.

Special Features

The university's location is in a major metropolitan area, known for its close proximity to major resort communities, and provides excellent opportunities for students to fulfill their 1,000-hour work requirement. It also provides the school with a rich supply of knowledgeable industry leaders for guest lectureships, property tours and mentoring.

Financial Aid and Scholarships

The University of Denver maintains a full-time financial aid office that can provide information on scholarships, loans, grants and other types of financial aid. There are numerous industry funded scholarships available to HRTM majors.

Approximate Tuition and Fees

Tuition: For 1998-99 $6,072 per quarter; heath fee: $84 per quarter and housing $$1915-$2360 per quarter.

Admissions

Students must provide either ACT or SAT scores, high school records and three references for admission consideration. Admission is granted by the admission office of the university and not by the school o Hotel, Restaurant and Tourism Management. However, once admitted to the university there are no additional requirements for admission to the School of Hotel, Restaurant and Tourism Management.

Graduation Requirements

Graduation requires completion of 185 quarter credits, comprised of approximately one third arts and science, one third business management and on third hospitality management. Students must also complete 1,000 hours of work experience and maintain a 2.0 average or better in the major courses, in business courses and overall.

University of Dundee

College: University of Dundee
Program Enrollment: 125
Institutional Enrollment: 8,500
Degree Awarded: Master of Arts (Hons)
Degree Category: Hotel and Catering Management
Program Accreditation: Hotel Catering & Institutional Management Association
Institutional Accreditation: Univerity of Dundee

Contact: Dr. Phil Lyon, Head of School, School of Management and Consumer Studies, University of Dundee, 13 Perth Road, Dundee, Scotland, DD1 4HT; phone +44 1382 345275; fax +44 1382 200047

Institution Description

The School was established in 1974 as part of the Duncan of Jordanstone College. Since 1988 all degree programmes offered by the College were validated by the University of Dundee. On August 1, 1994, the College merged with the University. The University is centrally located in Dundee and was a University College of the University of St. Andrews until 1967 when it became a University in its own right. The School now has two MA (Hons) programmes and is developing international educational links and internships.

Program Description

The programme in Hotel and Catering Management concentrates on operations, finance & control and management studies in years one and two. In the third year, these study areas merge into operations management and finance plus an elective study field. In the honours years, students study strategic management and industry studies with a further elective and a dissertation. The full 3/4 year programme is cohesive and fully satisfies the needs of the hotel and catering industry.

Special Features

Internships, most of which take place overseas, are organized and supervised by the School. Excellent modern training facilities including a production kitchen and restaurant. Research activities are encouraged and being developed.

Financial Aid and Scholarships

A variety of financial aid programmes are available, including loans, access grants and bursaries. Sponsorship by industry (notably Gleneagles Hotel).

Approximate Tuition and Fees

$9,000 per year; books $100 per year; accomodation (self catering residences) $50 per week.

Admissions

Applicants are normally 18 years of age or older and have been in full-time education. Entry requirements as normally expected for universities within the UK. Applications from *mature* students are actively encouraged. Articulation and transfer arrangements are in place.

Specialization Area

Students must choose an elective in years three and four. The current range consists of: Small Business management; Advanced Food and Wine Studies; Managerial Communication Skills.

Graduation Requirements

Internship requirements: satisfactory completion of 20 weeks. Study period including internship: three years (MA); four years (MA Hons).

University of Guelph

College: Social and Applied Human Sciences (CSAHS)
Program Enrollment: 600
Institutional Enrollment: 10,750 undergraduates; 1,700 graduates
Degree Awarded: Bachelor of Commerce
Degree Category: School of Hotel & Food Administration (HAFA)
Institutional Accreditation: Ontario Ministry of Colleges & Universities
Contact: Valerie Allen, Associate Professor, School of Hotel & Food Administration, University of Guelph, Guelph, Ontario N1G2W1, Canada. Phone (519) 824-4120, Ext. 8710; Fax: (519) 823-5512. Web site: http://www.uoguelph.ca/HAFA/

Institutional Description
The University of Guelph, situated 60 miles west of Toronto, has a diverse range of academic research and degree programs in management, the arts, and the physical, biological, agricultural and social sciences. The University follows the semester system and approximately 40 percent of students live in campus residences. The HAFA program, in its 27th year, enrolls nearly 600 undergraduates and about 25 graduate students.

Program Description
The Bachelor of Commerce degree was the first hospitality university degree program in Canada. The four-year program combines courses in hospitality and tourism management with courses in the arts and sciences. Such breadth assures that graduates will have a firm base of knowledge, as well as the necessary analytical skills to deal with the growing complexity of business. A paid co-op program, Executive in Residence Program, Management Development Program, strong Alumni networking and industrial connections, make for an outstanding program.

Special Features
The program makes extensive use of the case method of study and, through its advanced management courses maintains close links to industry.

Financial Aid and Scholarships
Besides the financial aid available through the university, the school has a large number of scholarships, which are awarded on the basis of academic achievement and industrial experience.

Approximate Tuition and Fees
Tuition fees per semester: residents, about CDN $2,000; visa students, about CDN $9,000.

Admissions
Admission to the program is based on the completion of high school graduation, applicants must satisfy certain subject requirements. Documented work experience in the hospitality industry is a consideration in the admissions process. Students usually enter the program in September each year.

Graduation Requirements
Graduation requires that students have completed 40 courses, of which 28 are core requirements.

University of Hawaii at Manoa

College: School of Travel Industry Management
Program Enrollment: 400
Institutional Enrollment: 11,790 undergraduate; 5,220 graduate
Degree Awarded: Bachelor of Science
Emphases/Specializations: Hotel Management; Restaurant/Institutional Food service Management; Tourism Management; Transportation Management
Program Accreditation: Accreditation Commission for Programs in Hospitality Administration (ACPHA)
Institutional Accreditation: Western Association of Schools and Colleges
Contact: Chuck Y. Gee, Dean, School of Travel Industry Management, University of Hawaii at Manoa, 2560 Campus Rd., Honolulu, HI 96822; phone (808) 956-8946

Institution Description

Founded in 1907, the University of Hawaii at Manoa (UHM) has emphasized throughout its history studies related to Hawaii's distinctive geographical and cultural setting including ocean and earth sciences, Asian and Pacific studies and, of course, the travel industry. Located in Manoa Valley, UHM is near downtown Honolulu and Waikiki, the center of Hawaii's tourism industry.

Program Description

The Travel Industry Management (TIM) School pioneered an academic and training program bringing together all components of the industry--hotel, restaurant, transportation and tourism management. All of its programs have an international perspective and encompass both public and private sectors. Through the internship program, students put classroom theories to practice and gain on-the-job experience.

Special Features

TIM offers outstanding laboratory, library and computer facilities. The internship and placement office provides special internship opportunities abroad, and career search and job placement assistance.

Financial Aid and Scholarships

In addition to assistance available through the university's financial aid office, the TIM School offers a number of scholarships, Awards are based on academic merit, achievement in extracurricular and work arenas, and financial need.

Approximate Tuition and Fees

Tuition for full-time students who are residents of Hawaii is $1,464 per semester; for nonresidents, $4704 per semester. Tuition for part-time students who are residents of Hawaii is $122 per credit; for nonresidents, $392 per credit. Fees are approximately $60 per semester.

Admissions

Students are admitted to TIM at all class levels. Courses, including English composition and literature, speech, financial and managerial accounting, micro and macroeconomics, computer science, business law, and calculus are completed during the freshmen and sophomore years. A minimum cumulative 2.5 GPA is required for admission.

Graduation Requirements

Graduation requires completion of a minimum of 124 semester hours. Requirements include 16 hours of preprofessional courses, 40 hours of general education, 14-16 hours of foreign language, 12-15 hours of electives, 42 hours of TIM courses, and 800 hours of work experience.

University of Houston

College: Conrad N. Hilton College of Hotel and Restaurant Management
Program Enrollment: 900: 820 graduate; 80 graduate
Institutional Enrollment: 32,000, Undergraduate 25,000 Post-Baccalaureate, 1,500 Graduate 4,000, Doctoral 1,500
Degree Awarded: Bachelor of Science; Master of Hospitality Management
Degree Categories: Hospitality Management
Emphasis/Specialization: N/A
Program Accreditation: N/A
Institutional Accreditation: Southern Association of Colleges and Schools
Contact: Dr. Alan T. Stutts, Dean, Conrad N. Hilton College of Hotel and Restaurant Management, University of Houston, Houston, TX 77204-3902; phone (713) 743-2610; fax (713) 743-2498; e-mail BSHRM@uh.edu; website http://www.hrm.uh.edu

Institution Description

The University of Houston (UH) is a nationally recognized urban research and teaching university. Its activities encompass undergraduate, graduate and professional education; basic and applied research programs; and public service programs. The university's graduate professional education; basic and applied research programs and public service programs.

Program Description

The College of Hotel and Restaurant Management emphasizes broad information skills and in-depth studies in food and beverage management, lodging management, accounting and finance, marketing, facilities management, law, and information systems.

Special Features

The university maintains a $28.8 million hotel and restaurant management training facility on campus.
The University of Houston Hilton and Conference Center has 86 guest rooms, 22 conference and meeting rooms with over 35,000 square feet of meeting and convention space, two full-service restaurants, a faculty club, an archive and library, three ballrooms, classrooms and laboratories.
The College houses the Hospitality Hall of Honor which features displays of historical information, personal and corporate memorabilia, and other items of interest. Each year a gala event brings industry leaders to the College for an annual induction ceremony. Our 20 full time professors have outstanding academic credentials and bring with them over 200 years of significant industry experience which is applied in both classroom and research activities.

Financial Aid and Scholarships

A large number of competitive scholarships are available. Application deadline for college scholarships is March 1. Financial Aid is also available to those who qualify.

Admissions

Freshman admission is based on rank in class, SAT/ACT scores, and high school core requirements. Transfer applicants with 15 or more college semester credit hours must have a cumulative GPA of 2.5 to be admitted directly into Hotel and Restaurant Management.

Tuition and Fees

Per year: Tuition for Texas residents, $2,000; nonresidents, $8,500; international students, $9,000; room and board, $4,200.

Specialization Area

Hotel & Lodging Management
Restaurant & Foodservice Management

Graduation Requirements

132 semester hours: 68 hours of General Education courses and 64 hours of Hotel and Restaurant Management Courses, including 36 advanced hours.

University of Illinois at Urbana-Champaign

Hospitality Management Program

Program Enrollment: 75
Institutional Enrollment: 27,000 undergraduate, 8,200 graduate
Degrees Awarded: Bachelor of Science
Degree Categories: Food Science and Human Nutrition
Emphases/Specializations: Hospitality/Foodservice Management
Institutional Accreditation: North Central Association of Colleges and Universities

Contact: Beth Reutter, Coordinator of Hospitality Management, University of Illinois, 363 Bevier Hall, 905 South Goodwin Ave., Urbana, IL 61801; phone: (217) 333-2024

Institution Description

Founded in 1867 as a land-grant institution, the University of Illinois at Urbana-Champaign (UIUC) is one of the nation's major comprehensive universities.

Program Description

UIUC's Hospitality Management option is multi-disciplinary, combining the advantages of a liberal arts education with a business and science-based course of study. A specialization in business adminstration complements a strong foodservice systems emphasis. Excellent on-site foodservice facilities, as well as internships, provide practical experience.

Special Features

Hands-on experience is provided through the management of Bevier Cafe and Spice Box, which houses a luncheon cafe, fine dining restaurant, and catering operation.

Financial Aid and Scholarships

UIUC maintains a financial aid office to help students. The William Myer's, Katsina's and Monical Pizza Scholarships are based on potential for success in the hospitality industry. Jonathan Baldwin Turner Scholarships are offered to incoming freshmen with high academic achievements.

Approximate Tuition and Fees

Undergraduate tuition and fees are $1,654 per semester for Illinois residents; out-of-state tuition is approximately three times that of Illinois residents.

Admissions

Admission to UIUC is highly competitive and is based on a combined selection index that includes high school GPA, rank in class, as well as ACT scores. Applicants must complete a specific number of units in high school preparatory courses, and may be required to submit a statement of professional interest. Transfer applicants must have completed at least 60 hours of baccalaureate credit and meet department requirements for GPA and work experience.

Graduation Requirements

Graduation requires the completion of 126 semester hours, which includes 45 hours of general education, 21 hours of business-related courses, and 35 hours of hospitality-related course work. Students must also complete a 320 hour practical work experience and a 320 hour professional work experience.

University of Kentucky

Hospitality Management

College: Human Environmental Sciences
Program Enrollment: 120
Institutional Enrollment: 17,250 undergraduate; 4,300 graduate
Degree Awarded: Bachelor of Science
Degree Category: Hospitality Management a *AA and Tourism*
Institutional Accreditation: Southern Association of Colleges and Schools

Contact: Claire D. Schmelzer, PhD Program Director, Hospitality Management, College of Human Environmental Sciences, 120 Erikson Hall, University of Kentucky, Lexington, KY 40506-0050; phone (606) 257-4965; fax (606) 257-4095

Institution Description

The University of Kentucky (UK), which is in the heart of Kentucky's Bluegrass region, is the state's only comprehensive, land-grant research university. It has an enrollment of over 23,000 students. Residence halls and Greek housing accommodate 6,400 students. Laboratories, recital halls, computer banks, art galleries and recreational facilities make UK the best equipped educational institution in Kentucky.

Program Description

The Hospitality Management program, located within the Nutrition and Food Science Department, provides students with the background and expertise to enter any area of the hospitality industry. Courses in management, marketing, finance, accounting, human resources, and the technical aspects of hospitality operations are included in the curriculum. Independent study opportunities and field work in a variety of industry settings are integral parts of the program.

Special Features

Fine restaurants, hotels, clubs, and other hospitalityrelated businesses in the Lexington, Louisville and Cincinnati areas provide excellent opportunities for internships and employment. Students interested in tourism can work with professionals at city convention and visitors' bureaus, the Kentucky Tourism Council, and the State Cabinet for Tourism.

Financial Aid and Scholarships

Full financial aid services are available through the university. A variety of scholarships are offered by the College of Human Environmental Sciences, state and local organizations, and the hospitality industry.

Admissions

Students accepted to UK may be automatically accepted into Hospitality Management. Students must have a 2.0 GPA to transfer into the college and program.

Graduation Requirements

The successful degree candidate will have completed 128 hours while maintaining a GPA of at least 2.0. The academic hours are comprised of the university studies requirement, six hours of college requirements, and the premajor and major program requirements which include at least 24 hours of coursework from the College of Business and Economics and 32 hours in the hospitality management core. Students are encouraged to choose electives from related disciplines.

University of Massachusetts-Amherst

Department of Hotel, Restaurant and Travel Administration

College: College of Food and Natural Resources
Program Enrollment: 500
Institutional Enrollment: 18,000 undergraduate; 5,000 graduate
Degrees Awarded: Bachelor of Science, Master of Science
Degree Categories: Hotel and Restaurant Administration; Travel and Tourism
Institutional Accreditation: New England Association of Schools and Colleges
Program Accreditation: Accreditation Commission for Programs in Hospitality Administration
Contact: Frank P. Lattuca, Head, Department of Hotel, Restaurant and Travel Administration, University of Massachusetts, Flint 107, Amherst, MA 01003-2710; phone (413) 545-1389; fax (413) 545-1235

Institution Description

The University of Massachusetts-Amherst is the land-grant flagship campus of the commonwealth's higher education system. It is a research institution that offers a comprehensive undergraduate program. There are 98 undergraduate degree programs, 69 master's degree programs and 48 doctoral degree programs.

Program Description

The Department of Hotel, Restaurant and Travel Administration requires students to pursue a degree program involving business, general education and hospitality operations courses. In addition to the formal educational requirements, the program puts a high emphasis on work experience, campus activities, professional development and student/faculty contacts. Over 50 courses are offered directly in the department.

Special Features

Students are encouraged to study abroad, engage in a cooperative education activity, internship, and participate in student clubs and organizations that will directly benefit them.

Financial Aid and Scholarships

The university has available all normal federal, state and competitive scholarships. The department also makes available some industrysponsored awards to students in the program.

Approximate Tuition and Fees

Tuition and fees for Massachusetts residents is $5,400; for nonresidents, $12,100. Room and board is $4,200.

Admissions

Applications for entering freshmen are welcomed from high school graduates with a good high school record. SAT or ACT exams are required. Students with 12 or more credits are considered as transfer students. Students from Maine, Vermont, Connecticut, and Rhode Island who enroll in hotel, restaurant and travel administration pay in-state tuition. Hotel, Restaurant and Travel Administration is a competitive enrollment major.

Graduation Requirements

To graduate a student needs 120 credits and a 2.0 GPA (45 in residence). Thirty-nine credits are in general education, six in writing, 18 in the School of Management, and 49 in Hotel, Restaurant and Travel Administration. A minimum of 800 hours of evaluated work experience in the industry is required.

University of Minnesota, Crookston

Hotel, Restaurant, and Institutional Management

College: Hotel, Restaurant, and Institutional Management
Program Enrollment: 80
Institutional Enrollment: 2,000
Degrees Awarded: Bachelor of Science (B.S.); Associate in Applied Science (A.A.S.)
Degree Categories: Hotel, Restaurant, and Institutional Management
Emphases/Specialization's: Dietetic Technician (A.A.S.)
Program Accreditation:
Institutional Education: North Central Association of Colleges and Secondary Schools
Contact: Ken W. Myers, Department Head, HRI Department, University of Minnesota, 2900 University Avenue, Crookston, MN 56716-5001; phone: (218)281-8200; fax:(218)281-8050 e-mail: Web page: http://webhome.crk.umn.edu/~kmyers

Institution Description

The University of Minnesota Crookston is a polytechnic institution granting career-oriented degrees that focus on "real world" applications with an extensive use of technology. The technology incorporated into the curriculum provides each full-time student with a 486-model notebook computer.

Program Description

The HRI B.S. program consists of 120 credits, 45 of which are general education courses. The remaining 75 credits include in depth courses in finance, hospitality law, rooms division management, menu design, restaurant operational management, global tourism, layout & design, catering, cases & trends, etc. Students complete an internship experience.

Special Features

A modern conference center provides both food production and dining room service experiences. Notebook computers allowing technological applications in areas from accounting to menu design.

Financial Aid and Scholarships

UMC offers students many financial aid and scholarship programs. More than 87 percent receive financial aid and over 75 percent of freshmen receive scholarships.

Admissions

Students with no prior college work will be admitted if they have: (a) graduated from an accredited or approved high school or have a GED, and (b) submitted results from the ACT Assessment. Students with prior college work should have transcripts submitted for review.

Tuition and Fees

In-State: $3,900 per year; Out-of-State: $294/credit; Room and Board: $4,300; Other Fees: Student Service Fee-$255, Technology Fee- $960.

Specialization Area

Hotel & Lodging Management; Restaurant & Foodservice Management.

Graduation Requirements

The A.A.S. degree must have a minimum of 64 semester credits with a GPA of 2.00 (C). The B.S. degree must have a minimum of 120 semester credits with a minimum GPA of 2.00 (C).

University of Nebraska-Lincoln

Restaurant/Foodservice Administration

College: Human Resources and Family Sciences
Program Enrollment: 25
Institutional Enrollment: Undergraduate - 20,000; Graduate - 5,000
Degrees Awarded: Bachelor of Science; Master of Science
Degree Categories: Restaurant/Foodservice Administration, Dietetics
Emphases/Specializations: Foodservice Management
Institutional Accreditation: North Central Association of Colleges and Schools
Contact: Fayrene Hamouz, Associate Professor, 316 Leverton, University of Nebraska-Lincoln, Lincoln, NE 68583-0806; phone (402) 472-1582; FAX (402) 472-1587; Fhamouz@unl.edu

Institution Description
The University of Nebraska-Lincoln is a comprehensive, public, land-grant university with a three fold mission: teaching, research and service. It is one of four units of a multicampus system.

Program Description
The Restaurant/Foodservice Administration Program provides a well-rounded background in general education, foodservice management and business. Students complete a 12 week practicum.

Special Features
The program maintains student organizations (professional and social), attends the National Restaurant Show and provides placement assistance.

Financial Aid and Scholarships
Students are encouraged to apply for financial aid and scholarships through the appropriate university office.

Admissions
Admission to the program requires graduation from an accredited high school with successful completion of high school core courses. Students begin the restaurant management sequence as freshman.

Tuition and Fees
In-State	$1,500 per semester.
Out-of-State	$3,600 per semester.

Specialization Area
Restaurant & Foodservice Mgmt.

Graduation Requirements
Graduation requires the completion of 128 semester hours, which includes 46 hours of general education, 35 hours of professional and 21 hours of business.

University of Nevada, Las Vegas

William F. Harrah College of Hotel Administration

College: William F. Harrah College of Hotel Administration
Program Enrollment: 1,830
Institutional Enrollment: Undergraduate: 21,000; Graduate: 3,200
Degree Awarded: Bachelor of Science
Degree Categories: Hotel Administration
Emphases/Specializations: Accounting; Computers; Clubs; Food & Beverage; Entertainment; Human Resources; Gaming; Conventions/Trade Shows; Travel and Tourism; Hotel Management; Sport & Leisure Services
Institutional Accreditation: Northwest Association of Schools and Colleges

Contact: Dr. Stuart H. Mann, Dean; William F. Harrah College of Hotel Administration; University of Nevada, Las Vegas; 4505 Maryland Parkway; Box 456039; Las Vegas, NV 89154-6039; phone (702) 895-3616; fax (702) 895-3127; e-mail: hoaadvis@nevada.edu

Institution Description

The campus is located within a few miles of 120,000 hotel rooms and countless restaurants. Eight dormitories supplement an unlimited number of apartments to offer either a residential or urban environment. The college is housed in a 100,000 square-foot facility.

Program Description

The William F. Harrah College of Hotel Administration houses three departments: Hotel Management; Food and Beverage Management; and Tourism and Convention Administration. In addition to the basic hospitality curriculum, special interests are met through electives, which are approximately 25 percent of total credits. Required work experiences are easily met through local employment; many students work to meet expenses. Special internships are also available in local hotels, labor unions, clubs, the convention authority and so forth.

Special Features

The college has more than 44 full-time faculty members, all with industry experience. Our students come from all over the world. There are 50 countries representing 26% of our undergraduate student body. Students from Nevada represent 26% of all students. Transfers are accommodated. Summer programs abroad are also available.

Financial Aid and Scholarships

Scholarships totaling over $200,000 are awarded annually by the college based on academic, professional and service achievement merit, regardless of need. Applications are processed by the university's financial aid office.

Admissions

Admission to the college requires a 2.5 GPA from high school or university/junior college record. ACT or SAT is required. Admission to a special second baccalaureate degree program is available with a 2.5 GPA. High school recommendation; college-bound curriculum.

Tuition and Fees

In state: $69 per credit hour
Out of State: $2885 per semester

Specialization Area

Hotel & Lodging
Restaurant & Foodservice Management
Travel & Tourism Management
Culinary Arts

Graduation Requirements

128 semester 42 in hotel, 18 in business and economics, 10 in science and mathematics, 28 in arts and letters, 15 hotel electives, 15 free electives (that may be in hotel management). Students must work and have a 2.5 GPA for graduation. Honors program available.

University of New Hampshire

Department of Hospitality Management

College: Whittemore School of Business and Economics
Program Enrollment: 150
Institutional Enrollment: 11,500 undergraduate; 750 graduate
Degrees Awarded: Bachelor of Science in Hospitality Management; Master of Business Administration; Ph.D. in Economics
Institutional Accreditation: New England Association of Schools and Colleges, American Assembly of Collegiate Schools of Business (AACSB), Accreditation Commission for Programs in Hospitality administration (ACPHA)

Contact: Raymond J. Goodman, Jr., Ph.D., Professor and Chair, Department of Hospitality Management, University of New Hampshire, McConnell Hall, Durham, NH 03824; phone (603) 862-3303

Institution Description

The campus, 200 acres in size, is surrounded by more than 3,000 acres of fields, farms and woodlands owned by the university. The university's approximately 570 fulltime faculty members provide a ratio of one full-time faculty member to about 17 full-time students. The Department of Hospitality Management has five full-time faculty members.

Program Description

The Hospitality Management Department prepares students for management positions in the service sector, specifically in the hospitality industry. The program includes a mix of professional experience along with classroom activities. Students are fully integrated in the business school and its curriculum.

Special Features

A distinguishing aspect of the program is the quality time spent outside of class on various activities related to the major. Study abroad opportunities and internships are also available. The department is in joint operations with the New England Center for Continuing Education, a 110-room hotel and conference center with 14 meeting rooms and a 350-seat dining room. Students use the center as a practice laboratory, both in their classes and for independent studies and internships.

Financial Aid and Scholarships

Financial aid is available to hospitality management students through the financial aid office. A wide range of scholarships are offered to students, including several scholarships reserved only for hospitality management students.

Approximate Tuition and Fees

Tuition for in-state residents is $5,140. Out-of-state residents, $13,860 per year.

Admissions

Most competitive applicants rank in the top 20 percent of their classes. The average SAT scores are 1,100 combined, and depending on the competitiveness of the high school, an applicant should have a B+ or better average. Experience in the hospitality field is helpful but not required. Admission to a bachelor's degree program is based upon successful completion of a four-year secondary school program of college preparatory coursework. Primary consideration is given to academic achievement and aptitude. Consideration is also given to character, leadership, initiative, and special aptitudes and talents.

The University of New Haven

Hotel, Restaurant, Tourism and Dietetics Administration

College: School of Hotel, Restaurant, Tourism and Dietetics Administration
Program Enrollment: 150 undergraduate; 15 graduate
Institutional Enrollment: 3,400 undergraduate; 3,600 graduate
Degrees Awarded: Bachelor of Science; Master of Science; Associate of Science; Certificate
Degree Categories: Bachelor in Hotel and Restaurant Management, Concentration in Tourism, General Dietetics; Associate in Hotel and Restaurant Management, Executive Master's in Hospitality and Tourism
Institutional Accreditation: New England Association of Schools and Colleges; National Association of Independent Colleges and Universities
Contact: LeRoy Sluder, Coordinator of Hotel, Restaurant Management, University of New Haven, 300 Orange Ave., West Haven, CT 06516; phone (203) 932-7362; fax (203) 932-7083; e-mail: lerosl@earthlink.net

Institutional Description
The University of New Haven (UNH) is a private, coeducational university with a contemporary and innovative view of higher education. The undergraduate programs are designed to provide students with the professional training they will need for career success.

Program Description
The School of Hotel, Restaurant, Tourism and Dietetics Administration serves the food service, lodging, tourism, health care and recreational industries. The curriculum is designed to develop team-building, problemsolving and critical thinking skills. Courses in Marketing, Human Resource Management and Leadership combine theory and application to ensure a comprehensive understanding of major service sector concepts and to prepare students for a hospitality career.

Special Features
Computer lab; 45-seat food service lab.

Financial Aid and Scholarships
The University of New Haven offers a comprehensive financial aid program, with students receiving assistance in the form of grants, scholarships, student loans and part-time employment. Funds are available from federal and state governments, private sponsors and universities resources. Many of the university's full-time undergraduate students receive some form of financial assistance. Most financial aid awards are based on an individual applicant's demonstration of need.

Approximate Tuition and Fees
Tuition for full-time students (12-17 hours) is $6,950 per semester.

Admissions
The admissions office considers out-of-state applicants on the same basis as Connecticut residents. The university recognizes both the College Entrance Examination Board's Advance Placement Program and the College Level Examination Program.

Graduation Requirements
A degree will be conferred when a student has satisfied all program requirements and met the following university requirements: earned a cumulative quality point ratio of no less than 2.0 in all degree courses; earned a cumulative quality point ratio of no less than 2.0 in the student's major; and passed the university's Writing Proficiency Exam.

University of New Orleans

School of Hotel, Restaurant and Tourism Administration

College: College of Business Administration
Program Enrollment: 400
Institutional Enrollment: 16,100 undergraduate; 3,991 graduate
Degrees Awarded: Bachelor of Science; Master of Business Administration HRT concentration
Degree Category: Business Administration
Emphases/Specializations: Hotel/Restaurant and Tourism Administration
Program Accreditation: Accreditation Commission for Programs in Hospitality Administration; American Assembly of Collegiate Schools of Business
Institutional Accreditation: Southern Association of Colleges and Schools
Contact: Dr. Jeffrey D. Schaffer, Director, School of Hotel, Restaurant and Tourism Administration, College of Business Administration, University of New Orleans, New Orleans, LA 70148, phone: (504)280-6385; fax: (504) 280-3189

Institution Description

The University of New Orleans (UNO) is the second largest university in Louisiana with 523 full-time and 192 part-time faculty members, and 618 non-academic staff. UNO has six colleges: Business Administration, Education, Engineering, Liberal Arts, Sciences and Urban and Public Affairs. Professional education is provided by the schools of Urban and Regional Studies; Hotel, Restaurant and Tourism Administration; and Naval Architecture and Marine Engineering. UNO offers bachelor degrees in 60 fields of study, master's degrees in 55 fields, and doctorates in 12 fields of study.

Program Description

UNO's School of Hotel, Restaurant and Tourism Administration (HRT) provides students with a business degree specialization in hospitality management. Six concentration areas include Lodging Operations Management; Food and Beverage Operations Management; Tourism, Meeting and Convention Management; Gaming Operations Management; and Club Operations Management. The city of New Orleans' great hotels, restaurants and tourism attractions constitute an outstanding "living laboratory" for UNO students.

Financial Aid and Scholarships

UNO maintains a financial aid office to assist students with financial needs. The School's Scholarship Committee assists HRT majors in applying for industry, hospitality associations and university scholarships.

Approximate Tuition and Fees

Tuition for residents with 12 or more semester hours is $1,181; for nonresidents $3,944. Dormitory costs including a meal plan are $1,575. All fees subject to change.

Admissions

Admission to the university and to all its programs is open to all persons regardless of race, creed, color, sex, age, marital status, handicap, veterans's status, or national origin who meet the admission requirements and qualifications of the university. All first-time freshmen must meet the following requirements for admission to UNO: a composite score of 20 on the ACT (950 on the SAT), or a cumulative grade point average of 2.0 on a scale of 4 in the 17_ units described in the university's catalog. Transfer students are admitted in accordance with the policy described in the university's catalog.

Graduation Requirements

Graduation requires the completion of 129 semester hours, which include 47 semester hours of general education, 42 hours of business, and 40 hours of hotel, restaurant and tourism. An 800-hour hospitality work experience is also required. The MBA requires the completion of 33 semester hours, which include 24 hours of graduate business courses and 9 hours of graduate HRT courses.

University of Queensland

Hospitality Management, Tourism Management, Leisure Management and Travel Management

College: Department of Hospitality, Tourism & Property Management
Program Enrollment: 350 intake per year
Institutional Enrollment: 20,000 undergraduate, 5,000 graduate
Degrees Awarded: Bachelor of Business, (Honours) Master of Business
Degree Categories: Hospitality Management, Tourism Management, Travel Management, and Leisure Management
Emphases/Specializations: Food and Beverage; Accommodation and Special Events Management, Sustainable Development and Tourism planning.
Program Accreditation: Catering Institute of Australia
Institutional Accreditation: International Association of Hotel management Schools; Tourism Training Australia (Hospitality Division)
Contact: Prof. Stephen Craig-Smith, Department Head, Department of Hospitality, Tourism and Property Management, University of Queensland, Gatton College, QLD 4345; Phone (07) 5460 1371; fax (07) 5460 1171

Institution Description

The University of Queensland is the largest and oldest in the state and is one of the seven major research universities of Australia. Its 25,000 students are taught in seven major faculties. Tourism, Hospitality, Travel and Leisure are taught by the Department of Hospitality, Tourism and Property Management in the Business, Economics and Law faculty. It is possible to progress from bachelors to doctoral level in all areas of study.

Program Description

Gatton College's hospitality, leisure, travel and tourism management degrees are built on a solid academic foundation together with specialised areas of study. The main components are (1) general business studies – business law, accounting, marketing, economics and finance; (2) human resource management; (3) food and beverage management; (4) lodging/property management; (5) tourism management, travel management and leisure studies and (6) industry

Special Features

The undergraduate program requires a period of industry internship that ensures our graduates are well received by the industry.

Financial Aid and Scholarship

Australian students only are eligible for Austudy, which is means-tested study assistance.

Approximate Tuition and Fees

Australian students: none (HECS applies – approximately US$1,650 per year). Overseas students: US$7,600 per year. Room and board: US$3,000. Other fees: student services fee US$85 per year.

Admissions

Entry to our courses is highly competitive, and admissions will be made on the basis of academic merit.

Graduation Requirements

Graduation requires successful completion of 250 credit points of study, including eight weeks of industry internship for Hospitality Management.

University of San Francisco

Hospitality Management Program

College: McLaren School of Business
Program Enrollment: 80
Institutional Enrollment: 7,803 total; 3,572 Undergraduate
Degree Awarded: Bachelor of Science in Business Administration
Major: Hospitality Management; a minor in Hospitality Management available (18 units)
Degree Category: Hospitality Management
Emphases/Specialization: Food & Beverage, Hotel, Sales & Marketing, Accounting
Program Accreditation: American Assembly of Collegiate Schools of Business
Institutional Accreditation: Western Association of Schools and College
Contact: Thomas Costello, Director, Hospitality Management Program, McLaren School of Business, University of San Francisco, 2130 Fulton Street, San Francisco, CA 94117-1045, phone (415) 422-2581, fax (415) 422-6935, admissions telephone (415) 422-6563, e-mail hospitality@usfca.edu, website www.usfca.edu/mclaren/HOSP/Hospitality.html

Institution Description

Founded as the first institution of higher education in San Francisco by the Jesuit Fathers in 1855, the University of San Francisco (USF), long-established as an institutional leader in the fields of law, business, the sciences, liberal arts and nursing, is a private university offering a wide range of undergraduate and graduate programs.

Program Description

The Hospitality Management Program is based in USF's McLaren School of Business, offering a curriculum rich in tradition, well grounded in values, leading with fundamentals, yet charged with creative "newness". The program utilizes the foundation of Jesuit liberal arts education to enrich and broaden the student's ability to relate in an ethnically diverse culture. Our objective is to help the student think like a manager and to make sound, value-based decisions for long-term success. The Program approaches this task with a curriculum reflecting a "real world" industry orientation combined with practical application.

Special Features

San Francisco's world-class hotels, restaurants, convention center and wineries are used by students for field trips, research and industry-related work experience. On-campus classroom facilities include a demonstration kitchen and a dining room. Class size averages 20 students. Twenty-five percent of the program's population is international, reflective of the global scope of the industry. Students gain access to industry leaders through industry-related events, executive dinners, career fairs and participation in mentorship programs. Hospitality Management Students have historically achieved a 98% job placement rate by graduation.

Financial Aid and Scholarships

USF's Office of Financial Aid is fully committed to easing the cost of a private education through a full range of financial aid, scholarship, loan and work-study opportunities for those who qualify. For further information, call (415) 422-6303. Over $65,000 in Hospitality Management scholarships and loans were awarded to students for the 1998/1999 academic year.

Approximate Tuition and Fees

Full time student (12-18 units per semester) $16,750

Admissions

Admission for freshmen is based on a student's overall secondary school record, results of either the SAT or ACT (TOEFL is required for international applications), letters of recommendation and other information collected in the application. Transfer students must have a minimum cumulative 2.0 grade point average on all transferable coursework and be in good academic standing at the last institution attended.

Graduation Requirements

128 units are needed for graduation: 60 units in general education courses and electives, 45 units in business core requirements, 23 units in Hospitality Management courses. 800 hours of industry-related work/internship experience is required.

University of South Carolina

School of Hotel, Restaurant and Tourism Administration

College: Applied Professional Sciences
Program Enrollment: 275
Institutional Enrollment: 16,000 undergraduate; 10,000 graduate
Degree Awarded: Bachelor of Science
Degree Category: Hotel, Restaurant and Tourism Administration
Program Accreditation: Accreditation Commission for Programs in Hospitality Administration (ACPHA)
Institutional Accreditation: Southern Association of Colleges and Schools; Accreditation Commission for Programs in Hospitality Administration
Contact: Sandra K. Strick, Ph.D., Interim Chair, Hotel, Restaurant and Tourism Administration, University of South Carolina, Columbia, SC 29208; phone (803) 777-6665; fax (803) 777-1224; e-mail: strick@gwm.sc.edu

Institution Description
The University of South Carolina is the largest university in the state. The main campus is located in the capital city, Columbia. The university has 17 academic units, including a School of Medicine and widely acclaimed programs in engineering and international business.

Program Description
The Hotel, Restaurant and Tourism Administration Program presently offers one comprehensive baccalaureate degree incorporating knowledge in the administration of hotels, restaurants and tourism facilities. In addition to the traditional liberal arts requirements, students are required to take 14 courses in the major, including an internship, to broaden industry exposure and professional commitment.

Special Features
The program includes: an institute for tourism research, two complete autonomous food laboratory kitchens, and extensive student club activities.

Financial Aid and Scholarships
The university, college, and hospitality industry provide numerous sources of financial aid and scholarships through both endowments and direct funding.

Approximate Tuition and Fees
In-state tuition is $3,530; out-of-state tuition, $7,242 per year.

Admissions
The Hotel, Restaurant and Tourism Administration Program adheres to the university admission requirements for freshmen and transfer students, while internal transfers must have a minimum of 2.2 GPA (4.0 system). All students are admitted to the lower division until they meet the requirements for upper division or professional status.

Graduation Requirements
Graduation requires a minimum of 127 semester hours, which includes 58 hours in general education and related areas, 54 hours in professional areas, and 15 hours of electives.

The University of Southern Mississippi

Department of Hospitality Management

College: Health and Human Sciences
Program Enrollment: 200
Institutional Enrollment: 15,000
Degree Awarded: Bachelor of Science
Degree Categories: Hospitality Management
Emphases\Specializations: Lodging/Restaurant and Tourism Management Program Accreditation: N/A
Institutional Accreditation: The Commission on Colleges of The Southern Association of Colleges and Schools
Contact: Dr. Joe Hutchinson, Chair, Department of Hospitality Management, USM, Box 5176, Hattiesburg, MS 39406-5176, Phone: (601) 266-6762; Fax: (601) 266-6707.

Institution Description

The University of Southern Mississippi (USM) is quickly becoming one of the nation's top research and teaching universities. Founded in 1910, USM has greatly expanded its educational programs and its physical plant over the last twenty years. Serving in excess of 15,000 students in Hattiesburg and on the Mississippi Gulf Coast, USM offers 160 bachelor, masters and doctoral degree programs.

Program Description

USM's degree in Hospitality Management (HM) prepares students for life-long successful careers as leaders within the hospitality and tourism industry. The curriculum in HM is interdisciplinary, drawing from business, science, and the liberal arts. Balancing theory with practice, students obtain both practicum and internship experiences. Spurred by the gaming industry, the growth of new hospitality and tourism positions has far exceeded the supply of qualified managers in this region of the United States.

Hattiesburg Campus: The program in Hattiesburg is in a traditional four-year residential setting with a full complement of campus activities and services. The program is supported through the operations of the Charcoal Room, an academic food service laboratory, the Mississippi Tourism Resource Center and the Applied Research Division of the National Food Service Management Institute.
Gulf Park Campus: The HM program in Long Beach is for juniors and seniors only, with lower-level courses offered at nearby community colleges. This program is ideal for students who want to gain a degree while working full-time in the hospitality industry on the Mississippi Gulf Coast, a growing gaming, meetings, and golf resort.

Special Features

Fine Dining Restaurant – Hattiesburg Campus
Culinary Academy – Gulf Coast Campus

Financial Aid and Scholarships

More than thirty scholarships are available annually for HM students. Other scholarships are available on a competitive basis to students within the College in addition to the full range of financial assistance available through the Office of Financial Aid at USM.

Admissions

Admission to the Department of Hospitality Management is open to all students who meet the general admission requirements of the University.

Tuition & Fees

(1998-1999) In-State: $1,435; Out-of-State: $2,986; Room and Board: $1,425 per semester.

Specialization Area

Hotel & Lodging Management; Restaurant & Foodservice Management; Travel & Tourism Management

Graduation Requirements

Graduation requires the successful completion of between 128 and 137 credit hours depending on specialization: 45 hours of University core (liberal arts), 400 hours of required practicum and a senior level internship.

University of Southwestern Louisiana

College: College of Applied Life Sciences
Program Enrollment: 150
Institutional Enrollment: 16,600 undergraduate; 1,362 graduate
Degree Awarded: Bachelor of Science (B.S.), Master of Human Resources (M.S.)
Degree Categories: Hospitality Management (Hotel, Restaurant, and Tourism Management)
Program Accreditation: American Association of Family and Consumer Science
Institutional Accreditation: Southern Association of Colleges and Schools
Contact: Virginia Lawrence M.H.M. , Hotel Restaurant Management, School of Human Resources, College of Applied Life Sciences, University of Southwestern Louisiana, Lafayette, LA 70504; phone (318) 482-6579

Institution Description

Established in 1898, the University of Southwestern Louisiana (USL) is a comprehensive, coeducational, public institution of higher education offering Bachelor's, Master's and Doctoral Degrees. USL reaffirms as its primary purpose the examination, transmission, preservation and extension of mankind's intellectual traditions. Thus, USL emphasizes teaching, learning, scholarship, research and public service.

Program Description

USL's Hospitality Management (HRTM) program provides training in management of hotels/resorts, restaurants and tourism operations. The HRTM program includes: (1) Liberal Studies courses; (2) College of Business courses and; (3) HRTM courses in the following areas; operations management, culinary arts, human resources, management/training, and internship experiences, special event production and tourism sciences.

Special Features

USL's HRTM faculty place the highest priority on working one-on-one with students in HRTM courses and laboratories, professional and career advising, placement in internships, and career planning and placement.

Financial Aid and Scholarships

USL's Financial Aid Office makes available numerous opportunities, and the HRTM Program offers several scholarships based on both academic achievement and hospitality industry experience.

Approximate Tuition and Fees

In State: $1,781.50 per year; Out of State: $3,581.50 per year; Room and Board: $1,735 per year; Books and Supplies $700.00 per year.

Admissions

Admission to USL is in transition from an open access to a selective admissions institution. Current regular admissions requirements include: (1) graduation from an accredited high school with a minimum GPA of 2.0 on a 4.0 scale with specific core courses completed; or (2) the student may have a minimum ACT composition score of 20 or be in the upper 25% of the class.

Graduation Requirements

Graduation requires the successful completion of 139 semester hours and includes: 39 hours of Liberal Studies courses; 30 hours from the College of Business; 62 hours of HRTM courses; and 1500 hours of documented hospitality work experience.

University of Surrey

Undergraduate Programs in Hotel, Catering, International Hospitality and Tourism Management

College: School of Management Studies for the Service Sector
Program Enrollment: 180 each year
Institutional Enrollment: Undergraduate 5,000; **Postgraduate**PGTaught – 1500, PG Research – 1,000
Degrees Awarded: Bachelor of Science
Degree Categories: Hotel and Catering Management, International Hospitality and Tourism Management, Retail Management.

Contact: Dr Andrew Lockwood, Undergraduate Program Co-ordinator, School of Management Studies for the Service Sector, University of Surrey, Guildford, Surrey, GU2 5XH, England; phone +44-(0)-1483-876351; fax +44-(0)-1483-259387; email A.Lockwood@surrey.ac.uk

Institution Description
The University of Surrey is one of Europe's largest, longest standing and best known providers of graduates in hotel, catering and tourism management. It has a reputation based on over 30 years of history of excellence in the provision of education and research in fields related to hotels and tourism.

Program Description
The philosophy of our courses is to provide a comprehensive business management education for potential and practicing managers in the hospitality, tourism and retail fields, covering . Undergraduate programs run over three or four years. The four-year courses include an integrated period of professional experience.

Special Features
Integrated period of professional training on our four-year undergraduate programs. Extensive facilities, including excellent computer laboratories, food science laboratories, food production and service laboratories, and one of the best hospitality libraries in Europe. Campus university with all facilities based on one main site, providing accommodation for the majority of our students. Excellent employment record on graduation.

Financial Aid and Scholarships
A limited number of scholarships offering some support toward tuition fees are available to well qualified students from Southeast Asia.

Admissions
Undergraduate programs require students to be a minimum of 18 years of age and hold British "A" levels or their international equivalents. Special-entry and mature candidates are considered on an individual basis.

Tuition and Fees
In-state n/a
Out-of-state $15,000
Room and Board $8,500
Other fees $1,500 books etc.

Specialization Area
Hotel and lodging management, restaurant and foodservice management, travel and tourism management.

Graduation Requirements
Degrees are obtained on the British system. Students must achieve 120 credits each year, normally from 12 courses, over the three / four years of the program to graduate. Final awards depend on a combination of coursework and final examinations.

University of Technology, Jamaica

Program Enrollment: 580
Institutional Enrollment: 7,540
Degrees Awarded: B.S. in Hospitality & Tourism Management; B.S. In Food Service Management
Degree Categories: Food and Beverage Management, Tourism Management, Culinary Management, Hotel and Resort management
Institutional Accreditation: Ministry of Education, Jamaica

Contact: Mrs. Una Lambert, Head, School of Hospitality a& Tourism management, University of Technology, Jamaica, 237 Old Hope Road, Kingston 6, Jamaica, W1, phone: (809) 92-71680-8; fax: (809) 92-71615 and (809) 92-71925

Institution Description

The University was established in 1958 as an institution of further education, and recruits students at the post-secondary level for training in Architecture, Building, Commerce, Computing, Engineering, Hospitality and Food Science, Health and Applied Sciences and Teacher Training. The University was conceived as a center for the training of skilled personnel at the level of the U.K. Higher National Certificate/Diploma. While the concept remains valid, a wide variety of other technical and professional courses have been added so that there are over one hundred (100) different course options now available as a result of the University's response to national and regional manpower needs.

Program Description

The programs offered by the School of Hospitality & Tourism Management are for four (4) years duration and prepares students to assume the responsibilities of middle managers or supervisors in a variety of Hospitality/Food Service Organizations and the health sector. All phases of Hospitality Education are addressed in a concise curriculum, which emphasizes the development of skills and techniques necessary. Certificate courses in specialized aspects of Catering are offered over a two-year period via full-time or day release delivery. The School collaborates with the Community Colleges at the first and second years and has transfer agreement at the third year level.

Special Features

The School of Hospitality and Tourism Management provides students with hands-on experience in food preparation and service at the campus A la Carte Restaurant. The Baking School provides similar experiences in small quantity and commercial baking. Students can transfer credits to American and European University Degree Programs. They complete an internship program of two (2) summers in the industry, which is arranged by the University. Programs are non-residential. Students may participate in many extra-curricular club activities.

Financial Aid and Scholarships

Non-Jamaican nationals are usually self-sponsored. Scholarships and financial aid are available to Jamaican nationals from various international and Government agencies and Jamaican Firms.

Tuition and Fees

Tuition for Jamaican students is J$70,325 and for internationals US$3,000-US$7,500 for the current year. Costs for boarding, uniform, and books are additional fees.

Admission Requirements

Five (5) GCE O Levels A, B, and C or CXC General Proficiency I and II or equivalent. For other courses admissions vary according to the requirement of each course.

Graduation Requirements

Graduate students must satisfactorily complete the curriculum specification for each course.

The University of Tennessee -Knoxville

College: Human Ecology
Program Enrollment: 175
Institutional Enrollment: 19,000 undergraduate; 6,000 graduate
Degree Awarded: Bachelor of Science
Degree Categories: Hotel and Restaurant Administration
Emphases/Specializations: Hotel Management; Restaurant Management; Food Systems Management

Institutional Accreditation: Southern Association of Colleges and Universities
Contact: Dr. Nancy Fair, College of Human Ecology, University of Tennessee, Knoxville, TN 37996-1900; phone (423) 974-4357; fax (423) 974-5236; e-mail GOTOBUTTON BM_1_ nbfair@utk.edu

Institution Description

Continuing a tradition of service begun in 1794, the University of Tennessee's Knoxville (UTK) campus carries out a unique higher education mission in Tennessee, the Volunteer State. Leadership in graduate and professional studies, research and creative activity, and public service enriches selective undergraduate programs and identifies UTK as the state's "campus of excellence."

Program Description

The Hotel and Restaurant Administration (HRA) Program offers a strong, broad-based curricula, providing students with an academic background that allows them the flexibility to successfully enter the many segments of the hospitality industry. The program builds on a base of general education and management courses with industry specific courses covering foodservice, lodging, tourism, hospitality marketing, human resource management and hospitality law. Two work experiences, including the 350-hour internship, are required of all HRA students, providing students an opportunity to apply principles learned in the classroom to the work place.

Special Features

Part of the mission of the HRA program is to support student development through teaching excellence, sound academic advising and individualized career counseling. This focus on personalized service exists throughout the College of Human Ecology and the HRA program at UT.

Financial Aid Scholarships

Scholarships are available through the university financial aid office, the College of Human Ecology and the HRA program.

Approximate Tuition and Fees

In-state tuition is $1,082 per semester; out-of-state, $3,147 per semester.

Admissions

Admission to the HRA Program is selective and based on meeting minimum GPA requirements, general education and preprofessional courses. Progression into the program is usually at the beginning of the sophomore year.

Graduation Requirements

Graduation requires the completion of 128 semester hours, which includes 58 hours of general education courses, 19 hours of business administration courses, and 36 hours of HRA courses.

The University of Texas at San Antonio

College: College of Business
Program Enrollment: 20
Institutional Enrollment: Undergraduate: 16,500; Graduate: 2,500
Degrees Awarded: Bachelor of Business Administration (BBA)
Emphases/Specializations: NA
Program Accreditation: American Assembly of Collegiate Schools of Business
Institutional Accreditation: Commission on Colleges of the Southern Association of Colleges and Schools
Contact: Dr. Thomas F. Cannon, Interim Program Director, Tourism Management, College of Business, The University of Texas at San Antonio, San Antonio, TX 78249-0631; phone (210)458-7102; fax (210)458-5783; e-mail tcannon@utsa.edu

Institution Description

The University of Texas at San Antonio has grown rapidly since its establishment in 1969, reaching an enrollment of nearly 19,000 students. Students from the San Antonio area are joined by students from across Texas, almost every state in the United States and several other countries.

Program Description

UTSA's Tourism Management Program (TM) builds on the fundamental foundation of a College of Business Management degree. Students are required to complete a program of study in the arts and sciences, business, and tourism/hospitality fields.

Special Features

Independent studies, internships, job opportunities, Student Association for Travel & Tourism, scholarships, 200 industry hours required, full-time and adjunct industry faculty, program advising.

Financial Aid and Scholarships

The University of Texas at San Antonio financial aid office offers information on numerous financial aid and scholarship programs.

Admissions

The admissions committee reviews students' high school program of study, SAT scores, recommendations and extracurricular activities. Admission to the College of Business requires the completion of 45 semester credit hours, a 2.5 grade point average, and the completion of selective core courses.

Tuition and Fees

In-State: $600 plus fees (9 sem. hrs.); Out-of-State: $1,920 plus fees (9 sem. hrs.)
Other Fees: approximately $300

Specialization Areas

Travel & Tourism Mgmt.

Graduation Requirements

A Bachelor of Business Administration in Tourism Management currently requires 129 hours composed of 54 hours of University Core Curriculum, 36 hours from the College of Business.

University of Victoria

Bachelor of Commerce Program with a Concentration in Hotel & Restaurant Management

College: Faculty of Business
Program Enrollment: 750 (50 Hotel & Restaurant Management Students)
Institutional Enrollment: 17,000 full-time and part-time undergraduate and graduate students
Degrees Awarded: Bachelor of Commerce
Degree Category: Hotel & Restaurant Management Program

Contact: Mr. William B. Pattison, Chair, Hotel & Restaurant Management Program, PO Box 1700, STN CSC, Victoria, BC V8W 2Y2 Canada, (250) 472-4617, (250) 721-7221

Institution Description
The University of Victoria is located on the Southern tip of Vancouver Island on Canada's spectacular west coast. UVic was established in 1963 and since has been rated the best comprehensive University for two consecutive years (Macleans Magazine - Canada's national weekly). The University offers excellent facilities, including recreational services, state of the art computer labs, cultural centres, its own night club, and superior student residences.

Program Description
This specialized concentration in the Bachelor of Commerce program is open only to graduates of recognized Hotel and Restaurant or Hospitality Administration two-year college diploma programs. The program combines the best of college and university training to give students both a practical understanding of the industry and a solid broad based foundation in business. The program also boasts an international emphasis with the option to participate in a foreign exchange.

Special Features
The program is unique in that it combines industry experience with top management training. Two mandatory coop work terms ensure a competitive edge after graduation. Also, Industry Case Workshops provide opportunities to study current issues in the industry, apply learned concepts, and nurture networking opportunities.

Financial Aid and Scholarships
The University of Victoria offers a wide range of bursaries and scholarships to students just entering the program, undergraduates, and graduate students.

Admissions
Admission to the Hotel & Restaurant Management Program is based on completion of a two year accredited diploma program. Successful candidates then enter the third year of the Bachelor of Commerce program, completing the degree program in approximately two years.

Approximate Tuition and Fees
The total cost of the two year program is approximately $6000 for Canadian students and $18000 for International students.

Specialization Area
Hotel & Lodging Mgmt

Graduation Requirements
Graduation requires that students complete a total of 60 units of course work; 30 units block transferred from the participating college and 30 units completed at the University of Victoria, with a core course concentration in commerce and hospitality. Students are also required to complete two Coop Work Terms and two Industry Case Workshops.

Ursuline College

Travel and Tourism Management

College: Division of Professional Studies
Program Enrollment: 30
Institutional Enrollment: 1,312; Undergraduate: 1,152 Graduate: 160
Degrees Awarded: Bachelor of Arts; Certificate
Degree Categories: Business
Emphases/Specializations: Travel and Tourism Management
Program Accreditation: North Central Association of Colleges and Schools
Institutional Accreditation: North Central Association of Colleges and Schools
Contact: Colleen Kearney, Director of Admission, Ursuline College, 2550 Lander Road, Pepper Pike, Ohio 44124; phone 440.449.4203, toll free 1-888-URSULINE, FAX 440.684.6138, e-mail ckearney@ursuline.edu

Institution Description

Founded in 1871, Ursuline College is the oldest Catholic women's college in the country. The College remains committed to providing a superior education with contemporary applications for career development. Ursuline offers a personalized education with small classes and accessible faculty. While most of the students are women, the College admits men.

Program Description

The program focuses on the disciplines of administration, management, finance, marketing, and accounting. The goal is to provide students with opportunities to gain a broad, liberal arts background combined with fundamental skills for successful employment in the Tourism industry. Students who already have a Bachelor's degree may earn a certificate.

Special Features

Cleveland, home of the Rock and Roll Hall of Fame, provides students many opportunities for experience, including internships, at outstanding locations, and jobs after graduation.

Financial Aid and Scholarships

Ursuline College participates in all Federal and State grant and loan programs. The College offers a liberal scholarship program, based on merit, to students who major in Travel and Tourism Management. Students who wish to live on campus may also qualify for a resident hall grant.

Admissions

Students should have a 2.5 GPA, score at least 17 on the ACT or 900 on the SAT, one letter of recommendation, and an essay. Official copies of transcripts from high school and all colleges should be submitted to the Director of Admission. Early enrollment is suggested.

Tuition and Fees

In-State: $391 per credit hour; Out of State: $391 per credit hour; Room and Board: $4,460 per year; Other Fees: varies

Specialization Area

Travel and Tourism Management

Graduation Requirements

Minimum of 128 hours for BA degree; GPA of 2.0 in the major and QPA of 2.0 in all work done at Ursuline. Minimum of 43 hours must be completed at Ursuline and half the requirements for a major. Maximum of 64 hours may be transferred to fulfill degree requirements.

Utah Valley State College

Hospitality Management

Program Enrollment: 110
Institutional Enrollment: 16,000
Degrees Awarded: Bachelors in Science, Associate in Science, Associate in Applied Science, Certificate, Diploma
Degree Categories: Bachelor in Science, Hospitality Management; Associate in Science Hospitality Management; Associate in Applied Science, Hospitality Management, Culinary Arts; Certificate, Hospitality Management, Culinary Arts; Diploma, Hospitality Management, Culinary Arts.
Program Accreditation: Commission on Accreditation of Hospitality Management Programs (CAHM), Educational Institute: of the American Hotel & Motel Association.
Institution Accreditation: Northwest Association of Schools and Colleges
Contact: Douglas Miller, Program Coordinator, Hospitality Management, Utah Valley State College, 800 W. 1200 S., Orem, Utah 84058; phone (801) 222-8859, fax (801) 764-7218, millerdo @ uvsc.edu

Institution Description
Utah Valley State is an accredited, state college that provides curricula in business, health, science, general education, and paraprofessional. UVSC provides educational training designed to meet the requirements of business and industry. UVSC is located 30 miles from Salt Lake City and Utah's famous ski resorts.

Program Description
UVSC's Hospitality Management Program builds on a solid foundation of business education, liberal arts, and Educational Institute courses of the American Hotel & Motel Association. Students can choose between an emphasis in general hospitality management or a speciality in Food and Beverage Management with strong culinary arts training.

Special Features
UVSC is the only School in Utah with a four-year or two-year degree in hospitality management and therefore has excellent working relationships with industry and government organizations.

Financial Aid and Scholarships
Fully staffed financial aid office. Excellent opportunities with various local government and industry associations as well as national scholarship agreements.

Admissions
Open door policy for both resident and non-resident. Excellent opportunities for foreign students.

Tuition & Fees
Tuition and fees is $790.00 resident, and $2,460.00 non-resident per full-time semester.

Specialization Area
Hotel and Lodging Mgmt., Restaurant & Foodservice Mgmt., Culinary Arts.

Graduation Requirements
Bachelors degree requires 121/126 credit semester hours. Associate degree requires 66/73 semester hours. Both degrees also require industry work experience hours to be determined by advisor. A 2.0 GPA is required for graduation.

Virginia State University

Hotel, Restaurant and Institutional Management (HRIM)

School: School of Agriculture, Science and Technology
Program Enrollment: 50
Institutional Enrollment: 4,200
Degree Awarded: Bachelor of Sciences (BS)
Institutional Accreditation Program: Southern Association of Colleges and Schools Accrediting Commission for Programs in Hospitality Administration (ACPHA)

Contact: Dr. Cynthia R. Mayo, Department Coordinator, Hotel, Restaurant and Institutional Management, Virginia State University, P. O. Box 9211, Petersburg, VA 23806, Phone: (804) 524-5761 Fax: (804) 524-5048

Institution Description

Virginia State University was founded on March 6 1882, with an enrollment of 126 students. Now operating with 4,200 students, this Historically Black University continues in excellence by embracing students who are eager to learn and take responsibility for their education. VSU students learn and take responsibility for their education. VSU mission states, "To promote and sustain academic programs that integrate instruction, research, and extension...public service in a design most responsible to the needs and endeavors of individuals and groups within its scope of influence. The University is dedicated to providing for its students an education which challenges their intellect and prepares them to become knowledgeable, perceptive and humane citizens who are secure in their self-awareness, equipped for personal fulfillment sensitive to the needs and aspirations of others, and committed to assuring productive roles in an ever changing global society" (University Catalog, 1994-1995).

Program Description

Established in September, 1980 as an interdisciplinary program in the School of Business, the Hotel, Restaurant and Institutional Management(HRIM), the program at VSU moved to what is known today as the School of Agriculture, Science and Technology in September, 1984. Opportunities in the Hospitality Industry continue to expand and this program is designed for those students who wish for professional preparation in the field. The HRIM program will emerge as "A Center of Excellence" in hospitality, which embraces global, team building behavior and relevant concepts. The HRIM program is integrative and global which promotes concepts of interpersonal, technological and educational aspects of hospitality management. The programs mission, "To prepare students to be effective and empowered leaders, through the integration of teaching, research and community service, and assume productive roles in an ever-changing global society."

Special Features

The HRIM program at VSU requires a completion of 600 hours of industry experience. This aspect toward graduation allows every student the opportunity to have hands on experience for a concentrated area in the hospitality field. All students are encouraged to network by attending various conferences while at VSU. Each student is assigned an advisor who counsels the students in courses and higher education, internship searches and career placement.

Financial Aid and Scholarships

The financial aid department provides a biannual list of scholarships and different forms of finical aid. The department offers scholarships which are given by various industry organizations.

Approximate Tuition and Fees

In-state tuition is $4,222 per year; out-of-state tuition is $6,645. Room and board is $2,503 per year.

Admissions

Virginia State university seeks to admit students who demonstrate an interest in learning as evidence by their achievement in high school and other activities. The University considers the applicant's scholarship record, character, personality, social maturity and academic potential in making admission decisions.

Graduation Requirements

Graduation requires a completion of 120 semester hours maintaining a 2.0; 39 hours in general education courses; 70 hours of HRIM/Business courses; 6 hours of HRIM electives; and 5 hours of internship.

Webber College

Hospitality Business Management/International Tourism Management/ Sport & Club Management

College: College of Business
Program Enrollment: 150
Institutional Enrollment: 471
Degrees Awarded: Master of Science; Bachelor of Science; Associate of Science
Degree Category: Business Administration
Emphases/Specializations: Hospitality Business Management; International Tourism Management; Sport & Club Management; Accounting; Finance; Management; Marketing
Institutional Accreditation: Southern Association of Colleges and Schools
Contact: Prof. Oscar A. Sampedro, DBA, MHM, CHA, FMP, CHE Director Hospitality Business Management, Webber College, P.O. Box 96, 1201 North Scenic Highway, Babson Park, Florida 33827; Phone (941)638-1431, fax (941)638-2823, Admissions: 1-800-741-1844, Web Site: www.webber.edu

Institution Description

Webber College, a privately endowed, nonprofit, independent, coeducational college of business, was founded in 1927. Classes operate on a semester basis with new semesters beginning in September and January. A summer semester (term A and B) is also held. Both evening and day classes are offered.

Program Description

Webber College, "A Tradition in Global Business Education," combines general education topics, business courses and tailored electives with the area of specialization selected by the student to provide a diversified and strong degree. The degree, coupled with internship programs and key contacts made through membership in industry associations, prepare graduates for entry-level management positions.

Special Features

Webber College is located in central Florida, the world's number one tourist destination. The 110-acre campus is situated on the shores of beautiful Lake Caloosa, just an hour (or less) away from Orlando, Tampa and major attractions, hotels, resorts, restaurants, clubs, destination management companies, transportation companies, and from Gulf and Atlantic Ocean beaches. The college is easily accessible by car from the Florida Turnpike, I-75, I-4, State Road 60, or U.S. Highway 27. Webber is served by Orlando and Tampa International Airports, as well as the Amtrak Station in nearby Winter Haven.

Financial Aid and Scholarships

Approximately 90 percent of Webber College Students receive financial aid, scholarships and grants.

Approximate Tuition and Fees

Tuition (12-16 credit hours) is $4,080 per semester. Housing costs range from $$990 to $1,090 per semester depending on the choice of accommodations. Meal plans are also available.

Admissions

Regular acceptance to the college requires a minimum of 860 on SAT, 18 on ACT, a GPA of 2.0, a letter of recommendation, class rank, student essay, official transcripts and an application for admission. International students are required to submit a completed application, a certified English translation of their transcripts, a certified statement of financial support, and have a minimum score of 500 on the TOEFL (Test of English as a Foreign Language). Transfer students: A maximum of 60 hours from a junior college and 90 hours from a senior college may be transferred to Webber for a baccalaureate degree.

Graduation Requirements

The Associate of Science degree requires 60 credit hours and a 2.0 GPA or higher. The Bachelor of Science degree requires 120 credit hours and a 2.0 GPA or higher. Thirty of the last 33 semester hours must be taken at Webber College for graduation.

West Liberty State College

Hospitality & Tourism Management

College: School of Business Administration
Program Enrollment: 40 students
Institutional Enrollment: 2500 students
Degrees Awarded: Bachelor of Science in Business Administration
Degree Categories: Hospitality & Tourism Management Specialization
Emphases/Specializations: Hospitality & Tourism Management

Institutional Accreditation: North Central Association of Colleges and Schools, National Council for Accreditation of Teacher Education, National Association of Schools of Music, National League of Nursing
Contact: Elizabeth A. Robinson, Interim Dean and Chairperson -- Department of Administrative Systems, West Liberty State College, West Liberty, West Virginia 26074: phone (304)336-8152; Fax(304)336-8418; e-mail robinsea@wlsc.wvnet.edu

Institution Description

West Liberty, founded 1837, is located in a beautiful, safe rural setting in the northern panhandle of WV, fifty miles southwest of Pittsburgh, PA. WL is known for its programs in business, teacher education and science. One-half of the students reside on campus while the remainder commute from surrounding areas.

Program Description

The curriculum combines a Business Studies Core providing a solid base in business principles and a Specialization which emphasizes the management of the various components of the travel industry including the management of hotels & resorts, travel services and food service along with the promotion of destinations.

Special Features

The program requires the completion of a 450-hour internship at an approved travel industry facility. Students are also encouraged to participate in the activities of The Travel Club. Students in this program actively participate in the day-to-day operations of Liberty Oaks, a beautiful bed and breakfast facility located on the campus.

Financial Aid and Scholarships

Federal aid programs are available in the form of grants, loans, and work-study jobs. Some academic scholarships are available through an application procedure conducted by the Director of Admissions.

Admissions

High school diploma (2.0 GPA min.) Or at least 17 on ACT or minimum of 810 (combined verbal/math) on SAT.

Approximate Tuition & Fees

In-State $2,190 per year; Out-of-State: $5,630 per year
Room and Board $3,200 per year.

Specialization Area

Hospitality & Tourism Management

Graduation Requirements

To earn a B.S. in Business Administration with a Specialization in Hospitality & Tourism Management, the student must complete the following: General Studies Core - 49 hours; Business Studies Core - 48 hours; HTM Specialization - 33 hours (including the 6 academic hour internship). This program (130 semester hours) can be completed in four years (eight academic semesters).

Western Carolina University

Hospitality Management

Program Enrollment: 50
Institutional Enrollment: 6,000
Degree Awarded: Bachelor of Science
Degree Category: Hospitality Management
Departmental Accreditation: American Home Economic Association
Institutional Accreditation: Southern Association on Colleges and Schools

Contact: Dr. Jinlin Zhao, Program Coordinator for Hospitality Management, Human Environmental Sciences, Western Carolina University, 113 Belk Building, Cullowhee, NC 28723; Phone: 828-227-2156, Fax: 828-227-7705

Institution Description

Western Carolina University, with a student population of approximately 6,000 students, is a constituent institution of the University of North Carolina system located in the mountain 50 miles southwest of Asheville near the Great Smokey Mountains National Park and Approximately 150 miles north of Atlanta.

Program Description

The program includes courses in Food Service Management, Lodging Management, Tourism, Environmental Health, Marketing, Cost Control, Human Resource Management, Strategic Management and Law. A minimum of 270 hours of internship in lodging management and foodservice management is required.

Financial Aid and Scholarships

Financial aid and scholarships are available to qualifying students. Application forms may be obtained from the university's Financial Aid Office.

Admissions

An application may be secured by writing the university's admissions department. Transcripts from high school or previous college should be sent to admissions along with either SAT or Act test scores.

Tuition & Fees

Per Semester for Full-time Student (according to 98/99 University Catalogue)

North Carolina student	$459.00
Out-of-State student	4,094.00
Required fees	440.50

Residence Hall Double Room Rate $740.00
Board (Declining Balance-Standard Option) $723.00

Graduation Requirements

To graduate, students must complete a total of 128 hours, which includes 41 hours of general education courses, 64 hours of hospitality program courses, 11 hours of program requirements, and 12 hours of electives. This includes six hours of internship or two cooperative education experiences.

Widener University

School of Hospitality Management

Program Enrollment: 275
Institutional Enrollment: 2,200 undergraduate; 5,500 graduate
Degree Awarded: Bachelor of Science
Program Accreditation: Accreditation Commission for Programs Hospitality Administration (ACPHA)
Institutional Accreditation: Middle States Association of Colleges and Schools
Contact: Nicholas J. Hadgis, Dean, Widener University, School of Hospitality Management, One University Place, Chester, PA 19013, Phone: (610) 499-1103; fax (610) 499-1106

Institution Description
Widener is a small, private, comprehensive university with undergraduate programs in arts and sciences, engineering, nursing, management, and hospitality management, and graduate programs in business, education, engineering and the law. Sixty-five percent of undergraduate students live on campus. The cosmopolitan student body comes from 30 states and 34 other countries.

Program Description
The curriculum is designed to produce well-educated citizens as well as competent managers. Required courses cover three basic areas: hospitality management, business administration, and liberal arts and general education. Students may follow the general Hospitality Management curriculum or may use their electives to create concentrations in the following areas: hotel and resort management; restaurant management; casino hotel and gaming operations; private club management; tourism and leisure services; contract services management; or healthcare food services management.

Special Features
An integral feature of the school's curriculum is an entire semester of full-time paid clinical experience in the industry.

Financial Aid and Scholarships
The school and university endeavor to provide a financial aid package of work, grants and/or loans that will enable the student to help meet collegiate expenses.

Approximate Tuition and Fees
Tuition is $15,750 per year; room and board, $6,510 per year; and general fees, $200 per year.

Admissions
Requirements for admission are a C+ GPA or better in a solid secondary academic program that includes a minimum of three years of academic math and one year of lab science. An average of 900 is required on the SAT. There is a $25 nonrefundable application fee. Transfers are welcome at all levels. Minimum 2.0 GPA is required for transfer.

Specialization Area
Hotel & Lodging Management
Restaurant & Foodservice Management

Graduation Requirements
Graduation requirements consist of successful completion of 127 credit hours of coursework. Sixty credit hours are in the field of hotel and restaurant management, while the balance is in the three areas of humanities, social science and science/technology. Additionally, a minimum of 1,400 hours of industry employment is required.

Youngstown State University

The Hotel, Restaurant, and Event Management Program Associate Baccalaureate College of Health and Human Services

Program Enrollment: 110
Institutional Enrollment: 12,500
Degrees Awarded: Associate and Bachelor
Degree Categories: Associate of Applied Science in Hospitality Management, Bachelor of Science in Applied Science in Hospitality Management
Emphases/Specializations: Lodging Administration, Food and Beverage Management, Event Management
Institutional Accreditation: North Central Association of Schools and Colleges
Contact: Robert C. Campbell, Associate Professor - Human Ecology, Coordinator, Hotel, Restaurant, and Event Management, State University, Youngstown, OH 44555; phone, (330)742-3338/3344; fax (330)742-2309; e-mail: Hotelprof@aol.com

Institution Description
Youngstown State University is a dynamic, urban university with substantial housing for resident students. The Hotel, Restaurant & Event Management program is one of the fastest growing programs on campus, stressing on-the-job application to classroom experiences. The program takes advantage of its ideal location, halfway between New York City and Chicago, by emphasizing hotel administration. The Northeast Ohio setting offers much in the way of experience, entertainment, and career opportunities.

Program Description
The associate-degree program offers a well-rounded industry education. All coursework completed in the associate-degree program transfers to the bachelor-degree program. Assistance is provided in finding paid internships and for placement of graduates. The program features an active student organization, the Hospitality Management Society.

Special Features
Faculty recognize the value of work experience subsequent and/or concurrent with study in Hospitality Management. Graduation credit is given with approval of a faculty committee. Students have an option of completing both the associate's and/ or bachelor's degree program without loss of credit. The Hotel, Restaurant and Event Management program is developing smooth articulation for their students.

Admissions
Youngstown State University is an open admission university.

Graduation Requirements
The AAS program requires 99 quarter hours; the BS in AS program requires 186 quarter hours.

Graduate Degree-Granting Programs

Please note: All listings are correct at time of publication based on information submitted by each school.

Auburn University

Hotel and Restaurant Management Program

Program Enrollment: program began in Fall 1994
Institutional Enrollment: 19,142 undergraduate; 2,633 graduate
Degree Awarded: Master of Science, Ph.D.
Degree Category: Nutrition and Food Science with an emphasis in Hotel and Restaurant Management
Institutional Accreditation: Southern Association of Colleges and Schools
Contact: Sareen Gropper, Graduate Program Officer, Department of Nutrition and Food Science, 328 Spidle Hall, Auburn University, Auburn, AL 36849; phone (334) 844-4261; fax (334) 844-3268

Institution Description

Auburn University is a comprehensive, land-grant university committed to the pursuit of excellence through teaching, research and extension. Auburn offers 138 baccalaureate degree programs, 60 master's degree programs, and the doctorate in 38 areas.

Program Description

The Master of Science with an emphasis in Hotel and Restaurant Management is designed to immerse students in the issues considered critical to success at the highest levels of hospitality management. The program also promotes the independent thinking demanded by a changing industry.

Special Features

A high level of electives in the program allows customization of a student's program of study and encourages an interdisciplinary approach to problems in hospitality management. Auburn's proximity to several major metropolitan areas and resorts provides ample access to hotels, restaurants and clubs.

Financial Aid and Scholarships

A number of graduate assistantships are available to qualified applicants in the Department of Nutrition and Food Science. Additional assistantships are provided through grants and contracts through external sources. Those receiving assistantships are eligible for Alabama resident fees.

Approximate Tuition and Fees

Both on-campus and off-campus housing are available to graduate students. The estimated cost for one year of study, including fees and room and board is $20,120.

Admissions

Minimum requirements include a baccalaureate degree from an accredited four-year college or university, satisfactory GRE General Test scores, and three letters of recommendation. For admission to all programs, international students are required to submit scores on the Test of English as a Foreign Language (TOEFL), unless they have completed a degree at a U. S. institution. Formulae combining undergraduate grade point averages and GRE scores are used to determine eligibility for domestic students.

Graduation Requirements

Programs of study are individually planned to meet the needs of each student. The Master of Science degree program requires a minimum of 46 hours and offers both thesis and nonthesis options. Nonthesis students complete a scholarly project as part of the program requirements.

Blackpool and The Fylde College

(An Associate College of Lancaster University)
BA (Hons) Hospitality Management (3 years), BA (Hons) Hospitality Management (International Hotel Management) (4 years); BA (Hons) Hospitality Management with Tourism (4 years)

College: Hospitality Management Department
Program Enrollment: 50 (with one third direct entry to year two)
Institutional Enrollment: 20,000 with circa 1,000 full time undergraduate
Degrees Awarded: Bachelor of Arts
Degree Categories: Hotel and Catering Management, Hospitality Management, International Hotel Management, Hospitality Management with Tourism
Emphases/Specializations: Food and beverage management, human resources, management information systems, marketing, tourism planning and management, culinary arts and leisure enterprises management
Program Accreditation: The College is an Associate College of Lancaster University, whose degrees we offer and deliver. Our diploma/certificate programs are approved by BTEC/Edexcel.
Contact: Mr. John B. Mooney, Head of Hospitality Management Study Unit, Blackpool and The Fylde College, Ashfield Road, Bispham, Blackpool FY2 OHB Lancashire, England. Tel: (01253) 352352 Ex.2367 Fax (01253) 356127; E-mail: JMO@BLACKPOOL.AC.UK

Institution Description
Established over 50 years ago, Blackpool and The Fylde College is now an Associate College of Lancaster University, one of the UK's leading universities. It is an established leader in the field of hospitality management and offers a wide range of undergraduate programmes covering Culinary Arts, Hotel, Catering and Tourism Management . The Hospitality Management department is located in a purpose built and designed campus in Europe's largest seaside resort, which receives 16 million visitors per year.

Program Description
The BA programmes seek to prepare students for management positions in hospitality and leisure enterprises. Students work experience and academic backgrounds are utilised in the overall learning process. Business theory is taught in a purpose built environment dedicated to the hospitality industry. The department's faculty are research active.

Special Features
Undergraduate students will find that unique educational opportunities are available through an excellent faculty, supported by a long history of high quality provision in this area. There is a first class recently modernised facility located in the UK's largest holiday resort so there is no better place to study the hospitality industry than in Blackpool, where tourism is the main driver of the local economy. Case studies and live projects are a feature of the interdisciplinary approach that comprises the essence of our approach to learning. Small classes and personal attention are an important feature of the tutorial support provided to our students.

Financial Aid and Scholarships
The College offers a limited number of bursaries to non UK/EC students each year. These are available upon application after the establishment of appropriate entry requirements. Opportunities for part-time employment are available in local industry.

Admissions
Admission is based upon attainment at high school or in post-high school programmes, together with motivation towards a management career in the hospitality industry. Entry, with credit based on prior qualifications and/or experience is possible, and may result in the period of study to graduation being reduced.

Tuition & Fees
EC and in state circa £3,000 pounds sterling; Overseas circa £6,500 pounds sterling. Living in Blackpool is relatively inexpensive. For example rent, food and heating would currently cost about £50 pounds sterling weekly.

Specialization Area
Hospitality and Tourism Management.

Graduation Requirements
Completion of 36 credits for full honours programme. Interested applicants should request current details.

Centre International de Glion (Switzerland)

Hospitality and Tourism Management Education

Program: Hospitality Administration - 3 Semesters; Hospitality and Tourism Management - 6 Semesters
College: CENTRE INTERNATIONAL DE GLION (SWITZERLAND), Hospitality and Tourism Management Education
Institutional Enrollment: Undergraduate 600
Degrees Awarded: The Glion Associate Degree in Hospitality Administration; The Glion Bachelor Degree in Hospitality and Tourism Management; The Bachelor of Science (Honors) in International Hospitality Management, University of Wales (UK)
Degree Categories: The Glion Associate Degree in Hospitality Administration; The Glion Bachelor Degree in Hospitality and Tourism Management; The Bachelor of Science (Honors) in International Hospitality Management, University of Wales (UK)
Program Accreditation: The Bachelor of Science (Honors) in International Hospitality Management, University of Wales (UK)
Contact: Mr. Tim Wolfe, Marketing & Communications Director

Institution Description

The Centre International de Glion (CIG) is a residential institution with a teaching faculty in hotel, restaurant, tourism and health care management. Its consulting department provides management and administrative expertise to hospitality and tourism industries and specialized training programs in Switzerland and abroad. CIG is an advanced professional school for tomorrow's managers.

Program Description

The six-semester degree program in hospitality and tourism management develops management skills and helps students master an extensive range of tools and techniques. It opens the door to any professional career in the field of hospitality and tourism. Both programs include practical training periods. The three-semester hospitality administration program, more condensed, concentrates on professional know-how and techniques. It opens the way to administrative careers in hotels, restaurants, tourism and health care enterprises.

Special Features

Bilingual scholastic environment. Choice of language : courses in French or English. Encouragement to develop knowledge of the other language. Familiarization with the trade, personal contacts with professional managers, study trips.

Financial Aid and Scholarships

Scholarships may be available from certain countries, or through international chains.

Admissions

Applicants must be at least 18 years old and hold a qualification such as a European baccalaureate, A'levels, U.S. College Board or equivalent. For other applicants, the Center requires an admissions test after an interview. Fluent English or French required.

Tuition and Fees

Out-of-State with Room and Board : Tuition Fees CHF 20'950 - plus Flat Service Fee CHF 3'950.- (payable in Swiss francs only)

Specialization Area

Hotel & Lodging Management, Restaurant & Foodservice Management, Travel & Tourism Management and Culinary Arts.

Cornell University

Hotel Administration

College: School of Hotel Administration
Program Enrollment: 850 undergraduate; 110 graduate
Institutional Enrollment: 12,950 undergraduate; 5,500 graduate
Degrees Awarded: Bachelor of Science; Master of Management in Hospitality; Master of Science; Doctor of Philosophy
Degree Categories: Hotel Administration
Emphases/Specializations: Operations Management, Human Resource Management, Financial Management, Information Systems, Food and Beverage Management, Marketing, Property Asset Management, Entrepreneurship
Program Accreditation: Middle States Association of Colleges and Schools
Contact: Mrs. Cheri Farrell, Director of Student Services, School of Hotel Administration, Cornell University, Statler Hall, Ithaca, NY 14853; phone (607) 255-6376; fax (607) 255-4179; http:/hotelschool.cornell.edu/mmh/

Institution Description

Located in the Finger Lakes Region of upstate New York, Cornell University, the largest school in the Ivy League, comprises 13 colleges and schools that offer instruction in virtually every field. Its numerous interdisciplinary programs provide wide ranging opportunities for study that cut across traditional department boundaries. Members of the current faculty have been awarded numerous Nobel Prizes, Pulitzer Prizes, MacArthur Fellowships, and more.

Program Description

The first of its kind, the School of Hotel Administration at Cornell University has a tradition of academic excellence dating back to 1922. It is distinctive for the breadth of its curriculum, the size and credentials of its faculty, the diversity of its student body, and the splendor of its facilities.

Special Features

Statler hall includes classrooms, laboratories, the school's library (the largest of its kind, with a collection numbering over 25,000 volumes), and an extensive computer center. Adjacent to Statler Hall is the 150-room Statler Hotel and J. Willard Marriott Executive Education Center, a full-service hotel and state-of-the-art management training facility for the hospitality industry.

Financial Aid and Scholarships

Undergraduate financial aid at Cornell University, including the School of Hotel Administration, is awarded solely on the basis of financial need. Financial aid packages generally include loans, employment and grants. Ensuring adequate financial aid for its students is a priority of the School.

Approximate Tuition and Fees

Tuition & fees: $21,914; room and board, $7,110; books and other expenses, $1,925.

Admissions

Admission to the undergraduate program is selective, and decisions are made by a faculty committee based on the applicant's educational goals, prior academic record, college entrance tests (either the SAT or ACT), relevant work experience in the hospitality industry, extracurricular activities, recommendations, and the results of a required personal interview.

Graduation Requirements

Undergraduate students must complete eight terms in residence, or the requirement designated for transfer students; complete the prescribed course curriculum and attain a cumulative GPA of at least 2.0; achieve a GPA of at least 2.0 in the final semester; qualify in one language other than English; complete the university's physical education requirement, usually during the first year of residence (including a swim test); and complete two units of practice credit (work in the industry) before registering for the senior year.

Eastern Michigan University

Hotel and Restaurant Management

College: Health and Human Services
Program Enrollment: 120 undergraduates; 20 graduates
Institutional Enrollment: 24,000; Undergraduate: 19,000; Graduate: 5,000
Degrees Awarded: Master's of Science Degree
Degree Categories: Hotel and Restaurant Management
Emphases/Specializations: Hotel and Restaurant Management
Institutional Accreditation: North Central Association of Colleges and Secondary Schools
Contact: Giri Jogaratnam, PhD, Coordinator – Hotel and Restaurant Management, Eastern Michigan University, 206 Roosevelt Hall, Ypsilanti, MI 48197; phone (734) 487-1226; fax (734) 484-0575

Institution Description

As one of the state's four regional universities, Eastern dates back to 1849 when it trained teachers for the public schools. Now a multipurpose university with five colleges, it offers over 180 fields of study. Today's students include residential and commuter students, both full-time and part-time, from traditional college age to mature adults returning to complete their college education. Additional information available at WWW.EMICH.EDU

Program Description

Eastern offers a 30-credit Master's degree that aims to provide a balance between courses in Hotel and Restaurant Management and student selected cognates. The program is designed to give the students varied options that best serve their individual needs. From 2 to 10 credits of cognate coursework is allowed. A 6-credit thesis or 3-credit culminating independent study is required of all students.

Special Features

To accommodate students that work full-time, most classes are offered in the evenings or on Saturdays. Classes of 10 to 15 students are common and allow for individual participation and class discussion. Personal advising and contact with faculty is emphasized. Graduate Catalog available at WWW.EMICH.EDU

Financial Aid and Scholarships

Students have access to Graduate Assistantship positions on campus that provides 18 credits of tuition plus an annual stipend. Other fellowships and grants are available to those who qualify. Scholarships from various hotel and restaurant professional associations are also available to students.

Admissions

An undergraduate Grade Point Average (GPA) of 2.75 is required. Transfer students from four-year institutions can expect some courses to transfer. Contact program coordinator with course descriptions and syllabi for details. International students need a 550 TOFEL score or 80 on MELAB and 4.5 on the TWE.

Tuition and Fees

In-State: $150 per credit hour
Out-of-State: $350 per credit hour
Room and Board: $1400
Other Fees: $75

Specialization Areas

Hotel and Lodging Management
Restaurant and Foodservice Management

Graduation Requirements

Complete all required courses totaling 30 credit hours and maintain a Grade Point Average (GPA) of 3.0 or higher. Must also successfully complete thesis or culminating independent study.

Ecole de Savignac

Ecole Supérieure Internationale de Dirigeants d'Entreprises de l'Hôtellerie et de la Restauration

Program Enrollment: 90 students
Degree Awarded: Diplôme Ecole de Savignac (master degree)
Degree Categories: hospitality and catering management
Emphases/Specializations: hotel and lodging management;restaurant and food service management; hospitality and food service management

Program Accreditation: France — diploma of hotel and restaurant management officially recognised by the French education authorities.
Contact: Philippe BÉTHUNE, director, Ecole de Savignac, 24420 SAVIGNAC LES EGLISES, France; phone: (33) 05-53-05-08-11; fax: (33) 05-53-05-39-65

Institution Description

Founded in 1988, the Ecole de Savignac is a hotel and management school situated in the heart of the Périgord region in south-west France. The Ecole de Savignac has nationally recognised masters programs in hospitality management. The Ecole de Savignac has strong links with universities abroad and especially with Johnson & Wales University (Rhode Island).

Program Description

The focal point of the Ecole de Savignac 's two-year-post-graduate program focuses on top level management in hotel, restaurant, foodservice and tourism fields.

These hospitality management programs include innovative techniques in hotel and catering administration, company management, marketing, human resources management, financial management, professional environment, personal development, professional ambition.

A lot of national and international companies collaborate with the school and are involved on a permanent basis in the program.

Special Features

Exchange programs with overseas hospitality universities, an educational program in which students can alternate studies with professional placement experiences.

The aim of the Ecole de Savignac is also to help students' development through high level teaching and the little number of students who are enrolled each year get individualized career counselling.
On the campus are all the ultra-modern and comfortable facilities for the students accommodation.

Financial Aid and Scholarship

Some preferential loans may be obtained with the support of the school. Some foreign students can be supported by their government.

Approximate Tuition and Fees

Tuition: US$6,900 per year
Room and full board: US$4,400 per year
Students are paid during their internship management courses.

Admissions

The Ecole de Savignac admits up to 45 students per year. Candidates must hold a Bachelor Degree or equivalent from other countries (graduate-level degree), and be highly motivated.

Applications are accepted throughout the year and are subject to examination. Successful candidates are interviewed and assessed on their qualifications and aptitude for business management. Interviews are held all year round at Savignac. Savignac also welcomes applicants with hospitality experience who wish to widen their qualifications.

Graduation Requirements

Students must complete the two-year-program which represents about 2,600 hours of instruction. These are continuous controls to monitor student's progress.

The George Washington University School of Business and Public Management Department of Tourism and Hospitality Management

Master of Tourism Administration

Program Enrollment: 60
Institutional Enrollment: 20,000
Degree Awarded: Master of Tourism Administration (MTA)
Emphases/Specializations: Destination Management, Travel Marketing, Event Management, Sport Management, Hotel Management, Ecotourism, Cultural Heritage Tourism, Airline Industry Management, Other Individualized Fields
Institutional Accreditation: ASCSB (The American Assembly of Collegiate Schools of Business)
Contact: Larry Yu, Ph.D., Director, Master of Tourism Administration Program, 600 21st Street NW, Washington, DC 20052; phone (202) 994-6281; fax (202) 994-1630; E-mail: lyu@gwu.edu

Institution Description
Located in the nation's capital, the George Washington University attracts students from all 50 states, the District of Columbia, and 100 countries. Surrounded by business organizations, government agencies and professional associations, the GW School of Business and Public Management captures the best of both public and private management.

Program Description
As the first master's program in tourism administration in the world, the program offers a challenging academic learning experience with a dynamic faculty. Students study tourism and hospitality management by combining the latest theoretical knowledge with solid professional experience through class projects and internships.

Special Features
The program offers many concentrations in tourism/hospitality management with unparalleled opportunities for internships, personalized advising and mentoring by faculty and alumni.

Financial Aid and Scholarships
Graduate Assistantships, J. Willard Marriott, Jr. Foundation Scholarship, Tourism and Hospitality management Fellowship. Federal and private loans are also available to graduate students.

Admissions
Admissions to the MTA Program require the following: a resume, undergraduate transcript, GMAT or GRE test score, TOEFL score for international students, three letters of recommendation, Statement of Purpose, and financial statement for international students.

Tuition and Fees
Please contact the program director for the latest tuition and fees information.

Specialization Areas
Destination Management; Travel Marketing; Event Management; Sport Management; Hotel Management; Airline Industry Management; Ecotourism Management; Cultural Heritage Tourism Management

Graduation Requirements
The program requires a total of 36 credit hours: 12 credits for core courses, 18 credits for concentration courses and electives, and 6 credits for capstone courses. Students must meet the practicum requirement of at least 145 hours.

Georgia State University

School of Hospitality Administration

College: J. Mack Robinson College of Business
Program Enrollment: 250 undergraduate; 30 graduate
Institutional Enrollment: 22,800 undergraduate; 6,800 graduate
Degree Awarded: Master of Business Administration
Concentration Category: Hospitality Administration
Institutional Accreditation: Southern Association of Colleges and Schools

Contact: Michael M. Lefever, Director, School of Hospitality Administration, J. Mack Robinson College of Business, Georgia State University University Plaza, Atlanta, GA 30303-3083, phone: (404) 651-3512; fax: (404) 651-3670

Institution Description

Georgia State University is a public urban research university located in downtown Atlanta. It is the second largest among 78 accredited institutions of higher education in the state. In an average semester, over 2,000 course selections are scheduled between 7 a.m. and 10 p.m., providing one of the most flexible academic time schedules for the working student. Fifty-three percent of the students work full-time and 25 percent work part-time.

Program Description

The program introduces students to management and administrative careers in the following industry segments: lodging; commercial and institutional food service; fair and trade show management; meeting planning; private club management; and tourism.

Special Features

The diversified curriculum is designed to expose students to varied hospitality and tourism industry career opportunities. A required work study component encourages students to diversify their career perspectives. The school offers the most extensive listing of courses in fair and trade show management in the United States.

Financial Aid and Scholarships

The School of Hospitality Administration distributes scholarships and stipends in amounts ranging from $100 to $1,500, based on academic achievement, service and financial need. Graduate students are encouraged to apply for Research Assistant positions, which grant a tuition waiver.

Approximate Tuition and Fees

Matriculation for Georgia residents is $101.00 per semester hour. Nonresident matriculation and tuition is $360.00 per semester hour.

Admissions

Consideration is given to the applicant's academic record, scores on the Graduate Management Admission Test (GMAT), educational background and objectives, experience in business or government and professional activities.

Graduation Requirements

The Master of Business Administration degree is awarded upon completion of a prescribed program ranging from 39 to 60 semester hours of credit, depending on the academic background of students and on options selected by the students.

Glasgow Caledonian University

PgD/MSc Hospitality Management

College: Faculty of Business
Program Enrollment: 30
Institutional Enrollment: 11,000; Undergraduate: 10,000; Graduate: 1,000
Degrees Awarded: PG Certificate, PG Diploma and MSc in Hospitality Management
Degree Categories: Hospitality Management
Emphasis Specializations: The program covers a wide range of hospitality sub-sectors

Program Accreditation: Exemption from HCIMA examinations
Institutional Accreditation: N/A
Contact: Joan Elwood, Department of Hospitality, Tourism and Leisure Management, Glasgow Caledonian University, 1 Park Drive, Glasgow, G3 6LP, UK. tel 041 337 4318, fax 041 337 4000, E-mail: J.Elwood@gcal.ac.uk

Institution Description

Glasgow Caledonian University is committed to excellence in learning and teaching at undergraduate post-graduate and professional levels. The Department of Hospitality, Tourism and Leisure Management is one of the largest providers of academic and commercial research and consultancy services in the UK.

Program Description

Modules of study include Services Marketing and HRM, Operations and Financial Management, Hospitality Operations, Hospitality Issues, Information Strategies, Strategic Management and one optional module including Supervised work experience. International and information technology dimensions are built into modules. The dissertation component provides an opportunity for in-depth research.

Special Features

Field based exercises, occasional group based consultancy work, supervised work experience, industry visits and guest lectures.

Financial Aid

Only available to Scottish residents.

Admissions

A University degree (Hons or Ord) in any discipline (except hospitality management) or equivalent, e.g. Diploma and management experience. The programme admission policy seeks to encourage applicants who have the academic ability and vocational motivation to benefit from the programme.

Tuition and Fees

Diploma: European Union £2775 Overseas £7150, MSc European Union £3275 Overseas £7900.

Specialization Area

N/A.

Graduation Requirements

For the qualification of MSc students must successfully complete all modules including dissertation.

Golden Gate University

Hotel, Restaurant, and Tourism Management

College: School of Technology and Industry
Program Enrollment: 25
Institutional Enrollment: 4,000 Undergraduates; 5,500 Graduates
Degrees Awarded: Master of Science
Degree Categories: Master in Hospitality Administration and Tourism
Institutional Accreditation: Western Association of Schools and Colleges
Contact: John T. Self, Ph.D., Department Chair, Hotel, Restaurant, and Tourism Management, Golden Gate University, 536 Mission Street, San Francisco, CA 94105; phone (415) 442-7802; fax (415) 442-7049

Institutional Description

Founded in 1853, Golden Gate University is the fourth oldest and fifth largest private university in California. Its mission is to prepare students for successful careers in professional fields through programs of exceptional quality that integrate theory with practical experience. It is one of the leading centers for higher education in business management, public administration and law in the Western United States.

Program Description

The HRTM department offers the finest internships available and an advisory board of Industry leaders available for mentoring. The program is located within the school of Industry and Technology and teaches the full range of managerial skills with a practical industry orientation. All faculty are practitioners in the field. The case study method of instruction is used to teach students how to put theory into practice.

Special Features

Classes are kept small and are taught by both industry professionals and faculty who have advanced degrees and extensive industry experience. San Francisco provides a unique learning laboratory, with world class hotels, restaurants, wineries and tourist destinations accessible to our students.

Financial Aid and Scholarships

GGU has extensive financial assistance programs available for students. In addition, the HRTM Program offers several scholarships based on academic achievement, financial need and hospitality industry experience.

Approximate Tuition Fees

Graduate tuition is $1,455 per course for both in-state and out-of-state.

Admissions

Baccalaureate degree required from an accredited institution. Demonstrate academic and professional capability to study at the graduate level; TOEFL results and proof of financial support required for international students.

Graduation Requirements

The MS degree requires completion of twelve units of Foundation Program courses and 30 units in the Advanced Program.

Griffith University

Master of Hospitality Management

College: School of Tourism and Hotel Management
Program Enrollment: 450 students (enrolled in Bachelor of Hotel Management)
Institutional Enrollment: Undergraduate 18,126; Graduate 3,000
Degrees Awarded: Bachelor of Hotel Management; Bachelor of Business in Restaurant and Catering Management; Bachelor of Business in Tourism Management; Bachelor of Business in Club Management; Master of Hospitality Management; Master of Tourism Management
Degree Categories: Tourism and Hospitality Management
Emphases/Specializations: Hotel, Restaurant and Catering, Tourism and Club
Program Accreditation: HCIMA
Institutional Accreditation: State Government of Queensland, Australia
Contact: Dr. Beverley Sparks, Head of School of Tourism & Hotel Management, PMB 50, Gold Coast Mail Centre, Qld 9726 Australia

Institution Description

Griffith University is a six campus university located in the South East corner of the State of Queensland, Australia. The University, long noted for its teacher education and innovative programs in both its undergraduate and graduate curricula. The School of Tourism and Hotel Management is located on the Gold Coast (approximately 70 klms South of the Brisbane Campus). The Gold Coast is a national and international tourist destination.

Program Description

Griffith's Tourism and Hospitality Management programs is based on a solid academic foundation consisting of university core components, courses required for a minor in Business Administration with subjects in operations management and administration, computer applications and marketing in addition to hospitality and tourism internships.

Special Features

THM degrees provide five different emphasis areas from which to choose, Tourism, Hotel, Club and Restaurant and Catering Management.

Financial Aid and Scholarships

Both the university financial aid office and private industry make available numerous opportunities for students with scholarships and prizes offered based on academic achievement.

Admissions

Based on academic achievement in formal education or on experience and other achievements. Applications are made through the Queensland Tertiary Admissions Centre.

Tuition and Fees

Undergraduate (HECS) 0$3356-$5593 per year for a full time student, can be paid upfront or deferred.

Graduation Requirements

Graduation requires the successful completion of a combination of subjects totally 240 credit points and includes over 600 hours of industry experience.

Institut de Management Hotelier International

Cornell University School of Hotel Administration and Ecole Superieure des Sciences Economiques et Commerciales (ESSEC)

Program Enrollment: 120 Master's students
Institutional Enrollment: 18,500 at Cornell; 3,000 at ESSEC
Degree Awarded: French Master's-level degree
Degree Category: International Hotel Management
Program Accreditation: Minister of Higher Education, Republic of France
Institutional Accreditation: Middle States Association of Colleges and Schools (Cornell); Minster of Higher Education, Republic of France (ESSEC); AACSB (ESSEC)
Contact: Michael Nowlis, Director, Institut de Management Hotelier International, Cornell-ESSEC, Avenue

INSTITUT DE MANAGEMENT HÔTELIER INTERNATIONAL

Bernard Hirsch, BP 105, 95021 Cergy-Pontoise, Cedex, France; phone (331) 3443 3171; fax (331) 3443 1701; E-mail: infoimhi@edu.essec.fr

Institution Description

The Institut de Management Hotelier International (IMHI) is a Master'slevel program jointly administered by Cornell University's School of Hotel Administration and ESSEC Graduate School of Management. As an independent Ivy League institution and the largest land-grant university in the state of New York, Cornell has 13 colleges and school. ESSEC is a private business school composed of 6 different programs. ESSEC also participates as a member of the French "grandes ecoles."

Program Description

Unique in Europe; IMHI is designed to integrate modern American Management principles with the European tradition of service and dedication to excellence. The IMHI focus is on international hospitality at the management level.

Special Features

IMHI's international emphasis prepares students to work in the global hospitality industry. Student enrollment is comprised of 20 different nationalities. Students benefit from an international faculty which stresses interactive and applied teaching methods including simulations, case studies and field projects. A large proportion of elective courses allow students to tailor a program of study to their professional needs. In addition, students benefit from strong ties with the international hospitality industry which IMHI has established.

Financial Aid and Scholarships

A small number of scholarships and loans may be obtained from IMHI. Many students are supported by their home governments, by company sponsorships or by preferential student loans.

Admissions

Admission to IMHI is highly competitive. Admission decisions are based on the candidate's undergraduate academic performance, examination (GMAT or TAGE-MAGE) results, work experience as well as a series of personal interviews at the school. English is the language of instruction and fluency is a prerequisite. Average GMAT score is 500.

Graduation Requirements

Graduation requires the successful completion of 34 courses, each of which represents 30 contact hours. Of the total number of courses, 13 are required and 21 electives are selected from over 50 hospitality-specific courses at IMHI or over 200 management courses at ESSEC. In addition, students must complete a 12-week management internship during the summer between their two years of study.

Iowa State University

Hotel, Restaurant, and Institution Management

College: Family and Consumer Sciences
Program Enrollment: 20 graduate; 275 undergraduate
Institutional Enrollment: 4,000 graduate; 20,000 Undergraduate
Degrees Awarded: Master of Science; Doctor of Philosophy (joint-major)
Degree Categories: Master's in Hotel and Restaurant Management, or Foodservice Systems Management; Doctorate in Hotel, Restaurant, and Institution Management with a joint-major in another discipline
Emphases/Specializations: None
Program Accreditation: Accreditation Commission for Programs in Hospitality Administration (ACPHA)
Institutional Accreditation: North Central Association of Colleges and Schools
Contact: Mary B. Gregoire, PhD, Department Chair, Hotel, Restaurant, and Institution Management, 11 MacKay Hall, Iowa State University, Ames, IA 50011-1120; phone (515) 294-1730; fax (515) 294-8551; E-mail: mgregoir@iastate.edu

Institution Description
Iowa State University is a public, land-grant research university consisting of the Colleges of Agriculture, Business, Design, Education, Engineering, Family and Consumer Sciences, Liberal Arts and Sciences, and Veterinary Medicine. The student body represents a rich diversity of age groups, socioracial ancestry, ethnic heritage, and international cultures.

Program Description
Graduate programs in Hotel, Restaurant, and Institution Management (HRIM) focus on providing the theoretical and applied knowledge needed for careers in foodservice and hospitality management and education. Leadership development and research completion are important components of the program.

Special Features
Individualized programs of study are planned with faculty advisors.

Financial Aid and Scholarships
In addition to university and college scholarships, graduate assistantships are available for teaching, research, and administrative assignments.

Admissions
Admission to the Master of Science program usually requires a 3.0 GPA. The GRE or GMAT is required. A minimum TOEFL score of 550 on the paper test or 213 on the computer test is necessary for international students. Three references, a statement of goals, and a résumé are requested. Additional requirements for doctoral work are a minimum 3.25 GPA in master's degree program, professional experience in the hospitality field, and minimum TOEFL score of 600 on paper test or 250 on computer test for international students.

Tuition and Fees
In-state tuition — $1,583; out-of-state tuition — $4,662. Graduate assistants pay the in-state tuition, less 50%, if appointment is half-time.

Specialization Area
Hotel and Lodging Management, Restaurant and Foodservice Management

Graduation Requirements
The Master's degree program requires the completion of at least 30 semester credits and includes either a thesis or creative component. The doctoral program requires an approved program of study which includes 18 to 20 credits for dissertation research.

Johnson & Wales University

Alan Shawn Feinstein Graduate School

Graduate School Enrollment: 538

Hospitality Program Enrollment: 103

Institutional Enrollment: 11,599

Degrees Awarded: Master of Business Administration (MBA), Master of Arts (MA), Doctorate of Education (EdD)

Degree Categories: Hospitality Administration (M.B.A); International Business (M.B.A.); Organization & Management (M.B.A.); Accounting (MBA); Teacher Education (MA); Educational Ledership (EdD)

Institutional Accreditation: Johnson & Wales University is accredited by the New England Association of Schools and Colleges, Inc(NEAS&C) through its Commission on Institutions of Higher Education; and is accredited by the Accrediting Council for Independent Colleges and Schools(ACICS). In addition, the hospitality programs at the Providence, Rhode Island campus are accredited by the Accreditation Commissions for Programs in Hospitality Administration(ACPHA).

Contact: Allan Freedman, Director, Feinstein Graduate Admissions. To receive a catalog write to: Johnson & Wales University, Feinstein Graduate Admissions, 8 Abbott Park Place, Providence, RI 02903, E-mail: gradadm@jwu.edu; fax (401) 598-4773; web address: www.jwu.edu.; phone (401) 598-1015 or 1-800-DIAL-JWU ext. 1015 (toll-free in the US)

Institutional Description

Johnson & Wales University, founded in 1914, is a private, coeducational institution offering practical career education in business, foodservice, hospitality, business, and technology. Associate, bachelor, master, and doctorate degree programs prepare students for careers in the United States and around the world.

Program Description

The Alan Shawn Feinstein Graduate School offers a MBA program in Hospitality Administration. The MBA program prepares students for numerous career opportunities in the hospitality industry. The hospitality field has broadened to include services in institutional settings, multi-level care environments, and institutional dining facilities as well as restaurants, hotels, and tourist-attractive facilities. The hospitality field is one of the most rapidly growing industries worldwide and needs managers well educated in the field. The program is offered on both a day and evening schedule. The day program starts only in the September term and can be completed in just 12 months.

Special Features

Accelerated day programs that allow students to graduate in twelve months. Convenient day or evening classes to accommodate any schedule. Terms instead of semesters, permitting students to complete more courses in less time diverse student population, including international students representing fifty-six countries. Lifetime career placement.

Financial Aid and Scholarships

JWU has a fully staffed financial aid and planning office to assist qualified students in meeting educational expenses. Students accepted into The Alan Shawn Feinstein Graduate School are eligible to apply for a Graduate Assistantship through the Feinstein Graduate Admissions Office. These positions are available on a competitive basis and are awarded according to the student's skills and experience.

Tuition and Fees

Graduate tuition for the 1999-2000 academic year for day school is $246 per quarter credit hour ($1,107 per course). The general fee (for day school only) is $175 per term. Graduate evening school tuition is $200 per quarter credit hour ($900 per course). Tuition and fees are subject to change annually.

Admissions

All applicants for the Alan Shawn Feinstein Graduate School must submit a signed application, official transcripts, three letters of recommendation. Scores from the Graduate Management Admissions Test (GMAT) may be submitted for consideration but are not required for admission. Applicants who are not U.S. citizens or permanent residents of the U.S. must meet the same admission requirements as all applicants, in addition to providing the following: a score of at least 550 on the written TOEFL or 210 on the computerized TOEFL or plan to enroll in our ESL program, declaration of financial support, and a financial statement that supports the information given in the declaration of financial support.

Graduation Requirements

All master's degree programs require the completion of 54 quarter credits, which is equivalent to 36 semester credits.

Kansas State University

Foodservice and Hospitality Management

College: Human Ecology
Program Enrollment: 18 master's; 11 doctoral
Institutional Enrollment: 17,500 undergraduate and 3,000 graduate
Degrees Awarded: Master of Science; Doctor of Philosophy
Degree Categories: Foodservice and Hospitality Management
Emphases/Specializations: Foodservice Management; Lodging; Tourism; Dietetic Education; Hospitality Education; Distance Education
Institutional Accreditation: North Central Association of Colleges and Schools
Contact: Dr. Carol Shanklin, Graduate Program Director, Department of Hotel, Restaurant, Institution Management and Dietetics, 103 Justin Hall, Kansas State University, Manhattan KS 66506-1404; phone (785) 532-2206; fax (785) 532-5522; E-mail: shanklin@humec.ksu.edu; http://www.ksu.edu/humec/hrimd/hrimd.htm

Institution Description

Kansas State University (KSU), one of the first land-grant institutions, is comprised of nine colleges and offers more than 200 undergraduate majors and options and advanced degrees in 107 areas. Faculty at KSU are dedicated to excellence in teaching, student advising, research, extension education and scholarly achievement.

Program Description

The graduate program emphasizes managerial, research, and conceptual skills and encompasses all aspects of foodservice and hotel management. The program focuses on developing qualities of leadership and providing the essential knowledge and skills for careers in foodservice or hotel management, dietetic or hospitality education, or research.

Special Features

Students confer with their faculty advisor to plan an individualized program of study to meet the student's personal and professional goals.

Financial Aid and Scholarships

KSU oversees an extensive financial assistance program for students. Graduate teaching and research assistantships are available on a competitive basis.

Admissions

Applicants should have a B.S. degree from an accredited institution, a GPA of 3.0 on a 4.0 base, and prerequisite knowledge in field, and industry experience. Applicants should submit application form, official transcript(s), resume, statement of objectives, and GRE or GMAT scores. International students must submit TOEFL scores.

Tuition and Fees

In-State Tuition - $1463 for 12 semester hours; Out-of-State Tuition- $4208 for 12 semester hours; Graduate assistants pay reduced tuition and fees.

Specialization Area

Hotel and Lodging Management; Restaurant and Foodservice Management

Graduation Requirements

Master's degree options: 30 hours of graduate credit consisting of 24 hours of graduate coursework and six hours of research for a thesis 36 hours of graduate coursework and a comprehensive examination. The doctoral program requires 60 hours of coursework beyond a B.S. degree and 30 hours of dissertation research.

Michigan State University

The School of Hospitality Business

College: The Eli Broad Graduate School of Management
Program Enrollment: 14 MBA and MS candidates
Institutional Enrollment: 33,420 undergraduate; 7,838 graduate
Degrees Awarded: Masters of Business Administration; Master of Science in Foodservice Administration
Degree Category: Hospitality Business, Foodservice Management
Emphases/Specializations: Hospitality Business; Foodservice Management
Program Accreditation: American Assembly of Collegiate Schools of Business
Institutional Accreditation: Association of American Universities; North Central Association of Colleges and Schools

Contact: Ronald F. Cichy, PhD, CHA, CHE, Director, The School of Hospitality Business, 231 Eppley Center, Michigan State University, East Lansing, MI 48824-1121; phone (517) 353-9211; FAX (517) 432-1170

Institution Description

As a pioneer land-grant institution and a respected research and teaching university, Michigan State University (MSU) is committed to leadership and developing knowledge. MSU strives to discover practical uses for theoretical knowledge. In fostering both research and its applications, MSU continues to be a catalyst for positive intellectual, social, and technological change.

Program Description

The mission of The School of Hospitality Business at MSU is to be the leader in hospitality business education through teaching, research, and service. Our curriculum is unique because it integrates Eli Broad Graduate School of Business requirements with major courses in hospitality business.

Special Features

As the top ranked busines college-based school in the world, The School of Hospitality Business offers an exceptionally well-crafted curriculum taught by innovative professors. While the MBA curriculum encourages dual concentration areas, the MS curriculum provides flexibility to meet many varied career goals. The faculty includes leading textbook authors, sought-after consultants, and respected researchers.

Financial Aid and Scholarships

MSU offers a comprehensive financial assistance program, including fellowships and limited graduate assistantships. These are available upon application after establishing a minimum GPA.

Approximate Tuition and Fees

Tuition is approximately $9,100 per year for full-time, in-state graduate students. Most students take 14-16 credits per semester.

Admissions

Admission to The School of Hospitality Business is selective and based on meeting minimum undergraduate GPA requirements, plus minimum GMAT scores and three letters of recommendation for the MBA; or minimum GRE scores and three letters recommendation for the MS. Students having less than six months of full-time work experience in the hospitality industry prior to enrolling are requires to complete an internship as part of their graduation requirements.

Graduation Requirements

The Master of Business Administration candidate requirements are 36 semester credits of core, 12 credits of major, and 6 credits of environment of business/international business (54 credits total). The Master of Science candidate requirements are 30 credits total.

New York University

Center for Hospitality, Tourism and Travel Administration

College: School of Continuing and Professional Studies; Center for Hospitality, Tourism and Travel Administration
Program Enrollment: 103 Master's students (62 Hospitality; 41 Tourism and Travel)
Institutional Enrollment: 38,000 in degree programs
Degrees Awarded: M.S. In Hospitality Industry Studies; M.S. In Tourism and Travel Management
Degree Category: Hospitality Industry Studies; Tourism and Travel Management
Institutional Accreditation: New York University is a member of the Association of American Universities and is accredited by the Middle States Association of Colleges and Schools. Graduate and Professional accrediting agencies recognize its degrees in all categories.
Contact: Mark Warner, D.P.A., Director of Graduate Studies, Center for Hospitality, Tourism and Travel Administration, New York University, 48 Cooper Square, Room 103, New York, NY 10003-7154; phone (212) 998-9107; fax (212) 995-4676; E-mail: chtta.sce@nyu.edu

NEW YORK UNIVERSITY
Center for Hospitality, Tourism and Travel Administration

Institution Description
New York University (NYU) is a private metropolitan university that offers the advantages of a great urban setting to a highly diverse student body. It currently enrolls nearly 38,000 students in degree-conferring divisions. They come from all 50 states and more than 120 foreign countries. Classes are conveniently located in New York City, one of the greatest hotel and tourist centers of the world.

Program Description
The graduate program offers two Master's Degrees, a M.S. In Hospitality Industry Studies and a M.S. In Tourism and Travel Management. Each of the Master's degrees requires completion of a 39 credit course of study which includes general core courses and professional core courses in areas such as global strategic marketing systems, asset management, hotel financing and feasibility, destination management, and applications in advanced technological systems. The program provides our students a graduate education committed to developing world class leaders who have the analytical and conceptual tools necessary to succeed in the hospitality and tourism industry.

Special Features
The city's extraordinary resources enrich the academic programs, while offering limitless opportunities for work experience. The Center's Advisory Board is comprised of world-renowned industry leaders. Through professional development programs, lecture series, and one-on-one research projects, we afford students opportunities to meet and work with these and other acclaimed industry leaders. Our motto reads: "The city is our laboratory...the industry is our faculty...and our students are the future of the profession."

Financial Aid and Scholarships
Scholarships, grants, loans, and financial aid for prospective and continuing students is available and competitive with other major educational institutions. Graduate assistantships are awarded on the basis of financial need, academic achievement, and availability of funds.

Approximate Tuition and Fees
Graduate tuition is $610 per credit (1998-99).

Admissions
The Master's degree applicant must have a baccalaureate degree from an accredited institution. A number of factors are considered when evaluating appliations. These include previous academic achievement, scores from GMAT or GRE, the nature and extent of previous work experience, and letters of recommendation. International applicants must submit scores from the TOEFL examination.

Graduation Requirements
The M.S. In Hospitality Industry Studies and the M.S. Tourism and Travel Management requires 39 credits, a cumulative G.P.A. Of 3.0, and the course of study must be completed within four years. In addition pre-requisite course work may be necessary based on applicant's precious academic concentration, work experience, and English proficiency.

Niagara University

Institute of Travel, Hotel and Restaurant Administration

College: Institute of Travel, Hotel and Restaurant Administration
Program Enrollment: 210
Institutional Enrollment: Undergraduate: 2300; Graduate: 750
Degrees Awarded: Bachelor of Science; Master of Business Administration
Degree Categories: Hotel and Restaurant Administration; Travel and Tourism Administration
Emphases/Specializations: Hotel and Restaurant Administration, Travel and Tourism, Food Service Administration, Financial Management, Marketing, Hospitality and Gerontology, Recreation and Leisure
Program Accreditation: Accreditation Commission for Programs in Hospitality Administration
Institutional Accreditation: Niagara University holds memberships in the American Council on Education and the Commission on Independent Schools and Colleges. It is accredited by the Middle States Association of Schools and Colleges.
Contact: Carl D. Riegel, Ed.D., Professor and Director, Institute of Travel, Hotel and Restaurant Administration, Niagara University, NY 14109-2012; phone (716) 286-8270; fax (716) 286-8277

Institution Description
Niagara University, founded in 1856, is a private liberal arts university following the Vincentian tradition. The university consists of five academic colleges and offers over 50 undergraduate and numerous graduate degrees. It is located in western New York just minutes from Niagara Falls, 20 minutes from Buffalo and 90 minutes from exciting Toronto.

Program Description
The Institute, established in 1968, prepares students for careers in hospitality and tourism enterprises. The curriculum combines a strong grounding in the liberal arts with a core of courses in business and administration. Students pursue specialized study in either Tourism or Hospitality Administration and then use electives to add an area of emphasis. There is a work experience requirement and students are strongly encouraged to take advantage of the many cooperative education opportunities.

Special Features
The program offers study abroad experiences, extensive cooperative education opportunities, an honors program, small classes, numerous professional organizations and outstanding placement assistance.

Financial Aid and Scholarships
In addition to federal and state aid, Niagara University provides grants to students based on both need and merit. Furthermore many Institute students receive generous assistance from private foundations and organizations. In total, about 90% of Niagara's students receive financial aid in one form or another.

Admissions
Admission is based on previous academic performance, SAT or ACT test scores, references and a writing sample. Although the Institute makes admission decisions, prospective students should apply to the University Admissions Office. Favorable decisions are based upon evidence that applicants will be able to successfully complete their program of study.

Tuition and Fees
Annual tuition for the 1998-99 academic year is $12,886 and additional fees average $450. For students choosing to live in the residence halls, room and board is $6,078.

Specialization Areas
Hotel and Lodging Mgmt., Travel and Tourism Mgmt. and Restaurant and Foodservice Mgmt

Graduation Requirements
Graduation requires the successful completion of 123 semester hours of which 60 are in general education and 63 are in the major. In addition Institute students must complete a minimum of 800 clock hours of approved work experience. Some areas of emphasis may require more academic credits or additional internships.

Oklahoma State University

School of Hotel and Restaurant Administration

College: College of Human Environmental Sciences
Program Enrollment: 187 undergraduate; 35 graduate
Institutional Enrollment: 20,000 undergraduate; 4,300 graduate
Degrees Awarded: Masters of Science; Doctor of Philosophy
Degree Categories: Hospitality Administration
Emphasis/Specialization: Restaurant, Hotel and Tourism
Institutional Accreditation: North Central Association of Colleges and Schools
Program Accreditation: Accreditation on Commission for Programs in Hospitality/Administration (ACPHA)

Contact: Patrick J. Moreo, Ed.D., CHA, Professor and Director, School of hotel and Restaurant Administration, Oklahoma State University, 210 Human Environmental Sciences West, Stillwater, OK 74078-6173; phone (405) 744-6713; fax (405) 744-6299; E Mail: cah@okstate.edu; Internet www.okstate.edu/hes/hrad/mshrad.html

Institution Description

A land-grant institution, Oklahoma State University (OSU) is a large, comprehensive university. Its size does not minimize the amount of personal attention to which each student is entitled. The individual is more than just a number in this university. OSU is nationally recognized for its coeducational residences halls, outstanding Allied Arts program and well balanced social activities. the Student Guide to Americas 100 Best College Buys in 1999 says the nation's best college value is Oklahoma State University.

Program Description

The School of Hotel and Restaurant Administration at OSU is one of the oldest and most highly recognized of its kind in the nation. Students plan their programs of study and research with help and guidance from the principal faculty advisors and committee. Students design programs based on their academic backgrounds, professional experiences, career goals and objectives. the M.S. degree in Hospitality Administration offers great flexibility and may be earned by one of the following plans: thesis, report, or creative component.

Special Features

An additional 22,500-square foot hospitality industry educational facility was opened in 1990, featuring formal service and multiunit foodservice and hotel front office training laboratories.

Financial Aid and Scholarships

The School of Hotel and Restaurant Administration has several assistantships, fellowships, and scholarships available to qualifying students. Research assistants work with faculty members on research projects. teaching assistants teach or assist with undergraduate courses or laboratories. Out-of-state fees are waived for students on at least a quarter time assistantship. Graduate students can compete for college and university scholarships and fellowships from professional organizations.

Approximate Tuition and Fees

Tuition and fees for 1998-99 are $117.73 per credit hour for in-state residents and $291.84 per credit hour for nonresidents per semester. Full-time tuition (9 credit hours) is approximately $1,059.57 for residents and $2,626.56 for nonresidents.

Admissions

Applications from individuals with a variety of undergraduate degrees are welcome. A completed application consist of: 1) OSU application form; 2) application fee; 3) three references; 4) official copies of transcript(s); 5) GRE scores (1500 required) or GMAT scores (525 required); and 6)TOEFL scores are required when English is a second language (550 required) 7) statement of background and professional goals, and 8) statement of intent.

Graduation Requirements

Graduate degrees require a minimum of a 3.0 GPA in all coursework and research.

Oxford Brookes University

International Hotel and Tourism Management Program

Program Enrollment: 30 Master's
Institutional Enrollment: Undergraduate - 12,000; Graduate - 1,200
Degrees Awarded: Master of Science in International Hotel and Tourism Management
Degree Categories: Pass or with Distinction
Master's Program Accreditation: Hotel and Catering International Management Association
Institutional Education: Oxford Brookes University

Contact: Dr. Angela Roper, Program Director, School of Hotel and Restaurant Management, Oxford Brookes University, Gipsy Lane, Headington, Oxford, OX3 0BP; phone: +44 (0) 1865 483804; fax: +44 (0) 1865 483878; email: admin@hrm.brookes.ac.uk; website: http://www.brookes.ac.uk/schools/harm

Institution Description

Established in 1865, Oxford Brookes is a coeducational, state-aided university operated by its own board of governors. Brookes offers a wide range of undergraduate and graduate programs in the sciences, business, education, communications and nursing. The School is recognised as an Area of Outstanding Quality.

Program Description

A one year full-time program of study (48 weeks). The program provides intellectual development, cultural awareness and a sensitivity to the ethos of hospitality organisations. Graduates will be equipped to be effective practitioners, approaching managerial decisions through reflection and critical evaluation and applying strategic and tactical methods to business problems.

Special Features

Brookes offers opportunities for graduate study in a city with a long history of academic excellence.

Financial Aid and Scholarships

A number of national governments make scholarships available for selected students.

Admissions

Applicants should normally have:
- a university degree in an appropriate discipline, or equivalent qualification;
- two years' work experience in the hospitality industry;
- and if your main language is not English, TOEFL 550 or equivalent.

Special access programs are available to students from different backgrounds to the above.

Tuition & Fees

In-State: $10,451
Out-of-State: $10,451
Room and Board: according to choice
Other Fees

Specialization Area

Hotel & Lodging Mgmt; Restaurant & Foodservice Mgmt
Travel & Tourism Mgmt

Graduation Requirements

Successful completion of the program including an individual dissertation.

Purdue University

Restaurant, Hotel, Institutional, and Tourism Management (RHIT)

College: School of Consumer and Family Science
Program Enrollment: Master's 42; Doctorate 8
Institutional Enrollment: 30,159 undergraduate; 6,719 graduate
Degrees Awarded: Bachelor of Science; Doctor of Philosophy
Degree Categories: Nonthesis, thesis
Emphases/Specializations: Hotel Management; Restaurant Operations; Marketing; Human Resources; Tourism
Institutional Accreditation: North Central Association of Colleges and Schools
Contact: Thomas E. Pearson, Director of Graduate Programs, Restaurant, Hotel, Institutional, and Tourism Management, Purdue University, 1266 Stone Hall, West Lafayette, IN 47907-1266; phone (765) 494-4643; fax (317) 494-0327; e-mail pearsont@cfs.purdue.edu; website http://www.cfs.purdue.edu/RHIT/

Institution Description

Located in the heart of the Midwest, Purdue was founded in 1869 as a land-grant university. Maintaining a tradition of providing superior education through its 14 schools offering 6,700 courses, Purdue ranks in the upper 15 universities awarding the doctoral degree. This beautifully landscaped campus offers infinite social and cultural events and is located in a major metropolitan center 125 miles southeast of Chicago and 5 miles northwest of Indianapolis.

Program Description

Ranked among the top ten hospitality programs in the nation, the RHIT master's program is designed to prepare professionals for senior positions in the hospitality and tourism industries. The RHIT doctoral program is ranked third nationally and is designed to develop scholars for research and teaching careers. Due to strong individual support provided by the department, admission to the doctoral program is competitive and limited.

Special Features

The RHIT Computer Resource Center integrates the latest computer technology into classroom usage and research. A $1.2 million renovation of the RHIT cafeteria and restaurant kitchens provide a state-of-the-art training facility. RHIT graduate students develop industry and research networks through unique interaction with the RHIT Advisory Board and The RHIT Recruiting Center. All graduate level faculty have hospitality industry experience. Students have access to courses throughout the university (after meeting prerequisites), allowing full development of an area of specialization.

Financial Aid and Scholarships

A variety of financial aid is available. Teaching assistantships support the department's instruction of the required undergraduate foods courses; research assistantships through individual faculty projects and endowments are also available. In addition, graduate scholarships and fellowships are available through the department and school. All RHIT Ph.D. students receive financial assistantships.

Admissions

Baccalaureate degree required for M.S. program; M.S. degree required for doctoral program; both from accredited institutions; GPA-3.0/4.0; GMAT or GRE test ranking 50th percentile. TOEFL results and proof of financial support required for all international applicants.

Approximate Tuition and Fees

In-state tuition is $3,564 per year; out-of-state tuition is $11,784 per year.

Specialization Area

Hotel & Lodging Mgmt., Restaurant & Foodservice Mgmt., and Travel & Tourism Mgmt.

Graduation Requirements

A minimum of 33 graduate credit hours is required for the M.S. program. The Ph.D. requires approximately 60 credit hours of work beyond the master's degree, including a dissertation and one year's residency at the West Lafayette campus. All students must maintain a B average for all graduate work and pass comprehensive written and oral exams as requested by the committee.

Rochester Institute of Technology

Hospitality-Tourism Management: Service Management; Human Resource Development; Instructional Development

College: Applied Science and Technology
Program Enrollment: 68 master's
Institutional Enrollment: 11,864 undergraduate; 2,153 graduate
Degrees Awarded: Master of Science
Degree Categories: Hospitality/Tourism Management; Service Management; Career and Human Resource Development; Instructional Technology
Emphases/Specializations: Health and Nutrition; Food Service/Restaurant management; Hotel/Resort Management; Travel/Tourism Management; Meeting Planning/Conference Management; Human Resource Management; Personnel and Training; Organization Development
University Accreditation: Middle States Association of Colleges and Schools
Contact: Richard F. Marecki, Ph.D., Chair; (716)475-6017; Dianne C. Mau, Program Chair, CHRD/FHTM (716)475-5036; C.J. Wallington Ph.D., Program Chair, IT/FHTM (716)475-2893; Anne Zachmeyer, Graduate Programs Assistant; (716)475-5062; Rochester Institute of Technology, School of Food, Hotel and Travel Management, 14 Lomb Memorial Drive, Rochester, NY 14623

Institution Description
Rochester Institute of Technology (RIT) is a private coeducational university located in upstate New York. Founded in 1829, RIT has been a pioneer in career-oriented and cooperative education. RIT consists of seven colleges. Wallace Memorial Library is a high technology, media resource center with a collection of over 5000,000 items. Information Systems and Computing provide services on VAX/VMS and VAX/Ultrix (Unix) Systems.

Program Description
All students prepare for professional and leadership positions in their respective capacities and industries. Graduates step into mid-level training and service management positions emphasizing quality and supervision. Coursework focuses on analytical techniques and problem-solving strategies related to customer satisfaction. Students also focus on designing training and performance improvements and learning to maximize human resources to achieve organizational goals. Each program offers a traditional program full-time or part-time), as well as an accelerated Executive Leader option.

Special Features
The department has dedicated state-of-the-art computer labs tied to file servers and RIT mainframes. The Executive Leader Master's program, for individuals with three to five years of work experience, is completed over two summers of part-time study.

Financial Aid and Scholarships
RIT maintains a financial aid office. Each program offers scholarship (on merit). The Hospitality-Tourism programs also offers graduate assistantships. Minority scholarships are also available.

Admissions
Requirements include: a bachelor's degree from an accredited institution, GPA of 3.0 or higher, official undergraduate transcript, two professional recommendations, and the results of either GRE or Miller's Analogy Test. International students must score a minimum of 550 on TOEFL.

Tuition and Fees
Graduate tuition is $18,765. The programs can be completed in one year of full-time study.

Graduation Requirements
Graduation requires completion of either 48 or 52 credit hours, which includes either a graduate project or graduate thesis. Cooperative placement is elective. Electives may be taken from the College of Business's Master of Business program.

Roosevelt University

The Manfred Steinfeld School of Hospitality & Tourism Management

College: Evelyn T. Stone University College
Program Enrollment: 50 Graduates; 250 Undergraduates
Institutional Enrollment: 2,400 Graduates; 4,300 Undergraduates
Degrees Awarded: Master of Science in Hospitality Management (MSHM); Master of Business Administration (MBA) with a Major in Hospitality Management; Executive Certificate in Hospitality Management
Degree Category: Hospitality Management
Emphases/Specializations: Lodging Management, Foodservice Management, Meeting Planning, Convention and Trade Show Management
Institutional Accreditation: North Central Association of Colleges and Schools: National Council for Accreditation of Teacher Education.
Contact: Gerald F. Bober, EdD, Professor and Director, Manfred Steinfeld School of Hospitality & Tourism Management, Roosevelt University, 430 South Michigan Avenue, Chicago, IL 60605; phone (312) 341-4321; fax (312) 341-2417; email: Gbober@roosevelt.edu

Institution Description

Housed in Louis Sullivan's landmark Auditorium Building in Chicago's Loop with a second campus in northwest suburban Schaumburg, Roosevelt University (RU) is an independent, nonsectarian, metropolitan institution founded in 1945 as a pioneer in offering education to working adults and non-traditional students. Flexible class schedules meet the needs of working and commuting students. A residence hall is available at the Loop campus.

Program Description

These programs seek to nurture and enhance professional leadership ability through a core of professional development course work, along with area studies in Lodging Management, Foodservice Management, and Meeting Planning, Convention and Trade Show Management. Elective courses may include Professional Education, Business, Training and Development, or other areas selected with advisor consent.

Special Features

Meeting Planning, Convention and Trade Show Management with the opportunity for paid internships in all aspects of the industry in a major urban market.

Financial Aid and Scholarships

RU offers a number of scholarships, awards, grants, loans and graduate assistantships for degree seeking students needing financial assistance. RU's Financial Aid Office can be reached at (312) 341-3565.

Admissions

Requirements include: a baccalaureate degree from an accredited institution, a completed application with professional resume attached, and official transcripts from each institution attended. A personal advising interview with the program director, Dr. Bober, is also required of all applicants.

Tuition and Fees

For 1998-1999, tuition is $445 per semester hour of graduate course work.

Specialization Areas

Hotel & Lodging Management
Restaurant & Foodservice Management
Meeting Planning, Convention and Trade Show Management

Graduation Requirements

Completion of thirty (30) semester hours of course work, plus required pre-requisite courses, maintaining an overall 3.0 grade point average (GPA).

Schiller International University

International School of Tourism and Hospitality Management (I.S.T.H.M.)

College: International School of Tourism and Hospitality Management (I.S.T.H.M.)
Program Enrollment: 176 undergraduates; 32 graduates
Institutional Enrollment: 934 undergraduate; 254 graduate
Degrees Awarded: Associate of Science; Bachelor of Business Administration: Master of Business Administration; Master of Arts; Diploma
Degree Categories: International Hotel and Tourism Management
Emphases/Specilizations: International residence and foreign languages, international internships
Program Accreditation: Accrediting Council for independent Colleges and Schools; Hotel, Catering and Institutional management Association (London) Travel and Tourism (London)
Contact: Wilfried Iskat, PhD, CHA, FMP, FHCIMA, Dean, International School of Tourism and Hospitality Management , 453 Edgewater Drive, Dunedin, FL 34698; phone (727)736-5082; fax (727) 736-6263; tollfree (USA only) 1(800) 336-4133; email: ISTHM@msn.com or wilfred_iskat@schiller.edu

---

Institution Description
Founded in 1964, and with students from more than 100 nations enrolled, SIU offers the opportunity for an American education in an international setting with English as the language of instruction at all eight campuses in six countries: Tampa Bay Area, Florida, USA; Central London, England; Paris and Strausbourg, France; Heidelberg, Germany; Engelberg and Leysin, Switzerland; and Madrid, Spain. Students are encouraged to transfer freely between SIU's campuses.

Program Description
SIU offers the Master of Business Administration (MBA) degree in international Hotel and tourism Management in Florida and London and the Master of Arts (MA) degree in the same field in London. The MBA requires some background in business-related courses; however, the necessary courses can be completed as part of an MBA preparatory program. The MBA in this field includes five courses focused specifically on hotel/restaurant mangement operations, plus 10 other in international business administration. The Master of Arts requires no prior business background and includes 11 courses in the hotel/restaurant management area, plus four others chosen from the areas of international business administration, economics, and international relations and diplomacy.

Special Feature
SIU offers the MBA in International Business in madrid, Heidelberg, Strabourg, and Lyesin (near Geneva, Switzerland), as wel as in London and Paris. Both the MBA and MA degrees are one-year programs.

Financial Aid and Scholarships
Schiller offers both scholarships and work-study opportunities and participates in government-sponsored loan programs.

Approximate Tuition and Fees
No in-state-out-of-state differentials, but the fee structure applies to the Florida and European campuses. 1999-2000 undergraduate per academic year: Florida, US$12,400; Europe, US$13,400. Room and board: Florida US$5,200; Europe, US$8,700. other fees: US$390.

Admissions
A bachelor's degree or the equivalent is required. For the MBA, submission of GMAT score is also required. For non-native English speakers, proof of advanced knoledge of English is required, (TOEFL). Those with a good intermediate knowledge can take a course in English as a Foreign Language while beginning working on their degree. Others can enroll initially at one of our English Language Institutes.

Graduation Requirements
MBA: 45 semester credit hours consisting of 15 graduate level courses in hotel.tourism management and international business administration. MA:45 semester credit hours consisiting of 15 graduate-level courses in hotel/tourism managment and international business administration, plus the option of taking graduate-level courses in economic and/or international relations and diplomacy.

Southern Cross University

International Tourism/Hotel Management

College: School of Tourism and Hospitality Management
Program Enrollment: 1000
Institutional Enrollment: 10,000
Degrees Awarded: Master of International Tourism Management, Master of International Hotel Management, and Master of Convention and Event Management
Degree Categories: International Tourism Management, International Hotel Management and Convention and Event Management
Emphases/Specializations: International Hotel Management, Convention and Event Management, Tourism Marketing and Planning, International Tourism Management, International Tourism Studies.
Program Accreditation: Winner of New South Wales Award for Excellence (Industry Education) in Tourism 1997 and 1998. Finalist (Industry Education) in the Australian Tourism Awards in 1997 and 1998.
Institutional Accrediation: N/A
Contact: Professor Gary Prosser, Head, School of Tourism and Hospitality Management, Southern Cross University, PO Box 157, Lismore, NSW, 2480, Australia. Ph: +61 26620 3354, Fax +61 266 22 2208

Institutional Description
Southern Cross University is a government regulated and funded university with an unequivocal commitment to excellence. Located on the beautiful East Coast of northern New South Wales, there are campuses in Lismore, Coffs Harbour and Sydney. Southern Cross University is the South Pacific's largest provider of university level tourism education.

Program Description
The courses have been designed in consultation with business and industry leaders to reflect the most recent international developments in industry practice and technology. The three programs share common units in Management, Marketing and International Tourism Studies, which provide a foundation for specialist units in Tourism Management, Hotel Management and Convention and Event Management.

Special Features
Study on-campus or by distance education with personal support; multiple exit points for different qualifications; flexible course structure; credit for previous study and experience; industry relevant management qualifications.

Financial Aid and Scholarships
The Australian Government provides financial assistance to international students through a range of scholarship programs.

Admissions
Candidates may be graduates from any discipline or have equivalent professional qualifications, preferably in the tourism and hospitality industries. Applicants must meet the university's English requirements.

Tuition and Fees
Fees are approximately A$19,200 per year or A$1,600 per unit payable in installments.

Specialization Area
Travel and Tourism Management

Graduation Requirements
Graduation for a Masters degree requires the successful completion of 12 units. A Graduate Certificate may be obtained after completing four units and a Graduate Diploma after completing eight subjects. An accelerated program is available that allows a candidate to complete the full Masters program in one year.

Svenska Handelshögskolan

Swedish School of Economics and Business Administration

Program Enrollment: (Only in Vasa) 25 Bachelor of Tourism Administration (BTA); 20 Master of Tourism Management (MTM); 10 MSc (econ.)
Institutional Enrollment: in Vasa 450 Graduate; 16 Postgraduate; in Helsinki-1,500 Graduate; 69 Postgraduate
Degree Categories: BTA, MTM, MSc (econ.), Doctorate of Economics
Contact: MSc (econ.) and Doctorate of Economics: Professor Lars-Johan Lindqvist, Ph. D., phone: +358-6-3533 712; BTA and MTM: Director of Program, MSc Jan Koskinen; P.O.BOX 287, FIN 65101 VASA, FINLAND; phone: +358-6-3533 704; fax: +358-6-3533 702

Institution Description

Svenska handelshögskolan, SHH, (Swedish School of Economics and Business Administration) is the oldest Business School in Scandinavia. The school was founded in 1909, and it gives education in two locations, in Helsinki, the capital of Finland, and since 1980 also in Vasa.

Program Description

The main programs are Master of Science in Economics, Doctorate of Economics and Tourism as specialty.

Special Features

After graduating from BTA, students can transfer to MTM, and after graduating from MTM, students can apply for the right to continue MSc (econ.).

Approximate Tuition and Fees

SHH is owned by the Finnish Government and the MSc and Doctorate education are free of charge. The BTA and MTM programs are meant for students with a vocational education and minimum of three years of working experience. The tuition for the BTA program is FIM 9,000, and for the MTM program FIM 10,000.

Texas Tech University

Restaurant, Hotel and Institutional Management

College: College of Human Sciences
Program Enrollment: 25 master's
Institutional Enrollment: 22,000 undergraduate; 3,400 graduate
Degree Awarded: Master of Science
Degree Category: Restaurant, Hotel and Institutional Management
Institutional Accreditation: Southern Association of Colleges and Schools
Contact: Graduate Advisor, Restaurant, Hotel, and Institutional Management, Texas Tech University,

Box 41162, Lubbock, TX 79409-1162; phone (806) 742-3068; fax (806) 742-3042; Internet: www.ns.ttu.edu/dept/enrhm/rhim

Institution Description

Texas Tech is one of the state's four major comprehensive universities and academically the most diverse. The university provides students with a range of programs and the opportunity for a liberal education. Texas Tech is located in Lubbock, a sun belt city with a population of over 200,000.

Program Description

The restaurant, Hotel, and Institutional Management (RHIM) Program offers a multidisciplinary approach to hospitality education. The curriculum is designed to prepare the student to meet both current and future hospitality needs. The program emphasizes problem-solving and creativity, and critical thinking skills.

Special Features

A strong emphasis is given to the integration of practical information with technical knowledge. The RHIM program offers a master's degree. Students may enroll in a traditional on-campus program, completing a research or a professional degree track. Opportunities for employment as a teaching or research assistant are available. Students may also choose to enroll in a distance education master's degree through the Center of Education Online. These graduate students must have had five years professional experience. They complete their education through executive style and web-based classes.

The RHIM program can also make available an innovative doctoral degree. This degree program prepares graduates for excellence in both research and teaching. The theoretical framework for the degree is teaching/education, with an 18-hour specialization in hospitality management. This program provides graduates with the needed expertise to enter a variety of career areas.

Financial Aid and Scholarships

Texas Tech maintains a fully staffed financial aid office. The RHIM Program offers several competitive scholarships to students.

Admissions

Admission to the graduate program is granted by a committee of graduate faculty in the department of proposed study. Admission is based upon the GRE or GMAT and undergraduate GPA. Application to graduate school is available at www.texastech.edu.

Graduation Requirements

A Master of Science (thesis) degree requires a minimum of 34 semester hours of graduate courses chosen in consultation with a graduate advisory committee selected by the student. A Master of Science (nonthesis) degree requires a minimum of 37 semester hours of graduate courses chosen in consultation with a graduate advisory committee selected by the student.

The University of Calgary

World Tourism Education and Research Centre
Tourism and Hospitality Management; Urban and Regional Planning; Environmental Science

Colleges: Faculty of Management, Faculty of Environmental Design

Program Enrollments: 20 Tourism and Hospitality Mgmt; 200 Urban and Regional Planning, Environmental Science

Institutional Enrollment: 18,000 Undergraduate, 2,500 graduate

Degrees Awarded: Master of Business Administration (MBA); Master of Environmental Design (MEDes); PhD in Management (PhD)

Degree Categories: MBA and PhD in Tourism and Hospitality Management; MEDes in Urban and Regional Planning, or Environmental Science

Program Accreditation: World Tourism Organization; American Assemble of Collegiate Schools of Business; Canadian Institute of Planners

Contact: Mr. Lorn Sheehan, Tourism and Hospitality Management, Faculty of Management, The University of Calgary, Calgary Alberta, Canada T2N 1N4; phone (403)220-8310

Institution Description
Conceived in 1945 and established as a fully separate institution in 1966, the University of Calgary is a coeducational, nondenominational, public institution. The campus is located in the city of Calgary at the foot of the Rocky Mountains. The university was the site of sports venues during the 1988 Olympic Winter Games, and in 1989 was designated a World Tourism Education Centre by the World Tourism Organization, a United Nations affiliate.

Program Description
The MBA tourism program includes general management and tourism courses in: policy planning and development in tourism; management of the service process; and international tourism. The MEDes program has a course sequence for students interested in the environmental, economic, socio-cultural and physical planning and design dimensions of tourism. Students complete interdisciplinary courses, tourism courses and a master's degree project. Students in the PhD program pursue tourism studies within a functional area of management. Students in the PhD program pursue tourism studies within a functional area of management. Students are exposed to the interaction of tourism and management in a rigorous academic setting.

Special Features
Students in the two master's programs can take courses from both programs to develop an interdisciplinary perspective. There are three student organizations: Tourism Association of Students in Commerce, Tourism Studies Association and TTRA International Student Chapter. Several noncredit programs are also available.

Financial Aid and Scholarships
A number of scholarships, fellowships, bursaries and special awards are available, as well as graduate research, teaching and service assistantships.

Approximate Tuition and Fees
Canadian students: US $2638 per year, international students: US $5004 per year; room and board: US $5,000 per year.

Admissions
Applicants to the master's programs must hold a bachelor's degree (or equivalent) from a recognized institution. Academic performance in the last two years of undergraduate study, a personal statement of career objectives, and letters of reference are considered. MBA applicants must obtain a GMAT score of 500 or better. PhD applicants, in addition to the above, must hold a master's degree (preferably in a related discipline).

Graduation Requirements
Graduation from both master's programs requires a minimum full-time study period of two consecutive four-month terms (both programs are normally completed in two years). The MBA program is offered with a thesis-based option. The MEDes program requires a master's degree project. Graduation from the PhD program requires a minimum study period of four full-time, four month terms. A student's program will consist of coursework in a major or minor field of business and research presented in the form of a dissertation adjudicated by a final examination committee.

University of Central Florida

Hospitality Management

Program Enrollment: 350
Institutional Enrollment: 25,000 undergraduate; 5,200 graduate
Degree Awarded: Bachelor of Science in Business Administration with specialization in Hospitality Management; MBA with specialization in Hospitality Management; PhD in Hospitality Management
Degree Category: Business, Hospitality Management
Emphases/Specializations: Accommodation Management; Foodservice Management; Tourism Management; Convention and Conference Management; Time Share Management

Program Accreditation: American Assembly of Collegiate Schools of Business; Accreditation Commission for Programs in Hospitality Administration
Institutional Accreditation: Southern Association of Colleges and Schools
Contact: Taylor Ellis, PhD, Interim Chair, Department of Hospitality Management, College of Business Administration, University of Central Florida, Orlando, FL 32816-1400; phone (407) 823-2188; fax (407) 823-5696

Institution Description

The University of Central Florida is a comprehensive urban university located in Orlando and is one of ten state universities in the State. The University offers bachelor, master and doctoral level degrees in five colleges with 60 different academic majors. Besides its emphasis on Hospitality Management, the university has established a national presence in computerized simulation and training, artificial intelligence in engineering, and the fine arts. The university is located on a 1,445 acre campus in the northeastern section of the city and students have easy access to all the attractions of the Greater Central Florida area. There are over 50 buildings, a new student union, and residential housing available for students. UCF has both intercollegiate and intramural athletics and a wide variety of other activities available for its students. In addition to the main campus, the University offers undergraduate and graduate coursework at its Cocoa and Daytona Beach Campuses.

Program Description

Orlando is a remarkable and unique place to major in Hospitality Management. Majors have the opportunity to work with and learn from the top managers of some of the leading organizations in all major segments of the hospitality industry. The major combines practical work experience with a newly redesigned academic curriculum that was developed in collaboration with industry leaders. Students, like all College of Business students, experience the innovative and nationally acclaimed BE 2000 educational curriculum in which they develop competency in teamwork, communication, creativity and adapting to and managing change. Hospitality Management students can also pursue their specific interests in convention and meetings management, foodservice operations, lodging and motel/hotel management, Time Share, and travel and tourism by taking specialized coursework in these areas.

Special Features

Study abroad programs are available in cooperation with a number of schools across the world. Student exchange opportunities are also available to any student meeting the equivalent of the Associate of Arts degree program requirements for College of Business admission. The department houses the Dick Pope, Sr. Institute for Tourism Studies, modern computer and foodservice teaching labs, and offers co-op and internships opportunities in the more than 400 hotels, 1,400 restaurants and 50 theme parks located in the Greater Orlando area.

Financial Aid and Scholarships

There are a number of industry-funded scholarships totaling more than $60,000 per year available to hospitality management majors. In addition, there are numerous university scholarships and community financial aid programs available.

Approximate Tuition and Fees

In-state undergraduate tuition is $64.32 per credit hour. Out-of-state tuition is $261.34 per credit hour. Fees are approximately $200 per semester. On campus room and board is an additional $2,200–$2,800 per semester.

Admissions

Admission to UCF and the program is limited and based on meeting both minimum GPA and SAT or ACT scores. Students whose native language is not English must submit a minimum TOEFL score of 550.

Graduation Requirements

One hundred and twenty credits, approximately half of which are in the liberal arts/general education areas and the remainder in business administration and hospitality management courses are required for graduation. The State of Florida requires students to pass the College Level Academic Skills Test (CLAST) and satisfy the Gorden Rule writing requirement.

University of Denver

School of Hotel, Restaurant and Tourism Management

College: Business Administration
Program Enrollment: 25
Institutional Enrollment: 4,000 undergraduate; 2,500 graduate
Degree Awarded: Master of Science in Resort and Tourism Management/MBA w/specialization
Degree Category: Business Administration
Program Accreditation: American Assembly of Collegiate Schools in Business
Institutional Accreditation: North Central Association of Colleges and Schools
Contact: Robert M. O'Holloran, Ph.D., Director, School of Hotel, Restaurant and Tourism Management, University of Denver, Denver, CO 80208; phone (303) 871-4268

Institutional Description
The University of Denver, recognized both nationally and internationally for its academic excellence, is a medium-sized, private university in a metropolitan setting. The university is a comprehensive university with a variety of programs at the undergraduate and graduate level. The university is scaled to human size where the student is individually important, the classes small and faculty attention available.

Program Description
The Master of Science in Resort and Tourism Management develops professionals in the Management of resort properties and tourism destination areas. This program places emphasis upon operational planning and management and actual operational experiential learning at internship sites. This multi-disciplinary program is made up of three parts. The first is made up of courses from the MBA program, the second is made up of specialized courses in resort and tourism management including internships and the third is a guided elective portion which is made up of course work taken outside the School of HRTM.

Special Features
The proximity to major resorts and tourism destination areas provides access to internship sites and to leaders in the industry who can enrich the program through their participation.

Financial Aid and Scholarships
The University of Denver provides several types of financial assistance to qualified students. Available assistance includes scholarships, graduate assistantships, Stafford loans (formerly Guaranteed Student Loans), Carl Perkins loans (NPSC) and Colorado-resident grants.

Approximate Tuition and Fees
Tuition for 1999-2000 for full time students is $6,072 per quarter; for part-time students, $506 per quarter hour. Tuition charges are the same for all students.

Admissions
Requirements include: a baccalaureate degree from an accredited institution and a complete application, including transcripts from each institution attended, GMAT or GRE results, recommendations, essays and a nonrefundable application fee. Complete applications should be received in the Graduate School of Business office by June 1 for admission for the Autumn Quarter. International students must provide TOEFL test results (a minimum score of 550 is required).

Graduation Requirement
Completion of 60 quarter credit hours for MS & 80 quarter credit hours for MBA specialization maintaining an overall 3.0/4.0 grade point average (GPA).

University of Guelph

Hotel & Food Administration

College: Social and Applied Human Sciences (CSAHS)
Program Enrollment: 600
Institutional Enrollment: 10,750 undergraduates; 1,700 graduates
Degree Awarded: Bachelor of Commerce
Degree Category: School of Hotel & Food Administration (HAFA)
Institutional Accreditation: Ontario Ministry of Colleges & Universities
Contact: J. E. (Joe) Barth, Graduate Coordinator, School of Hotel and Food Administration, University of

Guelph, Guelph, Ontario N1G2W1, Canada, Telephone (510) 824-4120, ext. 4867; Fax (519) 823-5512; e-mail: jbarth@uoguelph.ca; Web site: http://www.uoguelph.ca/HAFA/Graduate/index.html

Institutional Description

The University of Guelph, situated 60 miles west of Toronto, has a diverse range of academic research and degree programs in management, the arts, and the physical, biological, agricultural and social sciences. The University follows the semester system and approximately 40 percent of students live in campus residences. The HAFA program, in its 27th year, enrolls nearly 600 undergraduates and about 25 graduate students.

Program Description

The MMS program offers both a major paper and thesis track. The major paper track consists of one full year (three semesters) of study. The 1year major paper track prepares individuals for careers in the hospitality and related industries.

The thesis track consists of four semesters of study taken over two years. Curricula are individually planned. The thesis track is intended for individuals interested in careers in research and education.

Required courses for both degrees include finance, marketing, operations management, organizational behavior and research methods. Both teamwork and individual contributions are evaluated. Class sizes are less than 30 students in most courses.

Special Features

The program makes extensive use of the case method of study and, through its advanced management courses maintains close links to industry.

Financial Aid and Scholarships

Financial aid for both Canadian and foreign students is available on a competitive basis in the form of scholarships, teaching and research assistantships. Canadian students may qualify for student loans.

Approximate Tuition and Fees

Tuition fees for Canadian students are $1,575 CDN per semester. Visa (foreign) students pay $2,333 CDN (approximately $1,600 US) per semester. Total cost for the 1-year track (including accommodation, food, books, tuition, fees, etc.) is approximately $20,000 CDN ($13,700 US).

Admissions

Admission requirements include an undergraduate (baccalaureate) degree from a recognized university or college with a B average for the last two years, two letters of reference and a statement of purpose. Interviews may be requested. Full-time hospitality work experience is advantageous. Hospitality industry executives with strong track records are occasionally admitted under special criteria. The program is designed for students with hospitality, business or liberal arts degrees. Some foundation courses in hospitality or business may be required.

Graduation Requirements

The 1-year track consists of 10 courses (30 credit hours) and a major paper of publishable quality on an applied topic. The 2-year thesis track consists of 9 courses (27 credit hours) and a thesis. Two (2) semesters of full-time residency are required. Any foundation courses required are in addition to the above.

University of Hawaii at Manoa

Travel Industry Management

Program Enrollment: 20 masters
Institutional Enrollment: 11,790 undergraduate; 5,220 graduate
Degree Awarded: Master of Professional Studies
Degree Category: Travel Industry Management
Emphases/Specializations: Hotel and Restaurant Management; Tourism and Travel; Transportation; Travel Industry Education
Institutional Accreditation: Western Association of Schools and Colleges
Contact: Chuck Y. Gee, Dean, School of Travel Industry Management, University of Hawaii at Manoa, 2560 Campus Rd., Honolulu, HI 96822; phone (808) 956-8946

Institution Description

Founded in 1907, the University of Hawaii at Manoa (UHM) has throughout its history emphasized studies related to Hawaii's distinctive geographical and cultural setting including ocean and earth sciences, Asian and Pacific studies and, of course, the travel industry. Located in Manoa Valley, UHM is near downtown Honolulu and Waikiki, the center of Hawaii's tourism industry.

Program Description

The Master of Professional Studies (MPS), offered by the School of Travel Industry Management (TIM), provides a foundation for the understanding of management and operations in the hospitality and service industries. The objective is to prepare graduates to meet the economic, social and environmental challenges of the future. The program includes the study of functional areas such as strategic planning, investment and development, marketing, and management as they apply to hospitality, travel and tourism-related enterprises and organizations.

Special Features

Graduate students will find that unique educational opportunities are available through an outstanding faculty, one of the largest special reference collections and Hawaii's thriving tourism industry. The school is one of 12 institutions worldwide to be designated an International Center for Tourism and Training by the World Tourism Organization.

Financial Aid and Scholarships

A limited number of graduate assistantships, tuition waivers and scholarships are available through the TIM School. Student employment is also available on campus. The East-West Center and university financial aid office offer other types of aid.

Approximate Tuition and Fees

Tuition for full-time students who are residents of Hawaii is $1,956 per semester; for non residents, $4,920 per semester. Part-time tuition is $1,630 and $410 per credit for Hawaii and non-Hawaii residents, respectively. (Fees are approximately $60 per semester.)

Admissions

Selection is competitive and is based on undergraduate work, GMAT or GRE scores and professional work experience. At least two years of industry experience are recommended. Applicants with degrees in fields unrelated to the travel industry will be required to complete prerequisite coursework.

Graduation Requirements

The 36-hour Master of Professional Studies Degree program offers both thesis and nonthesis options. All students complete the managerial core (21 credits), and one of four specializations (9 or 12 credits). Thesis students complete a major research project (6 credits). Non thesis students complete a research monograph (3 credits) on a topic of special interest to the student in addition to course requirements.

University of Houston

Hotel and Restaurant Management

College: Conrad N. Hilton College of Hotel and Restaurant Management
Program Enrollment: 900: 820 graduate; 80 graduate
Institutional Enrollment: 32,000
Undergraduate: 25,000
Post-Baccalaureate: 1,500
Graduate: 4,000
Doctoral: 1,500
Degree Awarded: Bachelor of Science; Master of Hospitality Management
Degree Categories: Hospitality Management
Emphasis/Specialization: N/A
Program Accreditation: N/A
Institutional Accreditation: Southern Association of Colleges and Schools
Contact: Dr. Alan T. Stutts, Dean, Conrad N. Hilton College of Hotel and Restaurant Management, University of Houston, Houston, TX 77204-3902; phone (713) 743-2610; fax (713) 743-2498; e-mail BSHRM@uh.edu; website http://www.hrm.uh.edu

Institution Description

The University of Houston (UH) is a nationally recognized urban research and teaching university. Its activities encompass undergraduate, graduate and professional education; basic and applied research programs; and public service programs. The university's graduate professional education; basic and applied research programs and public service programs.

Program Description

The College of Hotel and Restaurant Management emphasizes broad information skills and in-depth studies in food and beverage management, lodging management, accounting and finance, marketing, facilities management, law, and information systems.

The university maintains a $28.8 million hotel and restaurant management training facility on campus. The University of Houston Hilton and Conference Center has 86 guest rooms, 22 conference and meeting rooms with over 35,000 square feet of meeting and convention space, two full-service restaurants, a faculty club, an archive and library, three ballrooms, classrooms and laboratories. The College houses the Hospitality Hall of Honor which features displays of historical information, personal and corporate memorabilia, and other items of interest. Each year a gala event brings industry leaders to the College for an annual induction ceremony. Our 20 full time professors have outstanding academic credentials and bring with them over 200 years of significant industry experience which is applied in both classroom and research activities.

Financial Aid and Scholarships

A large number of competitive scholarships are available. Application deadline for college scholarships is March 1. Financial Aid is also available to those who qualify.

Admissions

Freshman admission is based on rank in class, SAT/ACT scores, and high school core requirements. Transfer applicants with 15 or more college semester credit hours must have a cumulative GPA of 2.5 to be admitted directly into Hotel and Restaurant Management.

Tuition and Fees

Per year: Tuition for Texas residents, $2,000; nonresidents, $8,500; international students, $9,000; room and board, $4,200.

Specialization Area

Hotel & Lodging Management
Restaurant & Foodservice Management

Graduation Requirements

132 semester hours: 68 hours of General Education courses and 64 hours of Hotel and Restaurant Management Courses, including 36 advanced hours.

University of Massachusetts-Amherst

Hotel, Restaurant and Travel Administration

Program Enrollment: 35 masters
Institutional Enrollment: 18,000 undergraduate; 5,000 graduate
Degrees Awarded: Master of Science
Degree Category: Hotel, Restaurant and Travel Administration
Emphases/Specializations: Marketing; Human Resource Management; Computer Science; Finance; Management Information Systems; Accounting; Education; Tourism
Institutional Accreditation: New England Association of Schools and Colleges
Contact: Frank P. Lattuca, Department Head; or Linda Shea, Graduate Program Director, Department of Hotel, Restaurant and Travel Administration, University of Massachusetts-Amherst, Amherst, MA 01003-2710; phone (413) 545-4047 (Lattuca); or (413) 545-4039 (Shea); fax (413) 545-1235

Institution Description

There are 98 undergraduate degree programs, 69 master's degree programs, and 48 doctoral degree programs.

Program Description

The department offers the Master of Science degree. There are two tracks in the master's program, one leads to the completion of a thesis while the other does not. In either case, students complete a common core of courses. Furthermore, there is considerable flexibility for students to select many other courses on campus that will strengthen individual areas of specialization.

Special Features

Program offerings are tailored to the needs of individual students, incorporating elements of traditional structure and modern flexibility.

Financial Aid and Scholarships

The university has available all normal federal, state and competitive grants and scholarships. The department offers a significant number of teaching and research assistantships.

Approximate Tuition and Fees

Resident tuition is $2,775 and non-resident tuition is $5,824. Students with teaching/research assistantships receive tuition waivers as well as a monetary stipend. A number of research assistantships are available with the University Campus Center, which houses the Hotel, Food, Catering and Conference Service Departments. Students participating in the New England Regional Program receive substantial reductions in tuition.

Admissions

Applications from individuals with a variety of undergraduate degrees are welcome. A completed application consists of: (1) the application form; (2) two references; (3) two sets of official transcripts of all collegelevel work; and (4) an official report on the GMAT. TOEFL scores are required of all international applicants.

Graduation Requirements

Master's students must complete 36 credits of course work depending on areas of competency. If necessary, students may be required to take foundation courses as prerequisites to graduate courses.

University of Nevada, Las Vegas

William F. Harrah College of Hotel Administration

College: William F. Harrah College of Hotel Administration
Program Enrollment: 65-75 master's; 10 Ph.D.
Institutional Enrollment: Undergraduate: 21,000; Graduate: 3,200
Degree Awarded: Master of Science; Master of Hospitality Administration; Ph.D.
Degree Categories: Hotel Administration; Hospitality Administration
Emphases/Specializations: Flexible, individually tailored programs allow for a range of emphases in hotel, restaurant, gaming and hospitality education. UNLV has developed a specialty in delivering graduate programs to industry professionals through the Internet and intensive delivery formats.
Institutional Accreditation: Northwest Association of Schools and Colleges

Contact: Dr. John Bowen, Director of Graduate Studies and Research; William F. Harrah College of Hotel Administration; University of Nevada, Las Vegas; 4505 Maryland Parkway; Box 456013; Las Vegas, NV 89154-6013; phone (702) 895-3161; fax (702) 895-4109; e-mail bowen@ccmail.nevada.edu

Institution Description

As a specialized program in a city of hotels and restaurants, the college has been able to attract a strong faculty and a diversified student body, and has been able to develop a curriculum that carefully balances professional needs with academic expectations.

Program Description

The program is designed for the individual who has gained practical experience either in industry or in hotel/restaurant education and who now wishes to supplement that hands-on background with stringent academic preparation.

Special Features

Small classes, a faculty with multiple years of industry experience, a facility that includes everything from computer labs to test kitchens, and a location with over 30 million visitors annually, assure unique educational projects. There is no better place to study the hospitality industry than in Las Vegas, where tourism drives the economy. Las Vegas is a "living laboratory" with over 120,000 hotel rooms, major trend-setting restaurants, and home to major conventions and trade shows. The college receives excellent support from the business community.

Financial Aid and Scholarships

Low tuition, opportunity to work, graduate assistantships, and financial aid make the program easily affordable.

Admissions

Admission to the Master of Science program requires one year of management work experience, a GPA of 2.75 in the last two years of undergraduate work, an admissions essay, professional references, and test scores from either the GRE or the GMAT. Admission to the Ph.D. program requires a Master's degree, M.S. level thesis (or equivalent), a GPA of 3.0 for all post-baccalaureate work, an admissions essay, professional references, and a minimum GMAT score of 550.

Tuition and Fees

In state: $95 per credit hour
Out of State: $2885 per semester

Graduation Requirement

For the master's degree, approximately 36 credits, plus prerequisites, depending on previous academic preparation. Students may select a thesis or a professional paper with additional credits. Work requirements must be met prior to admission. Contact the office for Ph.D. requirements.

The University of New Haven

Hotel, Restaurant, Tourism and Dietetics Administration

College: School of Hotel, Restaurant, Tourism and Dietetics Administration
Program Enrollment: 15
Institutional Enrollment: 3,400 undergraduate; 3,600 graduate
Degree Awarded: Executive Master of Science in Tourism & Hospitality or Executive M.S. In Tourism & Hospitality with Research Concentration
Degree Categories: Hospitality and Tourism
Institutional Accreditation: New England Association of Schools and Colleges; National Association of Independent Colleges and Universities
Contact: Constantine E. Vlisides, Ph.D., Graduate Coordinator, University of New Haven, 300 Orange Avenue, West Haven, CT 06516; phone (203) 9327362; fax (203) 932-7083; e-mail: gradinfo@charger.newhaven.edu

Institutional Description

The University of New Haven (UNH), founded in 1920 is a private, coeducational university with a contemporary and innovative view of higher education. UNH has five schools: Arts & Science; Business; Engineering; Hotel, Restaurant, Tourism and Dietetics, and Professional Studies. Located near Long Island Sound and a little over 1 hour from New York City and 2 hours from Boston, UNH provides unique professional experiences.

Program Description

The goal of the Executive Master of Science in Tourism and Hospitality is to provide students with tools that enable them to manage in hospitality and tourism organizations. The program provides opportunities for students to develop specific professional competencies through focused coursework. Designed for the entry and middle level manager to enhance course and operational goals.

Special Features

Trimester schedule; non-traditional format for the working professional, allowing accelerated completion in 18 months without the research concentration.

Tuition and Fees

Executive Master—30 credits $15,750
48 credits (with research concentration) $20,520

Admissions

Applicants to Graduate School are required to hold a baccalaureate degree from an accredited college or university. Admission decisions are based primarily on an applicant's undergraduate record. In support of their applications, students must submit scores from GMAT or Graduate Record Examination (GRE), or the Miller Analogy Test (MAT). Three to five years experience in the field or related field.

Graduation Requirements

A degree will be conferred when a student has satisfied all program requirements and met the following university requirements: minimum of a 30 graduate credit residency, and completion of all requirements within 5 years. A quality point ratio of 3.0 ("B" average) is required for degrees awarded by the Graduate School. For the Research Concentration, a 48 graduate credit residency must be met.

University of Queensland

Hospitality Management, Tourism Management, Leisure Management and Travel Management

College: Department of Hospitality, Tourism & Property Management
Program Enrollment: 350 intake per year
Institutional Enrollment: 20,000 undergraduate, 5,000 graduate
Degrees Awarded: Bachelor of Business, (Honours) Master of Business
Degree Categories: Hospitality Management, Tourism Management, Travel Management, and Leisure Management
Emphases/Specializations: Food and Beverage; Accommodation and Special Events Management, Sustainable Development and Tourism planning.

Program Accreditation: Catering Institute of Australia
Institutional Accreditation: International Association of Hotel management Schools; Tourism Training Australia (Hospitality Division)
Contact: Prof. Stephen Craig-Smith, Department Head, Department of Hospitality, Tourism and Property Management, University of Queensland, Gatton College, QLD 4345; Phone (07) 5460 1371; fax (07) 5460 1171

Institution Description

The University of Queensland is the largest and oldest in the state and is one of the seven major research universities of Australia. Its 25,000 students are taught in seven major faculties. Tourism, Hospitality, Travel and Leisure are taught by the Department of Hospitality, Tourism and Property Management in the Business, Economics and Law faculty. It is possible to progress from bachelors to doctoral level in all areas of study.

Program Description

Gatton College's hospitality, leisure, travel and tourism management degrees are built on a solid academic foundation together with specialised areas of study. The main components are (1) general business studies – business law, accounting, marketing, economics and finance; (2) human resource management; (3) food and beverage management; (4) lodging/property management; (5) tourism management, travel management and leisure studies and (6) industry.

Special Features

The undergraduate program requires a period of industry internship that ensures our graduates are well received by the industry.

Financial Aid and Scholarship

Australian students only are eligible for Austudy, which is means-tested study assistance.

Approximate Tuition and Fees

Australian students: none (HECS applies – approximately US$1,650 per year). Overseas students: US$7,600 per year. Room and board: US$3,000. Other fees: student services fee US$85 per year.

Admissions

Entry to our courses is highly competitive, and admissions will be made on the basis of academic merit.

Graduation Requirements

Graduation requires successful completion of 250 credit points of study, including eight weeks of industry internship for Hospitality Management.

University of South Carolina

School of Hotel, Restaurant and Tourism Administration

College: College of Applied Professions
Program Enrollment: 30
Institutional Enrollment: 16,000 undergraduate; 10,000 graduate
Degree Awarded: Master of Hotel, Restaurant and Tourism Administration (MHRTA)
Degree Category: Hotel, Restaurant and Tourism Administration
Emphases/Specializations: Lodging; Food Service; Tourism
Institutional Accreditation: Southern Association of Colleges and Schools
Contact: Charles Partlow, Director, MHRTA Program, Hotel, Restaurant and Tourism Administration, University of South Carolina, Columbia, SC 29208; phone (803) 777-6665; fax (803) 777-1224; e-mail: partlow@gwm.sc.edu

Institution Description

With nine campuses, the University of South Carolina is the largest university in the state. The program is located on the main campus in the capital city, Columbia. The university has 17 academic units, including a School of Medicine and widely acclaimed programs in engineering and international business.

Program Description

The Master of Hotel, Restaurant and Tourism Administration is a professional program designed to prepare students for advanced careers in the hospitality and tourism industry. Students receive thorough training in the functional areas of hospitality management, as well as extensive knowledge in the fields of lodging, food service, and tourism. Flexibility in program design also allows for area specialization.

Special Features

Individualized attention from graduate faculty; Capstone Dining Facility, a restaurant and food production lab run by HRTA students under supervision of faculty and graduate assistants; HRTA Annual Career Fair and placement services; location in Columbia—a major corporate and legislative hub—just two hours from many beach and mountain resorts; Institute for Tourism Research, which provides opportunities to work on research, education and service programs for South Carolina's fastest growing industry—tourism.

Financial Aid and Scholarships

The school offers a number of research and teaching assistantships for those who qualify. Further information on scholarships, grants and other forms of financial aid may be obtained through the Office of Student Financial Aid and Scholarships, USC, Columbia, SC 29208; phone (803) 777-8134.

Approximate Tuition and Fees

For the 1998-99 academic year, in-state tuition is $193 per credit hour for up to 9 credit hours ($404 out-of-state), and $1,947 total for 11 or more credit hours ($4,057 out-of-state).

Admissions

Applicants must have at least one year of management experience in the hospitality industry. Acceptable undergraduate GPA and GMAT scores, along with letters of recommendation, a 500-word essay explaining professional goals and objectives, and a personal interview, are also required.

Graduation Requirements

Successful completion of 36 semester hours of approved graduate credit with at least a B average and a comprehensive final exam are required. This is a nonthesis program, but case studies, team project papers and presentations are required in several classes.

University of Surrey

Masters and Doctoral Programs in Tourism and Hospitality Management

College: School of Management Studies for the Service Sector
Program Enrollment: 120 Masters, 10 Doctoral each year
Institutional Enrollment: Undergraduate: 5,000; Postgraduate: PGTaught – 1500, PG Research – 1,000
Degrees Awarded: Master of Science (MSc), MPhil, PhD
Degree Categories: Tourism Management, Tourism Planning and Development, Tourism Marketing, International Hotel Management, Tourism and Hospitality Education, Health Care Management, Food Management, Leisure Culture and Tourism Management
Contact: Dr. David Gilbert, Postgraduate Program Coordinator, School of Management Studies for the Service Sector, University of Surrey, Guildford, Surrey, GU2 5XH, United Kingdom; phone +44-(0)-1483-259651; fax +44-(0)-1483-259387: E-mail D.Gilbert@surrey.ac.uk

Institution Description

Granted its Charter in 1966, the University of Surrey was the first in England to offer a comprehensive range of undergraduate, masters and doctoral qualifications in tourism and hotel management. Located only thirty minutes by train from London in the pleasant Surrey countryside, this modem campus university offers excellent facilities all on the same site.

Program Description

The Masters program is split into a taught element and a research dissertation. The taught element consists of core modules in subjects such as research methods, prescibed modules relevant to the degree stream, and electives at the student's choice. The dissertation is conducted under the supervision of our experienced academic staff.

Special Features

The School is recognized as a key Education and Training centre by the WTO and was graded as "excellent" in teaching by the HEFCE. It attracts students from over 50 different countries.

Financial Aid and Scholarships

None available through the School.

Admissions

The minimum entry requirement for the MSc program is an undergraduate honors degree at a lower/higher second class level. A minimum TOEFL score of 550, or the computer based equivalent of 213, is required for students for whom English is not their first language. A wide range of equivalent international qualifications will be considered on an individual basis.

Approximate Tuition and Fees

In-state	n/a
Out-of state	$12,250
Room and Board	$8,500
Other fees	$1,500 books, etc.

Specialization Area

Hotel and lodging management, restaurant and foodservice management, travel and tourism management.

Graduation Requirements

Students must obtain 180 credits for MSc graduation; 120 from the taught courses and 60 from the dissertation. An average mark of 50% must be obtained throughout all assessments. MPhil/PhD students are examined on their research thesis by a panel of internal and external examiners.

The University of Tennessee - Knoxville

Hotel and Restaurant Administration and Recreation Programs

Program Enrollment: 30 masters
Institutional Enrollment: 19,000 undergraduate; 6,000 graduate
Degrees Awarded: Master of Science
Degree Categories: Master in Recreation, Tourism and Hospitality Administration with concentrations in Hospitality Administrations; Tourism; Recreation Administration; Therapeutic Recreation

Institutional Accreditations: Southern Association of Colleges and Schools
Contact: Dr. Nancy Fair, College of Human Ecology, University of Tennessee, Knoxville, TN 37996-1900; phone (423) 974-4357; fax (423) 974-5236; e-mail: GOTOBUTTON BM_2_ nbfair@utk.edu

Institution Description

The University of Tennessee, Knoxville, is the official land-grant institution for the state of Tennessee. It is a comprehensive institution offering a wide range of graduate programs leading to the master's and doctoral degrees. The university offers master's programs in 93 fields and doctoral work in 52. Approximately 5,700 graduate students are enrolled both on and off campus. The graduate school brings together faculty and graduate students as a community of scholars with a common interest in creative work and advanced study. The university employs a variety of modes, traditional and nontraditional, in offering quality programs designed to serve students.

Program Description

The University of Tennessee has a reputation as a leader in graduate studies because of an outstanding faculty with excellent student/faculty ratios. In addition, the students enjoy flexible programming with maximum personal attention. Individual goals are considered, coupled with high quality instruction and diverse research options.

Special Features

In addition to microcomputer and mainframe access, students benefit from modern teaching and research laboratories and established contacts with the local, regional and national foodservice, lodging, tourism, and recreation industries.

Financial Aid and Scholarships

Graduate teaching and research assistantships (includes stipend plus tuition waiver) in the department or with university foodservices, graduate fellowships, numerous scholarships, student loans and employment opportunities, are available.

Admissions

Undergraduate coursework appropriate to major, GRE (1,000 combined score on verbal and quantitative sections preferred), minimum 2.5 GPA, work experience related to major.

Graduate Requirements

Master's thesis option: 33 semester hours, 16 hours in department thesis, oral comprehensive examination. Master's nonthesis option: 36 semester hours, 20 hours in department, nonthesis project, written comprehensive examination.

Indexes

Please note: Specialization indexes are based on information submitted by each school.

Geographical Index

UNITED STATES

ALABAMA
The University of Alabama
Auburn University
Faulkner State Community College

ARIZONA
Central Arizona College
Pima County Community College District

ARKANSAS
Arkansas Tech University
Garland County Community College

CALIFORNIA
Bakersfield College
California State University, Long Beach
California State Polytechnic University, Pomona
Golden Gate University
Mission College
Monterey Peninsula College
Oxnard College
University of San Francisco
Santa Barbara City College
United States International University

COLORADO
Colorado Mountain College
University of Denver
Fort Lewis College

CONNECTICUT
Briarwood College
International College of Hospitality Management, *"Cesar Ritz"*
Manchester Community Technical College
Naugatuck Valley Community-Technical College
Norwalk Community-Technical College (NCTC)
University of New Haven

DELAWARE
University of Delaware
Delaware County Community College
Delaware State University

DISTRICT OF COLUMBIA
The George Washington University
The George Washington University School of Business and Public Management
Howard University

FLORIDA
Bethune-Cookman College
The University of Central Florida
The Florida State University
Pensacola Junior College
Saint Thomas University
Schiller International University
Webber College

GEORGIA
Georgia State University
Georgia Southern University

HAWAII
Brigham Young University - Hawaii
University of Hawaii at Manoa

ILLINOIS
The Cooking and Hospitality Institute of Chicago
Eastern Illinois University
University of Illinois at Urbana-Champaign
Lexington College
Lincoln Land Community College
National Restaurant Association Educational Foundation
Parkland College
Roosevelt University
Southern Illinois University-Carbondale
William Rainey Harper College

INDIANA
Ball State University
Purdue University

IOWA
Iowa State University

KANSAS

Cloud County Community College
Johnson County Community College
Kansas State University

KENTUCKY

Morehead State University
Sullivan College
Transylvania University

LOUISIANA

Louisiana State University at Eunice
University of New Orleans
Nicholls State University
University of Southwestern Louisiana

MAINE

University of Maine at Augusta
York County Technical College

MARYLAND

Morgan State University

MASSACHUSETTS

Endicott College
University of Massachusetts-Amherst
Massachusetts Bay Community College

MICHIGAN

Central Michigan University
Eastern Michigan University
Educational Institute of the American Hotel & Motel Association
Ferris State University
Grand Rapids Community College
Grand Valley State University
Macomb Community College
Michigan State University
Siena Heights University
Washtemaw Community College

MINNESOTA

University of Minnesota, Crookston

MISSISSIPPI

Northeastern State University

MISSOURI

Central Missouri State University
Saint Louis University
St. Louis Community College at Forest Park

NEBRASKA

University of Nebraska-Lincoln
Southeast Community College

NEVADA

University of Nevada, Las Vegas

NEW HAMPSHIRE

University of New Hampshire

NEW JERSEY

County College of Morris
Fairleigh Dickinson University
Middlesex County College
Nassau Community College

NEW MEXICO

New Mexico State University

NEW YORK

Broome Community College
Canisius College
Cornell University
The Culinary Institute of America
Erie Community College, City Campus
Mohawk Valley Community College
New York Technical College
New York University
Niagara University
Paul Smith's College: The College of the Adirondacks
Plattsburgh State University of New York
Rochester Institute of Technology
Schenectady County Community College
State University of New York College of Agriculture and Technology at Cobleskill
State University of New York at Morrisville
State University of New York College at Oneonta
State University of New York College of Technology, Delhi, NY
St. Johns University, New York
Syracuse University
Tompkins Cortland Community College
Trocaire College
Westchester Community College

NORTH CAROLINA

Appalachian State University
Asheville-Buncombe Technical Community College
Cape Fear Community College
North Carolina Central University
East Carolina University
North Carolina Central University
Wake Technical Community College
Western Carolina University

NORTH DAKOTA

North Dakota State University

OHIO

University of Akron
Ashland University
Bowling Green State University
Columbus State Community College
Kent State University
Ohio University
Sinclair Community College
Tiffin University
Ursuline College
Youngstown State University

OKLAHOMA

Oklahoma State University

OREGON

Mt. Hood Community College
Southern Oregon University

PENNSYLVANIA

Drexel University
East Stroudsburg University of Pennsylvania
Harcum College
ICS Learning Systems
Indiana University of Pennsylvania
Indiana University of Pennsylvania Academy of Culinary Arts
Keystone College
Luzerne County Community College
Marywood University
Pennsylvania College of Technology
Philadelphia OIC Opportunities Inn: The Hospitality Training Institute
The Restarant School
Westmoreland County Community College
Widener University

RHODE ISLAND

Johnson & Wales University

SOUTH CAROLINA

University of South Carolina

TENNESSEE

University of Tennessee-Knoxville
Volunteer State Community College

TEXAS

University of Houston
Stephen F. Austin State University
The University of Texas at San Antonio
Texas Tech University

UTAH

Utah Valley State College

VERMONT

Johnson State College
New England Culinary Institute
Southern Vermont College

VIRGINIA

J. Sargeant Reynolds Community College
James Madison University
Norfolk State University
Northern Virginia Community College
Tidewater Community College
Virginia State University

WASHINGTON

Highline Community College
Spokane Community College

WEST VIRGINIA

Davis & Elkins College
West Liberty State College

WISCONSIN

Gateway Technical College
Milwaukee Area Technical College
Mount Mary College
Waukesha County Technical College

INTERNATIONAL

ARGENTINA
CENCAP International School of Hotel and Tourism Management
Ott College

ARUBA
Aruba Hotel School

AUSTRALIA
Australian International Hotel School
Canberra Institute of Technology
Griffith University
International College of Hotel Management
University of Queensland
Southern Cross University

AUSTRIA
International Center for Hotel- and Tourism Training MODUL Vienna
School for Tourism - Vienna

BAHAMAS
Bahamas Hotel Training College

BRAZIL
SENAC – CET

CANADA
Algonquin College
Atlantic Tourism & Hospitality Institute
University of Calgary
Centennial College
George Brown College
University of Guelph
Humber College
New Brunswick Community College - St. Andrews
Northern Alberta Institute of Technology
Nova Scotia Community College Akerley Campus
Red Deer College
Regal Constellation College of Hospitality
Southern Alberta Institute of Technology
University of Victoria

FINLAND
Hagga Institute Polytechnic
Svenska Handelshögskolan

FRANCE
Ecole de Savignac
Institut de Management Hotelier International
Taylor's College, School of Hotel Management

GREECE
Alpine Center
BCA Business Studies Department of Hotel and Tourism Management

GUAM
Guam Community College

HONG KONG
Chinese University of Hong Kong
The Hong Kong Polytechnic University

INDIA
Indian Institute of Hotel Management

IRELAND
Galway-Mayo Institute of Technology

ISRAEL
Ben-Gurion University of the Negev
Tadmor Hotel School

JAMAICA
University of Technology, Jamaica

MAURITIUS
The Beachcomber Training Academy

THE NETHERLANDS
Hotelschool The Hague, International Institute of Hospitality Management
Universidad de las Americas-Puebla

Specialization Index

CULINARY ARTS

The Academy of Hotel Management and Catering Industry in Poznañ
Alpine Center
University of Akron
Asheville-Buncombe Technical Community College
Atlantic Tourism & Hospitality Institute
Bahamas Hotel Training College
Bakersfield College
Canberra Institute of Technology
Cape Fear Community College
Center for Culinary Arts, Manila
Central Institute of Technology, New Zealand
Central Arizona College
Centre International de Glion (Switzerland)
Colorado Mountain College
Columbus State Community College
The Cooking and Hospitality Institute of Chicago
The Culinary Institute of America (CIA)
Domino Carlton Tivoli International Hotel And Business Management School (DCT)
Endicott College
Erie Community College, City Campus
George Brown College
Grand Rapids Community College
Humber College
International College of Hospitality Management, "Cesar Ritz"
Johnson & Wales University
Les Roches
Lincoln Land Community College
Macomb Community College
Manchester Community College
Middlesex County College
Milwaukee Area Technical College
Mohawk Valley Community College
University of Nevada, Las Vegas
New Brunswick Community College - St. Andrews
New England Culinary Institute
Nicholls State University
Northern Virginia Community College
Norwalk Community-Technical College (NCTC)
Nova Scotia Community College Akerley Campus
Ott College
Paul Smith's College: The College of the Adirondacks
Pennsylvania College of Technology
Pensacola Junior College
Regal Constellation College of Hospitality
The Restaurant School
Santa Barbara City College
Schenectady County Community College
Sinclair Community College
Spokane Community College
State University of New York College of Technology, Delhi, NY
Sullivan College
University of Technology, Jamaica
Volunteer State Community College
Wake Technical Community College
Waukesha County Technical College
Westmoreland County Community College
William Rainey Harper College

HOTEL AND LODGING MANAGEMENT

RESTAURANT AND FOODSERVICE MANAGEMENT

The Academy of Hotel Management and Catering Industry in Poznań
The University of Alabama
Alpine Center
Andalus Institute for Technology and Training (AITT) Hospitality Programs
Appalachian State University
Arkansas Tech University
Asheville-Buncombe Technical Community College
Ashland University
Atlantic Tourism & Hospitality Institute
Auburn University
Australian International Hotel School
Bakersfield College
Ball State University
BCA Business Studies Department of Hotel and Tourism Management
Bethune-Cookman College
Bowling Green State University
Briarwood College
California State Polytechnic University, Pomona
California State University, Long Beach
Canberra Institute of Technology
Central Arizona College
Central Michigan University
Central Missouri State University
Centre International de Glion (Switzerland)
Cloud County Community College
Colorado Mountain College
Columbus State Community College
The Culinary Institute of America
University of Delaware
University of Denver
Domino Carlton Tivoli International Hotel And Business Management School (DCT)
East Carolina University
East Stroudsburg University of Pennsylvania
Eastern Michigan University
Endicott College
Erie Community College, City Campus
Fairleigh Dickinson University
Ferris State University
Gateway Technical College
George Brown College
The George Washington University
Georgia Southern University
Golden Gate University
Grand Valley State University
Griffith University
Guam Community College
University of Guelph
Hagga Institute Polytechnic
University of Hawaii at Manoa
Highline Community College
Humber College
ICS Learning Systems
University of Illinois at Urbana-Champaign
International College of Hospitality Management, *"Cesar Ritz"*
International Center for Hotel- and Tourism Training MODUL Vienna
Iowa State University
James Madison University
Johnson & Wales University
Johnson State College
Kent State University
Lexington College
Lincoln Land Community College
Louisiana State University at Eunice
Luzerne County Community College
Macombe Community College
Manchester Community College
Marywood University
Middlesex County College
University of Minnesota, Crookston
Mission College
Mohawk Valley Community College
Monterey Peninsula College
Morehead State University
Mount Mary College
Mt. Hood Community College
National Restaurant Association Educational Foundation
University of Nebraska

University of Nevada, Las Vegas
New Brunswick Community College - St. Andrews
University of New Orleans
Niagara University
Norfolk State University
North Carolina Central University
Northern Virginia Community College
Norwalk Community-Technical College (NCTC)
Ohio University
Oklahoma State University
Ott College
Oxford Brookes University
Parkland College
Paul Smith's College: The College of the Adirondacks
Pennsylvania College of Technology
Plattsburgh State University of New York
Purdue University
Red Deer College
The Restaurant School
Rochester Institute of Technology
Roosevelt University
University of San Francisco
Santa Barbara Community College
Schenectady County Community College
Schiller International University
Siena Heights University
Sinclair Community College
Southern Illinois University-Carbondale
University of Southern Mississippi
Southern Vermont College
Southwest Missouri State University
University of Southwestern Louisiana
Spokane Community College
State University of New York College at Oneonta
State University of New York College of Technology, Delhi, NY
Stephen F. Austin State University
St. Johns University, New York
St. Thomas University
University of Surrey
University of Technology, Jamaica
Tidewater Community College
Tiffin University
Tompkins Cortland Community College
Transylvania University
Trocaire College
United States International University
University of Victoria
Volunteer State Community College
Wake Technical Community College
Waukesha County Technical College
Webber College
Western Carolina University
Westmoreland County Community College
Widener University
William Rainey Harper College
Virginia State University
Youngstown State University

TRAVEL AND TOURISM MANAGEMENT

The Academy of Hotel Management and Catering Industry in Poznañ
The University of Alabama
Alpine Center
Andalus Institute for Technology and Training (AITT) Hospitality Programs
Appalachian State University
Atlantic Tourism & Hospitality Institute
BCA Business Studies Department of Hotel and Tourism Management
Ben-Gurion University of the Negev
Bethune-Cookman College
Briarwood College
The University of Calgary
Canberra Institute of Technology
Centennial College
Central Michigan University
Centre International de Glion (Switzerland)
Columbus State Community College
University of Denver
East Stroudsburg University of Pennsylvania
Endicott College
Fairleigh Dickinson University
Ferris State University
Garland County Community College
Gateway Technical College
The George Washington University
Golden Gate University
Grand Valley State University
Griffith University
Guam Community College
Hagga Institute Polytechnic
Harcum College
University of Hawaii at Manoa
Highline Community College
Hong Kong Polytechnic University, The
University of Houston
Humber College
International College of Hospitality Management, "Cesar Ritz"
International Center for Hotel- and Tourism Training MODUL Vienna
James Madison University
Johnson & Wales University
Johnson State College
Leeds Metropolitan University
Louisiana State University at Eunice
Luzerne County Community College
Manchester Community College
Mt. Hood Community College
University of Nevada, Las Vegas
New Brunswick Community College - St. Andrews
University of New Orleans
New York University
Niagara University
North Carolina Central University
Northern Virginia Community College
Norwalk Community-Technical College (NCTC)
Oklahoma State University
Ott College
Oxford Brookes University
Parkland College
Paul Smith's College: The College of the Adirondacks
Plattsburgh State University of New York
Purdue University
Rochester Institute of Technology
Roosevelt University
Schenectady County Community College
Schiller International University
Siena Heights University
Sinclaire Community College
Southern Cross University
Southern Illinois University-Carbondale
University of Southern Mississippi
University of Southwestern Louisiana
St. Johns University, New York
St. Thomas University
State University of New York College of Technology, Delhi, NY

Alphabetical Index

– A –

– B –

– C –

– D –

— L —

— M —

— N —

— O —

— P —

— Q —

– R –

– S –

– T –

– U –

– V –

– W –

– X –

– Y –

– Z –

WITHDRAWAL